THE COMPLETE
MICROWAVE
COOKBOOK

THE COMPLETE MICROWAVE COOKBOOK

Val Collins

with 110 illustrations,
50 in colour

DAVID & CHARLES
Newton Abbot London North Pomfret (Vt)

With all my grateful thanks to my husband for sampling all the food, helping with most of the washing up and putting up with the noise of the typewriter during his favourite television programmes.

Colour photography by John Plimmer

Line illustrations by Mona Thorogood

For information and advice on microwave ovens and accessories please send a 9 × 6in stamped addressed envelope to the Microwave Oven Association, 16a The Broadway, Wimbledon SW19 1RF

British Library Cataloguing in Publication Data
Collins, Val
  The complete microwave cookbook.
  1. Microwave cookery
  I. Title
  641.5′882   TX832

  ISBN 0-7153-8533-X

Phototypeset by MS Filmsetting Limited, Frome
Printed in the Netherlands
by Royal Smeets Offset BV, Weert
for David & Charles (Publishers) Limited
Brunel House Newton Abbot Devon

Published in the United States of America
by David & Charles Inc
North Pomfret Vermont 05053 USA

Contents

Introduction

Now that the microwave revolution has progressed to the point when the microwave cooker is part of the essential kitchen equipment in many homes along with the freezer, the fridge and the food processor, it is timely to take a fresh look at its place in kitchen technology. Gone are the days, fortunately, when the microwave oven was merely used to reheat food and for defrosting frozen goods. Certainly it does those jobs efficiently, but it has so much more to offer; its flexibility and adaptability surprises first-time users and delights the devotees.

In a nutshell, the microwave cooker provides a more nutritious meal, often cooked in less time than it took to prepare, using less electricity, with fewer dishes to wash up and a cool oven which cleans with a wipe. True, there are a few things which the microwave cooker just cannot cope with—yorkshire puddings, pancakes, roast potatoes, some pastries and foods that are deep-fried—but the vast majority of foods are dealt with quickly and effortlessly.

Like all pieces of cooking equipment, the microwave oven is as useful as you want it to be, but as you use it more and more you will find that it plays an increasingly prominent role, being absolutely invaluable when cooking for the family, special occasions and dinner parties.

Manufacturers and retailers now offer a wide range of ovens to meet most requirements. The neat, attractive appliance can be fitted into most situations and is as simple to install as plugging in your electric kettle. It can be placed on a working surface, be built into a suitable kitchen unit or form a composite part of a built-in conventional oven/microwave oven combination appliance. It can easily be placed on a serving trolley so that it can be wheeled from room to room, or taken out to the patio or garden to assist with the barbeque.

Prime cooking operations—thawing, heating, softening, melting, poaching, boiling, simmering, roasting, baking—can be carried out in seconds and minutes rather than minutes and hours with no more effort than it took to pop the food in the oven and operate the controls. With no temperatures to set and only timer controls to adjust, the microwave cooker is so easy to use that any member of the family can reheat refrigerated or frozen ready-prepared meals or snacks. Because food is cooked so quickly, fewer valuable nutrients are lost, and as all the heat is produced in the food itself and not wasted elsewhere, the microwave cooker is also very economical to use. On average, up to 75 per cent can be saved on normal cooking times and up to 50 per cent on your cooking fuel bill. And because so little heat is produced, the kitchen will remain cooler and cleaner—a boon in today's tiny kitchens or in kitchen/dining areas.

When asked what I really think about the microwave cooker, I liken it to other domestic revolutions—the fridge, the freezer and the telephone. Once you have had one, you never know how you managed without! It has become a permanent part of my daily life and I would like to share with other microwave cooks the ideas and recipes which I have developed over the years.

Comparative measurement charts

The following charts give comparative quantities for metric, imperial and some American measurements. The recipes throughout the book include reference to metric measurements which have been rounded off into units of 25 grams due to the fact that exact conversions do not always give acceptable working quantities. This means the overall volume of the cooked product does vary slightly but, in fact, has little effect on the final result.

It is important to weigh and measure as accurately as possible and not to mix metric and imperial weights in one recipe as all measurements are proportionate.

Length and weight
Imperial and American measurements in length and weight are the same.

Length

1·25cm	½in
2·5cm	1in
15·0cm	6in
17·5cm	7in
20·0cm	8in
22·5cm	9in
25·0cm	10in

Weight

Metric	Imperial	Metric	Imperial
25g	1oz	300g	11oz
50g	2oz	350g	12oz
75g	3oz	375g	13oz
100g	4oz	400g	14oz
150g	5oz	425g	15oz
175g	6oz	450g	16oz (1lb)
200g	7oz	475g	17oz
225g	8oz	500g ($\frac{1}{2}$kg)	18oz
250g	9oz	550g	19oz
275g	10oz	575g	20oz (1$\frac{1}{4}$lb)

Liquid and volume
Measurements in liquid and volume are different and these charts show the difference using the American 8 ounce measuring cup.

Liquid

Metric	Imperial	American
150ml	$\frac{1}{4}$pt	$\frac{2}{3}$ cup
275ml	$\frac{1}{2}$pt	1$\frac{1}{4}$ cups
425ml	$\frac{3}{4}$pt	2 cups
550ml	1pt	2$\frac{1}{2}$ cups
850ml	1$\frac{1}{2}$pt	3$\frac{3}{4}$ cups
1000ml (1 litre)	1$\frac{3}{4}$pt	4$\frac{1}{2}$ cups
1150ml	2pt	5 cups

Volume

	Metric	Imperial	American
butter	225g	8oz	1 cup
sugar	225g	8oz	1 cup
flour	225g	8oz	2 cups
icing sugar	225g	8oz	1$\frac{1}{2}$ cups
rice	225g	8oz	1 cup
dried fruits	225g	8oz	1$\frac{1}{2}$ cups
breadcrumbs	225g	8oz	4 cups
grated cheese	225g	8oz	2 cups

Spoon measures
Spoon measures are best used only for small quantities, and are always level unless otherwise stated when referred to in recipes throughout the book.

Spoon measures

Metric	Imperial	American
5ml tsp	1tsp	1tsp
15ml tbsp	1tbsp	1tbsp
1$\frac{1}{2}$ × 15ml tbsp	1$\frac{1}{2}$tbsp	2tbsp
2 × 15ml tbsp (or 30ml)	2tbsp	3tbsp
4 × 15ml tbsp (or 60ml)	4tbsp	5tbsp

Terminology
The following comparison of imperial and American terminology for basic ingredients may be useful to those of you who have access to American cookery books and recipes.

Imperial	American
double cream	heavy cream
single cream	light cream
soured cream	sour cream
demerara sugar	brown sugar
icing sugar	confectioners sugar
black treacle	dark molasses
golden syrup	light corn syrup
clear honey	thin honey
condensed milk	full cream sweetened milk
wholemeal flour	wholewheat flour
plain flour	all-purpose flour
self-raising flour	all-purpose flour with double acting baking powder
bicarbonate of soda	baking soda
minced beef	ground beef
grade 4 eggs	medium eggs
plain chocolate	bitter chocolate
vanilla essence	vanilla extract
cornflour	cornstarch
digestive biscuits	graham crackers
girdle scones	griddle scones
clingfilm	saran wrap
greaseproof paper	wax paper
kitchen paper	paper towels

Conventional oven temperatures

	°C	°F	Gas
Cool	110	225	$\frac{1}{4}$
	130	250	$\frac{1}{2}$
Slow	140	275	1
	150	300	2
Moderate	160	325	3
	180	350	4
Fairly hot	190	375	5
	200	400	6
Hot	220	425	7
	230	450	8
Very hot	240	475	9

Microwave energy

For thousands of years, the method of applying energy in the form of heat to cook food has hardly changed at all. Whether frying, boiling, stewing, baking or roasting by electricity, gas, solid fuel or even the open fire, the food depends on the conduction of the heat from its source to the surface and then the inside of the food. To accelerate the cooking process, the heat or oven temperature may be increased but this can cause excessive browning or overcooking of the outside of the food. Unlike conventional ovens, microwave cookers heat and cook food without applying external heat but by applying microwave energy.

Microwaves—or microwave energy—are non-ionising, electromagnetic, high-frequency radio waves and are non-cumulative. They are close to but not as powerful as infra-red rays and must not be confused with X-rays, gamma rays or ultra-violet rays which are ionising and are known to cause irreversible chemical and cellular changes to take place with little or no temperature variation.

Microwaves vibrate millions of times per second; that is, they have a very high frequency and very short wavelength—hence the term 'microwave'. At a frequency of 2·450MHz or megahertz ('hertz' after the German scientist Heinrich Hertz who first detected electromagnetic energy), microwave energy is absorbed by materials with a high water content—like most foods—and the effect is a rise in temperature. The molecules contained within the food tend to align themselves with the energy and move rapidly back and forth. This causes high-speed friction between the molecules, converting microwave energy into heat. A similar experience can be felt when rubbing your hands together; feel them become warm, and the faster you rub, the warmer they become.

Some materials such as metal and foil—and thus the metal construction of the microwave oven cavity—reflect microwave energy. Other materials such as glass, china, pottery, paper and some plastics allow microwaves to pass through—thus making suitable microwave cooking containers. The effect is, therefore, that microwave energy is only absorbed by the food in the oven making the microwave cooker a very effective and efficient cooking medium. An example of this is solar energy; or imagine standing in front of a window on a cold, sunny day. The sun's energy in the form of heat passes through the window without heating it and it feels cold to the touch; but the molecules in our body behave like tiny magnets, converting the energy from the sun into heat and we feel warm.

Safety
To try to put the safety aspect of microwave cookers into perspective, compare the chance of being physically damaged by microwave energy from a microwave cooker to the possibility of obtaining a skin tan from moonlight. The worst thing that could happen if you were exposed to microwave energy would be a nasty burn—and you would feel it just as if you had placed a hand or finger into a naked flame. It is far more dangerous to sunbathe in the direct glare of the sun for hours on end or subject oneself to a sunlamp. Protection from unnecessary exposure to microwave energy is a requirement in all microwave cookers.

Modern technology and statutory electrical safety standards have ensured that cut-out microswitches are built in and operate as soon as the door is opened, so that the microwave energy switches off immediately. It will not start again until the door is securely shut and the start or 'cook' button operated. The microwave cooker door is built to precise specifications to ensure that when shut, the oven cavity is effectively sealed against energy leakage. Cooking by microwave is safe—frequently safer than cooking conventionally when you take into consideration the relative lack of heat and, therefore, practically no risk of conventional accidental skin burns.

The microwave cooker

While a microwave cooker is basically very simple to use, it would take many pages of text to cover the full details of the intricate operation of this revolutionary appliance. The basic facts which need to be known by the cook, however, are reasonably easy to explain. All reputable manufacturers give detailed information on the installation, operation and care of each particular model while ensuring that it is electrically safe, complying with the British Electrotechnical Approvals Board requirements, and that it will be functional and give satisfactory service to the user. Before first using your microwave cooker, it is important to know how it operates and to understand all the facts given in the manufacturer's handbook.

Operation
In most models, cooking commences once the timer and power level have been set and the start or 'cook' button is operated. On completion of cooking, an audible warning indicates that the set cooking period has elapsed and the cooker turns itself off automatically. Alternatively, at any time during the cooking cycle, the cooker may be switched off by turning the timer back to zero (or the OFF position). In addition, the cooking period can be interrupted when required, simply by opening the oven door. This breaks contact with a number of safety interlock microswitches which are incorporated as part of the door safety mechanism. Any one of the microswitches will ensure that the microwave energy is switched off and

that the oven is no longer operating. Conversely, if one of the microswitches does not make contact when the door is closed, then the microwave cooker cannot be operated.

This diagram shows the main components of the microwave cooker although some designs may vary between the various manufacturer's models.

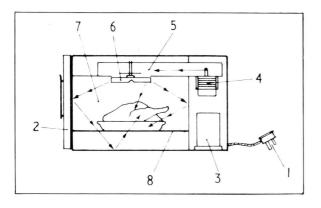

1 The plug top
When the plug top is inserted into the socket outlet and switched on, it enables the microwave cooker to be operated.

2 The oven door
As soon as the oven door is closed and the controls set, the 'cook' button or switch is operated and the energy begins to flow.

3 The transformer
The main function of the transformer is to convert the low voltage of the domestic electrical supply to the high voltages required by the magnetron.

4 The magnetron
This is the microwave energy generator. The magnetron receives the high voltage electrical supply and produces and transmits microwave energy.

5 The waveguide
The waveguide directs the microwave energy from the magnetron into the oven cavity.

6 The stirrer blade
The microwaves enter the oven cavity via the stirrer blade which ensures that the energy is evenly distributed throughout the oven cavity. Some models do not have a stirrer blade but rely on a turntable shelf to turn the food through the microwave energy (see page 12).

7 The oven cavity
The metal construction of the oven cavity directs the microwave energy through suitable cooking containers (see page 13) on to the food.

8 The oven shelf
All food for cooking is placed on the shelf which is so positioned within the oven cavity to gain max-

imum energy distribution and coverage. In some models, the oven shelf is in the form of a revolving turntable (see page 12).

The microwave cooker should never be operated when the oven is empty. If there is nothing to absorb the microwaves they will bounce off the oven cavity walls and reflect back on to the magnetron. This has the effect of shortening its life. A cup of water left in the oven when it is not in use just in case the cooker is accidentally switched on would be a wise precaution.

One of the characteristics of microwave energy is its ability to penetrate food items very quickly to a depth of about 2.5 centimetres (1 inch). Consequently the outer surface of the food will receive more heat than the centre and the rest of the cooking takes place by conduction. This is why sometimes it is recommended

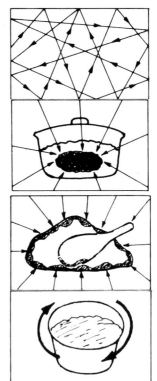

Microwave energy bouncing off the metal interior of the oven cavity

Microwaves passing through suitable cooking containers on to the food

The penetration of microwaves to a depth of about 2·5cm (1in)

The turning of dishes during the cooking cycle for even results

Trifle (page 168); Brandy Cider Cup (page 60); Honey-baked Gammon (page 105); Curried Chicken and Rice Salad (page 229); Devilled Almonds (page 197); Smoked Salmon Quiche (page 89)

to allow a standing time during or after cooking to let the heat equalise and be conducted from the outside of the food through to the centre. Some recipes suggest turning the dish or stirring the contents to assist this process. More information is given on this subject in Microwave Cooking Techniques on page 20.

Features

The application of microwave energy as a cooking medium was developed as a result of research work on radar during the Second World War, leading to the first cooker being produced in America in the late 1940s. As with many revolutionary domestic appliances, the microwave cooker has taken some time to gain respectability in the market place—over twenty-five years when you consider that the first domestic model was launched in 1955. It has now become a necessary piece of equipment, taking its rightful place in the kitchen as an adjunct to other cooking appliances.

How those early models differed from the modern microwave cooker we know today! As a result of recent technology a wide range of models is now available with a variety of additional features to the original standard unit with on/off controls:

Timer controls As most microwave cooking operations are gauged by time instead of time and temperature, the timer control is one of the most important features and is marked so that shorter heating or cooking periods can be set with a degree of accuracy.

Stirrer blade The stirrer blade is usually situated in the top of the oven cavity and ensures an even distribution of the microwave energy throughout the oven and, therefore, around the food to be cooked. Different manufacturers may refer to stirrer blades by other terminology but they all work on the same basic principle.

Turntable Some microwave cookers do not incorporate a stirrer blade but include a revolving turntable which also serves as the oven shelf. The turntable rotates the food in the oven through the microwave energy making sure that an even result is obtained.

Stirrer blade and turntable Both of these features are incorporated in some microwave cookers which in theory must be the ultimate combination for even distribution of the microwave energy for cooking, although in practice either one of the methods ensures that the microwave energy is evenly distributed around the food item being defrosted, reheated or cooked.

Variable power and defrost control These controls allow a greater flexibility of the cooking speed by varying the energy or power level into the oven cavity which can be compared with the equivalent of conventional oven settings. With many food items it is not necessary to vary the power level but it can be invaluable for those recipes or dishes which may benefit from a longer, slower cooking time.

Browning element A browning element is positioned in the top of the oven cavity to enable food to be browned on the surface before or after microwave cooking. This can be a convenient way of giving a microwave-cooked dish a traditional browned appearance and can be an advantage if your conventional cooker does not incorporate a grill element or burner.

Microwave/convection cookers These are microwave cookers with the addition of a conventional convection oven—usually forced air circulation via a fan—in the same compartment, giving you the choice of either or both modes of cooking. Usually the change from convection to microwave can be carried out independently or in automatic sequence. This type of microwave gives the best of both worlds in one compartment, enabling food to be browned conventionally and/or cooked quickly by microwave energy. It would be ideal for those who may have insufficient space for separate units in the kitchen.

Electronic programming Electronic programming relies on a microprocessor which enables multiple-sequence cooking to be carried out. By setting the program at the beginning of food preparation, the microwave cooker will automatically switch on, defrost, rest, cook—at different power levels if required—and finally switch off. Very often, it is also possible to program in certain cooking sequences which are then retained in a memory bank. This can be used most effectively for repeat food items such as proving bread doughs, or pre-programming a cycle for a dish which can then be effortlessly cooked by a member of the family while you are out.

Temperature probe A temperature probe allows you to set the oven to cook by temperature instead of, or in addition to, cooking solely by time. The probe is positioned into the food and the plug is inserted into the receptacle situated in the oven roof or wall. Once programmed, the probe will automatically switch off the microwave cooker as soon as the food has reached the pre-set temperature. Alternatively, it is possible to cook by time and temperature and check the exact temperature the food has reached when required. The temperature probe is usually a feature of microwave cookers with electronic programming and offers the advantage of leaving the food to cook in the microwave unattended. Further information is given in the section Cooking by Temperature on page 21.

Touch controls Touch controls are usually featured on the more sophisticated models with electronic programming. Without any control knobs, dials or switches, the microwave cooker is operated simply by touching the appropriate section of the control panel, and has the advantage of your being able to set times and power levels with great accuracy.

Sensor controls Sensor controls are normally only featured on microwave cookers with electronic programming. The sensory processor control detects the vapour (aroma, moisture or humidity) emitted from the food as it cooks and automatically adjusts the cooking times and power level for various food items and quantities. Some sensor controls work in conjunction with a weighing device. Food is placed on to the cooking shelf in the microwave oven and the weight of the food is automatically calculated before cooking takes place in the microwave cooker by sensor control.

Care and cleaning

Once the microwave cooker has been delivered, do follow the manufacturer's recommendations on the siting and installation of the appliance even though you will probably want to start using it straightaway. The instructions supplied with the microwave cooker will give detailed information on the care and cleaning of your particular model and should be carefully read.

The exterior of the cabinet normally only requires the occasional wipe over with a damp cloth and afterwards a dry and polish with a clean duster. If you wish to use a little spray polish, do not direct it straight on to the appliance but spray on to the duster instead, before applying it to the cabinet. This will ensure that polish is not inadvertently sprayed into any inlet or outlet air vent, which should also be kept clear of any dishes, tea towels, etc while the microwave cooker is operating.

One of the most important areas to keep clean inside the oven is the door seal which should be frequently wiped to clear any soilage which may have been deposited. Generally, microwave is a very clean method of cooking as most dishes are covered while heating or cooking, so preventing splashing of food on to the oven interior. In addition, with no radiant heat, any splashings which do occur are not burnt on, making soilage easy to remove with a moist, soapy cloth. If your oven incorporates a browning element, or is a microwave/convection model, then soilage may require more vigorous rubbing to remove. Avoid using abrasive cleaners other than those suggested by the manufacturer as these can scratch the interior surfaces.

Try to keep the microwave cooker as clean as possible as any soilage left in the oven will absorb microwave energy, slow down the cooking time and eventually become more difficult to remove. If this does happen, place a cup of water in the microwave, switch on and allow it to boil; the steam which is produced will assist in softening the soilage and it may then be wiped away more easily. Any condensation which occurs during the cooking process is quite normal and should be wiped away with kitchen paper towel or a dry cloth; alternatively, a piece of kitchen paper towel can be left in the oven during cooking which will help in absorbing the moisture from the food.

Removable oven shelves or turntables may be easily washed in the sink and dried before replacing in the oven; do read the manufacturer's instructions and recommendations before placing such items in the dishwasher.

Finally, keep a check on door seals and hinges which will need attention if they are faulty or have become rusty through neglect or lack of service. It is most unlikely that the glass or plastic door panel will fracture but, should this occur, do not use the microwave cooker and contact the service engineer straightaway.

Utensils

I find that less washing up is one of the great advantages of cooking by microwave, as many recipes can be cooked and served in the same dish; whether cooking for the family or entertaining guests, this is of tremendous benefit to the busy housewife. In addition to this, you will discover that washing up is generally easier as food does not stick or burn on, because heat is only produced within the food itself and there is no external heat applied to the dish inside the oven cavity.

Microwave energy is reflected from metal and so containers made from aluminium, tin, copper and stainless steel must not be used. But microwave energy passes through glass, pottery and china and provided they have no metal trim or manufacturer's mark in silver or gold on the base, they are ideal dishes for use in the microwave oven. However, some china

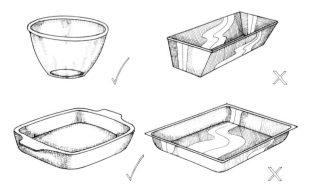

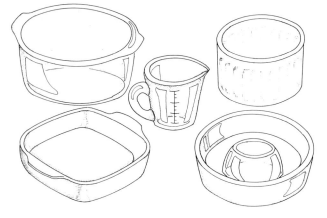

Microwave cooking containers and materials
Most cupboards have an assortment of glass or pottery bowls and pie dishes for fruit puddings and crumbles. A large shallow casserole dish with an upturned plate or saucer in the base makes an ideal roasting dish with trivet. Ovenproof glass and pottery flan dishes can be used equally well in the conventional oven or the microwave cooker for tarts or quiches; also oven-to-table casserole dishes are excellent for microwave cooking. Roasting and boiling bags are ideal for cooking some foods as they can be easily shaken or turned over to stir the contents during the cooking process, and clingfilm is an effective covering for puddings, casseroles and plate meals.

Glass Any type of glass utensil may be used providing there is no metal trim. Thus glass ovenware—eg Pyrex dishes, jugs, casseroles, plates, tumblers and bowls—can be used. Ceramic glass dishes also function extremly well in microwave cooking and make attractive serving dishes.

China and pottery These can be used in the same way as oven glassware providing there is no metal trim or manufacturer's mark or design in gold or silver. This can cause arcing—blue flashes of light—when the metal trim or pattern will discolour and peel. Some pottery can absorb more microwave energy than others, which slows down the cooking thus making these containers less efficient. They also may become fairly hot to the touch and the use of oven gloves is advisable.

Plastic Rigid plastic or heat-resistant plastic dinnerware can be used but may absorb some microwave energy and will be hotter to the touch than other dishes. Freezer containers or lightweight plastic containers can be used for short periods but the heat from the food they contain can cause them to melt during prolonged exposure to microwaves.

Do not use cream cartons, yoghurt pots or plastic bags as they will melt, but the 'boil-in' type bags are excellent although you must remember to prick them to allow steam to escape.

Do not use plastic or plastic freezer bags in the microwave cooker although frozen food wrapped in plastic bags may be placed into the oven for a short period in order to loosen the package before transferring its contents to another more suitable container.

Paper Many individual servings of food may be heated on serviettes or paper plates. Frozen gâteaux, pastries, sandwiches, etc may be placed on paper doyleys

and pottery containers are less efficient in use as they can absorb microwave energy. If in doubt, it would be worth carrying out this simple test to establish the suitability of a dish. Place the dish to be tested in the microwave oven together with a glass of water. Heat for $1\frac{1}{2}$–2 minutes after which time the water should be hot and the dish cool. If the reverse is found, ie the dish is hot and the water is cool, then microwave energy has been absorbed by the dish and should not be used. On the other hand, if both the water in the glass and the dish are warm then the dish could be used for cooking, but as it is absorbing some microwave energy it is less efficient and consequently cooking times would be longer.

Most containers remain relatively cool as microwaves pass through them to be absorbed by the food, but during cooking heat is transferred from the hot food to the dish and therefore it can get hot, so you may find the use of oven gloves necessary.

The majority of established kitchens have a selection of dishes and containers eminently suitable for use in the microwave, and I usually suggest sorting through these before considering buying any new ones. Suitable microwave containers and materials are listed below, but shapes and sizes of the dishes are important too. Regular-shaped dishes are generally better for the most even heating and cooking—round dishes are preferable to oval ones and straight-sided ones better than those which are curved. A container which is slightly rounded at the corners, rather than one with square corners, will help to prevent food from overcooking at these sharper edges. Larger, shallow dishes are preferable to smaller, deep ones as the greater surface area will allow more penetration of the microwave energy. Make sure that the container is large enough to hold the food to be heated or cooked, especially when thawing casseroles when the contents will require breaking down and regular stirring. Light pudding and cake mixtures rise extremely well, to almost double their volume, so remember to only half fill the container with the uncooked mixture.

Fish Chowder (page 71); Oatmeal Scone Round (page 182); Pears in Red Wine (page 164)

before defrosting in the microwave oven. Kitchen paper towels can be used to absorb moisture. Greaseproof paper can be used to cover food to prevent splashing in the oven, but kitchen paper towels are just as good and normally less expensive. Do not, however, place coloured or patterned kitchen paper towels close to food items as the colour may transfer on to the food. Baking parchment can be used most effectively for lining containers when cooking cakes and bread etc.

Wax-coated paper cups, plates and paper may be used for short periods only, as prolonged heating may cause the wax to melt.

Do not use paper and metal twist ties as they can burn very quickly. Make sure they are removed from plastic freezer bags before placing in the microwave oven to loosen.

Wicker and straw baskets These may be used in the microwave for short-term heating only as long exposure to microwave energy may cause them to dry out and crack. However, they are absolutely ideal when thawing or reheating bread or rolls before a meal or dinner party.

Heatproof spatulas and wooden spoons Plastic spatulas and wooden spoons may be used in the microwave cooker for stirring and mixing. If wooden spoons have absorbed grease or moisture they will become hot.

Clingfilm This is excellent for covering dishes and plate meals; however, as it is inclined to stretch and dilate during cooking due to the steam trapped underneath, it is advisable to slit the clingfilm with a knife or scissors before placing the dish in the microwave cooker. This is not necessary though when proving dough in the microwave oven.

Linings The use of clingfilm to line dishes has the advantage of enabling delicate cakes and puddings to be removed more easily from the container (especially when still warm) and placed the right way up on the cooling rack. Also it practically eliminates the need to

wash the dish afterwards. The one disadvantage of using clingfilm as a lining is that it is sometimes difficult to obtain neat corners and edges which may be important to the shape of the cooked result. In this case, it is preferable to line the base of the greased dish with greaseproof paper or baking parchment. It is better not to dust with flour, as this is inclined to result in a doughy crust forming on the outside of the baked product.

Roasting bags and boiling bags These are extremely convenient for cooking a variety of foods ensuring excellent results. Roasting bags are inclined to enhance the browning of joints and poultry and enable vegetables and fruits to be cooked with very little additional liquid.

Do not use the metal ties provided with the bags; elastic bands or string ties can be used instead.

Metal Metal pots and pans and other utensils with a high proportion of metal must *not* be used in the microwave oven. This includes tin, aluminium, copper and stainless steel cooking utensils. The reason for their non-use is that microwave energy is reflected from metal, thus preventing the food within the metal container from cooking, while the reflected microwave energy may cause damage to the magnetron.

Commercially frozen food in aluminium foil containers should be removed and placed in another dish. Never put an unopened can into the oven— always remove the contents and place in a suitable container.

Aluminium foil Small smooth pieces may be used to cover bones or narrower ends of poultry, meat or fish for part of the heating or cooking time to prevent overcooking. Care should be taken to ensure the foil is smoothed tightly around the ends. By using aluminium foil in this way you are in fact preventing the microwaves from reaching that area of the food as they are reflected from metal, thus slowing down the cooking time. Foil should not be allowed to touch the sides, rear, top or door of the cooker.

Always check with your manufacturer's instructions with reference to the use of aluminium foil in your particular model.

Metal skewers These may be used if they are placed carefully in large joints. The skewers must not touch one another or the metal sides, rear, top or door of the cooker. Providing these rules are followed kebab skewers may be used in the microwave oven, but if sparking or arcing occurs rearrange or remove the skewers.

Thermometers Thermometers which are specially designed for use in the microwave cooker are now available and should be used according to the manufacturer's instructions. Unless specially designed, other meat or sugar thermometers must not be used. Foods can of course be removed from the cooker and checked with a conventional cooking thermometer.

Specially designed microwave containers

A good choice of disposable and durable special microwave cooking containers and dishes is now widely available on the market. Decide on your particular needs and requirements before making a selection. Some of these utensils are intended for conventional as well as microwave cooking, while others are suitable for both microwave and the freezer, which are added advantages. Disposable plates, dishes and containers are ideal for heating snacks or shorter-term cooking operations.

Browning dishes

A browning dish makes it possible to prepare an entirely new range of dishes in the microwave cooker. It functions in a similar way to a frying pan or grill and is capable of browning, grilling or searing food items such as beefburgers, steaks, chops and chicken joints which attain the traditional golden-brown appearance normally associated with conventionally cooked foods. Larger joints of meat and poultry brown anyway during their longer cooking time.

In appearance it is a normal glass ceramic dish but has a special tin oxide coating on the base. This coating (on the underside of the dish) absorbs microwave energy when preheated, unlike the remaining surface of the glass ceramic dish which allows microwaves to penetrate. The bottom surface of the dish consequently gets very hot so that when foods are placed on to the hot surface, they brown in the same way as other foods do when immersed in a hot frying pan.

The temperature of the food, however, cools the browning dish, so before cooking a second batch the dish will require a second preheating time (about half the original time) before processing. When the dish containing the food is placed back in the oven, microwave energy cooks the food while the base of the dish continues to brown the underside.

Preheating The size and shape of the browning dish, the output of the microwave cooker, the type and quantity of the food being cooked and the degree of browning required will all affect the amount of preheating time required. When first using the browning dish, experiment a little so as to determine your personal preference. Try the minimum preheat time initially, but if you prefer a browner result, then increase the time—to 6 minutes for smaller dishes and up to 8 minutes for the larger ones. Instructions supplied with the dishes are usually fairly comprehensive and will give recommended preheating and cooking times for each particular shape and size of dish.

Putting a little butter or oil in the preheated dish immediately before adding the food improves the browning of many items, but in this case preheat the browning dish for 1 minute less than the normal time, and then add the butter or oil. When the food is first placed in the dish, flatten or press the food with a heatproof spatula against the hot base of the dish to increase the browning of the underside before placing it back into the microwave cooker.

Points to note
1 Do check with the instruction leaflet for your microwave cooker and be guided by the manufacturer's recommendations regarding the use of browning dishes in your particular model.
2 The feet on the base of the browning dish prevent it coming into direct contact with the oven shelf or a kitchen work surface, but care should be taken when it is hot to ensure that the dish is not placed on a surface which could be damaged by the heat emanating from the underside.
3 The base of the browning dish becomes very hot, so the use of oven gloves is advisable when handling the dish. While heating, the base of the dish will turn yellow but will return to its normal colour when cool.
4 The browning dish should not be preheated for longer than 6—8 minutes. IT IS NOT SUITABLE FOR USE IN A CONVENTIONAL OVEN OR ON A HOB.

5 The dish will require preheating again when cooking a second batch of food. Remove all excess food and drippings and preheat the dish for about half the original preheat time.

6 Turn the food over while there is still sufficient heat in the surface for browning the second side, but serve the food with the browned first side face up.

7 To increase browning of the underside, flatten or press the food with a spatula to gain more contact with the base of the dish before placing it back in the microwave cooker.

8 While browning food, some smoke may be caused but this is quite normal. To help prevent splashings on to the oven interior, cover the dish with its lid or kitchen paper towel.

9 Do not attempt deep-fat frying in the browning dish or in the microwave cooker at all as the temperature of the fat cannot be controlled.

10 Foods should be thawed before placing on the hot surface as any ice crystals present may prevent browning, although thinner foods, such as beefburgers or fish fingers, thaw out quickly during the cooking period.

11 The browning dish may be used as a casserole dish and is also useful for sautéing vegetables such as onions and mushrooms.

12 The browning dish may be washed in a dish washer or by hand, but harsh abrasives must not be used as they may damage the special browning surface. Usually stubborn soilage can be softened by soaking. If necessary, mild cleaners or a plastic scouring pad may be used.

13 The preheat and cooking times given in the Browning Dish Chart are intended only as a guide, as times vary depending on the size and shape of the dish, the output of the microwave cooker, the quantity of food being cooked and the degree of browning required. For those models with defrost control or variable power control all preheating and cooking is carried out on 100% (full) setting.

Browning dish chart

POWER LEVEL: 100% (FULL)

Food	Preheat	Butter or oil	First side	Second side
1 steak, 175–200g (6–7oz)	6–7 min	15g ($\frac{1}{2}$oz) butter or 1 × 15ml tbsp (1tbsp) oil	1$\frac{1}{2}$–2 min	1$\frac{1}{2}$–2 min
2 pork chops, each 225g (8oz)	5–6 min	15g ($\frac{1}{2}$oz) butter or 1 × 15ml tbsp (1tbsp) oil	3 min	8–10 min
4 beefburgers from frozen	6–7 min	15g ($\frac{1}{2}$oz) butter or 1 × 15ml tbsp (1tbsp) oil	1$\frac{1}{2}$–2 min	2–3 min
4 bacon rashers	5–6 min	15g ($\frac{1}{2}$oz) butter or 1 × 15ml tbsp (1tbsp) oil if required	1 min	30–45 sec
2 chicken pieces 225g (8oz) each	5–6 min	15g ($\frac{1}{2}$oz) butter or 1 × 15ml tbsp (1tbsp) oil	5 min	3–5 min
4 sausages, large	5–6 min	15g ($\frac{1}{2}$oz) butter or 1 × 15ml tbsp (1tbsp) oil	6–8 min	turning 3–4 times
4 cod portions in breadcrumbs	4–5 min	1 × 15ml tbsp (1tbsp) oil	2–3 min	3–4 min
6 fish fingers from frozen	5–6 min	Brush food with oil or melted butter	2 min	1–2 min
french toast, 2 slices	4–5 min	1 × 15ml tbsp (1tbsp) oil	45 sec	45–60 sec
1 pizza 17.5cm (7in), whole	3–4 min	15g ($\frac{1}{2}$oz) butter or 1 × 15ml tbsp (1tbsp) oil	3–4 min	—
oven chips 225g (8oz)	3$\frac{1}{2}$–4 min	—	2$\frac{1}{2}$–3 min	2$\frac{1}{2}$–3 min
2 eggs	2–3 min	15g ($\frac{1}{2}$oz) butter or margarine (prick yolks)	1$\frac{1}{2}$–1$\frac{3}{4}$ min	—

Examples of preheating and cooking times are given in this chart but further information for fish and meat are given in their relative sections (pages 84 and 99).

Guard of Honour (page 109) with Orange and Herb stuffing (page 141); Baked Onions (page 153); Chocolate Pots (page 158)

Microwave cooking techniques

Do not think that cooking by microwave means that you must learn completely new cooking techniques. Indeed, most of the basic rules still apply. It is just a case of adapting those rules and yourself to this new method of cooking food. Special points to watch for are given in the recipes but it is important to be aware of the factors which govern successful results.

Power of the oven and cooking times
Most microwave cookers have total power inputs of between 1,000 and 1,600 watts with outputs of between 500 and 700 watts respectively. The difference between the input and output power is used by the magnetron, stirrer blade, cooling fan, power converter and the interior and indicator lights.

It is the output power from the magnetron which controls the amount of microwave energy used in the oven cavity and the recipes in this book have been tested on microwave cookers with outputs of 650 watts. The instruction leaflet provided with your particular model should give details of the input and output power of the cooker, and timings on recipes should be adjusted accordingly. Cookers with lower outputs will require longer cooking times while higher outputs will need slightly shorter times. For example, a recommended cooking time of 10 minutes on 100% (full) setting for a microwave cooker with a power output of 650 watts would need to be adjusted to approximately 12–13 minutes for a 500 watt model and 8–9 minutes for a 700 watt cooker; shorter cooking times need less adjustment and longer times will require slightly more.

Starting temperature
Differences in the temperature of the food when placed in the microwave cooker will affect the length of cooking time required. The colder the food, the longer the heating time, so allowances must be made when using food directly from the refrigerator or freezer.

Turning and stirring
When food is placed into the oven cavity for heating, defrosting or cooking, microwave energy is directed into it from all directions including the base of the cavity beneath the glass shelf. However, due to the fact that microwaves penetrate the food only to a depth of 2.5cm (1in) it is quite likely that the entire outside surfaces of the food will heat through while the very centre remains relatively cool. The heating of the centre of the food relies on the conduction of heat through to this point, therefore the turning of the dishes or the stirring of some foods will be necessary during the heating process. The turning around of dishes means simply giving the dish a quarter turn

(90°) or a half turn (180°) on the oven shelf. Turning dishes is not always necessary if you have a microwave cooker with a turntable. Some foods such as joints of meat and large jacket potatoes may need to be turned *over* during the cooking process; this also applies when defrosting frozen foods such as steaks and chops etc to ensure even results are obtained.

Standing time
It is always better to undercook than to overcook the food, giving a little extra time if required. However, foods do continue cooking after their removal from the oven and some food items will require this standing, resting or 'heat equalisation' period to assist with the general heating or cooking process.

When defrosting a joint, for example, it may begin to cook around the edges before thawing completely in the centre, thus a period of standing time in between periods of exposure to microwave energy is required to allow more even defrosting. Due to the continuation of the heating or cooking process during the standing time, it is possible to keep foods quite hot while further dishes are being cooked in the microwave. This is, of course, very useful when preparing a meal. Some dishes—a cake or a pudding, for example—should be removed from the oven while the top is still slightly moist and left to stand until cooking is complete. Whether food is left to stand inside or outside the cooker is entirely up to you. It may be that you wish to leave the dish inside the oven out of the way, or you may have other food to cook in the meantime.

Utensils
The shape of the dish will affect timings in the microwave; also some utensils will absorb more microwave energy than others. In the latter situation, the cooking times will be affected. This is explained more fully under the section Utensils (page 13).

Quantity
As the quantity of food placed in the oven is increased, the length of cooking time needs also to be increased proportionately. For example, one jacket potato weighing 100–150g (4–5oz) will take 5–6 minutes, two will take 7–9 minutes and three will take 10–11 minutes, and so on. A rough guide would be to allow approximately between one-third and one-half extra time when doubling the quantity of food to be heated. Similarly, if you use less than the quantities given in the recipes in this book, then the cooking times must be reduced accordingly.

Shape
The shape of the food should be as uniform as possible to obtain the best results, but of course this will not always be possible. To protect legs and wings of

poultry or the thin ends of fish or a joint, such as a leg of lamb, from overheating, it is quite in order to wrap them with a small smooth piece of foil, which will slow down the cooking of these sections of the food. Generally, foods which have an overall longer, flatter surface area will heat more quickly than foods which are densely packed into a small dish.

Density and texture
Because microwave cooking is so fast, differences in densities and textures will show up much more quickly in the end result. You will soon find out that a slice of light-textured french or vienna bread will thaw and heat much more quickly than the sliced, prepacked variety and that a sponge cake will heat through faster than a meat pudding. This is because the lightness in the texture of the food allows the microwave energy to penetrate more easily.

Moisture
Moisture too can affect times as microwave energy reacts mainly on water molecules. Some of the recipes in this book have been adjusted to use more or less liquid than you are perhaps used to, in order to ensure successful results: for example, many vegetables can be cooked with very little water ensuring maximum flavour retention, whereas most cake mixtures have to be wetter than normal for a good even rise and a moist result.

Seasonings
Salt can have a toughening effect, especially on meat and poultry, so use minimal seasoning during the cooking process and, if in doubt, adjust the seasoning at the finish.

Covering the food
As, when cooking conventionally, lids on dishes or saucepans speed up the food heating process, so it is when cooking in the microwave. Whether a lid is placed on the casserole dish or the food is covered with clingfilm, steam is trapped inside and this will enable even and slightly faster results to be obtained. Covering food also allows minimal liquid to be used and ensures no flavour loss.

However, when heating through some items, for example crusty rolls or pastry dishes, it would be undesirable to trap the steam as this would prevent a crisp result. In these cases it would be preferable to cover the dish with a piece of kitchen paper towel, which would assist in absorbing the moisture given off from the food.

Cooking foods
All the different types of food which can be cooked by microwave are given in the various recipe sections. Prime cooking operations such as melting, softening, roasting, baking, boiling, simmering and poaching can be carried out very quickly and therefore give foods a fresher flavour with minimal loss of valuable nutrients.

The microwave cooker will cook anything in that it will turn food from a raw state into a cooked state, but experience has shown that some foods are better for being cooked conventionally—yorkshire puddings and roast potatoes are good examples. It therefore makes sense when cooking a traditional Sunday lunch to cook the beef, potatoes and yorkshire pudding in the normal way, saving the microwave free for the vegetables, sauces, gravy and dessert. Some other dishes for which you will still need your conventional cooker are pancakes, some pastry and foods which require deep-fat frying, for example fish in batter or breadcrumbs and chips.

Foods should be checked frequently until you become more experienced. Give half the recommended cooking time and then allow more time if necessary, remembering that food will carry on cooking for a short time after being removed from the oven. It is always better to undercook the food rather than to overcook as it is then almost impossible to rectify it. An indication that foods are overheating and too much time has been allowed is if you hear foods begin to 'pop'—remove from the oven straightaway and allow to stand to equalise the heat throughout.

Cooking by temperature
If your microwave cooker includes a temperature probe, the instructions supplied with your particular model will give detailed specific information on its use and care although I have included here some basic information for your guidance.

Generally, a probe gives best cooking results with foods of same densities, ie solid joints of meat (preferably without bone) or all liquid; for example, a casserole consisting of cubes of meat in a light stock is not recommended although of course a temperature probe can be used successfully when reheating foods of this type.

When using the temperature probe for dishes which need to be covered, clingfilm is ideal as the covering material as it can easily be pierced to allow the insertion of the probe into the food.

Positioning the probe: The pointed end of the metal thermometer should be inserted into the leanest/thickest part of the food and usually to a depth of at least 2.5cm (1in). When cooking meat, insert the probe into the centre of the joint—avoid inserting through fat and ensure that it is not in contact with bone as these tend to give false temperature readings.

For poultry, the probe should be positioned between the body and inner thigh of the bird. Minced meat casseroles and bolognaise sauces can be cooked successfully using the probe which should be placed in the centre of the dish. Cook on a low 30 or 50% power level to allow flavours to blend during the cooking period. Alternatively, some models have a facility whereby you can cook by temperature followed by time. Once food has reached the preset probe temperature, the food can be held at that temperature for a determined period of time to allow flavours to blend and sauces to thicken until ready for serving.

Temperature cooking chart: With the exception of meat and poultry items, all the temperatures given are intended as a guide, as much depends on personal preferences and the variety of recipes for each food type. Whether your oven is equipped with a temperature probe or you wish to use a separate microwave thermometer, the following gives recommended temperatures at the end of cooking for a variety of foods. Remember that the internal temperature of foods (particularly meat and poultry) will increase a further 5–10°C during the 10–15 minute standing time at the end of the cooking period.

Food item	Internal temperature at end of cooking
beverages	70–80°C
fish	65°C
meat	
beef—boneless roast	
rare	55–60°C
medium	65–70°C
well done	75–80°C
lamb—top leg roast	
medium	70–75°C
well done	75–80°C
pork—loin roast	75–80°C
veal	75–80°C
meat loaf	70–75°C
minced meat casserole, eg savoury mince	
bolognaise sauce	70–75°C
poultry	
chicken, whole	80–85°C
joint	80–85°C
turkey, whole	80–85°C
boneless roast	70–75°C
reheating, eg left-overs, canned foods, casseroles	70–80°C
soups	75–80°C

Heating foods

Whether you wish to reheat small portions of leftovers, the contents of a can of food or casseroles, the microwave oven will cope with them all without drying and loss of flavour. Dishes can be prepared in advance, refrigerated and then reheated when required which is a great benefit when entertaining, and the family can heat their own snacks and meals when you are not there. More information is given on this subject in the section Meal Planning on page 33. Foods should be covered where necessary (see Covering the Food on page 21) which will keep in the moisture and also prevent splashings in the oven interior. Pastry items and bread can either be covered with, or placed on, kitchen paper towels to absorb moisture and help obtain a crisp result. The Convenience Foods Guide on page 28 will give you an idea of timings and standing periods required when heating various food items.

Arrangement of food

When defrosting, heating or cooking a number of foods of the same type—rolls, buns, cakes, biscuits, jacket potatoes—they should be arranged in a circle on a plate or directly on the oven shelf and be of equal size and shape. If this is not possible, it may be necessary to rearrange the foods halfway through the heating process—outside ones to the inside and vice versa—to ensure that an even result is obtained. There may be occasions when you require to heat foods of varying type at the same time, for example some vegetables with a jug of sauce, or a sponge pudding with a bowl of custard. If different heating times are required, ensure that each item is removed from the oven as soon as it has heated sufficiently.

Appearance of food

With experience you will be able to tell if food is cooked by its appearance even though it does not take on the traditional golden-brown colour normally associated with conventionally cooked foods. You will

Veal and Ham Pies (page 245); Gannat (page 205); Chocolate and Biscuit Cake (page 177); Potted Tongue (page 52); Spiced Fruit Punch (page 58)

find that the fact the foods are cooked so quickly compensates for the lack of browning, and anyway this can be overcome very easily by garnishing and decorating dishes more attractively. Have available some ready-prepared toppings such as browned crumbs, chopped nuts, crushed cereals, brown sugar, apricot glaze, paprika, dried herbs, parmesan cheese, etc. When a cake is cooked in only a few minutes and coated in frosting or dusted with icing sugar when cool, this surely outweighs the fact that it is not golden brown in colour underneath, for it is virtually indistinguishable from one cooked conventionally.

Some longer cooking joints and poultry will brown to a degree but this can be enhanced by sprinkling with paprika before cooking or by the use of microwave seasonings and colourings or gravy brownings or sauces. If extra browning is required, food can be placed under a hot grill or in a preheated conventional oven for a few minutes at the end of the microwave cooking time. This is a way of combining speed of microwave with the browning acquired by cooking conventionally. More information is given on combining the two methods of cooking in the recipe section Microwave/Conventional Cooking on page 238. The browning of sausages, bacon, chops, etc can be carried out in the microwave by the use of a browning dish (see page 17).

Keeping foods hot
Dishes can be kept warm after heating or cooking by covering them with aluminium foil or can be simply left in the covered container during the final standing period. Remember that foods carry on cooking for a short while during this time so that it is possible to cook several items one after another and serve them all together when required. If the temperature of the food has dropped slightly, dishes can easily be put back into the oven for another minute or two to boost the serving temperature.

It is often quicker to heat or cook foods in small amounts rather than to overfill the oven with food, but if a large quantity of items are to be cooked, it is advisable to use the warming compartment or oven on your conventional cooker on a low setting to keep foods hot for an extended period prior to serving.

Defrost control

When defrosting food by microwave, it is so fast compared with normal methods that there is less flavour loss and the risk of bacterial growth is minimal by comparison.

In some models, the defrost control may be incorporated as part of the variable power control (page 25), or it may be a separate switch or setting when the microwave cooker features just one or two different power levels.

Check with your instruction booklet for the percentage output of the defrost control as this may vary according to the model. The times given in this book are for a defrost control with 50% power level. Times should be adjusted accordingly for defrosting at higher or lower percentage outputs.

When the defrost control is operated, the microwave energy is cycled on and off in the oven to slow down the heating process. Otherwise, if frozen food were subjected to microwave energy until it was completely defrosted, the outer edges would begin to cook before the centre was thawed. Therefore, the defrost control allows the heat to equalise within the frozen food by gradual conduction and no surface cooking should take place.

Defrosting
When defrosting some foods—joints of meat or poultry for example—additional standing periods are required to give a perfect thaw with no overheating of the outside edges. The food is then at an even temperature throughout, which ensures that when it is subsequently cooked, a good, even result is obtained. The number of heating and resting periods depends on the size or amount of food being defrosted, but generally the larger the item, the longer the periods of heating and of rest, with a final resting period being allowed before cooking or reheating.

Quicker defrosting is possible by simply placing frozen food into the microwave on defrost control until it is completely thawed, with one standing period halfway through; however, with this method less even results may be obtained. Alternatively, frozen food can be defrosted until it is warm to the touch on the outside edges and then left to stand at room temperature until it is completely thawed.

These defrosting methods are purely a matter of preference and time available, and with experience you will be able to determine which method you prefer. You will also find that many items—vegetables, small cakes, rolls, bread slices, for example—may be thawed in a matter of seconds or minutes by using a 100% (full) setting.

Most frozen foods should be placed in a suitable cooking container, first ensuring that it is large enough to hold the food once it has thawed—particularly important when defrosting soups, sauces, casseroles, etc—and allowing sufficient room for stirring the food without spillage. Commercially frozen foods in foil trays or containers should be removed and placed in a dish suitable for microwave cooking.

Foods should be covered during the defrosting period where necessary. In the case of pastry dishes and bread, kitchen paper towels can be used to absorb any moisture. Small, smooth pieces of aluminium foil (page 16) will protect the narrower ends of poultry, meat or fish for part of the defrosting cycle to prevent any cooking of these thinner parts.

You can check whether food is defrosted either by feel or by using a thermometer; if it needs a little extra time, just put it back into the oven for a short while longer. It is important that meat and poultry are completely thawed and at an even temperature throughout before cooking.

Defrosting and resting times are covered in more detail within the various recipe sections but the Convenience Foods Guide (page 28) deals with a range of commercially frozen foods and may be used as a general guide.

Heating and cooking
Some microwave cookers feature a defrost setting as the only alternative to 100% (full) power level. In addition to using it for defrosting, the control may be used for heating and cooking those foods which benefit from a slower heating or cooking period:

1 Softening butter, melting method cake mixtures, melting chocolate, combining butter and sugar for caramelising, melting jellies, melting cheese.
2 Cooking casseroles, either when using tougher cuts of meat or when it is important that seasoning and spices blend well, eg curries.
3 Cooking tougher joints of meat.
4 Heating or cooking egg-based custards or cream sauces and setting the fillings in pre-baked flan cases, eg quiches.
5 Reheating larger casseroles thereby eliminating some of the need to stir as heating of the centre will be through conduction.
6 Cooking larger, flatter dishes to prevent the outsides drying out before the centre is cooked, eg cheesecake, bread pudding.
7 Poaching large fruits, eg plums, greengages, peaches.
8 Warming bread or rolls in a basket.
9 Proving bread dough.
10 Poaching more delicate fish fillets or cutlets, eg salmon.

Whether you use the defrost control for some of the above items is a matter of choice. I have included some recipes for dishes which may be cooked on 50% (defrost) setting, but if adapting your own recipes,

allow approximately double the cooking time given for 100% (full) setting and refer to the Power Levels Time Chart on page 27.

Variable power control

The advantage of the variable power control featured on some models is that it enables a greater flexibility and control of the cooking speed. When a setting other than 100% (full) has been selected on the variable power control, the microwave energy is automatically cycled on and off at varying rates depending on the setting chosen. At the lower setting the energy is off longer than it is on. As the control is moved to the higher settings the energy is on for longer periods and at 100% (full) setting, the energy is on all of the time.

Choosing the setting is similar to selecting the oven temperature on your conventional cooker—the lower setting or temperature, the longer the cooking time; the higher the setting, the shorter the cooking time. When a variable power setting has been selected, the timer does not stop and start, but continues to move while the energy switches on and off in the oven.

It is important to understand the percentage outputs or power levels of your own microwave cooker and how these relate to the descriptions of the settings. This information should be given in the manufacturer's instructions to users.

Description of settings
There are many different ways that manufacturers portray the variable power control settings on the control panels of their microwave cookers. In addition, the electronic touch-control models enable any percentage level or setting to be selected just by touching the appropriate part of the control panel.

Below are a few examples of the description of settings used together with the approximate power (watts) outputs and percentage levels at those settings.

Power levels
Some foods require slower cooking to help tenderise them, such as the less expensive cuts of meat. Slower cooking also allows food flavours to blend thoroughly, meat sauces and curries for example, and some foods are heated through more evenly by using a

Description of settings

1	2	3	4	5	6	7
KEEP WARM	SIMMER/DEFROST	STEW	DEFROST	BAKE	ROAST	HIGH
LOW	LOW	MED–LOW	MEDIUM	MED–HIGH	HIGH	FULL
150 WATTS	200 WATTS	250 WATTS	300 WATTS	400 WATTS	500 WATTS	650 WATTS
(20–25%)	(30%)	(40%)	(50%)	(60%)	(75%)	(100%)

lower power level. The following may be a useful guide as to the use of the variable power control percentage levels:

10–20% This low setting may be used for defrosting joints very slowly and for keeping foods warm for up to half an hour.

30–40% This setting is often used for defrosting, cooking less tender joints, slow-simmering cheaper cuts of meat and for softening butter or cream cheese.

50–60% Use this setting for faster defrosting and simmering. It may also be used for defrosting and reheating frozen casseroles.

70–80% Most precooked foods and leftovers may be reheated using this setting. Use it also for roasting joints and for cooking foods which contain cheese or cream.

100% – Use for bringing liquids to the boil and for preheating a browning dish. Most joints of meat and poultry, vegetables and fish can be cooked on this setting. However, many dishes may have a better flavour, texture and appearance if one of the lower settings is used, in which case a longer cooking period would be required.

Power levels time chart
By using the chart given below, it is possible to adapt the cooking times given in this book to suit your own particular model. However, the timings given in the chart are intended only as a guide for much depends on the shape, density, texture and temperature of the food. The calculations have been based on a microwave cooker with an average power output of 650 watts and, of course, this may vary between different models. Allow slightly extra time if using a microwave cooker with a lower output and slightly less time if using a cooker with a higher output.

Unless otherwise stated, the recipes in this book have microwave cooking times given for 100% (full) setting.

If you wish to slow down the heating or cooking cycle by using one of the lower settings on the variable power control, this chart will give you the approximate times for the other percentage outputs. Remember to check with your instruction booklet for the description of settings/power levels and the percentage outputs of each one on your particular model. For times greater than 10 minutes, simply add together the figures in the appropriate column.

Power levels *(cooking time in minutes)*

10%	20%	30%	40%	50% (defrost)	60%	70%	80%	90%	100% (full)
10	5	$3\frac{1}{4}$	$2\frac{1}{2}$	2	$1\frac{3}{4}$	$1\frac{1}{2}$	$1\frac{1}{4}$	1	1
20	10	7	5	4	$3\frac{1}{4}$	$2\frac{3}{4}$	$2\frac{1}{2}$	$2\frac{1}{4}$	2
30	15	10	$7\frac{1}{2}$	6	5	4	$3\frac{3}{4}$	$3\frac{1}{4}$	3
40	20	13	10	8	7	$5\frac{1}{4}$	5	$4\frac{3}{4}$	4
50	25	17	12	10	8	7	6	$5\frac{1}{2}$	5
60	30	20	15	12	10	8	$7\frac{1}{2}$	$6\frac{1}{2}$	6
70	35	23	17	14	12	$9\frac{1}{4}$	$8\frac{3}{4}$	$7\frac{1}{4}$	7
80	40	27	20	16	13	11	10	9	8
90	45	30	22	18	15	12	11	10	9
100	50	33	25	20	16	13	12	11	10

Layered Rice Pudding (page 224); Beef and Walnut Burger (page 239); Jacket Potatoes with Sour Cream and Chives (page 150)

Convenience foods guide

Not all convenience foods are included, but use this chart as a handy reference guide.

Food	Quantity	Method	Defrosting time 50% (defrost)	Cooking time 100% (full)	Special points
MEAT *Reheat* cornish pasty	1	Stand on kitchen paper towel		$\frac{3}{4}$–1$\frac{1}{4}$ min	Stand for 2–3 min before serving
individual meat pie	1	Remove from foil tray, stand on kitchen paper towel		$\frac{3}{4}$–1$\frac{1}{4}$ min	Stand for 2–3 min before serving
family-size meat pie or quiche	450g (1lb)	Remove from foil dish and place on serving dish		6 min	Stand for 4 min halfway through and after cooking
4 beefburgers, canned	283g (10oz)	Place on dish or serving plate, cover		4 min	Turn over halfway through cooking
steak and kidney pudding, canned	440g (15$\frac{1}{2}$oz)	Remove from can, place in a bowl, cover		4–5 min	Stand for 5 min after cooking
soya protein mince or chunks, canned	425g (15oz)	Place in a bowl, cover		3–4 min	Stir once during cooking
Frozen roast meat in gravy	113g (4 oz)		5 min, stand for 4 min	1$\frac{1}{2}$ min	Separate slices after defrosting
	340g (12oz)		10 min, stand for 9 min	3$\frac{1}{2}$ min	
beefburgers	4	Place on kitchen paper towel		3–4 min	Turn over once during cooking
shepherd's pie	450g (1lb)	Remove from foil dish and place on serving plate or dish	6 min, stand for 6 min 3 min, stand for 6 min	5–6 min	Turn once during cooking
individual steak and kidney puddings	125g (5oz)	Remove from foil dish and place on serving plate	2 min, stand for 5 min 3 min, stand for 2 min	2$\frac{1}{2}$ min	Stand for 2 min before serving
individual meals 'boil in bag'	225g (8oz)	Slit bag and place on serving plate	6 min, stand for 6 min	2–2$\frac{1}{2}$ min	Stand for 2 min before serving
moussaka or lasagne	450g (1lb)	Remove from foil dish and place on serving plate or dish, cover	8 min, stand for 6 min 4–5 min	9 min	Stand for 1 min before serving
sausage rolls (cooked)	1	Place on kitchen paper towel	30–60 sec, stand for 1 min	15 sec	
	4		1$\frac{1}{2}$–2 min, stand for 3 min	30–30 sec	
FROZEN FISH 2 cod steaks	225g (8oz)	Place on plate or dish, cover	6 min, stand for 6 min	3 min	Turn over halfway through defrosting

Food	Quantity	Method	Defrosting time 50% (defrost)	Cooking time 100% (full)	Special points
'boil in bag' fish, eg smoked haddock	198g (7oz)	Slit top of bag and place on plate	6 min, stand for 4 min	6 min	Separate fillets after defrosting
fish steak in sauce 'boil in bag'	170g (6oz)	Slit top of bag and place on plate	4 min, stand for 4 min 2 min, stand for 5 min	1½ min	Shake contents of bag before serving
fish fingers	10	Arrange in circle on plate	6 min, stand for 4 min	1½–2½ min	Dot with butter before cooking
2 fish cakes	each 50g (2oz)	Place on plate	4 min, stand for 4 min	1–1½ min	Dot with butter before cooking
CANNED FOODS *Reheat* soup	275ml (½pt) 2 mugs or bowls	Pour into mug or soup bowl		3 min 5–6 min	Stir once during cooking
pasta, eg macaroni cheese	425g (15oz)	Place in bowl or serving plate, cover		4–5 min	Stir twice during cooking
spaghetti in tomato sauce	440g (15½oz)	Place in bowl or serving plate, cover		3–4 min	Stir once during cooking
baked beans	220g (7¾oz) 425g (15oz)	Place in a bowl, or on a plate, cover		1–1½ min 3–4 min	Stir once during cooking
peas or other small vegetables	425g (15oz)	Place in bowl, cover		4–4½ min	Stir twice during cooking
custard or milk puddings	440g (15½oz)	Place in serving jug or bowl		3 min	Stir once during cooking
sponge pudding	298g (10½oz)	Place in bowl or on a plate		2 min	Turn once during cooking
CAKES AND PUDDINGS Frozen home-made cake	1 slice	Place on serving plate	1–2 min		Time varies with size and type of cake
cream sponge	250g (9oz)	Place on serving plate	1–1½ min, stand until cream is completely thawed		Times given are sufficient to thaw the sponge only
cream doughnut	1 4	Place on kitchen paper towel	30 sec, stand for 4 min 1¼ min, stand 5 min		
jam doughnut	1 4	Place on kitchen paper towel	1½ min, stand 2 min 4 min, stand 4 min		
cheesecake with fruit topping	1	Place on serving plate	4 min, stand 5 min 2 min, stand 5 min		

Food	Quantity	Method	Defrosting time 50% (defrost)	Cooking time 100% (full)	Special points
Reheat mince pies, (cooked)	1	Place on kitchen paper towel		15 sec	Stand for 1–2 min before serving
	4			1 min	
Christmas pudding	1 whole 550–850ml (1–1½pt)	In pudding basin		2–3 min	Stand for 1 min before serving
	1 portion	On serving plate or dish		30–60 sec	Stand for 1 min before serving
BREAD PRODUCTS *Frozen* roll or large slice of bread	1 3	Place on kitchen paper towel or on oven shelf		10–25 sec 20–35 sec	Thawing time depends on density and type of bread
small loaf	1	Place on oven shelf	4–5 min, stand for 8–10 min		
large loaf	1		7–9 min, stand 12–16 min		
pizza, large small	1 1	Place on serving plate		5–6 min 3 min	
croissant	4	Place on kitchen paper towel	1½–2 min, stand 2 min	1 min	Stand 1–2 min before serving
MISCELLANEOUS butter or margarine, frozen	250g (8.8oz)	Place in dish or plate, remove any foil wrapping	30–45 sec, stand 1 min 30 sec, stand 1 min		
jelly	135g (4¾oz)	Break into cubes and place in bowl or measuring jug		15–30 sec	Stir well after heating and add remaining liquid quantity
chocolate	100g (4oz)	Break into squares and place in bowl		1–1½ min	Beat well after melting
toasted almonds	50g (2oz) blanched almonds	Place into boiling or roasting bag or on a plate		6 min or until toasted	Stir or shake frequently
chestnuts	10–12	Slit the skins, place on plate		1–1½ min	Shell and use as required
cream, frozen sticks	225g (8oz)	Place in bowl or measuring jug, cover	3–4 min, stand until thawed		Stir well every min, break down sticks with a fork. Beat frequently during the standing time
white sauce	275ml (½pt)	Place in bowl, cover	8 min, stand 5 min	4–5 min	Stir well and break down lumps with a fork. Whisk or beat well during the standing time

Claret Cup (page 61); Christmas Wine (page 60)

Summary of important notes

★ All cooking is carried out in the microwave cooker using 100% (full) power unless otherwise stated. Some microwave cooking instructions are given for models with variable power control settings, but it is still possible to cook the dish on models without this facility by referring to the Power Levels Time Chart on page 27 and calculating the time required for cooking on 100% (full) power. The automatic intermittent 'off' periods can be achieved manually by allowing the dish to rest at 1–2 min intervals throughout the cooking duration.

★ Metal baking tins or metal-trimmed dishes must not be used in the microwave cooker.

★ The recommended cooking times are intended as a guide only as so much depends on the power input to the microwave oven cavity: the shape, material and size of the dish; the temperature of the food at the commencement of cooking and the depth of food in the dish.

★ If the quantities of food placed in the cooker are increased or decreased, then the cooking times must be adjusted accordingly.

★ Always undercook rather than overcook the food by cooking for a little less time than the recipe recommends, allowing the extra time if required.

★ When reheating or cooking foods, best results are obtained if the food is at an even temperature throughout—particularly important when cooking foods after defrosting.

★ Some foods, ie casseroles, require stirring during defrosting, reheating or cooking to assist with the heating process. After cooking with microwave energy, heat equalisation or standing time is often recommended. This allows the distribution of heat evenly throughout the food.

★ Deep-fat frying must not be attempted as the temperature of the oil or fat cannot be controlled.

★ Microwave cooking does not brown some food in the traditional way, but dishes can be finished off in a conventional oven or under a grill if you feel it is preferred.

Recipe section

Meal planning

Does the thought of Christmas approaching delight you? Or, like me, fill you with apprehension and a degree of panic when thinking of cards to write, presents to buy and wrap, decorations for the house, the Christmas tree and the hundred and one other things required to ensure a happy time for all? For many of us, the Christmas meal is possibly the most important of the year, with family and friends gathered together to enjoy this annual feast. Unfortunately, for the housewife, it could mean weeks of preparation culminating in her spending a great many hours slaving in a hot kitchen and consequently missing most of the festivities. With the aid of the microwave and with no less thanks to the freezer, Christmas lunch or dinner need not be a headache at all.

We are all aware by now how the freezer has enabled us to prepare stuffings, sauces, sausage rolls and mince pies, etc, well in advance. With a microwave cooker, not only will it save time and energy in the preparation of most of these food items before freezing, but on the day, foods can be defrosted and reheated in the dishes in which they are to be served which obviously cuts down on washing up. Even the vegetables can be cooked by microwave earlier in the day and just reheated before serving. And think of the Christmas pudding which can be reheated in 3–4 minutes (depending on size) instead of the normal 3–4 hours' steaming on top of the cooker. A plate of cooked mince pies will be hot through in 1–2 minutes and these, with the pudding, can easily be heated in the microwave while the dishes from the main course are being cleared from the table.

Of course, Christmas is not the only time that the microwave will help in meal preparation. Complete meals of two, three or four courses can be cooked in the microwave with a little thought and planning. With experience, you will become more familiar with cooking and standing times. Dishes may be prepared in advance, so that they need only be placed back in the oven to be reheated or to boost the serving temperature without any harm to the food or loss of flavour. You will also find that some foods are better for being cooked conventionally. Yorkshire puddings and roast potatoes are good examples and, therefore, it makes sense if cooking a traditional Sunday lunch to cook the beef, potatoes and yorkshire pudding in the conventional cooker, leaving the microwave free for the vegetables, sauces, gravy and dessert. Foods which require deep-fat frying, fish in batter and chips for example, must be cooked conventionally as the temperature of the fat cannot be controlled in the microwave. Frozen chips, however, can be thawed in the microwave while the fat or oil is being heated conventionally which will shorten the frying time.

When first planning your menus, cook each course separately, then gradually progress until a complete meal is cooked by microwave. You may find that organising a time plan will help at first. Always serve at least one cold course, either a starter or a sweet, which can be prepared by microwave then refrigerated, and never worry about choosing to serve both of these courses cold if it saves time when entertaining. Defrost all foods first, except vegetables which can be cooked from frozen. When a large number of fresh vegetables are required, some may be partly cooked then left to stand while the rest are cooked. When using the microwave to cook a joint of meat or poultry, the vegetables should be cooked during its final standing time. As the microwave cooker automatically switches off at the end of any set cooking time, you can leave it to heat or cook the next course while eating the first without the worry of the food overcooking or spoiling.

You will find it helps to line up all the foods in their dishes in the order in which they are to be cooked and, where practicable, use clingfilm to cover dishes; also, use roasting bags or boiling bags which can be thrown away afterwards. Have aluminium foil ready so that you can wrap cooked items to keep them warm or, if there are a lot of dishes to be served, use the warming compartment or oven at a low setting on the conventional cooker.

Plate meals
Plate meals are an enormous help when members of the family require meals at difficult times. With the microwave you really can cook just once a day, and arrange meals on plates and refrigerate them to be reheated later or freeze them to use next week. Plate meals are ideal standbys for those members of the family who need to cook a meal for themselves when you are not there, and they will be delighted that there is only one plate to wash up!

When arranging a meal on a plate, place the food within the well of the plate as evenly as possible; if thin slices of meat are to be served, it is better to place them in the very centre with the gravy poured over and the vegetables around the outside. All items of food on the plate should be at the same temperature and cooked to the same degree to ensure an even result during reheating.

The plate should be covered while heating. Using 100% (full) setting the average plate meal (350–450g/12–16oz) will take approximately 3–4 minutes to reheat from room temperature and 4–5 minutes from a refrigerator; with a frozen plate meal, more even results will be achieved if it is defrosted first for 10–12 minutes using 50% (defrost) setting before reheating. Allow 1–2 minutes standing time before uncovering and serving. If you are heating two plate meals, one after the other, pop the first one back after the second one has heated and give it an extra $\frac{1}{2}$–1 minute to boost the temperature before serving. Alternatively, there are now plate-stacking rings available which make it possible to heat two or more plate meals at one time, although you will find that due to the extra load in the oven the reheating time will be proportionately longer.

Baby's meals
Once prepared, baby's bottles and feeds may be quickly heated in the microwave, providing they are in a container suitable for use in the microwave. However, sterilization of the bottles is not advised; it is generally recommended to sterilize by the usual conventional methods.

Depending on the type of milk used, a 275ml (8fl oz) bottle feed should be heated for 45–60 seconds on 100% (full) setting which will bring it to an even temperature for feeding. Similar heating times are required for baby's solid foods, although, of course, this will vary according to the type and quantity of the prepared foods.

In this section I have given examples of various menus and a suggested order of work and cooking. The length of time given for the preparation and cooking for each meal is intended as a guide, as much depends on whether or not you have other kitchen aids available, for example a food processor or blender etc. With experience you will be able to adapt your own menus and plan delicious microwave-cooked meals with the aid of all the other recipes in the book.

BREAKFAST (serves 4–6)

Porridge or Breakfast Grapefruit
*
Poached Eggs
Bacon and Tomatoes
Wholemeal Toast
*
Warm Rolls or Croissants
Preserves
*
Coffee

As there are a lot of cooking operations required to serve breakfast, it would be advisable to have a warming compartment or conventional oven on a low setting ready to heat the plates and keep the food warm. Otherwise, a bowl of hot water will heat plates, and dishes should be covered with aluminium foil to keep them hot prior to serving. Should it be necessary, food may be placed back into the microwave for a minute or two to boost the serving temperature.

In advance
Make a selection of jams and marmalades from the recipe section on page 184. The porridge can also be made in advance and just reheated for 2–3 min before serving.

Order of work (preparation and cooking time 40 min)
1 Prepare the porridge or grapefruit, bacon and

Breakfast Grapefruit (page 36); Porridge (page 36); Bacon, Tomatoes and Poached Eggs (page 36); Toast and Croissants (page 36); Pumpkin Marmalade (page 192)

tomatoes and place in their appropriate dishes ready for cooking.

2 Slice the bread for the toast and place the rolls or croissants in the basket.

3 Lay the table and have ready the toaster or grill for making the toast. Place plates into a warming compartment or oven on your conventional cooker or into a bowl of hot water.

4 If you have an automatic coffee maker, prepare and switch on. Otherwise, make a quantity of coffee, place into a suitable jug for reheating in the microwave when required.

5 Line up the foods and cook in the following sequence, removing one dish from the microwave when cooked and placing the next in the microwave straightaway. Keep the foods warm as described previously: a) porridge or grapefruit; b) bacon; c) tomatoes;

6 While the above dishes are cooking, make the toast and boil some water in the kettle for the eggs. Crack the eggs into the cups.

7 Serve the porridge or grapefruit, toast and coffee and place the eggs into the microwave to cook while eating the first course.

8 Serve the eggs, bacon and tomatoes while heating the rolls or croissants. Make more toast and coffee or reheat the coffee in the jug as required.

Alternative dishes for breakfast menus can be found in the appropriate recipe sections, eg Eggs and Cheese (page 73) and Fish (page 82).

Porridge *(serves 4–6)*
POWER LEVEL: 100% (FULL) *(colour page 35)*

175g (6oz) porridge oats
850ml (1½pt) water or milk and water
good pinch salt to taste
for serving: sugar and milk or cream

1 Mix the porridge with the water or milk and water in a bowl or dish. Stir in salt to taste.

2 Cover and cook for 6–8 min, stirring well 2–3 times throughout. Leave to stand for 4–5 min. Beat well and serve hot with sugar and milk or cream.

Breakfast grapefruit *(serves 6)*
POWER LEVEL: 100% (FULL) *(colour page 35)*

3 large grapefruit
demerara or caster sugar to taste
ground nutmeg for sprinkling, optional

1 Halve the grapefruit, remove the pips and loosen the flesh around the skin with a sharp knife. Place each half grapefruit into individual bowls or dishes and sprinkle with the sugar to taste.

2 Heat 3 together for 2½–3 min, rearranging or turning the dishes halfway through if necessary. Stand for 1 min before serving sprinkled with a little ground nutmeg if preferred

DO NOT FREEZE

Poached eggs *(serves 3–6)*
POWER LEVEL: 100% (FULL) *(colour page 35)*

boiling water
6 eggs, size 3

1 Pour about 6mm (¼in) boiling water into individual microwave egg dishes or ramekins or cups.

2 Crack an egg into each one and prick the yolks. Place the dishes in a circle on the microwave cooker shelf.

3 Cook uncovered for 2–2½ min depending whether preferred soft or well done. If the eggs are larger and/or taken straight from the refrigerator, allow a little longer cooking time—½–1 min.

4 Allow to stand for 2 min before removing from the cups with a draining spoon. Serve immediately.

DO NOT FREEZE

Bacon *(serves 3–6)*
POWER LEVEL: 100% (FULL) *(colour page 35)*

Derind 12 rashers bacon (weighing about 300–350g/10–12oz) and snip the fat. Arrange on a plate or microwave bacon rack and cover with kitchen paper towel. Cook 5–6 min, rearranging the rashers on the dish halfway through. Cook 1–2 min longer if preferred more crispy. Drain on kitchen paper towel and serve.

DO NOT FREEZE

Tomatoes *(serves 3–6)*
POWER LEVEL: 100% (FULL) *(colour page 35)*

Choose 6 ripe, even-sized tomatoes. Cut each tomato in half and arrange in a circle on a plate. Sprinkle with salt and pepper and top with slivers of butter (optional). Cook uncovered for 4–5 min, turning the plate halfway through if necessary. Stand for 1 min before serving.

DO NOT FREEZE

Warm bread rolls or croissants *(serves 3–6)*
POWER LEVEL: 100% (FULL) *(colour page 35)*

Place 6 bread rolls or croissants on a paper serviette or kitchen paper towel in a basket. Cover with kitchen paper towel and heat through for 1–1½ min. Stand for 2 min before serving.

LUNCH *(serves 4)*

Chilled Avocado Soup with Melba Toast

*

Ham Quiche
Potatoes in their Jackets with Aïoli
Tomato and Onion Salad

*

Plums with Yoghurt

The starter and sweet courses are optional, of course, on a lunchtime menu—either one or both may be served depending on the occasion, and very often fresh fruit and/or cheese is served instead of a dessert as a most acceptable finish to the meal.

In advance
Make the soup early in the day or even the day before and place to chill in the refrigerator; do not add the cream to the soup at this stage. Make the melba toast by conventional methods, and when quite dry, store in an airtight tin. Prepare and cook the flan case for the quiche the day before. Wash and stone the plums for the sweet and scrub the jacket potatoes. Make the aïoli and store, covered, in the refrigerator. Lay the table and put plates and dishes to warm.

Order of work (preparation and cooking time about 1 hr 10 min)
1 Place the jacket potatoes in their dish or boiling bag with the salted water ready for cooking later.
2 Prepare the ingredients for the tomato and onion salad. Arrange in the serving dish with seasoning but do not add the dressing or herbs. Cover the dish and set to one side.
3 Mince the onion, garlic and ham for the quiche and prepare the remaining ingredients for the filling.
4 Prepare and cook the plums with yoghurt. As soon as these have finished cooking, leave to one side ready for serving.
5 Cook the filling for the quiche and pour into the flan case. Continue to cook as given in the recipe.
6 While the quiche is cooking, remove the soup from the refrigerator and swirl in the cream. Add the french dressing and herbs to the salad.
7 As soon as the quiche is ready, cook the potatoes, leave to stand and then drain. During this time, serve the soup and melba toast for the first course.
8 Add the aïoli to the potatoes and serve with the quiche and salad.
9 Serve the plums when required after the main course.

Chilled avocado soup *(serves 4)*
POWER LEVEL: 100% (FULL)

15g (½oz) butter
1 small onion, peeled and finely chopped
1 large avocado pear, ripe
1 × 15ml tbsp (1 tbsp) lemon juice
150ml (¼pt) chicken stock (page 64)
150ml (¼pt) milk
150ml (¼pt) double cream
salt and freshly ground black pepper
a little green food colouring, optional
for serving: Melba Toast (page 38)

1 Melt the butter in a large dish for 30 sec. Add the onion, cover and cook for 3 min until soft.
2 Halve the avocado pear, remove the stone and scoop out the flesh with a spoon. Add to the onion with the lemon juice and mix together until blended.
3 Add chicken stock, milk and half the cream. Purée in a liquidiser or blender or pass through a sieve. Add seasoning and colouring if required.
4 Chill thoroughly and just before serving, swirl in the rest of the double cream.
5 Serve with melba toast.

DO NOT FREEZE THE SOUP WITH THE RESERVED CREAM–
SWIRL IN THE CREAM JUST BEFORE SERVING

Ham quiche *(serves 6)*
POWER LEVEL: 50% (DEFROST)

175g (6oz) Light Wholemeal
Pastry (page 248)
1 medium onion, peeled
1–2 cloves garlic
275g (10oz) cooked ham
2 × 5ml tsp (2tsp) dried herbs, eg oregano, basil
freshly ground black pepper
3 eggs, beaten
150ml (¼pt) milk
50g (2oz) cheese, grated
parmesan cheese for sprinkling
paprika pepper for sprinkling, optional
tomato slices for garnish

1 Roll out the pastry, line a 20cm (8in) flan dish and bake blind (page 248).
2 Mince the onion, garlic and ham. Mix well together and add the herbs, pepper, eggs, milk and grated cheese.
3 Cook the mixture on 50% (defrost) setting for 7–8 min or until heated through, stirring every 2 min.
4 Pour into the flan case and continue to cook for 11–13 min, turning every 3 min. Allow to stand for a few minutes.

5 Sprinkle with parmesan cheese and paprika pepper; alternatively, sprinkle with parmesan cheese and brown the top under a hot grill.
6 Serve hot or cold garnished with tomato slices.

VARIATION

Cooked chicken or turkey can be used instead of the ham.

Melba toast

Melba toast is made by conventional methods. Toast thin slices of white bread. Quickly remove the crusts and split the slices through the middle. Toast the uncooked sides under the grill or alternatively place in the oven until crisp and curling at the edges. Store in an airtight tin.

Potatoes in their jackets with aïoli (serves 4)
POWER LEVEL: 100% (FULL)

Choose small even-sized potatoes and scrub well. Place in a single layer in a casserole dish with a lid or boiling bag with 4–6 × 15ml tbsp (4–6tbsp) salted water. Cook for 9–12 min for 450g (1lb) or allowing 15–18 min for 675g (1½lb). Allow to stand for 5 min. Drain well and allow to cool slightly before topping with spoonfuls of Aïoli (page 141). Alternatively the aïoli may be handed separately.

DO NOT FREEZE

Plums with yoghurt (serves 4)
POWER LEVEL: 100% (FULL) AND 50% (DEFROST)

450g (1lb) dessert plums
1 × 5ml tsp (1tsp) cinnamon
sugar to taste
2 egg yolks
275ml (½pt) natural yoghurt
25–50g (1–2oz) caster sugar
½ × 5ml tsp (½tsp) vanilla essence
2 × 15ml tbsp (2tbsp) chopped walnuts

1 Wash and halve the plums. Remove stones and place the fruit in a 17.5cm (7in) round dish. Mix the cinnamon with the sugar and sprinkle over the plums. Cover and cook for 4 min on 100% (full)

setting, turning or stirring once throughout.
2 Beat the egg yolks with the yoghurt. Beat in the caster sugar and vanilla essence. Heat for 1½ min, whisking every 30 sec until heated through.
3 Pour the topping over the plums. Cook in the microwave on 50% (defrost) setting for 5 min until the topping is set.
4 Serve hot or cold sprinkled with the chopped walnuts.

DO NOT FREEZE

Tomato and onion salad (serves 4)

Allow 2 large beef tomatoes or 4–6 small salad tomatoes and cut into thin slices. Arrange the slices in the serving dish and sprinkle with a little salt and pepper. Slice a large spanish onion and push the slices through into rings. Place the onion rings over the top of the tomatoes and spoon over a little French Dressing (page 141) to taste. Sprinkle with a few chopped fresh herbs before serving.

DO NOT FREEZE

Peach and Ginger Crème Brûlée (page 160); Rum Truffles (page 196); Vegetable Moussaka (page 236)

DINNER *(serves 4)*

Scampi au Gratin
French Bread

*

Stuffed Tenderloins of Pork
Potatoes Almondine
Creamed Spinach or Broccoli Spears

*

Apple and Raspberry Purée Pudding

*

Coffee

Dinner should be a relaxed affair, whether it is a gathering of the family to enjoy the main meal of the day together, or guests invited for the evening to enjoy good food in a pleasant atmosphere with congenial company. When entertaining, plan your menu well in advance and prepare as much as possible the day before so that you leave plenty of time to yourself to relax and get ready for the evening. The menu I have given is a suggestion for a dinner party, but can easily be adapted for a main meal that the family will appreciate.

In advance
The day before, prepare the apple and raspberry purée mixture, pour into the ring mould and leave to set in the refrigerator. Prepare and shape the almondine potatoes and place into their heating/serving dish and cover; mix together the ingredients for the stuffing for the pork and store in the refrigerator with the potatoes.

Early on the day of the party, lay the table and if at all possible shut the door of the dining-room to keep the family out. Prepare the stuffed pork tenderloins and broccoli ready for cooking. If choosing to serve the spinach, this can be cooked and the cream and butter added, ready just to heat through later on.

Turn out the pudding on to its serving dish and pipe with the reserved cream. Place the pudding in the refrigerator, remembering to remove it about 1 hour before the meal is to be served. Slice the french bread, put it into a polythene bag and loosely twist the top. Place in a bread basket lined with a serviette. The bread slices are then ready to be shaken from the bag into the basket for heating through in the microwave later. Prepare and cook the scampi au gratin.

Finally, sort out all the dishes and plates required for the meal and take out the prepared foods from the refrigerator to allow to come up to room temperature. Don't forget to refrigerate white wine for about at least an hour before required and to open red wine in sufficient time to allow it to breathe.

Order of work (preparation and cooking time about 55 min)
1 Put dishes and plates to warm in the conventional oven on a low setting, arranging the oven shelves so that there will be sufficient room for the foods to keep warm after they are cooked in the microwave.
2 Cook the pork, wrap in foil and keep warm. Heat the potatoes uncovered and keep warm. Heat the spinach, cover and keep warm. Cook the gravy for the pork, pour into a jug and keep warm.

3 Heat the scampi and french bread and serve. If you have chosen broccoli instead of spinach, leave to cook in the microwave while you are eating the first course.

4 Clear the dishes from the first course. Drain the broccoli and remove the pork and potatoes (and spinach) from the oven and garnish as required. Serve the main course.

5 If you have an automatic coffee maker, put the coffee on to brew while the main-course dishes are being cleared from the table. Otherwise make a quantity of coffee in a suitable microwave jug for reheating later.

6 Serve the sweet course followed by the coffee when required.

Scampi au gratin *(serves 4)*

POWER LEVEL: 100% (FULL)

15g (½oz) butter
225g (8oz) peeled scampi or prawns
few drops of lemon juice
275ml (½pt) Béchamel Sauce (page 134)
1 × 15ml tbsp (1tbsp) browned breadcrumbs
1 × 15ml tbsp (1tbsp) grated parmesan cheese
for garnish: lemon twists and parsley sprigs

1 Melt the butter in a bowl or dish for 30 sec. Add the scampi, toss well in the butter, cover and cook for 1½–2 min.

2 Drain the scampi and place in a serving dish or individual au gratin dishes, and sprinkle with a few drops of lemon juice.

3 If necessary, heat the sauce through and spoon over the scampi. Sprinkle with browned breadcrumbs and parmesan cheese.

4 Cook, uncovered, for 1–2 min until heated through; alternatively brown the top under a hot grill.

5 Serve hot, garnished with lemon twists and parsley sprigs.

Stuffed tenderloins of pork *(serves 4–6)*

POWER LEVEL: 100% (FULL) AND 70%

3 pork tenderloins, weighing about 900g (2lb)
50g (2oz) butter
1 onion, finely chopped
2 × 5ml tsp (2tsp) chopped parsley
1 × 5ml tsp (1tsp) mixed dried herbs
2 × 5ml tsp (2tsp) chopped sage
½ lemon, grated rind and juice
salt and pepper
50g (2oz) fresh breadcrumbs
1 egg or 2 egg yolks for binding
1 glass dry sherry

1 × 15ml tbsp (1tbsp) flour
275ml (½pt) hot stock (page 64)
few drops soy sauce, optional

1 Cut off the narrow ends of the pork tenderloins so that you have about 100–150g (4–5oz) and mince or chop finely.

2 Split the tenderloins about two-thirds of the way through lengthways, open out and beat flat with a rolling pin.

3 Make the stuffing by melting 25g (1oz) butter in a large bowl for 1 min on 100% (full) setting. Add the onion, stir well, cover and cook for 3 min. Add the minced pork, herbs, lemon juice and rind, seasoning and breadcrumbs. Bind the mixture together with the egg.

4 Layer the stuffing between the pork slices, shaping them to form a loaf. Tie securely with fine string.

5 Melt the remaining butter in a dish large enough to take the pork. Add the meat and turn over in the butter. Pour over the sherry.

6 Place the meat uncovered in the microwave and cook on 70% setting for 30–35 min, or until the centre of the meat registers 75°C (170°F) on a meat thermometer or microwave temperature probe. Halfway through cooking, turn the joint over and baste with the juices. Protect the ends of the meat with small smooth pieces of aluminium foil for the rest of the cooking time if necessary.

7 At the end of the cooking time, wrap the meat in aluminium foil to keep warm while preparing the gravy.

8 Blend the flour into the meat juices in the dish and stir in the stock. Add seasoning to taste and a few drops of soy sauce will help to darken the gravy if preferred.

9 Cook in the microwave on 100% (full) setting for 3–4 min, stirring every minute until thickened and boiling.

10 Remove the string from the pork and serve whole or sliced. Spoon a little gravy round the meat and pour the rest into a sauce-boat or jug.

Potatoes almondine *(serves 4)*

POWER LEVEL: 100% (FULL)

Follow the method and ingredients for Creamed Potatoes (page 152), omitting the milk but stirring in the butter and seasonings to taste. Allow the mixture to cool then refrigerate until cold. Divide the mixture into small balls about the size of a walnut, rolling the balls between the palms of the hands and using a little flour if necessary to prevent the potatoes from sticking. Roll the balls in toasted flaked almonds. Place in their serving dish, in no more than two layers and heat through uncovered for about 3 min.

Broccoli spears *(serves 4)*
POWER LEVEL: 100% (FULL)

Place 450g (1lb) broccoli in a casserole dish with 4 × 15ml tbsp (4tbsp) salted water. Cover and cook for 8–12 min, allowing a little longer if necessary as the times will vary according to the size of the broccoli heads. Leave to stand for a few minutes, then drain and serve, sprinkled with a little ground black pepper.

Creamed spinach *(serves 4)*
POWER LEVEL: 100% (FULL)

Thoroughly wash 900g (2lb) fresh trimmed spinach and place into a large bowl with only the water clinging to the leaves. Cover and cook for 6 min, stir well and add $\frac{1}{2}$ × 5ml tsp ($\frac{1}{2}$tsp) salt. Cook covered for a further 6–8 min, stirring as necessary throughout. Drain well, squeezing out as much water as possible. Chop coarsely and stir in 25g (1oz) butter, $\frac{1}{4}$ × 5ml tsp ($\frac{1}{4}$tsp) ground nutmeg and 75ml ($\frac{1}{8}$pt) double cream. Stir well and heat for 1–2 min before serving.

Apple and raspberry purée pudding *(serves 6)*
POWER LEVEL: 100% (FULL)

450g (1lb) cooking apples, thinly sliced
225g (8oz) frozen raspberries
4 × 15ml tbsp (4tbsp) sugar
15g ($\frac{1}{2}$oz) gelatin
2 egg whites, stiffly beaten
275ml ($\frac{1}{2}$pt) double cream, whipped
1 × 15ml tbsp (1tbsp) caster sugar
few drops vanilla essence

1 Place the apples, raspberries and 4 × 15ml tbsp (4tbsp) sugar into a large bowl, mix well then cover and cook for 10 min, stirring halfway through.
2 Using a draining spoon, remove the fruit from the bowl and purée in a food processor or blender, or put through a sieve. This should make 700ml ($1\frac{1}{4}$pt) of purée but, if not, add some of the juice from the fruit. Leave the purée to cool slightly.
3 Measure 4 × 15ml tbsp (4tbsp) of the fruit juice into a small bowl or cup and sprinkle on the gelatin. Mix well and heat in the microwave for 15–30 sec until dissolved. Stir again and add to the purée.
4 Fold in the egg whites and half the cream. Stir with a metal spoon until blended and then pour the mixture into a 20cm (8in) ring mould. Leave to chill and set in the refrigerator.
5 Turn out on to a serving plate and pipe with the remaining cream which has been sweetened with the caster sugar and vanilla essence.

SUPPER *(serves 4)*

Hungarian Goulash
Buttered Noodles
Braised Red Cabbage
*
Peaches and Cream Pie

The term 'supper' means different things to different people. It can be a light snack before bedtime when perhaps a meal has been served earlier in the evening; supper can also be a more substantial one-course meal when the main meal of the day has been served at lunchtime. I often use 'supper' when inviting guests round for an informal evening—in this sense it indicates a more simple meal is to be served rather than one for a full-scale dinner party. The menu given here is intended as the latter sort, although it can easily be adapted to suit the occasion.

In advance
Both the goulash and braised cabbage freeze extremely well so take advantage of this and make well in advance. Remove the dishes from the freezer early in the day and leave to thaw at room temperature, but alternatively, if it is an impromptu occasion, both dishes may be defrosted and reheated in the microwave as given below. The peaches and cream pie can be made the day before if it is to be served cold, otherwise work to the following recommendations.

Order of work (preparation and cooking time about $1\frac{1}{2}$ hr)
1 Take the goulash and cabbage from the freezer, place in their serving dishes and defrost in the microwave using 50% (defrost) setting. Allow 15–20 min for the goulash and 12–15 min for the cabbage; alternate the dishes in the microwave while stirring one to break down the still-frozen parts. Leave to stand to equalise the temperature at the end.
2 While the 2 dishes are defrosting, prepare the ingredients for the peaches and cream and the topping. When the goulash and cabbage are standing at the end of the defrosting period, cook the peaches and cream, then add the topping and finish cooking the pie.
3 While the pie is cooking, place the noodles and salt in a dish or bowl and boil the water in a kettle. Put the plates to warm in a bowl of hot water or in a warming compartment.
4 Cover and heat the goulash for 6–8 min and the cabbage for 5–6 min on 100% (full) setting, stir-

Hungarian Goulash (page 44); Buttered Noodles (page 44); Braised Red Cabbage (page 44); Peaches and Cream Pie (page 44)

ring as necessary. Leave to stand, still covered.

5 While the goulash and cabbage are heating, lay the table and during the standing time cook the noodles.

6 Rinse the noodles under hot running water and drain them while the butter is melting in the microwave.

7 If necessary, boost the serving temperature of the goulash and cabbage by replacing in the microwave and cooking for 1–2 min.

8 Serve the main course and then the dessert.

Hungarian goulash *(serves 4–6)*
POWER LEVEL: 100% (FULL) and 30% *(colour page 43)*

1kg (2.2lb) braising steak, trimmed and cut into
   3.75 cm (1½in) cubes
2 large onions, sliced
6 × 15ml tbsp (6tbsp) oil or lard
850ml (1½pt) boiling beef stock (page 64) or water
salt
1 × 57g (2¼oz) can tomato purée
1½ × 15ml tbsp (1½tbsp) paprika pepper
3 × 5ml tsp (3tsp) caster sugar
1½ × 15ml tbsp (1½tbsp) plain flour
75ml (⅛pt) soured cream

1 Place the steak, onions and oil or lard into a large casserole dish. Cover and cook on 100% (full) setting for 6 min, stir well and continue to cook for a further 4 min.

2 Pour over the boiling stock or water, reserving about 75ml (⅛pt). Add salt to taste and stir. Cover and cook for 4 min.

3 Mix the tomato purée, paprika, sugar and flour together to make a paste and then stir in the reserved stock or water.

4 Mix the tomato purée mixture into the casserole, blending thoroughly. Return to the oven and cook, covered, for 4 min, stirring halfway through.

5 Reduce to 30% setting and continue to cook for 50–60 min, stirring occasionally, until tender.

6 Allow to stand for 15 min before stirring in the cream and serving hot.

Buttered noodles *(serves 4)*
POWER LEVEL: 100% (FULL) *(colour page 43)*

Place 350g (12oz) ribbon noodles into a large casserole dish or bowl. Add 850ml (1½pt) boiling water, salt and 1 × 15ml tbsp (1tbsp) oil. Stir well, cover and cook for 5–6 min until tender but with a 'bite'. Stand for 2 min and then drain and rinse under hot water. Drain well again and stir in 50–75g (2–3oz) butter which has been melted for about 2 min in the microwave. Serve hot straightaway.

Braised red cabbage *(serves 6–8)*
POWER LEVEL: 100% (FULL) *(colour page 43)*

575–675g (1¼–1½lb) red cabbage, finely shredded
150ml (¼pt) salted water
25g (1oz) butter
1 large onion, finely sliced
1 large cooking apple, sliced
2–3 × 15ml tbsp (2–3tbsp) wine vinegar
freshly ground black pepper
2 × 5ml tsp (2tsp) sugar
salt to taste
25g (1oz) butter, softened
15g (½oz) flour

1 Place the red cabbage and salted water into a large bowl, toss over, cover and cook for 5 min. Leave to stand for 5 min.

2 Melt the butter in a separate bowl or dish for 1 min, add the onion and apple and mix well together. Cover and cook for 5 min.

3 Drain the cabbage and add the onion and apple mixture. Add the wine vinegar, pepper and sugar. Cover and cook for 10 min, stirring well twice.

4 Adjust seasoning. Blend 15g (½oz) of the softened butter with the flour and stir this into the cabbage. Cook for 2–3 min until thickened. Stir in the remaining butter and serve hot.

Peaches and cream pie *(serves 8–10)*
POWER LEVEL: 50% (DEFROST) *(colour page 43)*

900g (2lb) peaches, fresh or canned, drained
50–100g (2–4oz) caster sugar
½ × 5ml tsp (½tsp) cinnamon
2 eggs, beaten
150ml (¼pt) soured cream
25g (1oz) plain flour
50g (2oz) wholemeal flour
pinch salt
75g (3oz) butter
75g (3oz) demerara sugar
for decoration: whipped cream

1 Halve and slice the peaches and arrange in the bottom of a 22.5cm (9in) dish. Sprinkle with caster sugar and the cinnamon.

2 Beat the eggs with the soured cream and pour over the peaches. Cook for 12–15 min on 50% (defrost) setting until set, giving a quarter turn every 3 min.

3 Mix together the flours and salt. Rub in the butter and stir in the demerara sugar to give a coarse crumb mixture.

4 Sprinkle the crumb mixture over the peaches and cook on 50% (defrost) setting for 7–8 min until the crumb topping is cooked.

5 Leave to cool slightly and serve with whipped cream or, when cold, pipe with whipped cream.

Appetizers and starters

I have included in this section a variety of hot and cold starters which can be quickly prepared using the microwave cooker. Many can be made in advance to serve cold, while others which are to be served hot can also be made beforehand and quickly reheated in the microwave when you and your guests are ready. You will find that some may also be used for snacks or light lunch or supper dishes. In other sections of the book—soups, fish and shellfish, vegetables, rice, pasta and pulses for example—there are many ideas for dishes which can also be served as a first course to a meal.

Appetizers—those tempting pre-meal nibblers with drinks—can be served as alternatives to the more usual selection of crisps, peanuts, olives and gherkins. They should be small and easy to manage by your guests. I have found it better to avoid any which are sticky or crumble at a touch. When time is precious, there are many toppings you can buy and prepare ready to serve on fingers of toast or savoury biscuits—prawns, shrimps, smoked salmon, pâtés, relishes, spreads, thinly sliced continental sausage, etc. When time allows, try some of the recipes included here: Devilled Crab Toasts, Taramasalata, Potted Tongue or any of the Pâtés. Very often I serve appetizers instead of a starter to a meal, particularly when the following course is large or rich. It also enables small eaters to pace themselves and gives ample time for the host or hostess to potter in the kitchen if necessary, finalising preparation for the next course before seating the guests at the table.

Pâté maison *(serves 6–8)*
POWER LEVEL: 50% (DEFROST)

Serve as an appetizer on freshly made toast or as a starter.

100g (4oz) pork
225g (8oz) veal
225g (8oz) lambs' liver
2 cloves garlic, finely chopped
1 × 5ml tsp (1tsp) dried thyme
$\frac{1}{4}$ × 5ml tsp ($\frac{1}{4}$tsp) nutmeg
salt and freshly ground black pepper
1 × 15ml tbsp (1tbsp) each brandy and madeira
2 × 15ml tbsp (2tbsp) double cream
1 egg, beaten
3 chicken livers, optional
3 slices bacon
for garnish: stuffed olives, gherkins and sprigs of
     parsley

1 Mince the pork, veal and liver. Place into a large bowl with the garlic, thyme, nutmeg, seasoning, brandy, madeira and cream.
2 Mix well together and stir in the egg. Take care not to overmix otherwise the mixture will become heavy.
3 Cut the chicken livers in half if used, and arrange them in the bottom of a suitable container—a deep round one or a glass loaf pan would be ideal.
4 Pile the pâté mixture into the dish and press down firmly. Remove the rind from the bacon rashers and arrange the bacon over the top of the pâté.
5 Cover and cook for 10 min, allow to stand for

5 min, then cook for a further 5–8 min. Allow to cool slightly then place weights on top of the pâté. Leave in the refrigerator overnight. Turn out and garnish before serving.

Devilled crab toasts *(makes about 24)*
POWER LEVEL: 100% (FULL)

Serve as an appetizer.

15g (½oz) butter
½ small onion, finely chopped
75g (3oz) can crabmeat
1 × 5ml tsp (1tsp) worcestershire sauce *or* few drops tabasco sauce to taste
pinch dry mustard
2 × 15ml tbsp (2tbsp) double cream
about 24 fingers toast or fried bread
for garnish: paprika pepper for sprinkling and parsley sprigs

1 Melt the butter in a bowl for 15–30 sec, add the onion, cover and cook for 3 min until tender.
2 Add the crabmeat, worcestershire or tabasco sauce, mustard and the cream. Mix well together and spread on to fingers of toasted or fried bread.
3 Sprinkle with paprika and garnish with parsley sprigs before serving.

Onions à la grecque *(serves 4–6)*
POWER LEVEL: 100% (FULL) *(colour opposite)*

450g (1lb) button onions or shallots
boiling water
2 × 15ml tbsp (2tbsp) olive oil
1 small onion, finely chopped
1 clove garlic, crushed
4 tomatoes, skinned, deseeded and coarsely chopped
salt and freshly ground black pepper
3 × 15ml tbsp (3tbsp) tomato purée
1 wineglass white wine
2 × 15ml tbsp (2tbsp) chopped parsley

1 Peel the onions and place in a large bowl or casserole dish. Pour on sufficient boiling water to cover. Cover the dish and bring the water up to the boil in the microwave; allow to stand for 3 min then drain.
2 Place the olive oil in a large serving dish with the chopped onion and the garlic. Cover and cook for 2 min.
3 Add the button onions or shallots, tomatoes, salt and freshly ground black pepper, cover and cook for 3 min.
4 Blend the tomato purée and the wine and add to the onions. Stir, cover and cook for 2–3 min.
5 Stir half the parsley into the dish and allow to cool,

then chill for 2 hours. Remove the onions from the dish and strain the sauce through a fine sieve.
6 Place the onions back into the serving dish and pour the strained sauce over the top. Sprinkle with the rest of the parsley before serving cold.

Chicken livers with sage *(serves 3–4)*
POWER LEVEL: 100% (FULL) *(colour opposite)*

25g (1oz) butter
2 lean bacon rashers, derinded and cut into strips
450g (1lb) chicken livers, cut into halves
salt and freshly ground black pepper
2 × 5ml tsp (2tsp) chopped fresh sage
1 × 15ml tbsp (1tbsp) sherry
2 × 5ml tsp (2tsp) flour
1 × 15ml tbsp (1tbsp) water
for serving: bed of well washed and shredded spinach tossed in oil and vinegar salad dressing, optional, and chopped sage

1 Melt the butter in a casserole dish or bowl for 1 min, add the bacon and cook, covered, for 2 min. Stir in the chicken livers and continue to cook for 5–6 min, stirring well halfway through.
2 Add salt and pepper to taste, and the sage and sherry. Blend the flour with the water and stir into the dish.
3 Cook for 2 min until thickened, stirring halfway through. Serve on a bed of spinach salad, and sprinkle with a little chopped sage.

Avocado and tuna cream *(serves 6)*
POWER LEVEL: 100% (FULL) *(colour opposite)*

1 large avocado pear, ripe
few drops lemon juice
75g (3oz) cream cheese
salt and freshly ground black pepper
150ml (¼pt) soured cream or natural yoghurt
100g (4oz) canned tuna fish, drained and flaked
150ml (¼pt) double cream, lightly whipped
few drops green food colouring, optional
15g (½oz) gelatin
75ml (⅛pt) water
for garnish: parsley sprigs, thin slices avocado, optional
for serving: fingers of toast

1 Halve and stone the avocado. Scoop out the flesh with a spoon into a large bowl. Add the lemon juice and mash down with a wooden spoon.

Onions à la Grecque; Chicken Livers with Sage; Avocado and Tuna Cream

2 Add the cream cheese and seasoning and blend well together. If preferred the mixture can be puréed in a blender or food processor. Add the soured cream or yoghurt and the tuna fish and mix well together. Carefully stir in the cream, and add a few drops of green food colouring if required.

3 Sprinkle the gelatin over the water in a bowl and heat in the microwave for 15–20 sec until the gelatin is dissolved. Stir until smooth.

4 Pour in a stream on to the avocado mixture, stirring continuously until blended together.

5 Turn into individual small dishes or 1 larger serving dish and chill for about 3 hr in the refrigerator before garnishing with parsley sprigs or thin slices of avocado and serving with fingers of toast.

Grapefruit in brandy *(serves 6)*
POWER LEVEL: 100% (FULL)

3 large grapefuit, peeled
75g (3oz) demerara sugar
150ml ($\frac{1}{4}$pt) water
1 × 5ml tsp (1tsp) cinnamon
3 × 15ml tbsp (3tbsp) brandy

1 Remove all the pith from the peeled grapefruit and carefully take out the core from the centre with a skewer. Cut the fruit into 1.25cm ($\frac{1}{2}$in) thick slices.

2 Add the sugar to the water with the cinnamon in a large, shallow dish.

3 Heat for 2 min, then stir until the sugar has dissolved in the water. Cook for a further 2 min, then lay the grapefruit slices into the syrup.

4 Cover and cook for 2–3 min, turning the slices over in the syrup halfway through.

5 Place the slices of grapefruit in a serving dish. Mix 3 × 15ml tbsp (3tbsp) of the syrup with the brandy and pour over the fruit.

6 Serve hot or chilled on their own.

Chicken and pork terrine *(serves 8)*
POWER LEVEL: 70%

1.5kg (3lb) chicken, cooked
450g (1lb) pork sausage meat
225g (8oz) cooked ham, diced
2 cloves garlic, finely chopped
2 eggs, beaten
1 × 5ml tsp (1tsp) dried tarragon
1 × 15ml tbsp (1tbsp) finely chopped parsley
2 × 15ml tbsp (2 tbsp) brandy, optional
salt and freshly ground black pepper
100g (4oz) butter, softened
225g (8oz) bacon rashers

1 Remove the meat from the chicken, discarding skin and bones, and roughly chop into small pieces.

2 Combine all the other ingredients except the bacon and mix well together.

3 Remove the rind from the bacon rashers and line a 1.7 litre (3pt) round casserole dish with half the rashers. Layer the chicken and sausage mixture into the casserole, starting and finishing with the sausage mixture. Cover with the remaining bacon rashers.

4 Cover and cook for 15 min, leave to stand for 10 min, then cook for a further 8–10 min. Allow to cool slightly before placing weights on top of the terrine. Leave in the refrigerator overnight.

5 Serve straight from the dish as a starter with salad.

Marinated lamb kebabs *(serves 4–6)*
POWER LEVEL: 100% (FULL)

These starters are marinated in wine and cooked at the last minute in the browning dish.

450g (1lb) lean lamb fillet
150ml ($\frac{1}{4}$pt) white wine
4 × 15ml tbsp (4tbsp) oil
1 × 5ml tsp (1tsp) worcestershire sauce
1 × 5ml tsp (1tsp) ground cumin seed
1 × 5ml tsp (1tsp) ground coriander seed
1 clove garlic, crushed
salt and freshly ground black pepper
for serving: shredded lettuce and lemon slices

1 Cut the lamb into small dice (about 1.25cm/$\frac{1}{2}$in), and place in a bowl.
2 Mix the wine, 2 × 15ml tbsp (2tbsp) oil, worcestershire sauce, cumin seed, coriander, garlic and the seasoning. Beat well together and pour over the lamb. Leave to marinate for several hours in the refrigerator or overnight if possible.
3 Remove the meat from the marinade and pat dry with pieces of kitchen paper towel.
4 Preheat the browning dish for about 6 min according to size, add the remaining 2 × 15ml tbsp (2tbsp) oil and the lamb.
5 Cover and cook for 1$\frac{1}{2}$ min, turn the meat over with a heatproof utensil and cook for a further 1$\frac{1}{2}$–2 min.
6 Serve straightaway on a bed of shredded lettuce and garnished with lemon slices.

Lemon and sardine pâté *(serves 4–6)*
POWER LEVEL: 100% (FULL)

50g (2oz) butter
75g (3oz) fresh brown breadcrumbs
1 lemon, grated rind and juice
100g (4oz) can sardines
salt and freshly ground black pepper
1 × 15ml tbsp (1tbsp) freshly chopped parsley
for garnish: lemon twists
for serving: fingers of hot toast

1 Melt the butter in a covered bowl for 1$\frac{1}{2}$ min until melted. Stir in the breadcrumbs, lemon rind and juice.
2 Bone the sardines if preferred, then mash down well with a little of the oil. Stir the sardines into the breadcrumb mixture, adding a little more oil if required to make a smooth mixture.
3 Beat in the seasoning to taste and parsley and spoon the mixture into 4 or 6 small dishes or 1 large dish.
4 Garnish with lemon twists before serving with fingers of hot toast.

Bacon stuffed tomatoes *(serves 6)*
POWER LEVEL: 100% (FULL)

6 rashers lean bacon
6 large, firm tomatoes
25g (1oz) butter
1 small onion, finely chopped
50g (2oz) fresh white breadcrumbs
salt and pepper
6 small rounds hot, buttered toast
for garnish: parsley sprigs

1 Remove the rinds from the bacon and place the rashers on a plate in a single layer. Cover with a piece of kitchen paper towel and cook for 5–6 min. Cook for another minute if preferred. Drain off the fat and cut the cooked bacon into strips.
2 Cut a thin slice from the top of each tomato and scoop out the flesh.
3 Melt the butter in a bowl for 1 min, add the onion, toss well in the butter, cover and cook for 3 min. Stir in the breadcrumbs, bacon, salt and pepper to taste and the tomato pulp.
4 Fill the tomato cases with the mixture and place in a circle on a plate.
5 Cover and cook for 3–4 min until heated through. Serve on rounds of hot buttered toast and garnish with sprigs of parsley.

Spicy meatballs *(serves 4–6)*
POWER LEVEL: 100% (FULL)

1 onion, minced
1 green chilli, minced
1 clove garlic, minced
450g (1lb) lean beef, minced
50g (2oz) fresh white breadcrumbs
$\frac{1}{2}$ × 5ml tsp ($\frac{1}{2}$tsp) ground cumin seeds
1 × 5ml tsp (1tsp) ground coriander seeds
$\frac{1}{2}$ × 5ml tsp ($\frac{1}{2}$tsp) turmeric powder
$\frac{1}{4}$ × 5ml tsp ($\frac{1}{4}$tsp) ground cloves
$\frac{1}{4}$ × 5ml tsp ($\frac{1}{4}$tsp) ground cinnamon
1 egg, beaten
salt and freshly ground black pepper
melted butter
for garnish: chopped parsley

1 Place the first 10 ingredients into a large bowl and mix well together.
2 Stir in the beaten egg and seasoning and when the mixture binds together, form into small balls about the size of a walnut.
3 Brush each meatball with the melted butter and place in a single layer in a shallow dish. Cook about 15 meatballs at a time for 5 min uncovered, turning the dish twice throughout.
4 Garnish with chopped parsley before serving hot.

Moules marinière *(serves 2–3)*
POWER LEVEL: 100% (FULL)

1.1 litre (2pt) mussels
25g (1oz) butter
1 small onion, finely chopped
1 small carrot, diced
1 celery stick, finely chopped
bouquet garni
salt and pepper
1 wineglass dry white wine
1–2 × 5ml tsp (1–2tsp) flour
for garnish: freshly chopped parsley

1 Scrub the mussels and rinse well in cold water. Discard any which are broken or not tightly closed, and scrape away the beards or tufts of hair with a sharp knife.
2 Melt the butter in a large bowl for 1 min. Add the vegetables, cover and cook for 2 min; add the bouquet garni, seasoning and white wine, cover and cook for 2 min until boiling.
3 Add the mussels, cover and cook until the shells are open, 3–3½ min approximately, tossing well half-way through. Allow the dish to stand for about 4 min.
4 Remove the top halves of the shells from the mussels, discarding any which have not opened during the cooking.
5 Place the mussels on to a serving dish. Strain the liquid from the mussels into a small bowl and blend in the flour. Cook for 1–2 min until thickened and pour over the mussels.
6 Serve hot garnished with chopped parsley.

DO NOT FREEZE

Gnocchi *(serves 6)*
POWER LEVEL: 100% (FULL) AND 70% *(colour opposite)*

550ml (1pt) milk
pinch nutmeg
100g (4oz) fine semolina
75g (3oz) cheddar cheese, finely grated
50g (2oz) butter
1 × 5ml tsp (1tsp) french mustard
salt and freshly ground black pepper
½ egg, beaten
paprika pepper for sprinkling
for serving: Tomato Sauce (page 134) or tomato salad

1 Heat the milk in a large bowl on 100% (full) setting for 4 min until hot. Sprinkle on the nutmeg and semolina and stir well together.
2 Cook uncovered for 3–4 min, stirring every minute until the mixture has come to the boil and thickened.
3 Beat in 50g (2oz) of the cheese, 25g (1oz) of the

butter, the mustard, seasoning and beaten egg. Beat until smooth.
4 Turn the mixture on to an oiled or non-stick baking tray and smooth out to a thickness of about 1.25cm (½in). Leave to cool and set.
5 When firm, turn out on to a chopping board or work surface and cut the mixture into small 3.75cm (1½in) circles or squares and arrange the pieces overlapping in a buttered, shallow dish.
6 Dot the surface with the remaining butter, sprinkle with the remaining cheese and the paprika pepper.
7 Cook uncovered for 10–12 min on 70% setting until hot through and the cheese is melted and bubbling. Alternatively, after heating through in the microwave, the top of the dish may be browned under a hot grill.
8 Serve hot with tomato sauce or a tomato salad.

Tomato and herb ring mould *(serves 4–6)*
POWER LEVEL: 100% (FULL) *(colour opposite)*

1 × 400g (14oz) can and 1 × 225g (8oz) can tomatoes
½ lemon, grated rind and juice
4 × 15ml tbsp (4tbsp) dry white wine
1 clove garlic, crushed
salt and freshly ground black pepper
150ml (¼pt) soured cream
2 × 15ml tbsp (2tbsp) freshly chopped mixed herbs, ie sage, chives, thyme
15g (½oz) gelatin
75ml (⅛pt) water
for serving: watercress

1 Place the tomatoes in a bowl with the lemon rind and juice, white wine, garlic and seasoning. Cover and cook for 5 min, stirring once throughout.
2 Add the soured cream and blend well together. Purée the mixture in a blender or food processor. Add the herbs.
3 Sprinkle the gelatin over the water in a bowl and heat in the microwave for about 30 sec until the gelatin is dissolved. Stir until smooth.
4 Pour the gelatin in a stream on to the tomato mixture, stirring continuously until blended together.
5 Pour into a ring mould and chill for several hours in the refrigerator before turning out on to a serving plate or dish.
6 Fill the centre of the tomato ring with watercress before serving.

DO NOT FREEZE

Gnocchi; Tomato and Herb Ring Mould

Salmon mousse *(serves 8)*
POWER LEVEL: 100% (FULL) *(colour page 127)*

15g ($\frac{1}{2}$oz) gelatin
75ml ($\frac{1}{8}$pt) white wine
275ml ($\frac{1}{2}$pt) cold Béchamel Sauce (page 134)
150ml ($\frac{1}{4}$pt) Blender Mayonnaise (page 137)
75ml ($\frac{1}{8}$pt) double cream
225g (8oz) cooked salmon, finely chopped or
   pounded
50g (2oz) peeled prawns or shrimps, coarsely
   chopped
salt and pepper
for garnish: thinly sliced cucumber and a few fresh
   prawns or shrimps
for serving: thin slices brown bread and butter

1 Mix the gelatin into the wine. Heat for 15–30 sec and stir well until dissolved. Stir into the béchamel sauce with the mayonnaise.
2 Lightly whip the cream and stir into the mixture with the salmon and coarsely chopped prawns or shrimps. Add seasoning to taste.
3 Turn the mousse into 8 individual ramekin dishes or 1 larger suitable dish and chill in the refrigerator until set.
4 Garnish with twists of thinly sliced cucumber and a few prawns or shrimps. Serve chilled with thin slices of brown bread and butter

Creamed sweetcorn *(serves 6)*
POWER LEVEL: 100% (FULL)

25g (1oz) butter
1 small onion, finely chopped
1 clove garlic, finely chopped, optional
450g (1lb) frozen sweetcorn, thawed
1 × 15ml tbsp (1tbsp) dry sherry or vermouth
150ml ($\frac{1}{4}$pt) thick double cream
1 egg yolk, beaten
salt and freshly ground black pepper
3 × 15ml tbsp (3tbsp) browned breadcrumbs
paprika pepper for sprinkling

1 Melt the butter in a large bowl for 1 min. Add the onion and garlic, toss well in the butter, cover and cook for 3 min.
2 Stir in the sweetcorn and the sherry or vermouth, cover and cook for 3–4 min. Stand for 2 min then drain off most of the juices. Beat the cream and egg yolk together.
3 Stir the cream and egg yolk into the sweetcorn and heat through for about 2 min stirring every 30 sec. Add seasoning to taste and divide the mixture between individual serving dishes. Sprinkle with the browned breadcrumbs and paprika pepper before serving hot or cold.

Bean salad *(serves 4–6)*
POWER LEVEL: 100% (FULL)

450g (1lb) french beans, trimmed and left whole
2 × 15ml tbsp (2tbsp) salted water
100g (4oz) cooked or canned red kidney beans,
   drained
6 × 15ml tbsp (6tbsp) olive oil
2 × 15ml tbsp (2tbsp) lemon juice or wine vinegar
salt and freshly ground black pepper
pinch sugar
2 × 15ml tbsp (2 tbsp) freshly chopped mixed herbs,
   ie chives, sage, thyme, parsley
for garnish: 1 hard-boiled egg, chopped

1 Wash the beans and place with the salted water in a serving dish. Cover and cook for 6 min, shaking or stirring the beans twice throughout. Leave to stand for a few minutes; the beans should be crisp.
2 Drain the beans and place in the dish with the red kidney beans.
3 Whisk the olive oil, lemon juice or wine vinegar, seasoning and sugar together. Beat in the herbs.
4 Pour the dressing over the beans and leave to cool. When cold toss the beans in the dressing.
5 Serve cold garnished with chopped hard-boiled egg.

Prawns in butter wine sauce *(serves 4)*
POWER LEVEL: 100% (FULL)

100g (4oz) butter
1 clove garlic, finely chopped
1 wineglass dry white wine
salt and freshly ground black pepper
450g (1lb) large fresh prawns, heads removed
for garnish: snipped parsley

1 Place the butter, garlic and wine in a large shallow dish. Cover and cook for 4–5 min, stirring well halfway through.
2 Add seasoning to taste and the prawns. Toss the prawns over in the sauce, cover and cook for 3 min, stirring once halfway through.
3 Allow to stand for 1 min before serving in individual bowls or plates and garnish with snipped parsley.

Potted tongue *(serves 4)*
POWER LEVEL: 100% (FULL) *(colour page 23)*

225g (8oz) cooked tongue
75g (3oz) unsalted butter
salt and pepper to taste
$\frac{1}{2}$ × 5ml tsp ($\frac{1}{2}$tsp) french mustard
pinch cayenne pepper
for garnish: parsley sprigs
for serving: hot toast

1 Mince or finely chop the tongue. Place the butter in a bowl, cover and heat in the microwave for 2 min until melted.
2 Beat together the tongue, melted butter, seasoning, mustard and cayenne pepper to give a smooth paste. If preferred, the mixture can be blended in a liquidizer or food processor.
3 Press the mixture firmly into a small dish and chill until firm. Garnish with parsley sprigs before serving with hot toast.

Mushrooms in garlic butter *(serves 4)*
POWER LEVEL: 100% (FULL)

175g (6oz) butter
2–3 cloves garlic, crushed or finely chopped
450g (1lb) small button mushrooms, wiped
salt and freshly ground black pepper
2 × 15ml tbsp (2tbsp) chopped parsley
for serving: crusty french bread

1 Place the butter in a bowl or dish, cover and cook for 3–3½ min until melted. Add the garlic, cover and cook for 1 min.
2 Add the mushrooms, toss well in the butter and garlic, and add seasoning to taste.
3 Cover and cook for 4–4½ min, stirring twice throughout. Leave to stand for 2–3 min before stirring in the chopped parsley.
4 Serve hot in individual au gratin dishes with crusty french bread.

Coquilles Saint-Jacques *(serves 4 or 8)*
POWER LEVEL: 100% (FULL)

Use either the deep shells or individual shell dishes for cooking and serving the scallops.

8 scallops and their shells (or individual shell dishes)
150ml (¼pt) white wine
1 small onion, grated
salt and freshly ground black pepper
1 bay leaf
225g (8oz) mushrooms, finely sliced
50g (2oz) butter
50g (2oz) flour
200ml (7½fl oz) milk
150ml (¼pt) single cream
1 egg yolk
few drops lemon juice
75g (3oz) cheese, grated
paprika pepper for sprinkling
for serving: brown bread and butter

1 Wash and dry the scallops and their shells, if used, and put to one side.
2 Pour the white wine into a large bowl with the onion, seasoning and bay leaf. Cover and cook for 3 min, stirring once halfway through.
3 Add the mushrooms and scallops, cover and cook for 5 min, stirring once halfway through. Leave to stand.
4 Melt the butter in a large bowl for 1½ min, stir in the flour and when blended gradually add the milk. Season lightly, cover and cook for 4 min, stirring every minute until the sauce thickens.
5 Blend the cream and egg yolk and add to the sauce with a few drops of lemon juice. Remove the bay leaf from the mushroom and scallop mixture; add to the sauce, mixing well together.
6 Divide the mixture between the 8 scallop shells, ensuring that 1 scallop is placed into each one.

7 Sprinkle with grated cheese and heat for 2–3 min until the cheese is melted and then sprinkle with paprika pepper. Alternatively, heat through and brown the top under a hot grill.

8 Allow 1 or 2 per person and serve with brown bread and butter.

DO NOT FREEZE

Smoked mackerel pâté (serves 4–6)
POWER LEVEL: 100% (FULL)

450g (1lb) smoked mackerel fillets
2 × 15ml tbsp (2tbsp) grated onion
1 × 15ml tbsp (1tbsp) lemon juice
175g (6oz) cream cheese
2–3 × 15ml tbsp (2–3tbsp) natural yoghurt
salt and freshly ground black pepper
for garnish: parsley sprigs
for serving: lemon wedges and fingers of toast

1 Skin the fish, cut into small pieces and place into a casserole dish with the onion and lemon juice. Cover and cook for 5 min, stirring once halfway through.

2 Drain the mackerel and then blend in a liquidiser or food processor with the onion, cream cheese and the natural yoghurt.

3 Season to taste and divide between individual ramekin dishes or place in a large serving dish. Leave to chill until firm.

4 Garnish with parsley sprigs before serving with lemon wedges and fingers of toast.

Marinated herrings (serves 4–8)
POWER LEVEL: 100% (FULL) AND 50% (DEFROST)

1 large onion, sliced
2 bay leaves
275ml ($\frac{1}{2}$pt) dry white wine
150ml ($\frac{1}{4}$pt) white wine vinegar
275ml ($\frac{1}{2}$pt) water
1 × 5ml tsp (1tsp) soft brown sugar
2 × 5ml tsp (2tsp) salt
6 black peppercorns
8 herring fillets
for serving: brown bread and butter

1 Place all the ingredients except the herrings into a large casserole dish. Cover and bring to the boil at 100% (full) setting, reduce to 50% (defrost) setting and cook for 5 min.

2 Add the herring fillets to the dish and continue to cook for a further 3 min. Leave to stand until cool.

3 Remove the cold herrings from the dish and place on a serving dish. Pour over the marinade and chill before serving with brown bread and butter.

Taramasalata (serves 6–8)
POWER LEVEL: 100% (FULL)

225g (8oz) smoked cod's roe, soaked overnight
100g (4oz) cooked potato
1–2 cloves garlic, crushed
juice half lemon
4–6 × 15ml tbsp (4–6tbsp) olive oil
salt and freshly ground black pepper
for garnish: black olives, lemon wedges and parsley sprigs
for serving: pitta bread

1 Peel the skin from the cod's roe and mash down well. Warm the potato for 30 sec and add to the cod's roe with the crushed garlic. Blend well together.

2 Add the lemon juice and olive oil alternately and taste for seasoning before adding salt and pepper. At this stage, the mixture may be blended in a food processor or liquidiser but a little additional lemon juice or oil or cold water will be needed to soften the mixture.

3 When quite smooth and the required consistency is obtained, pile the mixture into a dish and garnish with black olives and lemon wedges before serving.

4 Warm the pitta bread in the microwave—4 will take about 1$\frac{1}{2}$ min—and serve with the taramasalata.

Angels on horseback (serves 3–6)
POWER LEVEL: 100% (FULL)

6 lean bacon rashers, 225–275g (8–10oz) approximately
6 oysters
6 small rounds hot buttered toast
for garnish: watercress

1 Remove rinds from the bacon rashers and wrap each rasher around an oyster—roll up and secure the ends with cocktail sticks.

2 Place in a circle on a plate and cook uncovered, for 4–5 min, turning the plate halfway through if necessary. Drain on kitchen paper towel.

3 Place each 'angel' on a small round of buttered toast and garnish with watercress.

DO NOT FREEZE

Beverages, cups and punches

Preparing beverages in the microwave is quick and easy and especially ideal when just one or two mugs or cups are required. With the microwave, no longer will drinks need to be thrown away when they are cold—reheating is fast and the full flavour is retained.

This section contains a variety of hot and cold non-alcoholic drinks and a selection of alcoholic cups, punches and mulls. When entertaining, drinks which are to be served hot can be made beforehand when it is convenient, covered, and then reheated as necessary when you and your guests are ready. In particular, fresh coffee may be prepared in advance using your usual filter of percolator method, covered, and then reheated in a suitable jug prior to serving. Any remaining coffee can be quickly reheated later when offering your guests a second cup.

Milk heats more quickly than water although this depends on the starting temperature of the liquid. Make sure you allow sufficient room in the container for milk to boil if required. Drinks which are inclined to boil up should be heated uncovered, and if they do begin to overflow, opening the microwave oven door or switching off immediately should prevent the boil over. Although most drinks are heated on 100% (full) power level, larger quantities of milky drinks are best heated on a slightly lower setting and whisked or stirred occasionally throughout the heating period.

Here is a guide to heating times from cold carried out on 100% (full) power level:

Quantity	Cooking time
150ml ($\frac{1}{4}$pt) milk	1–1$\frac{1}{4}$ min
275ml ($\frac{1}{2}$pt) milk	2–2$\frac{1}{2}$ min
550ml (1pt) milk	4$\frac{1}{2}$–5 min
275ml ($\frac{1}{2}$pt) black coffee	3–3$\frac{1}{2}$ min
550ml (1pt) black coffee	4$\frac{1}{2}$–5$\frac{1}{2}$ min
1.1 litre (2pt) black coffee	6$\frac{1}{2}$–7$\frac{1}{2}$ min
1 mug or cup	1$\frac{1}{2}$–2$\frac{1}{2}$ min
2 mugs or cups	3–3$\frac{1}{2}$ min
3 mugs or cups	4–4$\frac{1}{2}$ min
4 mugs or cups	5–5$\frac{1}{2}$ min
5 mugs or cups	6$\frac{1}{2}$–7 min
6 mugs or cups	7$\frac{1}{2}$–8$\frac{1}{2}$ min

Instant coffee *(serves 1)*

POWER LEVEL: 100% (FULL)

1–2 × 5ml tsp (1–2tsp) instant coffee
sugar to taste, optional
175ml (6fl oz) water or milk and water

1 Blend the coffee with the sugar and a little of the liquid in a cup or mug.
2 Stir in the rest of the water or milk and water and heat for 1$\frac{1}{2}$–2 min. Stir well before serving.

Tea (*serves 1*)

POWER LEVEL: 100% (FULL)

175ml (6fl oz) water
1 teabag
sugar and milk or lemon, to taste

1 Heat the water in a cup for 2 min.
2 Add the teabag and leave to brew for 1 min.
3 Remove the teabag and add sugar and milk or lemon to taste.

Hot Bovril (*serves 1*)

POWER LEVEL: 100% (FULL)

175ml (6fl oz) water
1 × 5ml tsp (1tsp) Bovril

1 Heat the water in a cup or mug for 2 min.
2 Stir in the Bovril and serve straightaway.

Hot spicy milk (*serves 6*)

POWER LEVEL: 100% (FULL)

1 litre (1¾pt) milk
75g (3oz) black treacle
4 × 7.5cm (3in) cinnamon sticks
whipped cream
nutmeg

1 Place the milk and treacle in a large jug or bowl. Stir well and add the cinnamon sticks.
2 Heat for about 6 min until hot without boiling.
3 Remove the cinnamon sticks before pouring the drink into serving glasses or mugs. Top with a little whipped cream and sprinkle with grated nutmeg before serving.

Hot mocha (*serves 2*)

POWER LEVEL: 100% (FULL)

3 × 15ml tbsp (3tbsp) drinking chocolate
1 × 5ml tsp (1tsp) instant coffee
¼ × 5ml tsp (¼tsp) ground cinnamon
275ml (½pt) milk
2 × 5ml tsp (2tsp) whipped cream

1 Mix together the drinking chocolate, coffee and cinnamon.
2 Stir in a little of the milk to make a smooth paste. Gradually pour on the rest of the milk and heat for 2½ min without boiling.
3 Pour into serving glasses or mugs and top with a spoonful of whipped cream.

DO NOT FREEZE

Hot cocoa (*serves 3–4*)

POWER LEVEL: 100% (FULL)

2 × 15ml tbsp (2tbsp) cocoa
2 × 15ml tbsp (2tbsp) sugar
75ml (⅛pt) water
550ml (1pt) milk

1 Mix together the cocoa, sugar and water in a large jug, heat for 1 min.
2 Gradually stir in the milk, heat for 4½–5 min until hot. Do not allow the milk to boil.

DO NOT FREEZE

Grapefruit barley water (*makes about 2 litres/3½pt*)

POWER LEVEL: 100% (FULL)

15g (½oz) patent barley
1.7 litre (3pt) boiling water
juice of 3 grapefruit, 275ml (½pt) approximately
sugar or sweetener to taste

1 Blend the patent barley to a smooth paste with a little cold water in a measuring jug. Stir in a little of the boiling water and then add the rest gradually, stirring well until thickened. Transfer the liquid to a larger bowl as necessary.
2 Cover and cook in the microwave for 3–4 min, stirring once throughout. Add the grapefruit juice and sugar or sweetener to taste. Serve hot or cold.

Note: *Patent barley can be purchased at good chemist shops. Lemon juice or orange juice may be used instead of the grapefruit if preferred.*

DO NOT FREEZE

Hot apricot cider cup (*makes about 1¾ litre/2¾pt*)

POWER LEVEL: 100% (FULL)

1 litre (1¾pt) strong cider
15cm (6in) cinnamon stick
15g (½oz) blanched almonds
1 × 822g (1lb 13oz) can apricots
2 × 241ml (8½fl oz) bottles tonic water

1 Heat 275ml (½pt) cider with the cinnamon and almonds in a large bowl for 5 min.
2 Blend the apricots and juice in a liquidiser or rub through a nylon sieve. Add the apricots to the hot liquid.
3 Add the remaining cider and the tonic water. Heat in the microwave for 10–15 min. Stir well and remove the cinnamon stick before serving.

DO NOT FREEZE

Bitter lemon *(makes about $\frac{3}{4}$litre/$1\frac{1}{2}$pt)*
POWER LEVEL: 100% (FULL) AND 50% (DEFROST)

2 lemons, washed
550ml (1pt) water
100g (4oz) sugar
for serving: soda water or gin

1 Cut the lemons into pieces and place into a bowl with the water. Cover and bring to the boil in the microwave then reduce to 50% (defrost) setting and cook for 10 min or until the fruit is tender.
2 Add the sugar and stir until it is dissolved. Leave to cool.
3 Strain the drink before serving with soda water or gin.

DO NOT FREEZE

Mulled wine *(makes about 1 litre/$1\frac{3}{4}$pt)*
POWER LEVEL: 100% (FULL)

275ml ($\frac{1}{2}$pt) water
100g (4oz) sugar
4 cloves
7.5cm (3in) cinnamon stick
1 orange
1 lemon
1 bottle red wine
few lemon slices

1 Place the water, sugar and spices in a bowl and heat in the microwave for 4 min.
2 Slice the orange and lemon thinly and add to the spiced water. Leave to stand for 10 min.
3 Add the wine and heat for 4 min. Strain the mulled wine and heat for 2 min.
4 Garnish with extra lemon slices and serve hot.

DO NOT FREEZE

Spicy fruit cooler *(makes about $\frac{3}{4}$ litre/$1\frac{1}{2}$pt)*
POWER LEVEL: 100% (FULL)

275ml ($\frac{1}{2}$pt) orange juice
1 lemon, thinly pared rind and juice
150ml ($\frac{1}{4}$pt) pineapple juice
275ml ($\frac{1}{2}$pt) water
2 × 15ml tbsp (2tbsp) sugar syrup (page 61)
4 cloves
$\frac{1}{4}$ × 5ml tsp ($\frac{1}{4}$tsp) each ground cinnamon and mixed spice
1 split ginger ale
for serving: orange slices

1 Combine all the ingredients except the ginger ale and the orange slices in a large bowl. Cover and heat through for 5 min until warm. Leave to stand until cool.
2 Strain the liquid, add the ginger ale and serve decorated with orange slices.

DO NOT FREEZE

Spicy apple juice *(makes about 700ml/$1\frac{1}{4}$pt)*
POWER LEVEL: 100% (FULL)

450g (1lb) cooking apples
2 × 15ml tbsp (2tbsp) water
sugar to taste
150ml ($\frac{1}{4}$pt) white wine
generous pinch cinnamon
275ml ($\frac{1}{2}$pt) cider

1 Place apples, water and sugar in a covered container or roasting bag, cover and cook in the microwave for 5 min.
2 Blend the apples with the white wine and cinnamon in a food processor or liquidiser.
3 Stir in the cider and serve warm or cold.

DO NOT FREEZE

Spiced fruit punch *(makes about 1½ litres/2½pt)*
POWER LEVEL: 100% (FULL) *(colour page 23)*

275ml (½pt) orange juice
150ml (¼pt) pineapple juice
1 lemon, thinly pared rind and juice
¼ × 5ml tsp (¼tsp) each ground nutmeg and mixed
  spice
3 cloves
275ml (½pt) water
75g (3oz) sugar
550ml (1pt) ginger ale

1 Place the fruit juices, lemon rind and juice and the
   spices into a large jug.
2 Heat the water and sugar together for 2–3 min
   until hot, then stir well until the sugar is dissolved.
   Allow to cool slightly.
3 Add the cooled liquid to the fruit juices in the jug
   and chill in the refrigerator. Strain the punch and
   add the ginger ale.
4 Serve chilled with some crushed ice.

DO NOT FREEZE

Hot toddy *(serves 1)*
POWER LEVEL: 100% (FULL)

175ml (6fl oz) water
2 × 5ml tsp (2tsp) lemon juice
1 × 15ml tbsp (1tbsp) demerara sugar
2 × 15ml tbsp (2tbsp) whisky or rum
slice lemon

1 Heat the water in a jug or bowl for 2–2½ min until
   boiling.
2 Mix the lemon juice, demerara sugar and whisky or
   rum together in a heatproof glass.
3 Pour on the boiling water and serve garnished with
   a slice of lemon.

Wine punch *(makes about 700ml/1¼pt)*
POWER LEVEL: 100% (FULL)

550ml (1pt) red wine
75g (3oz) demerara sugar
2 × 5cm (2in) pieces cinnamon stick
1 lemon stuck with cloves
1 wineglass brandy

1 Place all the ingredients except the brandy into a
   large bowl.
2 Cover and bring to the boil in the microwave, cook
   for 2 min then allow to stand for 5 min.
3 Add the brandy, stir well and strain before serving
   hot.

DO NOT FREEZE

Gaelic coffee *(serves 2)*
POWER LEVEL: 100% (FULL) *(colour opposite)*

2 × 5ml tsp (2tsp) brown or demerara sugar
1½–2 cups strong black coffee
4–5 × 15ml tbsp (4–5tbsp) irish whisky
75ml (⅛pt) double cream

1 Divide the sugar and coffee between 2 irish coffee
   glasses. Stir the sugar in the coffee until dissolved.
2 Divide the whisky between the glasses and heat for
   about 2 min until hot.
3 Carefully float the cream over the back of a spoon
   on to the top of the coffee. If preferred, the cream
   may be whipped.

DO NOT FREEZE

Mulled cider *(serves 2)*
POWER LEVEL: 100% (FULL) *(colour opposite)*

275ml (½pt) cider or apple juice
2–4 cloves
2 × 2.5cm (1in) pieces cinnamon stick
whipped cream
nutmeg

1 Divide the cider or apple juice, cloves and pieces of
   cinnamon stick between 2 glasses or mugs. Heat for
   3½–4 min.
2 Top each glass or mug with a spoonful of whipped
   cream and a sprinkling of nutmeg before serving.

DO NOT FREEZE

Party egg nog *(serves about 8)*
POWER LEVEL: 100% (FULL) *(colour opposite)*

275ml (½pt) milk
3 eggs, separated
40g (1½oz) caster sugar
40g (1½oz) soft brown sugar
1 wineglass brandy
1 wineglass rum
150ml (¼pt) cream

1 Heat the milk in a large jug or bowl for about
   2½–3 min without boiling.
2 Whisk the egg yolks together with the sugars until
   blended, then add the brandy and rum gradually.
3 Carefully fold in the cream and stir in the heated
   milk. Whisk the egg whites until stiff and fold them
   into the nog.

DO NOT FREEZE

Gaelic Coffee; Party Egg Nog; Mulled Cider

Brandy cider cup *(makes about 1 litre/1¾pt)*
POWER LEVEL: 100% (FULL) *(colour page 11)*

½pt water
1 teabag
25g (1oz) sugar
juice 1 orange
½ wineglass brandy
550ml (1pt) cider
1 lemon, thinly sliced

1 Place the water in a bowl or jug in the microwave and heat for about 3½ min until boiling. Add the teabag and leave to brew.
2 Add the sugar and stir until dissolved. Remove the teabag.
3 Allow the liquid to cool then add the orange juice and the brandy.
4 Just before serving add the cider and garnish with the lemon slices.

DO NOT FREEZE

Hot gossip *(makes about ¾ litre/1½pt)*
POWER LEVEL: 100% (FULL)

1 orange stuck with cloves
1 bottle red wine
3 × 15ml tbsp (3tbsp) rum
2 × 15ml tbsp (2tbsp) demerara sugar

1 Place the orange in the microwave and cook uncovered for 4 min.

2 Heat the wine for about 5 min until hot but do not allow to boil.
3 Add the rum and sugar, stirring until the sugar is dissolved. Add the orange to the wine and serve hot in heatproof tumblers or punch glasses.

DO NOT FREEZE

Christmas wine *(makes about 1.1 litre/2pt)*
POWER LEVEL: 50% (DEFROST) *(colour page 31)*

½ bottle aquavit or gin
1 bottle burgundy
40g (1½oz) stoned raisins
50g (2oz) sugar
2 × 5ml tsp (2tsp) cardamom seeds, optional
3 cloves
small piece cinnamon
small piece lemon peel
for decoration: thin slices of orange, optional

1 Place half the aquavit or gin, burgundy, raisins and the sugar into a large bowl.
2 Tie the spices and lemon peel in a small muslin bag and add to the bowl.
3 Cover and cook for 30 min. Add the remaining aquavit or gin and remove the muslin bag. Before serving, ignite the wine with a long taper or a match (do not ignite in the microwave), then decorate with the orange slices. Serve in heat-resistant tumblers or punch glasses.

DO NOT FREEZE

Mulled ale *(makes about 1.1 litre/2pt)*
POWER LEVEL: 100% (FULL)

550ml (1pt) ale
4 × 15ml tbsp (4tbsp) brandy
2 × 15ml tbsp (2tbsp) rum
2 × 15ml tbsp (2tbsp) gin
25g (1oz) demerara sugar
275ml (½pt) water
1 lemon, thinly pared rind and juice
good pinch each ground nutmeg and cinnamon

1 Place all the ingredients into a large bowl. Cover and heat for about 8 min but do not allow to boil.
2 Strain and serve in heatproof tumblers or punch glasses.

DO NOT FREEZE

Rum punch *(makes about 1½ litre/2½pt)*
POWER LEVEL: 100% (FULL)

225g (8oz) sugar
850ml (1½pt) warm water
1 lemon, thinly pared rind and juice
2 oranges, thinly pared rind and juice
150ml (¼pt) strong tea
150–275ml (¼–½pt) rum

1 Place the sugar, warm water and the rind of the lemon and oranges into a large bowl, stir until the sugar has dissolved.
2 Cover and bring to the boil in the microwave, uncover and cook for 3 min.
3 Add the fruit juices, tea and the rum. Stir well and leave to stand for 5 min. Strain the punch and serve hot or cold.

DO NOT FREEZE

Claret cup *(makes about 1.1 litre/2pt)*
POWER LEVEL: 100% (FULL) *(colour page 31)*

75ml (⅛pt) sugar syrup (following recipe)
1 lemon, thinly pared rind and juice
1 orange, thinly pared rind and juice
1 bottle claret
275ml (½pt) tonic water
for serving: thinly sliced cucumber

1 Place the sugar syrup, lemon and orange rind in a bowl, cover and bring to the boil in the microwave. Reduce to 50% (defrost) setting and continue to cook for 5 min.
2 Add the lemon and orange juices and the claret.
3 Leave until cool and then chill. Just before serving add the tonic water and decorate with the cucumber slices.

DO NOT FREEZE

Sugar syrup *(makes about 275ml/½pt)*
POWER LEVEL: 100% (FULL)

450 g (1lb) sugar
275ml (½pt) water

1 Place sugar and water into a bowl, cover and heat for 3–4 min; stir well until sugar has dissolved.
2 Replace into the microwave uncovered, and bring to the boil. Boil steadily until a temperature of 105°C (220°F) is reached.
3 Unless a thermometer is used which is designed for use in the microwave, the temperature of the syrup should be taken with a sugar thermometer at intervals throughout the cooking period.
4 Use as required for drinks.

Hot buttered rum *(serves 2)*
POWER LEVEL: 100% (FULL)

2 × 15ml tbsp (2tbsp) demerara sugar
2 × 5ml (2tsp) butter
pinch each nutmeg and cinnamon
2 lemon slices
2 cloves
4 × 15ml tbsp (4tbsp) white rum
275ml (½pt) water or milk

1 Divide 1½ × 15ml tbsp (1½tbsp) demerara sugar between 2 heatproof glasses.
2 Cream the rest of the sugar with the butter, nutmeg and cinnamon.
3 Place a slice of lemon and a clove into each glass and add the rum and water or milk. Heat for 3–3½ min until boiling and stir well.
4 Top with the creamed mixture and serve sprinkled with nutmeg.

DO NOT FREEZE

Soups and stocks

Soups

Whether used as a starter to a meal or as a snack, home-made soups are always welcome and when prepared with a good stock are particularly nourishing and full of flavour. A soup can be served cold or chilled in the summer, or hot on a cold winter's day and, whether home-made or commercially prepared, when heated in the microwave it will retain its full flavour and colour.

Home-made soups can be made in advance and, if preferred, frozen in individual portions. If frozen in larger quantities, the soup should be broken down and stirred frequently during the defrosting process so that the outside liquid does not overheat before the centre portion is thawed. When reheating soups, ensure that the dish or bowl is covered for faster results and is large enough to allow for the expansion of the liquid; this is particularly important when heating milk-based soups.

Soups can be heated in the microwave in individual bowls or mugs, which is a great saving on washing up; one will take about 3 minutes and 2 will take about 5–5½ minutes. Shop-bought soups can be prepared in the microwave on 100% (full) setting as follows:

Canned condensed soups
Add hot water and whisk thoroughly before heating in a large jug or dish or soup tureen. The 275g (10oz) size will take about 6–7 minutes to come to boiling point but do not allow to overheat. Stir thoroughly halfway through the cooking time and whisk well before serving.

Packet soups
Empty the packet of soup mix into a large bowl or jug and gradually stir in the amount of water recommended on the packet. Leave to stand for 20–30 minutes which will allow the ingredients to soften. Stir well, cover the bowl or jug and bring to the boil in the microwave. This will take 8–10 minutes on 100% (full) setting depending on the quantity of soup. Cook for 1–2 minutes, stir or whisk well and leave to stand for 5 minutes before serving with a knob of butter or a spoonful of cream as preferred.

Stocks
Stocks, made from bones and a few vegetables, form the simple basis of home-made soups providing a source of natural goodness and excellent flavour. Small quantities of stock can be made in the microwave cooker, but larger quantities are best cooked conventionally on a hotplate or burner when they should be simmered for up to 4 hours to extract the full flavour. For convenience, bouillon or stock cubes may be used as alternatives to home-made stocks when time is short, although the finished dish will be somewhat lacking in texture and flavour.

Oyster Soup (page 65); Chestnut Soup (page 65); Consommé with Noodles (page 65)

White stock *(makes about 1 litre/1¾pt)*
POWER LEVEL: 100% (FULL) AND 50% (DEFROST)

Use when recipes require chicken stock.

450g (1lb) knuckle of veal or chicken bones, cooked
   or raw
knob of dripping or lard
½ leek, sliced
1 small onion, sliced
1 celery stick, sliced
1 carrot, sliced
1 bouquet garni
¼ × 5ml tsp (¼tsp) salt
6 black peppercorns
1 litre (1¾pt) water

1 Ask the butcher to cut the veal bones into
  convenient-sized pieces. Place the veal or chicken
  bones and dripping or lard into a large bowl, cover
  and cook on 100% (full) setting for 4 min, turning
  the bones over halfway through.
2 Add the remaining ingredients, cover and bring to
  the boil in the microwave (about 10–12 min).
3 Skim the surface of the stock, reduce to 50%
  (defrost) setting and continue to cook for 1 hour,
  topping up with hot water as necessary.
4 Strain the stock through a sieve or fine muslin,
  allow to cool then remove the fat from the surface.
5 Use as required, or when cool store in the refrigerator for 2–3 days or freeze.

Note: *The above recipe may be used as chicken broth,*
providing that chicken bones are used as the basic
ingredients.

Brown stock
Use when recipes require beef stock. Follow the recipe
for White Stock, replacing the veal or chicken bones
with marrow bones or shin of beef.

Fish stock *(makes about 550ml/1pt)*
POWER LEVEL: 100% (FULL) AND 30%

Use the trimmings of the fish such as bones, head and the
skin to make this fish stock. Almost any white fish can be
used, but as it does not keep well, the stock should
preferably be used on the day it is made.

450g (1lb) fish trimmings, washed well
550ml (1pt) water
salt
1 onion, finely chopped
1 stick celery, finely chopped
bouquet garni

1 Place the fish trimmings in a large bowl or jug with
  the water and a little salt. Cover and bring to the
  boil on 100% (full) setting in the microwave.
  Remove the bowl and take off any scum from the
  surface.
2 Add the onion, celery and bouquet garni, cover and
  cook on 30% setting for 30 min.
3 Strain the stock through a sieve or a fine cloth.
  Store in the refrigerator until required.

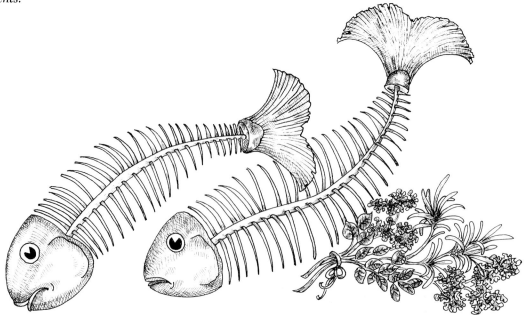

Oyster soup *(serves 3–4)*
POWER LEVEL: 100% (FULL) *(colour page 63)*

40g (1½oz) butter
2 shallots or small onions, finely chopped
½ × 5ml tsp (½tsp) paprika pepper
pinch ground mace
1 × 15ml tbsp (1tbsp) cornflour
425ml (¾pt) milk
small can evaporated milk
salt and pepper
12 oysters, fresh or canned
3–4 × 15ml tbsp (3–4tbsp) single cream

1 Melt the butter in a large bowl for 1–1½ min, stir in the shallots or onions, cover and cook for 5 min. Add the paprika pepper and the mace and continue to cook for 1 min.
2 Blend the cornflour with a little water and add to the onions with the milk and evaporated milk. Cook uncovered for about 6 min, until thickened and boiling. Stir in salt and pepper to taste. Allow to stand for 5 min.
3 Remove the oysters and their juices from their shells, or the canned oysters and juices, and add to the soup. Reheat for 1–2 min without boiling, and stir in single cream just before serving.

DO NOT FREEZE

Chestnut soup *(serves 4–6)*
POWER LEVEL: 100% (FULL) *(colour page 63)*

Rich and creamy, this soup may be served as part of the traditional Christmas fare. This quick version uses canned chestnut purée.

25g (1oz) butter
1 small onion, finely chopped
2 sticks celery, finely sliced
439g (15½oz) can chestnut purée
850ml (1½pt) boiling chicken stock (page 64)
salt and pepper
150ml (¼pt) hot milk
15g (½oz) unsalted butter *or* 3 × 15ml tbsp (3tbsp) double cream
for serving: small Croûtons (page 71)

1 Heat the butter in a large bowl for 1 min until melted. Add the onion and celery, cover and cook for 5 min.
2 Stir in the chestnut purée, boiling chicken stock and salt and pepper to taste.
3 Cover and cook for 5 min. Purée the soup in a blender or food processor and stir in the hot milk.
4 Reheat the soup for 2–3 min if necessary, and just before serving stir in the unsalted butter or double cream.
5 Serve with small croûtons cooked in butter.

Consommé with noodles *(serves 4)*
POWER LEVEL: 100% (FULL) *(colour page 63)*

850ml (1½pt) canned beef consommé
50g (2oz) thread egg noodles
salt and freshly ground black pepper
1 × 15ml tbsp (1tbsp) grated cheddar cheese
1 × 15ml tbsp (1tbsp) grated parmesan cheese

1 Place the consommé into a large bowl. Cover and bring to the boil in the microwave, about 7–8 min.
2 Add the noodles, stir well until softened, then cover and cook for 5 min. Add seasoning to taste.
3 Pour the soup into individual serving dishes and just before serving, sprinkle with the mixed grated cheeses.

Tomato soup *(serves 4)*
POWER LEVEL: 100% (FULL)

25g (1oz) butter
1 onion, finely chopped
25g (1oz) flour
2 × 400g (14oz) cans tomatoes, roughly chopped
3 × 15ml tbsp (3tbsp) tomato purée
150ml (¼pt) boiling water
1 beef stock cube, crumbled
1 × 5ml tsp (1tsp) dried oregano or basil
salt and freshly ground black pepper
for serving: Croûtons (page 71)

1 Melt the butter in a large bowl for 1 min. Stir in the onion, cover and cook for 4 min.
2 Stir in the flour, tomatoes, tomato purée, boiling water and the crumbled stock cube. Add the herbs and salt and pepper to taste.
3 Cover and bring to the boil, stirring twice throughout. Continue to cook for a further 3 min.
4 If preferred, the soup may be puréed in a blender or food processor. Serve straightaway with croûtons.

Blue cheese soup *(serves 4–6)*
POWER LEVEL: 100% (FULL)

25g (1oz) butter
1 × 15ml tbsp (1tbsp) chopped onion
25g (1oz) flour
425ml (¾pt) boiling chicken stock (page 64)
425ml (¾pt) milk
salt and freshly ground black pepper
pinch each ground bay leaves, cayenne pepper
½ × 5ml tsp (½tsp) mild mustard, optional
175g (6oz) blue cheese or stilton, crumbled
75ml (⅛pt) single cream
for serving: Croûtons (page 71) or toasted bread

1 Heat the butter in a large bowl for 1 min until melted. Add the onion, cover and cook for 1 min.

2 Stir in the flour and then add the chicken stock gradually. Add all the other ingredients except the cheese and cream.

3 Cover and cook for 5 min, stirring twice throughout. Add the cheese and continue to cook for a further 3 min.

4 If preferred the soup may be puréed in a blender or food processor. Reheat in the microwave if necessary.

5 Stir in the cream and serve hot with croûtons or toasted bread.

Beef soup *(serves 6) (colour opposite)*
POWER LEVEL: 100% (FULL) AND 50% (DEFROST)

This substantial main-course soup is topped with toasted cheese croûtes before serving.

2 × 15ml tbsp (2tbsp) oil
2 medium onions, finely chopped
2 medium carrots, finely chopped
1 clove garlic, crushed
350g (12oz) minced lean beef
50g (2oz) mushrooms, sliced
40g (1½oz) flour
1.1 litre (2pt) boiling beef stock (page 64)
1 × 213g (7½oz) can red kidney beans
salt and freshly ground black pepper
6 thick slices french bread, toasted
butter for spreading
a little english mustard, optional
100g (4oz) cheddar cheese, grated
for garnish: freshly chopped parsley

1 Place the oil, onions, carrots and garlic in a large bowl. Mix well together, cover and cook on 100% (full) setting for 6 min.

2 Add the beef and mushrooms, stir well, cover and cook for 6–7 min, stirring twice throughout and breaking down any lumps with a fork.

3 Stir in the flour and the stock. Cover and bring to the boil stirring twice throughout. Reduce to 50% (defrost) and continue to cook for 12–15 min until the meat is tender.

4 Stir in the red kidney beans and salt and pepper to taste. Heat for 2 min and leave to stand covered.

5 Place the toasted slices of french bread in a circle on a plate and spread with butter and a little mustard. Top with the grated cheese.

6 Cook uncovered for 1½–2½ min until the cheese is melted. Alternatively brown conventionally under a hot grill.

7 Float the toasted cheese croûtes on top of the soup and sprinkle with chopped parsley before serving.

DO NOT FREEZE WITH THE TOASTED CROÛTES AND CHEESE TOPPING

Bacon and bean chowder *(serves 4)*
POWER LEVEL: 100% (FULL) *(colour opposite)*

2 × 15ml tbsp (2tbsp) oil
1 onion, finely chopped
1 turnip, diced
225g (8oz) lean bacon rashers, derinded and cut into strips
100g (4oz) boiling sausage, sliced
1 × 15ml tbsp (1tbsp) tomato purée
700 ml (1¼pt) boiling chicken stock (page 64)
salt and freshly ground black pepper
225g (8oz) canned red kidney beans
1 × 15ml tbsp (1tbsp) cornflour
2 × 15ml tbsp (2tbsp) cold water
150ml (¼pt) hot milk

1 Place the oil in a large bowl with the onion. Toss the onion in the oil, cover and cook for 4 min.

2 Add the turnip, cover and cook for a further 4 min. Add the bacon, cover and cook for 4 min.

3 Add the sausage, tomato purée, stock and seasoning, cover and cook for 8 min, until the vegetables are tender. Stir in the beans and cook for a further 2 min.

4 Blend the cornflour with the water and stir into the soup until thickened. Add the hot milk, stir well and serve hot.

Chicken broth with dumplings *(serves 4)*
POWER LEVEL: 100% (FULL) *(colour opposite)*

40g (1½oz) butter
1 egg, beaten
40g (1½oz) plain flour
25g (1oz) self-raising flour
good pinch salt
½ lemon, grated rind
2 × 5ml tsp (2tsp) chopped parsley
1.1 litre (2pt) hot chicken broth (page 64)

1 Soften the butter in a small bowl by heating in the microwave for 10–15 sec. Beat in the egg, flours and the salt. Fold in the lemon rind and parsley.

2 Form the dumplings into tiny balls, the size of large peas.

3 Bring the chicken broth to the boil in a large covered bowl or tureen in the microwave. Drop the dumplings one by one into the broth, cover and cook for 5 min until the dumplings are well risen, stirring once halfway through.

4 Serve hot. The dumplings should be small, light and not too filling.

Bacon and Bean Chowder; Chicken Broth with Dumplings; Beef Soup

Onion soup *(serves 4)*
POWER LEVEL: 100% (FULL)

25g (1oz) butter
450g (1lb) onions, peeled and thinly sliced
25g (1oz) flour
salt and freshly ground black pepper
1 × 5ml tsp (1tsp) sugar
550ml (1pt) boiling chicken stock (page 64)
275ml (½pt) milk
for serving: Croûtons (page 71) or crusty french bread

1 Heat the butter in a large, shallow serving dish for 1 min. Toss the onion in the butter and cover and cook for 5 min.
2 Add the flour and mix into the butter and onion. Add salt and pepper to taste and the sugar.
3 Gradually add the stock and mix well together. Cover and cook for 10 min.
4 Heat the milk in a bowl or jug for 3 min and add to the soup. Blend in a liquidiser or food processor.
5 If necessary, heat in the microwave for 2–3 min before serving with croûtons or crusty french bread.

Highland hotpot *(serves 6)*
POWER LEVEL: 100% (FULL)

40g (1½oz) butter
2 × 15ml tbsp (2tbsp) oil
2 onions, finely sliced
1 stick celery, finely sliced
2 carrots, diced
1 turnip, diced
1 leek, finely sliced
450g (1lb) lean lamb, minced
1.1 litre (2pt) boiling beef stock (page 64)
salt and pepper
100g (4oz) frozen peas, thawed
100g (4oz) cauliflower, cut into tiny florets
2 × 15ml tbsp (2tbsp) chopped parsley

1 Place the butter and 1 × 15ml tbsp (1tbsp) of the oil into a large bowl and heat in the microwave for 1½ min.
2 Add the onions, celery, carrots, turnip and leek, toss well in the butter and oil. Cover and cook for 6 min.
3 In another bowl, place the remaining oil and the lamb. Mix well, cover and cook for 5–6 min until brown, stirring twice throughout and breaking down any lumps with a fork.
4 Mix the lamb with the vegetables, add the stock and seasoning to taste. Cover and cook for 15 min.
5 Add the peas and cauliflower florets. Mix well and continue to cook for a further 6–8 min until the vegetables are tender.
6 Correct seasoning and stir in the parsley.

Cream of chicken soup *(serves 4)*
POWER LEVEL: 100% (FULL)

25g (1oz) butter
1 onion, finely chopped
½ stick celery, chopped
25g (1oz) flour
550ml (1pt) boiling chicken stock (page 64)
175g (6oz) cooked chicken, finely chopped
150ml (¼pt) milk
3 × 15ml tbsp (3tbsp) single cream or top of the milk
for garnish: chopped chives

1 Melt the butter in a large bowl for 1 min. Add the onion and celery, cover and cook for 3 min.
2 Stir in the flour and gradually add the chicken stock and the chicken. Cover and bring to the boil in the microwave, stirring twice throughout. Continue to cook for a further 3 min.
3 Add the milk to the soup and at this stage the soup may be blended if preferred in a liquidiser or food processor.
4 Reheat the soup if necessary for 2–3 min and stir in the cream or top of the milk.
5 Sprinkle with chopped chives before serving.

Prawn bisque *(serves 6)*
POWER LEVEL: 100% (FULL)

This soup may be served hot or chilled.

25g (1oz) butter
1 onion, finely chopped
900g (2lb) tomatoes, fresh or canned
100g (4oz) canned pimentos, chopped
2 × 5ml tsp (2tsp) tomato purée
850ml (1½pt) boiling chicken stock (page 64)
salt and pepper
175g (6oz) peeled prawns
2 × 5ml tsp (2tsp) arrowroot
150ml (¼pt) double cream

1 Melt the butter in a large bowl for 1 min. Add the onion, toss well in the butter, cover and cook for 4 min until soft.
2 Skin the fresh tomatoes, cut into quarters and remove the seeds, or drain the canned tomatoes if used.
3 Add the tomatoes, pimentos, tomato purée, boiling chicken stock and seasoning. Cover and bring to the boil in the microwave and then cook for 5 min.
4 Stir in the prawns and purée the soup in a blender or food processor. To thicken the soup, blend the arrowroot with a little cold water and add to the soup in the blender or food processor.
5 Chill the soup if to be served cold. Whip the cream and stir into the soup before serving.

Cream of turnip soup *(serves 6)*

POWER LEVEL: 100% (FULL)

Use early turnips for this delicious vegetable soup.

50g (2oz) butter
350g (12oz) young turnips, peeled and diced
225g (8oz) potatoes, peeled and diced
1 leek, trimmed, washed and chopped
1 onion, peeled and chopped
25g (1oz) flour
2 litre (3½pt) boiling chicken (page 64) or vegetable
    stock
salt and freshly ground black pepper
2 egg yolks
3 × 15ml tbsp (3tbsp) double cream
for garnish: Croûtons (page 71)

1 Melt the butter in a large bowl for 1½–2 min. Add all the vegetables; toss well in the butter. Cover and cook for 12–15 min, shaking or stirring every 5 min.
2 Stir in the flour and blend in the boiling stock. Season to taste.
3 Cook for 15–20 min until the vegetables are tender. Purée the soup in a liquidiser or pass through a sieve.
4 Beat the egg yolks with the cream, add a little of the soup and stir until well blended. Add this to the soup and mix well. Correct seasoning.
5 Heat without boiling. Serve hot, garnished with croûtons or hand them separately.

Crab and sweetcorn soup *(serves 4)*

POWER LEVEL: 100% (FULL)

1 × 15ml tbsp (1tbsp) oil
1 onion, finely chopped
1 stick celery, chopped
425ml (¾pt) boiling chicken stock (page 64)
225g (8oz) sweetcorn, canned or frozen, thawed
salt and pepper
100g (4oz) crab meat
150ml (¼pt) milk
3 × 15ml tbsp (3tbsp) single cream or top of the milk
25g (1oz) flaked almonds, toasted

1 Heat the oil in a large bowl for 1–2 min, add the onion and celery, cover and cook for 3 min.
2 Add the chicken stock, sweetcorn and seasoning and cook for 5 min. Add the crab and cook for 2 min.
3 Blend the soup with the milk in a liquidiser or pass through a sieve. Reheat the soup for 2 min.
4 Stir in the cream and serve sprinkled with the flaked almonds.

Note: *If preferred, the soup may be served without puréeing. Use 550ml (1pt) boiling chicken stock and omit the milk. Thicken the soup with 2 × 5ml tsp (2tsp) arrowroot mixed with a little water, then stir in the cream or top of the milk. Mix the almonds into the soup before serving.*

DO NOT FREEZE

Bouillabaise *(serves 6)*
POWER LEVEL: 100% (FULL)

The flavour of the soup is made more interesting if as many varieties of fish as possible are included. Use the trimmings from the fish to make the stock.

2 × 15ml tbsp (2tbsp) oil
1 small onion, finely chopped
75g (3oz) leeks, finely chopped
2–3 cloves garlic, crushed
225g (8oz) can tomatoes
850ml (1½pt) boiling fish stock (page 64)
1 × 15ml tbsp (1tbsp) tomato purée
salt and freshly ground black pepper
2 × 15ml tbsp (2tbsp) chopped mixed fresh herbs, ie parsley, thyme, basil
1 bay leaf
450g (1lb) prepared mixed fresh fish, cut into small pieces
225g (8oz) peeled prawns
225g (8oz) frozen mussels, thawed
for serving: crusty french bread

1 Place the oil, onion, leeks and garlic into a large casserole dish, cover and cook for 3–4 min until the onion and leeks are transparent.
2 Add all the other ingredients except the prawns and mussels. Stir well, cover and bring to the boil and continue to cook for 6–7 min.
3 Stir in the prawns and mussels and cook for a further 2–3 min. Adjust seasoning and allow to stand for a few minutes.
4 Remove the bay leaf and serve hot with crusty french bread.

DO NOT FREEZE

Garlic soup *(serves 4)*
POWER LEVEL: 100% (FULL)

8–10 small cloves garlic, peeled and roughly chopped
850ml (1½pt) boiling chicken stock (page 64)
sprig thyme
sprig sage
1 clove
salt and pepper to taste
4 slices bread, brown or white
50g (2oz) cheese, grated
4 × 5ml tsp (4tsp) olive oil

1 Place the garlic, boiling chicken stock, thyme, sage and clove in a large bowl. Cover and cook for 10 min. Allow to stand for 3–5 min.
2 Strain the soup and add salt and pepper to taste.
3 Place the slices of bread on to a plate in a single layer, sprinkle with the grated cheese and the olive oil. Heat, uncovered for about 1 min until the cheese is softened.
4 Place one slice of bread into each individual serving bowl and pour over the soup. Leave to stand for a minute or two to allow the bread to swell.
5 Serve piping hot.

Leek and potato soup *(serves 4–6)*
POWER LEVEL: 100% (FULL)

675g (1½lb) leeks, washed and trimmed
225g (8oz) potatoes, peeled
40g (1½oz) butter
1 stick celery, finely sliced, optional
700ml (1¼pt) milk
salt and pepper
1 chicken stock cube
150ml (¼pt) boiling water
grated nutmeg for sprinkling

1 Slice the leeks finely and cut the potatoes into small dice.
2 Melt the butter for 1–1½ min, add the leeks, potatoes and celery. Mix well together, cover and cook for 10 min.
3 Heat the milk in a jug for 3 min and add to the vegetables.
4 Add salt and pepper, the chicken stock cube and boiling water.
5 Blend the soup in a liquidiser or food processor and adjust the seasoning.
6 Reheat for 1–2 min if necessary before serving sprinkled with a little grated nutmeg.

Lentil and ham soup *(serves 4)*
POWER LEVEL: 100% (FULL)

100g (4oz) lentils, soaked overnight
850ml (1½pt) boiling ham stock
1 onion, finely chopped
2 sticks celery, finely sliced
salt and freshly ground black pepper
¼ × 5ml tsp (¼tsp) dried mustard
100g (4oz) cooked ham, chopped
for garnish: chopped parsley

1 Drain the lentils and place in a large bowl with the ham stock, onion, celery, seasoning and mustard.
2 Cover and cook for 10 min. Add the ham, stir well and continue cooking for a further 3–5 min until the lentils are tender.
3 At this stage, the soup may be puréed if preferred in a blender or food processor. Otherwise serve straight away.
4 Serve hot sprinkled with chopped parsley.

Fish chowder *(serves 4)*
POWER LEVEL: 100% (FULL) *(colour page 15)*

1 × 15ml tbsp (1tbsp) cooking oil
2 bacon rashers, derinded and chopped
1 medium onion, chopped
2 sticks celery, chopped
350g (12oz) potatoes, cut into small dice
350g (12oz) white fish fillets, cut into 2.5cm (1in)
  pieces
550ml (1pt) boiling chicken or fish stock (page 64)
¼ × 5ml tsp (¼tsp) turmeric
¼ × 5ml tsp (¼tsp) dried thyme
1 bay leaf
salt and freshly ground black pepper
275g (10oz) can or jar baby clams or mussels,
  drained
150ml (¼pt) single cream
2 × 15ml tbsp (2tbsp) chopped parsley
for serving: crusty bread

1 Mix together the oil, bacon, onion and celery in a large casserole dish; cover and cook for 2 min.
2 Add the potatoes, mix well together, cover and cook for 11–12 min, stirring twice throughout.
3 Add the fish, stock, turmeric, thyme, bay leaf and seasoning. Cover and cook for 5–6 min.
4 Adjust seasoning and add the clams or mussels. Cover and heat through for 2 min.
5 Stir in the single cream and 1 × 15ml tbsp (1tbsp) chopped parsley. Sprinkle with the rest of the parsley and serve hot with crusty bread.

Spinach soup *(serves 4–6)*
POWER LEVEL: 100% (FULL)

40g (1½oz) butter
1 × 15ml tbsp (1tbsp) chopped onion
40g (1½oz) flour
salt and freshly ground black pepper
425ml (¾pt) hot chicken stock (page 64)
425ml (¾pt) milk
1 × 5ml tsp (1tsp) ground nutmeg
225g (8oz) frozen spinach, thawed
75ml (⅛pt) double cream

1 Heat the butter in a large bowl for 1–1½ min until melted. Stir in the onion, cover and cook for 1 min.
2 Stir in the flour and seasoning and add the hot chicken stock gradually. Add the milk and nutmeg.
3 Cover and cook for 5 min stirring twice throughout. Add the spinach, stir well and continue to cook for a further 5–6 min.
4 Purée the soup in a blender or food processor. Reheat in the microwave for 2–3 min if necessary.
5 Stir in the double cream to give a swirled effect before serving.

Curry soup (Mulligatawny) *(serves 4–6)*
POWER LEVEL: 100% (FULL)

This curry-flavoured soup was a particular favourite among the British in India. This version can be served hot or cold.

50g (2oz) unsalted butter
1 onion, finely chopped
1 carrot, finely chopped
1 clove garlic, crushed
25g (1oz) flour
2 × 5ml tsp (2tsp) curry powder
1 litre (1¾pt) hot beef stock (page 64)
2 × 15ml tbsp (2tbsp) mango chutney, finely
  chopped
4–6 × 15ml tbsp (4–6tbsp) cooked rice
for garnish: tiny cauliflower florets

1 Place the butter in a large bowl, heat for 1½ min. Add the onion and carrot, toss well in the butter, stir in the garlic.
2 Cover and cook for about 7–8 min until the vegetables are tender.
3 Stir in the flour and the curry powder, cook for 1 min, stirring halfway through. Gradually stir in the stock.
4 Bring the soup to the boil in the microwave, and continue to cook, covered, for 5 min.
5 Purée the soup in a blender or food processor and then stir in the mango chutney.
6 Heat the rice for 1–2 min then place a spoonful into each serving bowl. Top with the soup and serve garnished with tiny cauliflower florets.
7 If serving cold, after puréeing the soup in the blender or food processor, allow to cool and then chill in the refrigerator. Place a spoonful of the cold rice into each serving bowl and top with the cold soup. Serve cold garnished with the cauliflower.

Croûtons *(serves 2–3)*
POWER LEVEL: 100% (FULL)

1 large slice thick brown or white bread, crusts
  removed
25g (1oz) butter
paprika pepper for sprinkling, optional

1 Cut the slice of bread into small cubes.
2 Place the butter in a shallow dish and heat for 1 min in the microwave.
3 Add the bread cubes to the dish, toss the bread over in the melted butter and cook, uncovered for 1 min; turn the bread over and cook for a further 1 min.
4 Drain on kitchen paper towel, allow to stand for 1 min before sprinkling with paprika and serving hot with soup.

Minestrone soup *(serves 4–6)*
POWER LEVEL: 100% (FULL)

25g (1oz) butter
1 carrot, peeled and diced
1 onion, peeled and finely chopped
1 small leek, finely sliced
1 stick celery, finely chopped
1 clove garlic, finely chopped
550ml (1pt) boiling chicken stock (page 64)
15g ($\frac{1}{2}$oz) long grain rice
salt and pepper
225g (8oz) tomatoes, skinned and chopped
2 × 15ml tbsp (2tbsp) baked beans
for garnish: 1 × 5ml tsp (1tsp) chopped parsley
for serving: grated parmesan cheese

1 Melt the butter in a large bowl for 1 min. Add the carrot, onion, leek, celery and garlic. Toss well in the butter, cover and cook for 3 min.
2 Add boiling stock, rice and seasoning. Cover and cook for 5–6 min, stirring once halfway through.
3 Add the tomatoes and baked beans and continue to cook, covered, for a further 5–6 min.
4 Sprinkle with parsley and serve with grated parmesan cheese.

Celery and beetroot soup *(serves 4–6)*
POWER LEVEL: 100% (FULL)

1 onion, peeled and chopped
$\frac{1}{2}$ head celery, trimmed and finely sliced
225g (8oz) cooked beetroot, chopped
550ml (1pt) boiling chicken stock (page 64)
salt and pepper
1 bay leaf
bouquet garni
1 × 15ml tbsp (1tbsp) cornflour
150ml ($\frac{1}{4}$pt) milk
150ml ($\frac{1}{4}$pt) single cream
for garnish: freshly chopped chives

1 Place the onion, celery, beetroot and boiling stock into a large casserole dish or bowl. Add salt and pepper, bay leaf and bouquet garni.
2 Cover and cook for 12–13 min until the vegetables are tender.
3 Remove bay leaf and bouquet garni. Blend the soup in a liquidiser or food processor.
4 Blend the cornflour with the milk and then add to the soup in the bowl. Heat for 3–4 min or until slightly thickened and boiling, stirring twice.
5 Stir in the cream and serve sprinkled with chives.

Eggs and cheese

It is probably quite well established that a microwave cooker will produce perfect scrambled eggs in next to no time—cooked to a softer or dryer texture as preferred and leaving no sticky dish to wash up afterwards. In addition, the microwave will cook other egg dishes so that the yolks remain creamy and the whites set without becoming tough. However, eggs and cheese are both high-protein foods and, as such, are sensitive to heat.

As cooking is so fast in the microwave, it is advisable to slightly undercook as egg yolks tend to set more quickly than the whites, and cheese, if overcooked, tends to become leathery in texture. With some egg- and cheese-based dishes, lower power levels give the flexibility in control to ensure results which are near perfect every time.

When baking, frying or poaching eggs in the microwave, prick the yolks with a sharp-pointed knife or cocktail stick to prevent steam building up inside the yolk which causes the egg to explode. Similarly, eggs should never be boiled whole in their shells in the microwave except by the method I have given in this section.

The cooking times given for eggs are intended as a guide as much depends on how well done you like them, but remember to remove them from the oven just before they are set as they will carry on cooking for a short while afterwards. Leave them to stand for a minute before serving but if they are not set sufficiently for your liking, return them to the oven for a further 10–15 seconds.

Defrosting cheese

Most cheeses freeze quite well, especially the creamy varieties, brie and stilton for example. Cheddar cheeses are inclined to become crumbly in texture after thawing so are best used for cooking and are easier to handle frozen if already grated.

Frozen cheeses are best left to thaw naturally in the refrigerator or at room temperature. If required more quickly, the defrosting process can be started in the microwave by allowing 4–5 minutes at 30% setting for 275g (10oz) cheese and then allowing to stand until completely thawed. Watch the cheese during the defrosting process and be prepared to remove it from the microwave as soon as the cheese appears to melt on the outside edges.

Baked eggs *(serves 1 or 2)*
POWER LEVEL: 50% (DEFROST)

butter or margarine
2 eggs

1 Lightly grease 2 ramekin dishes or small cups or bowls with the butter or margarine.
2 Break the eggs into the dishes and prick the yolks.
3 Cover and cook for 2–2½ min, turning the dishes once halfway through.

Note: *Baked eggs may be used as hard-boiled eggs when required chopped, for use in salads or fillings.*

DO NOT FREEZE

Fried eggs *(serves 1 or 2)*
POWER LEVEL: 100% (FULL)

15g (½oz) butter or margarine
2 eggs

1 Melt the butter in 2 small shallow dishes or saucers. Break the eggs into the hot butter and pierce the yolks.
2 Cover and cook for 30 sec. Stand for 1 min, then turn the dishes and cook for 15–30 secs.

DO NOT FREEZE

Boiled eggs *(serves 2–4)*
POWER LEVEL: 100% (FULL)

Eggs in their shells should not normally be cooked in the microwave as steam builds up inside the shell which can cause the egg to explode. The following method is the only one which allows eggs to be cooked in their shells by covering each egg completely in aluminium foil.

4 eggs
boiling water

1 Wrap the eggs tightly in pieces of smooth foil to reflect the microwave energy. Place the eggs in a bowl or dish and just cover with boiling water.
2 Cover and cook for 3–4 min, stand for 2 min. Drain and unwrap the eggs and serve immediately.

DO NOT FREEZE

Poached eggs *(serves 2–4)*
POWER LEVEL: 100% (FULL) AND 50% (DEFROST)

boiling water
4 eggs
hot buttered toast, optional

1 Pour the boiling water into individual cups, ramekin dishes or small bowls to a depth of about 2.5cm (1in). Place the dishes in a circle on the microwave oven shelf and heat until boiling.
2 Carefully break the eggs into the dishes and prick the yolks. Cook on 50% (defrost) for 3–3½ min until the whites are set, turning each dish halfway through. Be careful not to overcook as the eggs will continue to cook slightly after removal from the microwave.
3 Drain the eggs and serve on hot buttered toast.

Note: *Cook 1 egg for 1–1½ min, 2 eggs for 1½–2 min.*

DO NOT FREEZE

Eggs lorraine *(serves 3 or 6) (colour opposite)*
POWER LEVEL: 100% (FULL) AND 50% (DEFROST)

Serve as a light lunch or supper dish.

knob butter
8 thin, lean rashers bacon
100g (4oz) gruyère cheese, thinly sliced
6 eggs
150ml (¼pt) single cream
salt and pepper
paprika pepper for sprinkling

1 Lightly grease a shallow 17.5–20cm (7–8in) round dish with half of the butter.

2 Remove the rinds from the bacon and place rashers in a single layer on a plate. Cover with kitchen paper towel and cook for 3–4 min on 100% (full) setting. Drain on kitchen paper towel.
3 Line the buttered dish with the bacon rashers and the cheese. Break the eggs and arrange 5 in a circle around the outside of the dish with 1 in the middle. Prick the yolks.
4 Pour the cream around the eggs and top with slivers of butter. Sprinkle with salt, pepper and paprika pepper. Cover and cook on 50% (defrost) setting for 12–15 min until the eggs are just set.
5 Allow to stand for 5 min before serving.

DO NOT FREEZE

Piperade *(serves 4)*
POWER LEVEL: 100% (FULL) *(colour opposite)*

3 × 15ml tbsp (3tbsp) cooking oil
2 medium onions, peeled and finely sliced
2 cloves garlic, crushed
2 red peppers, deseeded and sliced
4 tomatoes, skinned
salt and freshly ground black pepper
4 eggs
for serving: triangles of fried or toasted bread or fresh bread and butter

1 Heat the oil in a large bowl or dish for 1½ min. Add the onions and garlic, cover and cook for 3 min. Add the peppers and continue to cook for 3 min.
2 Chop the tomatoes and add them to the onions and peppers. Season lightly, cover and cook for a further 3–4 min until the vegetables are tender, stirring occasionally.
3 Whisk the eggs lightly in a bowl and pour over the vegetables; stir lightly as for scrambled eggs, cover and cook for 1 min, stir and cook for a further 1–2 min. When the eggs begin to thicken, the piperade is cooked.
4 Serve immediately with triangles of fried or toasted bread, or with plenty of fresh bread and butter.

DO NOT FREEZE

Eggs Lorraine; Piperade

Scrambled eggs (serves 2)
POWER LEVEL: 100% (FULL)

4 eggs
4 × 15ml tbsp (4tbsp) milk
pinch salt
25g (1oz) butter
hot buttered toast, optional

1 Beat together the eggs, milk and the salt. Melt the butter in a bowl or jug for 1 min. Pour in the egg mixture and cook for 1 min.
2 Stir well and cook for 2–2½ min, stirring every 30 sec. Cook for 15–30 sec longer if preferred more well cooked. Serve with hot buttered toast.

Note: *Halve the above cooking times for 2 eggs.*

DO NOT FREEZE

Peppered cheese soufflés (serves 4 or 8)
POWER LEVEL: 100% (FULL)

25g (1oz) butter
15g (½oz) flour
150ml (¼pt) milk
75g (3oz) cheese, finely grated
3 eggs, separated
seasoning
paprika pepper for sprinkling

1 Place the butter in a bowl and melt for 1 min.
2 Stir in the flour and gradually blend in the milk. Cook for 1½ min until thickened, stirring every 30 sec. Add the cheese.
3 Beat the egg yolks into the mixture one at a time and season.
4 Stiffly beat the egg whites, fold into the mixture and divide between 8 individual soufflé dishes or ramekin dishes.
5 Cook 4 at a time for 1–1½ min. Serve immediately, sprinkled with paprika pepper.

DO NOT FREEZE

Eggs en cocotte (serves 4)
POWER LEVEL: 50% (DEFROST)

150ml (¼pt) double cream
salt and pepper
garlic salt
paprika pepper
25g (1oz) butter
4 eggs
for garnish: 4 sprigs of parsley

1 Mix the cream with the seasonings to taste. Whip the mixture lightly until the cream is thick but not stiff.
2 Divide the butter between 4 ramekin or individual soufflé dishes and melt for 1 min. Brush the butter around the dishes and break an egg into each dish.
3 Pierce the yolk of each egg, then spoon over the cream mixture.
4 Cover and cook for 2–2½ min and stand for 1 min.
5 Sprinkle with more paprika and garnish with parsley before serving.

DO NOT FREEZE

Baked egg custard (serves 4–5)
POWER LEVEL: 100% (FULL) AND 50% (DEFROST)

425ml (¾pt) milk
3 eggs, lightly beaten
50g (2oz) sugar
few drops vanilla essence
ground nutmeg for sprinkling

1 Heat the milk in a measuring jug or bowl for 3 min on 100% (full) setting. Add the eggs, sugar and vanilla essence and whisk lightly.
2 Strain and pour the mixture into individual bowls or ramekin dishes. Sprinkle with nutmeg and cover.
3 Arrange in a circle in the microwave and cook on 50% (defrost) setting for 10–12 min, turning the dishes halfway through. If not quite set, allow an extra 1–2 min, or leave to stand.
4 Serve warm or leave to chill in the refrigerator.

DO NOT FREEZE

Eggs jacqueline (serves 4)
POWER LEVEL: 100% (FULL) AND 70%

Serve as a starter to a meal.

4 hard-boiled eggs
40g (1½oz) butter
½ × 5ml tsp (½tsp) paprika pepper
175g (6oz) peeled prawns
salt and freshly ground black pepper
350g (12oz) frozen asparagus spears
275ml (½pt) Béchamel Sauce (page 134)
for garnish: 1 × 15ml tbsp (1tbsp) parmesan cheese
  paprika pepper for sprinkling

1 Cut the eggs in half lengthways; remove and sieve the yolks.
2 Cream together the butter and paprika pepper and stir in the sieved egg yolks and 50g (2oz) of the prawns which have been finely chopped. Season to taste.
3 Stuff the egg whites with the prawn mixture.
4 Place the frozen asparagus spears into a dish with a little salt. Cover the dish and cook on 100% (full)

setting for 8–10 min, tossing well 2–3 times throughout.

5 Drain the asparagus spears and arrange them in the bases of 4 individual au gratin dishes or bowls. Top with the eggs and the remaining prawns.

6 Heat the béchamel sauce for 2–3 min if necessary and coat the eggs and prawns. Sprinkle with the parmesan cheese and paprika pepper.

7 Place the dishes in the microwave and cook uncovered on 70% setting for about 5 min until heated through. Serve straightaway.

DO NOT FREEZE

Anglesey eggs *(serves 4)*
POWER LEVEL: 100% (FULL)

Traditionally served for high tea, this welsh dish mixes leeks and cheese to provide a substantial meal.

6 leeks, washed thoroughly and sliced
4 × 15ml tbsp (4tbsp) salted water
450g (1lb) Creamed Potatoes (page 152)
8 hard-boiled eggs, sliced
275ml (½pt) Cheese Sauce (page 132)
2 × 15ml tbsp (2 tbsp) grated cheese

1 Place the leeks into a covered dish or a boiling bag with the salted water and cook until tender, about 7–10 min. Drain well.

2 Add the leeks to the creamed potatoes, beating well together until the mixture is light and fluffy. If preferred the vegetables may be puréed in a blender or food processor or beaten in a food mixer.

3 Arrange the slices of egg in the centre of a shallow, round dish and spoon the potato around them. Heat the sauce for 2–3 min if necessary and pour over the eggs.

4 Sprinkle with the grated cheese and cook, covered, for 3–4 min until heated through. Allow to stand for 3 min before serving.

DO NOT FREEZE

Eggs mornay *(serves 2 or 4)*
POWER LEVEL: 50% (DEFROST)

butter
4 eggs
275ml (½pt) Cheese Sauce (page 132)
1 × 15ml tbsp (1tbsp) grated cheese
1 × 15ml tbsp (1tbsp) browned breadcrumbs

1 Lightly grease a shallow dish with a little butter. Break the eggs into the dish, arranging them around the edge.

2 Heat the sauce if necessary for 3–4 min. Coat the eggs with the cheese sauce. Mix the grated cheese with the breadcrumbs and scatter over the top of the sauce.

3 Cook in the microwave for 10–12 min until the eggs are set. Serve straightaway.

DO NOT FREEZE

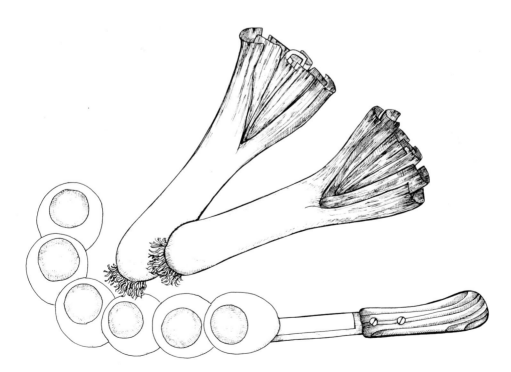

Hot and cold roquefort salad *(serves 4–5)*

POWER LEVEL: 50% (DEFROST) *(colour opposite)*

This salad-with-a-difference gives an unusual contrast between the melting, tangy dressing and the cool, crisp lettuce. Serve it as a starter or as a side salad.

150ml (¼pt) Blender Mayonnaise (page 137)
½ small onion, grated
50g (2oz) grated parmesan cheese
¼ × 5ml tsp (¼tsp) horseradish sauce
¼ × 5ml tsp (¼tsp) dried basil
75g (3oz) roquefort or blue cheese
75ml (⅛pt) double cream, whipped
crisp lettuce leaves, shredded and well chilled
chopped walnuts for sprinkling

1 Mix together the mayonnaise, grated onion, parmesan cheese, horseradish sauce and the dried basil.
2 Crumble the cheese and add to the mayonnaise mixture, stirring well together. Fold in the whipped cream.
3 Cover the dish and cook for about 2 min until just hot, stirring well halfway through. (Do not overcook or the mixture will separate.)
4 Arrange the lettuce on a serving plate or dish and top with the dressing. Sprinkle with chopped walnuts and serve straightaway.

DO NOT FREEZE

Cream cheese mousse *(serves 4)*

POWER LEVEL: 100% (FULL) *(colour opposite)*

This light, cheese mousse is very easy to make and can be served as a starter to a meal or as a main summer lunch dish with a green salad.

2 cans consommé, 550ml (1pt) approximately
225g (8oz) plain cream cheese
2 hard-boiled eggs, sliced
salt and freshly ground black pepper
for garnish: cream cheese for piping, thinly sliced cucumber and a lemon twist

1 Place the consommé into a jug or bowl and heat in the microwave until just melted, about 2 min. Stir well until smooth or heat for another 15–30 sec if necessary.
2 Stir half the consommé into the cream cheese until it is a smooth cream.
3 Arrange the slices of egg in the base of a white

Hot and Cold Roquefort Salad; Cream Cheese Mousse; Potted Cheese

soufflé dish and carefully pour over the cream cheese mixture. Chill until firm.
4 If the remaining consommé has begun to set, heat again until just melted but not hot and pour over the set mousse. Chill until firm.
5 Beat the cream cheese until soft. Decorate the mousse with piped cream cheese, thinly sliced cucumber and a lemon twist.

DO NOT FREEZE

Potted cheese *(serves 4–6)*

POWER LEVEL: 100% (FULL) *(colour opposite)*

25g (1oz) butter, approximately
2–3 × 15ml tbsp (2–3tbsp) brandy, port or wine, approximately
100–175g (4–6oz) leftover dry cheese
ground nutmeg, mace, paprika and black pepper to taste
50–75g (2–3oz) leftover stilton or blue cheese
one or more of the following additions to taste, optional: anchovy essence, tabasco sauce, crushed garlic, chopped parsley, chives, spring onion, dill, cumin, fennel, caraway, chopped nuts

1 Heat the butter and brandy, port or wine for 1–2 min. Stir well and heat again until hot, about 1 min.
2 Add the dry cheese and seasonings to taste. Mix well together until blended. It may be necessary to heat again for 15–30 sec at a time until the cheese is softened. Be careful not to overheat otherwise the mixture may separate.
3 Crumble in the stilton or blue cheese and blend well. If preferred, the mixture may be blended in a liquidiser or food processor.
4 If the mixture seems a little dry, add more butter and/or brandy, port or wine until a smooth paste is made.
5 Add one or more of the alternative additions to taste. Pack into small pots and chill before serving.

Chilled kipper soufflé *(serves 6)*

POWER LEVEL: 100% (FULL)

Serve as a starter or part of a buffet menu.

225g (8oz) frozen kipper fillets
1 small onion, chopped
1 lemon, grated rind
1 × 15ml tbsp (1tbsp) lemon juice
550ml (1pt) White Sauce (page 132)
4 eggs, separated
1 × 15ml tbsp (1tbsp) chopped parsley
salt and freshly ground black pepper
20g (¾oz) gelatin
2 × 15ml tbsp (2tbsp) water

for garnish: chopped parsley and lemon butterflies
for serving: brown bread and butter

1 Prepare a 14cm (5½in) soufflé dish by tying a double band of greaseproof paper around the outside of the dish to rise 5cm (2in) above the rim of the dish. Secure firmly with string.
2 Place the kipper fillets into a shallow casserole dish. Add the onion, lemon rind and juice. Cover and cook for 5–6 min until tender, turning once halfway through.
3 Skin the fish and blend in a liquidiser or food processor with the onion, lemon rind, juices, sauce and egg yolks. Stir in the parsley and season to taste.
4 Sprinkle the gelatin on to the water in a small bowl and heat for 10–15 sec. Stir until dissolved and then stir into the fish mixture. Chill until half set.
5 Whisk the egg whites until stiff and then fold into the fish mixture. Pour into the prepared soufflé dish and chill until set.
6 Carefully remove the greaseproof paper and press the chopped parsley around the edges. Garnish the top with lemon butterflies and serve with brown bread and butter.

Macaroni cheese supreme *(serves 4–6)*
POWER LEVEL: 100% (FULL)

The addition of ham and fresh tomatoes gives extra colour and flavour to a plain macaroni cheese.

225g (8oz) macaroni
550ml (1pt) boiling water
1 × 15ml tbsp (1tbsp) oil
1 × 5ml tsp (1tsp) salt
100g (4oz) cooked ham, diced
4 large tomatoes, skinned and chopped
425ml (¾pt) White Sauce (page 132)
175g (6oz) cheddar or double gloucester cheese, grated
salt and freshly ground black pepper
2 × 15ml tbsp (2 tbsp) browned breadcrumbs
paprika pepper for sprinkling
25g (1oz) melted butter

1 Place macaroni in a large, shallow dish. Pour over the boiling water and stir in the oil and salt. Cook for 10 min, then separate with a fork, and drain well.
2 Add the ham and tomatoes to the macaroni. Heat the sauce if necessary for about 5 min and stir in 100g (4oz) grated cheese.
3 Stir the sauce into the macaroni mixture, season to taste and place into a heatproof serving dish. Mix the remaining cheese with the breadcrumbs and sprinkle over the top.

4 Sprinkle on the paprika pepper and the melted butter and cook uncovered for 3–4 min until heated through. Alternatively, brown the top under a hot grill.

Swiss cheese fondue *(serves 4)*
POWER LEVEL: 50% (DEFROST)

1 clove garlic, crushed
100g (4oz) gruyère cheese, grated
100g (4oz) emmenthal cheese, grated
black pepper and grated nutmeg
175–225ml (6–8fl oz) dry white wine
squeeze lemon juice
2 × 5ml tsp (2tsp) cornflour
1 liqueur glass kirsch

1 Rub the garlic around the inside of a heatproof dish. Place the cheese, seasonings, wine and lemon juice into the dish.
2 Melt the cheese in the microwave for 10 min—the cheese and wine will not combine at this stage.
3 Blend the cornflour with the kirsch and add to the fondue; stir and cook for 6 min until slightly thickened.
4 Keep the fondue warm over a spirit lamp or dish warmer; serve with crusty bread.

DO NOT FREEZE

Plain omelette *(serves 1–2)*
POWER LEVEL: 100% (FULL)

15g (½oz) butter
4 eggs
2 × 15ml tbsp (2 tbsp) milk or water
salt and pepper

1 Melt the butter in a 20cm (8in) shallow dish for 30 sec. Mix all the other ingredients together in a separate bowl.
2 Brush the melted butter around the base and sides of the dish. Pour in the egg mixture.
3 Cover and cook for 1 min; stir gently bringing the sides of the omelette towards the centre. Cover and cook for a further 1 min. Uncover and cook for another 1–1½ min depending on whether a moist or dry omelette is preferred.
4 Fold into 2 or 3 before sliding on to the serving plate.

VARIATIONS FOR PLAIN AND FLUFFY OMELETTE

Cheese omelette: make the omelette as above, adding 3 × 15ml tbsp (3tbsp) grated cheddar or cheshire cheese before folding and serving the omelette.

Ham omelette: make the omelette as above, adding 3 × 15ml tbsp (3tbsp) finely chopped ham to the omelette before folding and serving.

Herb omelette: add 3 × 5ml tsp (3tsp) freshly chopped herbs to the eggs before cooking. If fresh herbs are not available, use 1 × 5ml tsp (1tsp) dried herbs.

Mushroom omelette: make the omelette as above, adding 3 × 15ml tbsp (3tbsp) sliced, fried mushrooms to the omelette before folding and serving.

Fluffy omelette *(serves 2)*
POWER LEVEL: 100% (FULL) AND 30%

15g (½oz) butter
3 eggs, separated
2 × 15ml tbsp (2tbsp) milk
salt and pepper

1 Melt the butter in a 20cm (8in) round, shallow dish for 30 sec.
2 Whisk the egg yolks, milk and seasoning together. In a separate bowl, whisk the egg whites until stiff.
3 Carefully fold the egg whites into the egg yolk mixture. Turn into the prepared dish, smooth the mixture over the dish.
4 Cook uncovered on 30% setting for 5–6 min until the centre of the omelette is set. Fold in half with a palette-knife before sliding on to a serving plate. If preferred, the top of the omelette may be browned under a hot grill.

DO NOT FREEZE THESE OMELETTES

Devilled egg bake *(serves 4)*
POWER LEVEL: 100% (FULL)

6 hard-boiled eggs
½ × 5ml tsp (½tsp) dried mustard
½ × 5ml tsp (½tsp) curry powder
2 × 15ml tbsp (2tbsp) melted butter
3–4 × 15ml tbsp (3–4tbsp) cream
275ml (½pt) White Sauce (page 132)
175g (6oz) cheddar cheese, grated
50g (2oz) pasta shells, cooked (page 216)
for garnish: few green or black olives

1 Cut the eggs in half lengthways. Remove and sieve the yolks. Add the mustard, curry powder and the melted butter. Stir in just sufficient of the cream to make a thick paste. Stuff this mixture into the halves of egg whites and place in a serving dish.
2 Heat the white sauce if necessary for 2–3 min, and stir in half the cheese and the pasta shells. Mix well together and add the remaining cream.
3 Pour the sauce over the eggs. Sprinkle with the remaining cheese and cook uncovered for 3–4 min until heated through.
4 Garnish with green or black olives before serving hot.

DO NOT FREEZE

Cream cheese and bacon tart *(serves 4–6)*
POWER LEVEL: 100% (FULL) AND 50% (DEFROST)

1 × 20cm (8in) baked flan case (page 248)
for the filling:
4 rashers streaky bacon, derinded and cut into strips
225g (8oz) cream cheese
1 egg
3 egg yolks
150ml (¼pt) double cream
3 tomatoes, skinned and sliced
salt and pepper
for garnish: chopped chives

1 Place the bacon in a small dish, cover with clingfilm or a lid and cook on 100% (full) setting for 2–3 min. Arrange the bacon in the bottom of the flan case.
2 Cream the cheese until soft, then add the egg and egg yolks. Beat well together and gradually add the cream. Season to taste.
3 Heat the egg mixture on 50% (defrost) setting for 3–4 min until warm, stirring every minute, then pour into the flan case over the bacon.
4 Arrange the tomatoes over the top of the tart and cook uncovered for 15–18 min until the filling is set. Allow to stand for 10 min.
5 Serve hot or cold garnished with chopped chives.

DO NOT FREEZE

Fish and Shellfish

Whichever variety you may select—a delicate white fish, a richer oily fish or one of the more delicious types of shellfish—all provide a good source of protein and add variety to the diet whether served as a starter, a main course, or a light lunch or supper dish. Probably more than most other foods, fish benefits from being cooked by microwave as the moist textures and delicate flavours are preserved by this cooking method.

Fish which are normally steamed, poached or baked are particularly good. Whole fish, fillets, steaks or cutlets of fish can be simply cooked without any additional liquid other than perhaps a few drops of lemon juice and/or coated with a little melted butter if preferred. A sprinkling of seasonings or herbs will enchance the flavour and apperance. Alternatively, fish may be poached in liquid, such as wine and cream, if a well-flavoured sauce is required.

Breadcrumbed fish may be dotted or brushed with a little butter before cooking, although the breadcrumbed coating will not become crisp unless using a browning dish. Deep-fat frying must not be attempted in the microwave cooker as the temperature of the oil or fat cannot be controlled.

Test fish and shellfish regularly during cooking as they can easily overcook. Remove the fish when barely done and then allow a standing period to finish cooking. To ensure that the fish cooks evenly, arrange the thicker portions of the fish near the edge of the dish with the thinner parts towards the centre. When cooking more than one at a time, the tail ends of thin fillets or whole fish may be overlapped or placed 'head-to-tail' to prevent overcooking of these thinner parts. Alternatively, thin strips of foil may be wrapped around the head and tail end of whole fish or the thinner ends of fillets for half the cooking period.

For best results cover the containers and rearrange the fish or turn the dish halfway through the cooking time although this may not be necessary if you have a microwave cooker with a turntable.

Defrosting

It is important to ensure that fish and shellfish are evenly thawed to obtain best results when they are cooked afterwards (see Fish Defrosting and Cooking Chart, page 84). Defrosting times will depend on the thickness of the fish, which should be placed in a single layer on a shallow dish or plate and covered. Frozen fish fillets should be separated as soon as possible during the defrosting process and the thinner tail ends can be wrapped in small pieces of foil to prevent them from thawing too quickly. The heads and tails of whole fish may also be wrapped in aluminium foil for about half the defrosting period. Thicker steaks, cutlets, whole fish or shellfish may need to be turned over half way through the thawing process.

Fish should be cold when thawed; if it is warm in parts, it has started to cook and it is then preferable to remove it from the microwave cooker and allow it to stand until completely thawed. After defrosting, the fish may be rinsed in cold water to remove any remaining ice crystals or refrigerated until required.

Prepared, cooked and frozen fish dishes should be defrosted using a 50% (defrost) setting although a lower setting may be preferred. Depending in the type

Cod Romana (page 85); Scampi Italian Style (page 85)

of dish, it is sometimes necessary to reheat gently using a 70% setting rather than heat too quickly on full power. This is particularly important to ensure that sauces do not overheat before the main fish ingredient has heated through. As when cooking, the dish should be covered during reheating and allowed to stand for a few minutes before serving.

Fish defrosting and cooking chart

Fish	Defrosting time 50% (defrost)	Cooking time 100% (full)
bass 450g (1lb)	5–6 min stand 15 min	5–7 min
bream 900g (2lb)	10 min stand 20 min 5 min stand 30 min	10–12 min
cod fillets 450g (1lb)	4–5 min stand 5 min	4–5 min
cod steaks 450g (1lb)	5 min stand 5 min	6 min
crab claws 450g (1lb)	5 min stand 5 min	2–3 min
crab, dressed 100g (4oz)	2 min stand 10 min	—
haddock fillets 450g (1lb)	4–5 min stand 5 min	4–5 min
haddock steaks 450g (1lb)	4–5 min stand 5 min	4–5 min
hake steaks 450g (1lb)	5–6 min, stand 5 min	7 min
kipper, 1	—	1–2 min
'boil in bag' kipper fillets 200g (7oz)	3 min stand 5 min	3 min
lobster in ice 350g (12oz)	10 min pour off water 6 min break off ice stand 15 min	—
mackerel 450g (1lb)	6–8 min stand 8–10 min	5 min
mussels 450g (1lb)	5 min stand 5 min	—
plaice fillets 450g (1lb)	4–5 min stand 5 min	4 min
prawns 450g (1lb)	5 min stand 5 min	—
salmon, smoked 200g (7oz)	2 min stand 10 min 2 min stand 15 min	—
salmon steaks 450g (1lb)	5 min stand 5 min	4–5 min
salmon trout 900g (2lb)	8–10 min stand 20 min 5 min, stand 30 min	8–10 min
scampi 450g (1lb)	5 min stand 5 min	2–3 min
sole 450g (1lb)	5–6 min stand 8–10 min	4 min
trout 450g (1lb)	6–8 min stand 8–10 min	7 min
fish in sauce 200g (7oz)	3 min stand 5 min	3–4 min

Browning dish chart
POWER LEVEL: 100% (FULL)

Food	Preheat	Butter or oil	First side	Second side
4 cod portions in breadcrumbs	4–5 min	1 × 15ml tbsp (1tbsp) oil	2–3 min	3–4 min
2 cod steaks in batter	4–5 min	1 × 15ml tbsp (1tbsp) oil	2 min	2–3 min
4 fish cakes	5–6 min	15g (½oz) butter	1½ min	1½ min
6 fish fingers from frozen	5–6 min	brush food with melted butter or oil	2 min	1–2 min
1 plaice fillet in breadcrumbs	4–5 min	1 × 15ml tbsp (1tbsp) oil	2 min	2 min
oven chips 225g (8oz)	3½–4 min		2½–3 min	2½–3 min

Cod romana *(serves 4–6)*
POWER LEVEL: 100% (FULL) *(colour page 83)*

The fish is lightly pre-fried using a browning dish.

675g (1½lb) fresh cod fillet, thick end
salt for sprinkling
1 × 15ml tbsp (1tbsp) seasoned flour
4 × 15ml tbsp (4tbsp) oil
2 small onions, sliced
2 large green peppers, deseeded and sliced
1 × 539g (1lb 3oz) can tomatoes, drained and
  quartered *or*
450g (1lb) tomatoes, skinned and quartered
salt and freshly ground black pepper
for garnish: 1 × 15ml tbsp (1tbsp) freshly chopped
  oregano or parsley

1 Remove the skin from the cod and cut the fish into
  3.75cm (1½in) pieces.
2 Sprinkle the fish with salt and leave for 30 min to
  draw out some of the moisture. Rinse well in cold
  water, pat the pieces dry and toss in the seasoned
  flour.
3 Preheat the browning dish for 6–8 min. Add
  2 × 15ml tbsp (2tbsp) oil and heat for 1 min. Add
  the fish, pressing it down against the hot base of the
  dish for 10–15 sec with a heatproof spatula. Turn
  the pieces over, press down well again, cover and
  cook for 2 min.
4 Drain well and remove the cod pieces from the dish.
  Add the remaining 2 × 15ml tbsp (2tbsp) oil to the
  dish, stir in the onions, cover and cook for 2 min.
  Add the peppers, cover and cook for 6 min.
5 Add the cod and tomatoes to the vegetables and
  mix carefully together. Season to taste, cover and
  cook for 4 min.
6 Serve hot sprinkled with chopped oregano or
  parsley.

Scampi italian style *(serves 4–6)*
POWER LEVEL: 100% (FULL) *(colour page 83)*

50g (2oz) butter
2 courgettes, sliced
1 small green pepper, deseeded and cut into strips
1 medium onion, chopped
2 cloves garlic, crushed
225g (8oz) tomatoes, canned or fresh, skinned
75ml (⅛pt) dry white wine
1 × 5ml tsp (1tsp) sugar
1 × 15ml tbsp (1tbsp) chopped parsley
salt and freshly ground black pepper
450g (1lb) peeled scampi (or prawns) fresh or frozen,
  thawed
100g (4oz) mozzarella cheese, thinly sliced
for serving: boiled rice (page 216)

1 Place the butter in a large dish or bowl, cover and
  heat for 1½–2 min. Stir in the courgettes and
  pepper, cover and cook for 4 min, shaking the dish
  once halfway through. Remove the vegetables.
2 Add onion and garlic to the dish, cover and cook for
  5 min. Add the contents of the can of tomatoes or
  fresh tomatoes quartered, wine, sugar, parsley and
  seasoning, cover and cook for 6–7 min.
3 Add scampi (or prawns) with the courgettes and
  pepper, cover and cook for 4–5 min.
4 Arrange the sliced cheese over the top and cook
  uncovered for about 3 min until the cheese is
  melted. Alternatively, brown under a hot grill.
5 Serve hot with boiled rice.

Mussels with rice *(serves 4)*
POWER LEVEL: 100% (FULL)

2 litre (4pt) mussels
25g (1oz) butter
1 onion, sliced
1–2 cloves garlic, crushed
1 carrot, finely sliced
bouquet garni
6 peppercorns
1 wineglass white wine
1 wineglass water
450g (1lb) tomatoes, skinned
salt and freshly ground black pepper
for serving: Rice Pilaf (method 5 and page 217) and
  slivers butter.

1 Scrub the mussels and rinse well in cold water.
  Discard any which are broken or are not tightly
  closed, and scrape away the beards or tufts of hair.
2 Melt the butter in a very large bowl for 1 min. Add
  the onion, garlic and carrot, cover and cook for
  3 min. Add the bouquet garni, peppercorns, wine
  and water, cover and cook for 3–4 min until
  boiling.
3 Add the mussels, cover and cook until the shells are
  open, 6 min approximately, tossing well halfway
  through. Allow to stand for a few minutes.
4 Cut the tomatoes into quarters and remove the
  seeds and small hard core.
5 Remove the mussels from their shells with a sharp
  knife and add them to the tomatoes. Strain the
  liquid from the dish into a jug or small bowl and use
  some of it with the chicken stock to make the pilaf.
6 When rice is cooked, fork in the mussels and
  tomatoes. Adjust seasoning and dot with silvers of
  butter. If the rice is a little dry, add about
  1 × 15ml tbsp (1tbsp) of the mussel liquid.
7 Cover and cook for 1 min to heat through; allow to
  stand for 5 min before serving.

DO NOT FREEZE

Stuffed herrings with gooseberry sauce
(serves 4)
POWER LEVEL: 100% (FULL) *(colour opposite)*

4 herrings
25g (1oz) butter
1 small onion, finely chopped
100g (4oz) white breadcrumbs
salt and freshly ground black pepper
1 × 15ml tbsp (1tbsp) chopped parsley
$\frac{1}{2}$ × 5ml tsp ($\frac{1}{2}$tsp) dried mixed herbs
2–3 × 15ml tbsp (2–3tbsp) hot water
275ml ($\frac{1}{2}$pt) Gooseberry Sauce (page 136)
for garnish: lemon slices

1 Clean and bone the herrings as described for the mackerel on page 92.
2 Melt the butter in a bowl for 1 min. Add the onion, toss well in the butter, cover and cook for 3–4 min until tender.
3 Stir in the breadcrumbs, seasonings and herbs. Add sufficient hot water to bind the stuffing together.
4 Divide the stuffing between the herrings, reshape the fish and place 'head-to-tail' in a large shallow casserole dish, overlapping slightly to protect the tail ends, or alternatively cover these thinner parts with small, smooth pieces of aluminium foil. Cover with greaseproof paper.
5 Cook for 8–10 min, rearranging the fish halfway through if necessary, by placing the centre ones to the outside. Leave to stand covered, for 5 min.
6 Pour the gooseberry sauce into a serving bowl or jug and heat through if necessary for 2–3 min although the sauce may also be served cold.
7 Garnish the herrings with lemon slices and serve with the sauce handed separately.

Shrimp cocottes *(serves 4)*
POWER LEVEL: 100% (FULL) *(colour opposite)*

Serve as a starter or light lunch or supper dish.

175g (6oz) canned shrimps
25g (1oz) butter
25g (1oz) flour
150ml ($\frac{1}{4}$pt) fish stock, made from shrimp liquid and water
150ml ($\frac{1}{4}$pt) single cream
1 × 15ml tbsp (1tbsp) dry sherry, optional
100g (4oz) mushrooms, sliced
salt and freshly ground black pepper
butter
25g (1oz) browned breadcrumbs
for garnish: parsley sprigs

1 Drain the liquid from the shrimps and make up to 150ml ($\frac{1}{4}$pt) with water.
2 Melt the butter in a bowl for 1 min, then stir in the

flour. Add the stock gradually, bring to the boil in the microwave, stirring frequently until thick, about 2–3 min.
3 Add the cream, sherry, if used, and the mushrooms and cover and cook for 3 min. Stir the shrimps into the sauce and add salt and pepper to taste.
4 Butter 4 individual cocotte dishes or ramekins and spoon the shrimp mixture into them. Sprinkle with the breadcrumbs and dot with a little butter.
5 Reheat for 1 min and serve garnished with parsley sprigs.

Haddock with bacon *(serves 2)*
POWER LEVEL: 100% (FULL) *(colour opposite)*

This makes a substantial breakfast, lunch or supper dish.

2 medium-sized smoked haddock
4 rashers lean bacon
butter
freshly ground black pepper

1 Rinse the haddock well in cold water and place in a large shallow dish. Cover and cook for 6–8 min, turning each haddock halfway through the cooking time. Leave to stand covered, for 5 min.
2 Remove the rinds from the bacon and place in a single layer on a plate or dish. Cover with kitchen paper towel and cook for about 3 min, allowing an extra $\frac{1}{2}$–1 min if the bacon is preferred more crispy. Drain well on kitchen paper towel.
3 Uncover the haddock, drain well and place on to serving plates. Add a knob of butter to each fish and sprinkle with ground black pepper.
4 Place the bacon rashers on top of the haddock and serve hot.

Tuna fish pie *(serves 4–6)*
POWER LEVEL: 100% (FULL)

1 × 298g (10$\frac{1}{2}$oz) can condensed cream of chicken soup
425g (15oz) canned tuna fish, approximately
1 small packet frozen peas, thawed
3 tomatoes, skinned and sliced
1 large packet potato crisps
2 × 15ml tbsp (2tbsp) finely grated cheese
for garnish: 1 × 15ml tbsp (1tbsp) chopped parsley

1 Empty the soup into a bowl or jug and heat through for 2$\frac{1}{2}$–3 min, stirring halfway through.
2 Drain and flake the tuna fish and place half in a layer into a heatproof pie dish.

Stuffed Herrings with Gooseberry Sauce: Haddock with Bacon; Shrimp Cocottes

3 Heat the peas for 2 min and place half on top of the fish. Add half of the tomatoes and top with half the soup and half the crisps.
4 Repeat the layers with the remaining ingredients, ending with the crisps. Sprinkle with the grated cheese.
5 Cook, uncovered for 2½–3 min until heated through and the cheese is melted.
6 Sprinkle with chopped parsley before serving hot.

Sweetcorn fish cakes (serves 6)
POWER LEVEL: 100% (FULL)

These fishcakes are cooked in a browning dish.

450g (1lb) cooked fish
450g (1lb) cooked potatoes
275g (10oz) canned sweetcorn
1 egg
½ lemon, juice and rind, finely grated
salt and pepper
2 × 5ml tsp (2tsp) chopped parsley
browned breadcrumbs for coating
6 × 15ml tsp (6tbsp) oil
for garnish: parsley sprigs

1 Flake the fish, removing any skin and bones. Mash the potato and mix together with the fish, sweetcorn, egg, lemon juice and rind, seasoning and parsley.
2 Turn the mixture on to a floured board or work surface and divide into approximately 12 piece. Shape each portion into a flat, round cake.
3 Dip each fish cake into the browned breadcrumbs, pressing the crumbs well into the cakes.

4 Preheat the browning dish for 6–8 min, depending on its size, add half the oil and heat for a further minute.
5 Add half the fish cakes to the browning dish, pressing each one down with a heatproof spatula. Cook for 2 min, turn the fish cakes over and cook for 2½–3 min. Drain on kitchen paper.
6 Repeat with the remaining fish cakes, scrape any residue from the browning dish first and preheat for a further 3–4 min.
7 Serve hot garnished with sprigs of parsley.

Crab gratinée (serves 4)
POWER LEVEL: 100% (FULL)

40g (1½oz) butter
1 small onion, finely chopped
100g (4oz) mushrooms, chopped
1 × 15ml tbsp (1tbsp) brandy
3 × 15ml tbsp (3tbsp) Tomato Sauce (page 134)
½ wineglass white wine
salt and pepper
pinch each cayenne pepper and curry powder
450g (1lb) crabmeat
1 × 15ml tbsp (1tbsp) browned breadcrumbs
for garnish: parsley sprigs

1 Melt 25g (1oz) butter in a large bowl for 1 min, stir in the onion, cover and cook for 4 min until softened. Add the mushrooms and cook for a further 3 min.
2 Stir in the brandy and the tomato sauce which has been sieved. Add the wine, seasoning, cayenne pepper, curry powder and the crabmeat.
3 Transfer the mixture into 4 individual au gratin dishes, 1 larger au gratin dish or a shallow casserole dish, cover and cook for 2 min. Sprinkle with the browned breadcrumbs, dot with the remaining butter and cook uncovered for a further 1 min.
4 Garnish with parsley sprigs before serving.

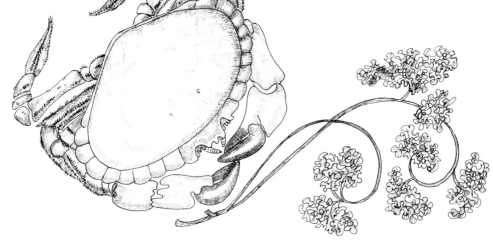

Smoked salmon quiche *(serves 6)*
(colour page 11)
POWER LEVEL: 100% (FULL) AND 50% (DEFROST)

20cm (8in) cooked flan case (page 248)
75g (3oz) smoked salmon, cut into strips
freshly ground black pepper
¼ cucumber, skinned and thinly sliced
150ml (¼pt) single cream
2 large eggs, beaten
3 × 15ml tbsp (3tbsp) milk
salt
1 × 15ml tbsp (1tbsp) chopped chives
for garnish: cucumber slices

1 Cook the flan case and arrange the smoked salmon pieces in the base. Sprinkle with freshly ground black pepper.
2 Arrange the cucumber slices over the salmon.
3 Heat the cream for 30 sec on 100% (full) setting, beat in the eggs and milk and add seasoning to taste. Pour the mixture into the flan case and sprinkle with the chopped chives.
4 Reduce to 50% (defrost) setting and cook, uncovered, for 12–15 min until the filling is set. It does not matter if it is still a little uncooked as it will finish setting during its standing time. Allow to stand for 10–15 min.
5 Serve hot or warm garnished with cucumber slices.

DO NOT FREEZE

Stewed eels *(serves 4–6)*
POWER LEVEL: 100% (FULL)

Ask the fishmonger to skin the eels for you.

900g (2lb) eels, skinned
550ml (1pt) hot water
1 onion, finely chopped
salt and pepper
40g (1½oz) butter, softened
40g (1½oz) flour
few drops lemon juice
2 × 15ml tbsp (2tbsp) chopped parsley

1 Wash the eels thoroughly and cut into 5cm (2in) lengths. Place into a casserole dish with the hot water. Add the onion and sprinkle with a little salt.
2 Cover the dish and bring to the boil in the microwave on 100% (full) setting then reduce to 50% (defrost) and simmer for 10–12 min.
3 Blend the butter with the flour and add this in small pieces to the dish, stirring all the time. Cook, uncovered for 2–3 min, stirring every minute until thickened. The sauce should have the consistency of thick gravy.
4 Stir in the lemon juice and parsley and adjust seasoning to taste with salt and pepper. Serve hot.

Haddock crumble *(serves 6)*
POWER LEVEL: 100% (FULL)

675g (1½lb) cooked haddock
3 hard-boiled eggs, roughly chopped
100g (4oz) peeled prawns, optional
275ml (½pt) Béchamel or White Sauce (page 134 and 132)
salt and freshly ground black pepper
40g (1½oz) butter
40g (1½oz) plain flour
40g (1½oz) wholemeal flour
50g (2oz) finely grated cheese
paprika pepper for sprinkling

1 Flake the fish removing any skin and bones. Mix well with the eggs, prawns, if used, and the béchamel or white sauce.
2 Season to taste and place in a round dish or pie dish.
3 To make the crumble, rub the butter into the flours with a pinch of salt. Stir in the grated cheese lightly.
4 Sprinkle the crumble over the top of the haddock mixture and sprinkle with a little paprika pepper.
5 Cook, uncovered, for 8–10 min until hot through and the crumble is cooked. Allow to stand for 3–4 min before serving hot.

Fillets of sole in cider *(serves 4–8)*
POWER LEVEL: 100% (FULL)

4 sole, filleted
1 medium onion, finely chopped
salt and freshly ground black pepper
275ml (½pt) dry cider
50g (2oz) mushrooms, finely sliced
3 × 5ml tsp (3tsp) cornflour
2 × 5ml tsp (2tsp) water
4 × 15ml tbsp (4tbsp) double cream
for garnish: parsley sprigs

1 Wipe or wash and dry the fish and place into a casserole dish with the onion, seasoning and the cider. Cover and cook for about 7 min, turning the dish once throughout if necessary. Allow to stand for a few minutes.
2 Remove the sole, place on to a serving dish and keep warm. Return the dish to the microwave and cook, uncovered, for about 5 min until the liquid quantity is slightly reduced.
3 Add the mushrooms, cover and cook for 2 min. Blend the cornflour with the water, stir into the sauce and cook for 1 min until thickened, stirring once halfway through.
4 Stir in the cream, adjust seasoning and spoon the sauce over the sole fillets. Garnish with a few parsley sprigs before serving hot.

DO NOT FREEZE

Trout in red wine sauce *(serves 4)*
POWER LEVEL: 100% (FULL) *(colour opposite)*

4 trout, about 150–175g (5–6oz) each
4 × 15ml tbsp (4tbsp) water
4–5 peppercorns
25g (1oz) butter
1 small onion, finely chopped
1 small carrot, cut into small dice or finely chopped
2 wineglasses red wine
15g ($\frac{1}{2}$oz) flour
salt and pepper
$\frac{1}{4}$ × 5ml tsp ($\frac{1}{4}$tsp) anchovy essence
1 × 5ml tsp (1tsp) chopped thyme
1 × 15ml tbsp (1tbsp) chopped parsley
for serving: Potatoes Parisienne (page 148),
    optional

1 Clean the fish, leaving the heads on. Wash and dry. Place in a shallow dish, add the water and peppercorns, cover and cook for 7–8 min, turning the dish or rearranging the trout halfway through. Allow to stand covered.
2 Melt half the butter in a bowl for 15–30 sec, add the onion and carrot, toss well in the butter, cover and cook for 3 min. Add the wine and cook, uncovered, for 5 min until the vegetables are tender and the liquid quantity is slightly reduced.
3 Blend the remaining 15g ($\frac{1}{2}$oz) butter with the flour. Drain the liquid from the trout and gradually blend this into the flour and butter. Stir into the vegetables and red wine.
4 Cook for about 2–2$\frac{1}{2}$ min until thickened and add the seasoning, anchovy essence and the herbs.
5 Coat the trout with the sauce and arrange the potatoes around the dish before serving.

Gratin of seafood *(serves 4)*
POWER LEVEL: 100% (FULL)

550g (1$\frac{1}{4}$lb) white fish
50g (2oz) button mushrooms, finely sliced
juice $\frac{1}{2}$ lemon
100g (4oz) peeled prawns or shrimps
salt and pepper
275ml ($\frac{1}{2}$pt) Béchamel Sauce (page 134)
2 × 15ml tbsp (2tbsp) browned breadcrumbs
1 × 15ml tbsp (1tbsp) each grated parmesan cheese
    and cheddar cheese
for garnish: sprigs parsley

1 Skin the fish fillets, wash and dry and place into the base of a casserole dish. Scatter the sliced mushrooms over the top and sprinkle with the lemon juice.
2 Add the peeled prawns or shrimps and add salt and pepper to taste. Cover and cook for 5–6 min, turning once halfway through. Allow to stand for 3–4 min.
3 Heat the sauce if necessary for 2–3 min until hot, stirring halfway through.
4 Drain the fish and transfer the mixture to 4 individual au gratin dishes if preferred, otherwise replace into the casserole dish.
5 Coat the fish mixture with the hot sauce and sprinkle with the browned breadcrumbs and the grated cheese.
6 Heat the individual dishes for 1 min each or the large dish for 2–3 min until the cheese has melted. Alernatively, brown under a hot grill. Serve hot, garnished with sprigs of parsley.

Devilled sardines on toast *(serves 4–5)*
POWER LEVEL: 100% (FULL) *(colour page 179)*

2 cans sardines, approximately 100g (4oz) each
15g ($\frac{1}{2}$oz) butter
1 small lemon, grated rind and juice
1 × 15ml tbsp (1tbsp) tomato ketchup
2 × 5ml tsp (2tsp) worcestershire sauce
good pinch dried mustard
2 × 5ml tsp (2tsp) chopped mixed herbs
for serving: 4–5 rounds hot buttered toast and
    ground black pepper

1 Drain the sardines well and carefully transfer them on to a plate. Pour over a little hot water to rinse off the excess oil and then drain again.
2 Melt the butter in a shallow dish for 15–30 sec, and stir in the remaining ingredients. Add the sardines to the dish and turn them over in the mixture.
3 Cover and cook for 2–2$\frac{1}{2}$ min. Serve on rounds of hot buttered toast and sprinkle with ground black pepper before serving.

Salmon with prawns in cream *(serves 4)*
POWER LEVEL: 100% (FULL)

4 × 175g (6oz) salmon cutlets, 2.5cm (1in) thick,
    approximately
25g (1oz) butter
100g (4oz) peeled prawns, fresh, or frozen thawed
freshly ground black pepper
275ml ($\frac{1}{2}$pt) single cream
for garnish: lemon wedges and sprigs of parsley
for serving: Sauté Cucumber with Mint (page 149) or
    cucumber salad

Chicken with Tarragon (page 117); Orange Cheese Flan (page 163); Trout in Red Wine Sauce (above)

1 Wipe the salmon cutlets. Place the butter in a large shallow dish and heat for 1 min until melted.

2 Brush the butter around the dish and add the salmon cutlets with the thicker parts towards the outside of the dish. Fill the cavities with the prawns. Brush the tops of the salmon cutlets and prawns with the butter.

3 Sprinkle with freshly ground black pepper, cover the dish and cook for 7 min. Allow to stand for 2 min.

4 Put the cream into a jug or bowl and heat for 1½ min. Pour the cream over the salmon and prawns, cover the dish and cook for 2 min. Allow to stand for 2 min.

5 Garnish with lemon wedges and sprigs of parsley and serve with sauté cucumber or a cucumber salad.

DO NOT FREEZE

Spanish lobster (serves 3–4)
POWER LEVEL: 100% (FULL)

2 × 15ml tbsp (2tbsp) oil
2 small onions, chopped
2 red peppers, deseeded and thinly sliced
6 tomatoes, skinned and chopped
salt and freshly ground black pepper
½ wineglass white wine
175–200g (6–8oz) lobster meat
2 × 15ml tbsp (2tbsp) chopped parsley
½ × 5ml tsp (½tsp) paprika pepper
1 × 15ml tbsp (1tbsp) brandy, optional
for serving: boiled rice (page 216)

1 Place the oil in a shallow dish, stir in the onions, cover and cook for 2 min. Add the peppers, cover and cook for 6 min.

2 Stir in the tomatoes, seasoning and wine, cover and cook for 4–5 min until the sauce is a pulp.

3 Add the lobster meat and carefully turn over in the sauce. Stir in the parsley, paprika pepper and brandy. Cover and heat through for 2 min.

4 Serve hot with boiled rice.

Plaice with cabbage (serves 4–6)
POWER LEVEL: 100% (FULL)

50g (2oz) butter
1 small onion, finely sliced
350–450g (¾–1lb) green cabbage, finely shredded
salt and pepper
675 (1½lb) plaice fillets
few drops lemon juice
275ml (½pt) Cheese Sauce (page 132)
1 × 15ml tbsp (1tbsp) parmesan cheese
paprika pepper for sprinkling

1 Melt the butter in a large casserole dish for 1½ min, stir in the onion, cover and cook for 3 min. Add the cabbage and seasoning. Mix well together, cover and cook for 8–10 min until tender, stirring 2–3 times throughout. Leave to stand.

2 Sprinkle the fish with seasoning and a few drops of lemon juice. Fold over the fillets, place in a dish or on a plate, cover and cook for 6–7 min.

3 Drain and place the fish on top of the cabbage. Heat the cheese sauce if necessary and spoon over the fish and cabbage.

4 Sprinkle with parmesan cheese and paprika pepper and heat through, uncovered, for 2–3 min or alternatively brown under a hot grill.

Prawns au gratin (serves 4)
POWER LEVEL: 100% (FULL) AND 70%

40g (1½oz) butter
450g (1lb) peeled prawns
salt and pepper
3 × 15ml tbsp (3tbsp) double cream
8 green lettuce leaves, shredded
paprika pepper for sprinkling

1 Melt the butter in a dish on 100% (full) setting for 1–1½ min, add the prawns, cover and cook for 2 min.

2 Season to taste and stir in the brandy; continue to cook for a further 2 min.

3 Add the cream and mix well together. In a separate bowl, cook the lettuce for 1½–2 min until softened and then stir into the prawn and cream mixture.

4 Reduce to 70% setting, cover and cook for 3–4 min until heated through. Stir frequently and do not allow to boil.

5 Sprinkle with paprika pepper before serving hot.

DO NOT FREEZE

Mackerel in mustard cream sauce (serves 4–8)
POWER LEVEL: 100% (FULL)

4 mackerel
50g (2oz) butter
1 medium onion, finely sliced
salt and freshly ground black pepper
15g (½oz) flour
2 × 5ml tsp (2tsp) french mustard
pinch sugar
275ml (½pt) water, or fish stock (page 64)
75ml (⅛pt) double cream
25g (1oz) cheese, grated

1 Clean the fish and remove the heads. Cut each of the fish open along the belly to the tail. Flatten out and ease the bones from the flesh and pull the backbone free. Remove any remaining small bones with tweezers. Cut each fish in half lengthways.

2 Place 40g (1½oz) butter into a large shallow dish and melt in the microwave for 1–1½ min. Add the onion slices, cover and cook for 3–4 min until tender. Remove the onions and keep warm.

3 Place the fish fillets 'head-to-tail' in the dish, overlapping slightly. Season well, cover and cook for 6–8 min turning the dish halfway through.

4 When cooked, drain off any liquid then scatter the cooked onions over the mackerel.

5 Melt the remaining butter in a bowl for 15–30 sec, stir in the flour and blend well together with the mustard and sugar. Gradually add the water or fish stock, cover and cook for 3–4 min until thickened, stirring every minute.

6 Add the cream and half the cheese. Adjust seasoning, stir well and spoon the sauce over the onions and mackerel.

7 Sprinkle with the rest of the cheese and cook uncovered in the microwave for 1–2 min, or alternatively brown under a hot grill.

Scallops provençale (serves 4)
POWER LEVEL: 100% (FULL)

25g (1oz) butter
1 onion, finely chopped
1 clove garlic, finely chopped or crushed
4 tomatoes, skinned and quartered
1 wineglass white wine
salt and freshly ground black pepper
1 × 5ml tsp (1tsp) paprika pepper
450g (1lb) scallops, washed
225ml (8fl oz) double cream
1 × 15ml tbsp (1tbsp) chopped parsley

for serving: boiled rice (page 216)

1 Melt the butter in a dish for 1 min. Toss the onion and garlic in the butter and cook, covered, for 4 min.

2 Add the tomatoes, wine, seasoning and paprika pepper and stir well together.

3 Add the scallops, cover and cook for 4–5 min. Stir in the cream and chopped parsley, reduce to 70% setting and cook for a further 3 min until heated through. Stir frequently and do not allow to boil.

4 Adjust seasoning and serve with freshly boiled rice.

Fish pudding au gratin (serves 4–5)
POWER LEVEL: 100% (FULL)

This pudding is very light in texture and makes a good lunch or supper dish.

450g (1lb) white fish fillets, cooked
75g (3oz) white breadcrumbs
1 × 15ml tbsp (1tbsp) chopped parsley
1 lemon, grated rind
salt and freshly ground black pepper
50g (2oz) butter
2 eggs, beaten
275ml (½pt) Cheese Sauce (page 132)
for garnish: browned breadcrumbs, grated cheese, paprika pepper and parsley sprigs

1 Lightly grease an 850ml (1½pt) pudding basin.

2 Flake the fish, discarding any skin or bones. Mix with the breadcrumbs, parsley, lemon rind and seasoning.

3 Melt the butter for 1–1½ min and add to the fish with the beaten eggs. Mix well together and place the mixture into the greased pudding basin.

4 Cover and cook for 4–5 min, turning once halfway through. Leave to stand for 3 min.

5 Heat the sauce if necessary for 2–3 min. Invert the

pudding on to a serving dish and coat with the sauce.

6 Garnish with browned breadcrumbs, a little grated cheese and sprinkle with paprika pepper. Heat for $1\frac{1}{2}$–2 min to melt the cheese or alternatively brown the top under a hot grill. Garnish with sprigs of parsley before serving hot.

Haddock with lemon sauce *(serves 4)*
POWER LEVEL: 100% (FULL) *(colour opposite)*

150ml ($\frac{1}{4}$pt) lemon juice
150ml ($\frac{1}{4}$pt) water
2 × 5ml tsp (2tsp) chopped parsley
675g ($1\frac{1}{2}$lb) haddock fillets
salt and pepper
40g ($1\frac{1}{2}$oz) butter
40g ($1\frac{1}{2}$oz) flour
150ml ($\frac{1}{4}$pt) milk
150ml ($\frac{1}{4}$pt) single cream
few drops yellow food colouring, optional
for garnish: grated lemon rind, finely chopped parsley

1 Place the lemon juice, water and parsley into a large shallow casserole dish. Arrange the haddock fillets 'head-to-tail' in the dish and sprinkle with a little salt and pepper.
2 Cover and cook for 6–7 min. Drain the fish and strain the liquid into a jug. Place the fish on to a serving platter or plates and keep warm.
3 For the sauce, melt the butter in a bowl or jug for 1–$1\frac{1}{2}$ min and stir in the flour. Add the reserved fish liquid and the milk gradually.
4 Cook for 3–4 min until thick, stirring frequently. Stir in the cream and heat for 1 min. Adjust seasoning and add a few drops of yellow food colouring.
5 Spoon the sauce over the fish and garnish with grated lemon rind and chopped parsley before serving.

Plaice duglére *(serves 4)*
POWER LEVEL: 100% (FULL)

8 fillets of plaice
1 onion, finely chopped
1 × 15ml tbsp (1tbsp) oil
400g (14oz) can tomatoes
100g (4oz) mushrooms, sliced
salt and freshly ground black pepper
75ml ($\frac{1}{8}$pt) water
150ml ($\frac{1}{4}$pt) dry white wine
1 × 15ml tbsp (1tbsp) chopped parsley
pinch tarragon
for garnish: chopped parsley and lemon slices

1 Wash and dry the plaice and arrange in a shallow casserole dish.
2 Place the onion and oil in a separate bowl, cover and cook for 4 min. Add tomatoes, mushrooms and salt and pepper, cover and cook for 5 min. Allow to stand for a few minutes.
3 Pour the water and wine over the fish, add a little seasoning, cover and cook for 5–6 min. Drain the fish and remove the skin if preferred.
4 Reduce the fish cooking liquid by boiling in the microwave, uncovered. Strain into the tomato sauce and add parsley and tarragon. Adjust the seasoning.
5 Heat for 1–2 min, stir well and pour over the plaice fillets. Garnish with chopped parsley and lemon slices before serving.

Sole thermidor *(serves 4)*
POWER LEVEL: 100% (FULL)

25g (1oz) butter
8 fillets sole, skinned
salt and freshly ground black pepper
1 small onion, finely chopped
25g (1oz) flour
150ml ($\frac{1}{4}$pt) milk
150ml ($\frac{1}{2}$pt) dry white wine
1 × 15ml tbsp (1tbsp) brandy
$\frac{1}{2}$ × 5ml tsp ($\frac{1}{2}$tsp) made mustard
3 × 15ml tbsp (3tbsp) double cream
25g (1oz) grated parmesan cheese
for garnish: parmesan cheese for sprinkling and a little paprika pepper

1 Melt the butter in a large shallow casserole dish for 1 min. Fold over the fish fillets and arrange them in the dish with the thinner parts towards the centre of the dish.
2 Brush the fish with the melted butter and sprinkle with salt and pepper. Cover and cook for 3–4 min, allow to stand for 3 min then remove the fish and keep warm.
3 Add the onion to the dish, cover and cook for 3–4 min until softened. Stir in the flour, add the milk and wine gradually, and cook for 3–4 min until thickened.
4 Stir in the brandy, mustard, cream and cheese and adjust the seasoning to taste. Reheat the sauce for 15–30 sec and carefully coat the sole fillets.
5 Sprinkle with extra parmesan cheese and a little paprika pepper before serving.

Haddock with Lemon Sauce (above); Raspberry Mousse (page 165)

Meat

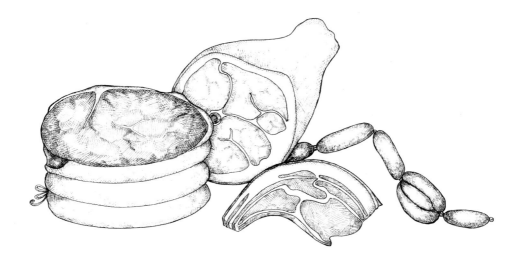

The microwave cooker produces excellent results whether you are cooking smaller cuts of meat or large joints but, as this cooking method does not tenderise meat in the same way as when roasting or grilling conventionally, prime cuts will give the best results. However, if you have a microwave cooker with a variable power control giving 50% output (often a defrost setting), or a lower 30% output, then perfect results can be obtained, even when casseroling the tougher, cheaper cuts of meat.

If your microwave cooker does not have lower variable power control settings, cheaper cuts can be tenderised or marinated in oil and vinegar for several hours, or minced or cut into very small pieces before cooking. In addition, casseroles are often more tender if they are left to cool naturally after cooking and then reheated before serving. This great advantage means that dishes can be prepared well in advance—when you have the time—then refrigerated or frozen to be reheated when required.

The advantage of roasting joints by microwave is that while the joint is resting during its final standing period, vegetables, sauces and gravies can be cooked to produce a complete microwave meal.

Cooking

For best results, a joint should be regular in shape so that it will have a better appearance and cook more evenly—rolled joints or top leg of lamb or pork are ideal. Irregular-shaped joints such as shoulder or leg of lamb may have the projecting part of the shoulder or narrow piece of the leg protected with smooth small strips of aluminium foil for half the cooking time.

Seasonings should be limited to spices and herbs as salt attracts moisture and can have a toughening effect to the outside of the meat during cooking. The exception to this is pork crackling, when salt rubbed into the scored skin will help it to crisp. But, if in any doubt, leave the seasonings to the end of the cooking time.

Meat can be open roasted by placing it on to an upturned small, flat dish or plate which is used as a trivet inside the roasting dish. Special microwave roasting dishes are now available on the market. These serve a similar purpose as the trivet in keeping the meat out of the juices during cooking. Open roasting is ideal when cooking pork with crackling as this method allows moisture to escape and gives a more crisp finish to the outside of the meat. When open roasting, cover the dish with greaseproof paper or kitchen paper towel to help prevent splashings of fat on to the oven interior. Alternatively, roasting bags may be used to cook joints but remember that wire ties must not be used—string or rubber bands are suitable instead. The roasting bag should be pierced or slit at the base so that the juices will run out into the cooking container away from the meat.

Larger joints should be turned over at least once during the cooking period, and a joint which has fat on one side only should be placed fat side down at the beginning of cooking and turned over halfway through so that the fat is then on the top. If cooking joints on 100% (full) setting, a standing time of 10–25 minutes halfway through cooking will assist in a more even result, particularly important for joints over 2kg (4lb) in weight. If using a 70% setting on a variable power control model, this standing period halfway through is not necessary; although all joints should be allowed to stand for 5–20 minutes at the end of the cooking period, left in the roasting bag or covered in aluminium foil to retain the heat. However, if the joint is cooked to the desired degree on completion of the cooking time it is not necessary to let it stand.

If the total cooking time is 15 minutes or more the joint will brown naturally, but for extra browning the joint may be placed in a conventional oven at a high temperature for 10–15 minutes at the end of the microwave cooking period, or placed under a hot grill. The careful use of gravy brownings, sauces or paprika, or microwave seasonings painted or sprinkled on to the surface of the meat will give a more attractive colour if preferred. Steaks, chops, sausages and escalopes may be browned during cooking by using a browning dish (page 99) or alternatively finished off under a hot grill after cooking by microwave.

The cooking times given in the following charts are when using a 100% (full) setting and a 70% setting. For those microwave cookers with a 'roast' setting, it is advisable to check with the manufacturer's recommendations regarding cooking times. If you have a microwave with 'full' and 'defrost' settings only, the joint may be cooked for half the time on 100% (full) setting and then reduced to 50% (defrost) for the remaining time. Alternatively, some joints benefit from a slow cooking process using the 50% (defrost) setting in which case the cooking time will be almost double that for 100% (full) setting. Much depends on the time available and your own preferences.

The use of a meat thermometer is helpful to determine the temperature at the centre of the food, particularly when defrosting and cooking larger cuts and joints. Only specially designed thermometers for microwave cookers may be left inside the oven while it is operating.

Ordinary meat thermometers must not be used in the microwave but can be inserted in to the centre of the joint when it has been taken out of the oven cavity. The following temperatures after the final standing time will help you to assess whether the meat is cooked. If your microwave cooker has the facility of a probe, set it to the temperatures given below, although it is advisable to check with the manufacturer's instructions before using.

BEEF
rare	60°C (140°F)
medium	70°C (160°F)
well done	80°C (175°F)
LAMB	80°C (175°F)
PORK	80°C (175°F)
VEAL	80°C (175°F)

When braising, casseroling or stewing meat best results are obtained using a 50% (defrost) setting or a lower 30% setting for the total cooking time. This will give a longer cooking period required for tenderising the meat and will also allow sufficient time for the food flavourings and seasonings to blend. The container should be covered with a lid for the entire cooking process to retain moisture and to prevent the liquid in the casserole from evaporating; and as the casserole is being cooked by microwave energy from all directions inside the oven—the top as well as the sides and base—it is best to ensure that the food is well covered with the cooking liquid so that the meat at the top does not overcook and toughen.

Defrosting
Defrosting can be carried out completely in the microwave cooker or by a combination of microwave defrosting and natural thawing, commencing the defrosting in the microwave and then leaving the meat to thaw thoroughly in the refrigerator, larder or at room temperature. Although thinner cuts of meat can be thawed and cooked in one heating operation, generally it is better to ensure that all meat is completely defrosted before cooking to obtain the most even results.

As when cooking by microwave, thinner ends of joints and smaller cuts can be protected with smooth pieces of aluminium foil during the defrosting process, to prevent the outer sections from beginning to cook while the centre parts are still thawing. It is acceptable if the outside of the meat does start cooking during defrosting, providing the meat is cooked immediately afterwards, although the partially cooked parts should be protected with aluminium foil during the cooking period.

The meat should turned halfway through the defrosting process to ensure even defrosting. Smaller cuts, such as chops, steak, liver and sausages, should be separated and turned as soon as possible after defrosting begins. When defrosting minced meat or sausage meat, the thawed portions should be scraped away and removed leaving the still-frozen part to be returned to the microwave.

Most meats require standing time to allow the heat to equalise during defrosting so that the outer portions do not overheat. With a defrost setting on a variable power microwave, this is automatically given during the off cycles at these lower power levels, but more even defrosting will be achieved if additional standing times are allowed as recommended in the charts below. The defrosting standing times given are the total resting time required and a better result is obtained if this time is spread evenly throughout the defrosting period. Longer periods of defrosting without standing times will obtain a quicker defrost but may result in a less even thawing. If in doubt, remove the meat from the microwave when it feels warm to the touch and allow to stand or complete thawing naturally.

Meat which is covered during defrosting—either with a lid on a casserole dish, with clingfilm or in a roasting bag—will retain more moisture and defrosting will be slightly faster. Casseroles should be placed in a dish large enough to take the thawed food and to allow room for stirring and breaking down the icy portions. During defrosting and reheating the casserole, allow approximately 2 min per 25g (1oz) using 50% (defrost) setting, or 1 min using 100% (full) setting.

The defrosting and cooking charts given here are based on meats which have been removed straight from the freezer for defrosting and are fully thawed before cooking. If meats are partially thawed before being placed in the microwave for defrosting or are not completely thawed before cooking then the times on the charts will require some adjustments to suit. For those microwave models with a defrost control or setting, you may find the information given on page 24 useful.

Points to remember

★ Meat and poultry should be fully thawed before cooking.

★ Standing time is required by most joints during the defrosting period to ensure even thawing.

★ In addition, meat benefits from a standing time at the end of the cooking process, but larger joints also require a standing time halfway through their cooking period.

★ Smooth pieces of aluminium foil may be used to protect the thinner or narrower ends of meat during defrosting and/or cooking.

★ Joints should be turned over halfway through the defrosting and/or cooking cycle.

★ A joint will have a better appearance and cook more evenly if it is a regular shape.

★ Allow an extra minute per $\frac{1}{2}$kg (1lb) when cooking stuffed poultry or joints.

★ The tenderness of meat casseroles is improved if the dish is left to cool after microwave cooking and then reheated when required.

★ The times given on the following charts are for both lower- and higher-output microwave cookers: the models with lower output will require the longer times and those with a higher output will require the shorter times, ie beef medium 5–7 min per $\frac{1}{2}$kg (1lb).

Defrosting and cooking joints

Meat	Defrosting time 50% (defrost)	Cooking time 100% (full)	Cooking time 70% setting	Internal temperature	Special points
	$\frac{1}{2}$kg (1lb)	$\frac{1}{2}$kg (1lb)	$\frac{1}{2}$kg (1lb)		
beef joints on bone	10–12 min Stand for 60–70 min	Rare—4–6 min Med—5–7 min Well—6–8 min Stand for 15–25 min	10–11 min 11–13 min 12–14 min Stand for 20 min	60°C (140°F) 70°C (160°F) 80°C (175°F)	Cover bone end with foil during defrosting
beef, rolled, boned	8–10 min Stand for 50–60 min	Rare—4–6 min Med—5–7 min Well—6–8 min Stand for 15–25 min	10–11 min 11–13 min 12–14 min Stand for 10–15 min	60°C (140°F) 70°C (160°F) 80°C (175°F)	Turn joint on sides during defrosting
lamb	6 min Stand for 30–40 min	7–9 min Stand for 15–30 min	11–13 min Stand for 20 min	80°C (175°F)	Cover knuckle end of lamb with foil once thawed
pork or ham	7–8 min Stand for 60–70 min	7–9 min Stand for 15–30 min	12–14 min Stand for 20 min	80°C (175°F)	Try to get an evenly shaped joint. Tie for roasting after thawing
veal	5 min Stand for 20–30 min	7–9 min Stand for 15–30 min	11–13 min Stand for 20 min	80°C (175°F)	Foreleg may need covering with foil during defrosting

Defrosting and cooking smaller cuts

Type or cut of meat	Defrosting time 50% (defrost)	Standing time	Special points	Cooking
fillet steak 2 × 200g (7oz)	6–8 min	12 min	Cover any thin ends with foil. Turn over halfway through	Use as required See recipes or browning dish chart
stewing or braising meat, eg beef or lamb 675g (1½lb)	11–12 min	10 min	Separate pieces of meat during defrosting	Use as required See recipes
minced beef 450g (1lb)	10–11 min	11 min	Break up during defrosting. Remove thawed meat from oven	Use as required See recipes
belly pork strips 450g (1lb) (4 strips)	4–5 min	5 min	Separate strips during defrosting	Use as required or cook for 8–10 min, turning during cooking
offal (liver and kidney) 450g (1lb)	9–10 min	4 min	Separate pieces during defrosting	Use as required See recipes
sausage meat 450g (1lb)	6–7 min	10 min	Break thawed sausage meat up and remove from oven during defrosting	Use as required
sausages 450g (1lb)	6–7 min	10 min	Separate during defrosting	Prick skins and cook for 9–10 min
bacon 225g (8oz)	4–5 min	5 min	Separate rashers during defrosting	5–6 min
lamb chops 2 × 100g (4oz)	4–5 min	5 min	Separate chops during defrosting	5–6 min
pork chops 2 × 225g (8oz)	6–8 min	10 min	Separate chops during defrosting	10–11 min

Browning dish chart
POWER LEVEL: 100% (FULL)

Food	Preheat	Butter or oil	First side	Second side
1 steak, 175–200g (6–7oz)	6–7 min	15g (½oz) butter or 1 × 15ml tbsp (1tbsp) oil	1½–2 min	1½–2 min
1 gammon steak, 175g (6oz)	5–6 min	15g (½oz) butter or 1 × 15ml tbsp (1tbsp) oil	3 min	3–4 min
2 pork chops each 225g (8oz)	5–6 min	15g (½oz) butter or 1 × 15ml tbsp (1tbsp) oil	3 min	8–10 min
2 chicken pieces each 225g (8oz)	5–6 min	15g (½oz) butter or 1 × 15ml tbsp (1tbsp) oil	5 min	3–5 min
4 sausages, large	5–6 min	15g (½oz) butter or 1 × 15ml tbsp (1tbsp) oil	6–8 min	turning 3–4 times
4 beefburgers, from frozen	6–7 min	15g (½oz) butter or 1 × 15ml tbsp (1tbsp) oil	1½–2 min	2–3 min

Food	Preheat	Butter or oil	First side	Second side
4 bacon rashers	5–6 min	15g (½oz) butter or 1 × 15ml tbsp (1tbsp) oil	1 min	30–45 sec
6 hamburgers or rissoles each 75–100g (3–4oz)	6–7 min	15g (½oz) butter or 1 × 15ml tbsp (1tbsp) oil	2 min	6–8 min
4 lamb chops each 100g (4oz)	5–6 min	15g (½oz) butter or 1 × 15ml tbsp (1tbsp) oil	3 min	8–10 min

Casserole of sausages (serves 3–6)

POWER LEVEL: 100% (FULL) AND 50% (DEFROST)

6 large pork sausages with herbs
6 thick lean bacon rashers, rinds removed
25g (1oz) butter
2 × 15ml tbsp (2tbsp) oil
1 large onion, finely chopped
1½ × 5ml tsp (1½tsp) dried sage
2 × 15ml tbsp (2tbsp) flour
425ml (¾pt) hot stock (page 64)
salt and freshly ground black pepper
150ml (¼pt) soured cream
for garnish: chopped parsley
for serving: Buttered Noodles (page 44)

1 Roll up each sausage with a rasher of bacon and tie with fine string or secure with wooden cocktail sticks.
2 Melt the butter and oil in a casserole dish for 2 min, stir in the onion and cover and cook on 100% (full) setting for 5 min. Add the dried sage and the sausages and continue to cook for 4 min.
3 Remove the sausages to a plate and stir the flour into the dish. Gradually add the stock, cover and bring to the boil about 3–4 min, stirring every minute.
4 Add the seasoning to taste. Return the sausages to the casserole and reduce to 50% (defrost) setting. Cover and cook for 15 min.
5 Stir the soured cream into the dish and allow to stand for 5 min. Reheat for 1–2 min if necessary before serving on a bed of buttered noodles, garnished with chopped parsley.

Minced beef casserole with dumplings

(serves 4–6)

POWER LEVEL: 100% (FULL)

1 × 15ml tbsp (1tbsp) oil
25g (1oz) butter
2 onions, chopped
50g (2oz) mushrooms, chopped
675g (1½lb) lean minced beef
1 × 15ml tbsp (1tbsp) flour
275ml (½pt) beef stock (page 64)
½ × 5ml tsp (½tsp) dried mixed herbs
2 × 5ml tsp (2tsp) worcestershire sauce
salt and freshly ground black pepper
for serving: Suet Dumplings (following recipe)

1 Heat the oil and butter for 1½ min in a large bowl or casserole dish. Add the onions, cover and cook for 6 min. Add the mushrooms and continue to cook for a further minute.
2 Stir the minced beef into the dish, mix well with the onion, cover and cook for 6–7 min until browned, stirring once or twice and breaking down any lumps with a fork.
3 Add the flour and stir in the stock. Add the herbs, worcestershire sauce and seasoning. Cover and cook for about 15 min until tender, stirring twice throughout.
4 Make up the dumplings and drop them on to the top of the meat. Cover and continue to cook for a further 4½–5 min until the dumplings are well risen. Serve straightaway.

Suet dumplings (serves 4–6)

POWER LEVEL: 100% (FULL)

100g (4oz) self-raising flour
½ × 5ml tsp (½tsp) salt
50g (2oz) shredded suet
1–2 × 5ml tsp (1–2tsp) dried mixed herbs, optional
cold water to mix

1 Sift the flour and salt; stir in the suet, herbs and sufficient cold water to form a soft manageable dough.
2 Knead lightly and form into walnut-sized balls, rolling between the palms of the hands with a little extra flour if necessary.
3 Drop the dumplings on to the top of a hot, simmering casserole or stew in a deep, large dish. Cover and cook until light and well risen, about 4½–5 min.

Stuffed hearts *(serves 4)*
POWER LEVEL: 100% (FULL) AND 30%

4 sheep's hearts
Sage and Onion Stuffing (page 141)
25g (1oz) butter
2 onions, finely sliced
275–425ml ($\frac{1}{2}$–$\frac{3}{4}$pt) boiling beef stock (page 64)
salt and pepper
bouquet garni
1 × 15ml tbsp (1tbsp) cornflour
for garnish: chopped parsley

1 Soak the hearts in cold salted water for 30 min and then clean thoroughly. Remove pipes and trim. Fill with the sage and onion stuffing and secure the tops with thread.
2 Melt the butter in a casserole dish for 1 min, add the onions, mix well and cook, covered, for 4 min.
3 Add the hearts and brush with the onion and butter juices. Cook, covered for 2 min, turning the hearts halfway through.
4 Add sufficient stock to cover the hearts. Season to taste and add the bouquet garni. Bring to the boil in the microwave, about 4 min.
5 Reduce to 30% setting and continue to cook, covered, for about $1\frac{1}{2}$–$1\frac{3}{4}$ hr until the hearts are tender. Leave to stand for 20 min.
6 Blend the cornflour with a little cold water and add to the dish. Cook until thickened, about $1\frac{1}{2}$–2 min, stirring halfway through.
7 Garnish with plenty of chopped parsley and serve hot.

Lamb chops with rosemary *(serves 4)*
POWER LEVEL: 100% (FULL) AND 70%

These barbecue-style lamb chops are cooked in the browning dish. The meat is left to marinate for several hours before cooking.

1 × 15ml tbsp (1tbsp) french mustard
1 × 5ml tsp (1tsp) soy sauce
$\frac{1}{2}$ × 5ml tsp ($\frac{1}{2}$tsp) chopped fresh rosemary *or*
$\frac{1}{4}$ × 5ml tsp ($\frac{1}{4}$tsp) dried rosemary
$\frac{1}{4}$ × 5ml tsp ($\frac{1}{4}$tsp) ground ginger
1 clove garlic, crushed
salt and freshly ground black pepper
2 × 15ml tbsp (2tbsp) white wine
2 × 15ml tbsp (2tbsp) wine vinegar
4 chump or leg of lamb chops, weighing about 175g (6oz) each
2 × 15ml tbsp (2tbsp) water
1 × 5ml tsp (1tsp) cornflour
2 × 15ml tbsp (2tbsp) single cream
$\frac{1}{2}$ × 5ml tsp ($\frac{1}{2}$tsp) brown sugar
for garnish: sprigs of rosemary
for serving: Jacket Potatoes (page 150)

1 Mix together the first 8 ingredients and pour over the chops. Leave to marinate for 3–4 hr. Drain off and reserve the marinade.
2 Preheat a browning dish for 6–8 min, depending on size, and brown the chops on both sides without adding any oil; press the chops down well against the hot base of the dish with a heatproof spatula. Do not place in the microwave to cook.
3 Pour over the marinade and water, cover the dish and cook for about 15–18 min on 70% setting, turning the dish or rearranging the chops halfway through. Test with a skewer and if not quite tender, allow a further 2–3 min cooking time.
4 Place the chops on a serving dish or platter and keep warm. Blend the cornflour with a little water and stir into the juices.
5 Cook, uncovered, for 1–2 min until thickened and boiling, stirring once halfway through. Adjust the seasoning and stir in the cream and brown sugar.
6 Pour the sauce over the chops and reheat if necessary for 2–3 min. Garnish with sprigs of rosemary and serve hot with jacket potatoes.

Shepherd's pie *(serves 4)*
POWER LEVEL: 100% (FULL)

1 onion, chopped
275ml ($\frac{1}{2}$pt) boiling stock (page 64)
1–2 × 15ml tbsp (1–2tbsp) worcestershire sauce
pinch nutmeg
1 × 15ml tbsp (1tbsp) fresh breadcrumbs
salt and pepper
350g (12oz) cooked meat, minced
450–675g (1–1$\frac{1}{2}$lb) cooked potato
25g (1oz) butter
1 egg, beaten
for garnish: ground nutmeg or paprika for sprinkling

1 Place the onion in a medium-sized dish with the stock and cook for 4 min.
2 Add the sauce, nutmeg, breadcrumbs, seasoning and the meat, mixing thoroughly.
3 Mash the potato; if the potato is cold, this will be easier if heated for 2–3 min in the microwave. Add the butter and egg.
4 Beat well and place on top of the meat in a suitable dish. Smooth the top of the potato and cook uncovered for 10–15 min.
5 Sprinkle with a little grated nutmeg or paprika before serving.

Note: *450g (1lb) fresh meat may be used in the recipe instead of cooked meat. At stage 2 above, cook the fresh meat with the onion etc, in the stock for 15 min. Stir 2–3 times throughout and break down any lumps with a fork. Thicken with 15g ($\frac{1}{2}$oz) flour and then finish the dish as above.*

Ragoût of kidneys *(serves 4)*
POWER LEVEL: 100% (FULL) *(colour opposite)*

450g (1lb) lambs' kidneys
50g (2oz) butter
1 onion, finely chopped
25g (1oz) flour
2 beef stock cubes
150ml ($\frac{1}{4}$pt) hot water
50g (2oz) button mushrooms, sliced
1 × 5ml tsp (1tsp) tomato purée
1 bay leaf
salt and freshly ground black pepper
for garnish: sprigs of parsley
for serving: boiled rice (page 216)

1 Halve the kidneys and remove the cores and any skin. Cut them into slices.
2 Melt 25g (1oz) of the butter in a bowl for 1 min. Add the kidneys and stir well. Cover and cook for 2$\frac{1}{2}$–3 min.
3 Melt the remaining butter for 1 min in a casserole dish, stir in the onion and cook, covered, for 3 min.
4 Stir in the flour and crumble the stock cubes over the onions. Stir in the hot water and cook for 1$\frac{1}{2}$–2 min until boiling and thickened, stirring every minute.
5 Add the kidneys to the onions with the mushrooms, tomato purée, bay leaf and seasoning to taste. Mix well together.
6 Cover and cook for about 10 min until the kidneys are tender. Leave to stand for 5 min.
7 Remove the bay leaf and adjust the seasoning. Serve garnished with parsley on a bed of rice.

Pork strogonoff *(serves 5–6)*
POWER LEVEL: 100% (FULL) *(colour opposite)*

900g (2lb) pork fillet or tenderloin
50g (2oz) seasoned flour
100g (4oz) butter
2 onions, finely chopped
225g (8oz) button mushrooms, finely sliced
225g (8oz) tomatoes, skinned and chopped
$\frac{1}{2}$ × 5ml tsp ($\frac{1}{2}$tsp) grated nutmeg
salt and freshly ground black pepper
275ml ($\frac{1}{2}$pt) soured cream
for garnish: paprika pepper for sprinkling and chopped parsley
for serving: boiled rice or tagliatelle (page 216)

1 Trim away any fat and cut the meat into strips about 6 × 25mm ($\frac{1}{4}$ × 1in). Toss the meat in the seasoned flour.

Meatballs in Mushroom Sauce; Pork Strogonoff; Ragoût of Kidneys

2 Melt the butter in a large shallow casserole dish for about 2$\frac{1}{2}$–3 min, stir in the onions, cover and cook for 3 min. Add the mushrooms and continue to cook for 3 min.
3 Add the meat to the dish, mix well together and cook for a further 6–8 min until tender, stirring well every 2 min. Allow to stand for 15 min.
4 Stir in the tomatoes, nutmeg, seasoning and soured cream. Heat through for 3–4 min, stirring once halfway through.
5 Allow to stand for 3 min before sprinkling with a little paprika and garnishing with chopped parsley. Serve with rice or tagliatelle.

VARIATION

Beef strogonoff: use beef fillet or rump steak instead of the pork and omit the tomatoes.

Meatballs in mushroom sauce *(serves 6)*
POWER LEVEL: 100% (FULL) AND 50% (DEFROST)
(colour opposite)

25g (1oz) butter
1 onion, finely chopped
675g (1$\frac{1}{2}$lb) minced beef or lamb
50g (2oz) brown breadcrumbs
1 × 5ml tsp (1tsp) dried oregano
1 × 5ml tsp (1tsp) worcestershire sauce
1 × 5ml tsp (1tsp) tomato purée
pinch dry mustard
salt and freshly ground black pepper
1 egg, beaten
1–2 × 15ml tbsp (1–2tbsp) plain flour
2 × 15ml tbsp (2tbsp) oil
1 can condensed cream of mushroom soup
5 × 15ml tbsp (5tbsp) water
100g (4oz) button mushrooms
for serving: pasta (page 216) or crusty bread

1 Melt the butter in a large bowl for 1 min on 100% (full) setting; add the onion, cover and cook for 4–5 min until tender.
2 Add the minced meat, breadcrumbs, oregano, worcestershire sauce, tomato purée, mustard and seasoning. Mix well together and stir in the egg.
3 Shape the mixture into 18 balls and toss in the flour. Place the oil into a large shallow dish and heat for 2 min. Add the meatballs in a single layer and turn in the oil. Cook uncovered for 4–5 min until brown, turning over halfway through.
4 Place the meatballs into a casserole dish. Place the soup, water and mushrooms into the first dish and mix together. Heat for 2–3 min and stir well. Pour over the meatballs.
5 Reduce to 50% (defrost) setting and cook for 35–40 min, stirring or turning the meatballs halfway through. Serve with pasta or crusty bread.

Beef provençale (serves 3–4)

POWER LEVEL: 100% (FULL) AND 30%

2 × 15ml tbsp (2tbsp) oil, approximately
450g (1lb) braising steak, trimmed and cut into
  cubes
1 large onion, finely sliced
½ red pepper, deseeded and diced
2 tomatoes, skinned and sliced
1 large carrot, diced
4 button mushrooms, cut into halves
1 rasher lean bacon, derinded and cut into strips
275ml (½pt) hot beef stock (page 64)
1 large wineglass red wine
2 × 5ml tsp (2tsp) tomato purée
½ × 5ml tsp (½tsp) each dried oregano and thyme
salt and freshly ground black pepper
for garnish: chopped parsley

1 Heat the oil in a large casserole dish on 100% (full)
  setting for 2 min, add the meat and toss in the oil.
  Cover and cook for 2–3 min until browned, stirring
  once halfway through. Drain and remove the meat.
2 Add all the vegetables and the bacon to the dish, stir
  well and add a little more oil if required. Cover and
  cook for 6–7 min until the vegetables have
  softened.
3 Stir in the stock, the remaining ingredients and the
  meat. Reduce to 30% setting, cover and cook for
  about 1¼–1½ hr until tender, stirring once or twice
  throughout. Leave to stand for 20 min before
  serving, sprinkled with chopped parsley.

Braised steak and kidney (serves 4–6)

POWER LEVEL: 100% (FULL) AND 30%

1 onion, sliced
2–3 × 15ml tbsp (2–3tbsp) oil
900g (2lb) braising steak and kidney, trimmed and
  cut into cubes
20g (¾oz) seasoned flour
425ml (¾pt) boiling beef stock (page 64)
salt and freshly ground black pepper
for serving: boiled potatoes or Dumplings (page 100)

1 Place the onion in a casserole dish or large bowl
  with the oil. Stir well, cover and cook for 4 min on
  100% (full) setting.
2 Toss the prepared steak and kidney in the seasoned
  flour and add to the dish with the onion. Stir in the
  stock.
3 Cover and cook for 10 min, stirring halfway
  through. Stir again and reduce to 30% setting.
  Continue to cook for 50–60 min until tender.
  Adjust the seasoning.
4 Allow to stand for 20–25 min before serving hot
  with boiled potatoes. Alternatively, add dumplings
  to the dish about 10 min before the end of the
  cooking time.

Steak and kidney pudding (serves 6–8)

POWER LEVEL: 70%

900g (2lb) Braised Steak and Kidney (preceding
  recipe)
200g (7oz) plain flour
25g (1oz) wholemeal flour
3 × 5ml tsp (3tsp) baking powder
pinch salt
100g (4oz) shredded suet
150ml (¼pt) water
for garnish: chopped parsley

1 Cook the steak and kidney and leave until cool.
2 Sieve the flours, baking powder and salt into a
  bowl. Add the shredded suet and mix well. Stir in
  the water and knead the mixture together to form a
  soft dough.
3 Lightly grease an 850ml (1½pt) pudding basin. Cut
  off about one-third of the pastry for the lid and roll
  out the rest into a circle to fit the bowl.
4 Line the bowl with the circle of pastry, moulding it
  well into the sides.
5 Drain most of the gravy from the meat and reserve.
  Place the meat into the bowl, then roll out the
  remaining pastry for the lid.
6 Dampen the edges of the pastry lid and fit over the
  pudding, pressing down well to seal the edges.
7 Cover well with clingfilm and cook for 10 min,

turning the bowl halfway through. Cover the top of the pudding with a smooth circle of aluminium foil to prevent the microwave energy overcooking the pastry lid.

8 Continue to cook for 5–8 min and then allow to stand for 20 min. Invert the pudding on to a serving plate and garnish with parsley before serving with the reserved gravy.

Spiced lamb with cream and almond sauce
(*serves 4–6*)

POWER LEVEL: 100% (FULL) AND 30%

An unusual lamb dish with an oriental flavour.

6–8 cloves garlic, crushed
2.5cm (1in) piece fresh ginger, minced
50g (2oz) ground almonds (or flaked almonds, see point 1 below)
6 × 15ml tbsp (6tbsp) water
3–4 × 15ml tbsp (3–4tbsp) oil
900g (2lb) boned lamb, leg or shoulder, trimmed and cut into cubes
6 whole cardamom pods
4 cloves
2.5cm (1in) stick cinnamon
1 large onion, finely chopped
1 × 5ml tsp (1tsp) ground coriander
2 × 5ml tsp (2tsp) ground cumin
$\frac{1}{4}$ × 5ml tsp ($\frac{1}{4}$tsp) each garam masala and cayenne pepper
salt
275ml ($\frac{1}{2}$pt) single cream
for serving: Bombay Potatoes (page 153) or boiled rice (page 216) and green salad

1 Mix together the garlic, ginger, almonds and water to make a thick paste. If preferred, the mixture can be puréed in a food processor or blender in which case flaked almonds can be used.

2 Heat the oil in a large shallow dish for 2 min on 100% (full) setting, add the lamb and turn over in the oil. Cover and cook for 5–6 min until lightly brown. Remove from the dish with a draining spoon.

3 Add the whole cardamom pods and cloves to the dish with the cinnamon and the onion. Cover and cook for 5 min. Stir in the rest of the spices, the almond mixture, the meat, salt to taste and the cream.

4 Reduce to 30% setting, cover and cook for about 1 hr until the meat is tender. Stir 3–4 times throughout. Leave to stand for 15 min.

5 Remove the whole cardamom pods, cloves and cinnamon before serving with the potatoes or rice and salad.

Honey-baked gammon (*serves 8*)
POWER LEVEL: 100% (FULL) OR 70% *(colour page 11)*

1 unsmoked gammon, weighing about 3kg (6lb)
juice of 1 orange
3 × 15ml tbsp (3tbsp) clear honey
150g (6oz) demerara sugar
for garnish: a few cloves, pineapple rings, cocktail cherries or mandarin segments

1 Soak the gammon in cold water for 24 hr, changing the water occasionally. Dry well and weigh the joint.

2 Tie the joint securely with string. Stand the joint on an inverted plate in a large dish.

3 Cover the top with greased greaseproof paper and cook for half these total cooking times—7–9 min per 450g (1lb) on 100% (full) setting or 10–12 min per 450g on 70%. Stand for 30 min. Carefully remove the skin then score the fat with a sharp knife making a diamond pattern.

4 While the joint is standing, heat the orange juice and honey together for 2 min. After the joint has completed the standing time, brush it with the honey and orange syrup and roll the gammon in 100g (4oz) of the sugar.

5 Return the gammon to the dish, turning the joint on to the other side, and finish cooking it for the remaining time.

6 Remove the gammon from the oven. Add the remaining sugar to the orange and honey mixture in the dish and cook the syrup for 3 min, stirring once during the cooking. Brush the fat with the glaze and leave to cool.

7 Decorate the gammon with the cloves and pineapple rings, cocktail cherries or mandarin segments, pinning them to the gammon with wooden cocktail sticks cut into halves. Serve cold.

Note: *A gammon which has been bought already cooked can be glazed and finished in the same way. Score the fat into diamond or square shapes and brush with the honey and orange mixture. Roll in the sugar and then cook in the microwave, uncovered, on 70% setting until the glaze has set and the fat has opened slightly. Leave to cool before decorating and serving.*

Boiled ham
POWER LEVEL: 100% (FULL) OR 70%

Soak the ham for 24 hr or at least overnight, changing the water occasionally. Weigh the ham after soaking and allow 7–9 min per 450g (1lb) on 100% (full) setting or 10–12 min on 70% setting.

Normally no water is required if a roasting or boiling bag is used for cooking the ham but, if preferred, add 150–275ml ($\frac{1}{4}$–$\frac{1}{2}$pt) boiling water to a large, deep casserole dish. This will extend the cooking time to 10–12 min per 450g (1lb) on 100% (full) setting or 15–18 min on 70% setting, to allow for the extra volume in the oven. Cover the dish and cook for half the cooking time, allow to stand for 20 min, then turn the joint over, cover and continue to cook for the remaining time. If the joint is large, a further resting period of 20 min may be required at the end of the cooking time. The internal temperature of the ham at the end of cooking should be 80°C (175°F). Pease pudding may be served as a traditional accompaniment to the ham (page 225).

Braised loin of lamb with beans *(serves 4–6)*
POWER LEVEL: 70%, 100% (FULL) AND 30% *(colour opposite)*

1½kg (3lb) loin of lamb, boned
freshly ground black pepper
1 × 15ml tbsp (1tbsp) oil
25g (1oz) butter
225g (8oz) haricot beans, soaked overnight
2 large carrots, diced
1 turnip, diced
1 bay leaf
275ml (½pt) hot chicken stock (page 64)
25g (1oz) softened butter
25g (1oz) flour
for garnish: 4 tomatoes, skinned and sliced and sprigs of parsley

1 Wipe the lamb, sprinkle with black pepper and then roll up and tie securely with string.
2 Heat the oil and butter for 1½ min, add the meat and brush with the fat or turn over in the dish. Cook uncovered on 70% setting for 15 min, turning the lamb over halfway through.
3 Remove the lamb and place the beans and vegetables into the dish. Stir, cover and cook for 5 min on 100% (full) setting, stirring once halfway through.
4 Replace the meat into the dish and add the bay leaf and stock. Reduce to 30% setting and cook, covered, for 40–50 min until the meat and vegetables are tender. Leave to stand for 10 min.
5 Place the meat on to a serving platter and drain the vegetables, reserving the juices. Arrange the vegetables around the meat on the platter and keep warm.
6 Remove the bay leaf from the juices. Blend together the softened butter with the flour and stir it into the juices.
7 Cook uncovered, for 2–3 min until thickened and boiling, stirring every minute. Taste and adjust the seasoning.
8 Garnish the meat and vegetables with tomatoes and parsley and serve hot with the sauce handed separately.

Gammon steaks with pineapple *(serves 4)*
POWER LEVEL: 100% (FULL) *(colour opposite)*

4 gammon steaks, weighing about 175g (6oz) each
16 cloves, optional
1 × 15ml tbsp (1tbsp) brown sugar
freshly ground black pepper
400g (14oz) can pineapple rings
2 tomatoes, halved
1 × 15ml tbsp (1tbsp) cornflour
for garnish: bunches watercress
for serving: Creamed Potatoes (page 152)

1 Snip the fat off the gammon steaks with scissors and stick the cloves into the steaks. Place a single layer in a large shallow dish.
2 Sprinkle the steaks with brown sugar and freshly ground black pepper. Drain the pineapple and pour the juice into the dish.
3 Cover and cook for 6–8 min, turning the dish or rearranging the steaks halfway through. Test with a skewer and if not quite tender allow another 2–3 min. Leave to stand for 3 min.
4 Place a ring of pineapple on the top of each steak and place a halved tomato into each ring. Cook uncovered for 2–3 min to heat through.
5 Remove the steaks from the dish with a draining spoon and place on a serving dish or platter. Blend the cornflour with a little water and stir into the juices.
6 Cook for 1–2 min until thickened and boiling, stirring once halfway through. Pour the sauce over the steaks and garnish with bunches of watercress. Serve hot with creamed potatoes.

Veal fricassée *(serves 4–5)*
POWER LEVEL: 100% (FULL) AND 30%

40g (1½oz) butter
550g (1¼lb) stewing veal, trimmed and cut into cubes
25g (1oz) flour
425ml (¾pt) stock (page 64)
2 × 5ml tsp (2tsp) lemon juice
salt and freshly ground black pepper
4–5 small onions
boiling water
100g (4oz) button mushrooms
2 × 15ml tbsp (2tbsp) double cream
1 egg yolk
75ml (⅛pt) milk
for garnish: chopped parsley and bacon rolls

Braised Loin of Lamb with Beans; Gammon Steaks with Pineapple

1 Melt the butter in a large shallow casserole dish on 100% (full) setting for $1-1\frac{1}{2}$ min. Add the veal, toss over in the butter, cover and cook for 4 min.

2 Stir in the flour, stock, lemon juice and seasoning. Mix well, cover and bring to the boil in the microwave, about 4–5 min, stirring halfway through.

3 Reduce to 30% setting and continue to cook for 1 hr. Peel the onions, place in a bowl and cover with boiling water. Leave to stand for 20 min, then drain.

4 Add the onions to the veal with the mushrooms and continue to cook for a further 30 min until the meat is tender.

5 Mix together the cream, egg yolk and milk. Stir into the dish and cook for a further 5 min, stirring halfway through. Garnish with bacon rolls and chopped parsley before serving.

Sweet and sour beef *(serves 4–6)*
POWER LEVEL: 100% (FULL) AND 30% *(colour page 131)*

40g ($1\frac{1}{2}$oz) butter
675g ($1\frac{1}{2}$lb) topside of beef, trimmed and cut into 2.5cm (1in) cubes
1 onion, finely chopped
2 sticks celery, finely chopped
225g (8oz) can pineapple chunks
salt and freshly ground black pepper
150ml ($\frac{1}{4}$pt) boiling beef stock (page 64)
2 × 15ml tbsp (2tbsp) cornflour
1 × 15ml tbsp (1tbsp) soy sauce
2 × 5ml tsp (1tsp) brown sugar
1 × 15ml tbsp (1tbsp) tomato ketchup
3 × 15ml tbsp (3tbsp) wine vinegar
for serving: boiled rice or noodles (page 216)

1 Melt the butter in a casserole dish on 100% (full) setting for $1-1\frac{1}{2}$ min. Stir in the beef and cook, covered for 5 min. Using a draining spoon, remove the meat from the dish.

2 Stir the onion and celery into the dish, cover and cook for 5 min.

3 Drain the juice from the pineapple and make up to 275ml ($\frac{1}{2}$pt) with water. Add to the onions and celery with seasoning, beef stock and the meat.

4 Reduce to 30% setting and cook, covered, for about 1 hr until the meat is tender, stirring halfway through.

5 Meanwhile, in a mixing bowl, stir together the remaining ingredients. When the meat is cooked, add the cornflour mixture to the casserole with the pineapple chunks.

6 Cook for 2–3 min, stirring every minute until boiling and thickened. Serve with boiled rice or noodles.

Sausage and bacon rolls *(serves 2–8)*
POWER LEVEL: 100% (FULL)

Serve as a main course with creamy mashed potatoes or as an accompaniment to poultry or game.

8 chipolata sausages
8 lean rashers bacon

1 Prick the sausages and remove the rind from the bacon. Wind the bacon around the sausages and secure each one with a wooden cocktail stick. Alternatively thread the sausage and bacon rolls on to skewers. (**Note:** if metal skewers are used, they must **not** be allow to touch the sides, back or door of the oven interior.)

2 Place the rolls on to a plate or suitable-sized dish and cover with kitchen paper towel. Cook for 9–10 min, turning the rolls over halfway through. Allow them to stand for 3 min before serving.

Calves' liver and onions *(serves 4)*
POWER LEVEL: 100% (FULL)

1 large onion, finely sliced
1 stick celery, finely sliced
2 × 15ml tbsp (2tbsp) oil
2 × 15ml tbsp (2tbsp) dry white wine
4 rashers lean bacon
450g (1lb) calves' liver
$\frac{1}{2}$ × 5ml tsp ($\frac{1}{2}$tsp) dried chervil
$\frac{1}{4}$ × 5ml tsp ($\frac{1}{4}$tsp) paprika
1–2 × 15ml tbsp (1–2tbsp) seasoned flour
1 tomato, skinned and chopped

1 Mix together the onion, celery, oil and wine in a mixing bowl. Cover and cook for 5–6 min until tender, stirring once halfway through. Leave to stand.

2 Remove the rind from the bacon and place the rashers on a plate or microwave bacon trivet or rack. Cook, uncovered, for 5–6 min until the bacon is crisp. Drain bacon and crumble; reserve the drippings.

3 Cut the calves' liver into even-sized pieces. Add the chervil and paprika to the seasoned flour. Toss the liver in the flour.

4 Place the drippings from the bacon into a shallow dish and add the liver, turning the liver over in the fat. Cover with greaseproof paper and cook for 3 min, turning the liver over halfway through.

5 Mix together the onion and celery mixture with the tomato and place over the top of the liver. Cover with the greaseproof paper and continue to cook for 4–5 min until the liver loses its pink colour. Allow to stand for 5 min.

6 Arrange in a serving dish or on a plate and sprinkle with the crumbled bacon.

Pork chops normande *(serves 6)*
POWER LEVEL: 100% (FULL) AND 30%

6 pork chops
25g (1oz) butter
1 × 15ml tbsp (1 tbsp) oil
1 onion, finely chopped
1 stick celery, finely sliced
1 medium-sized cooking apple, chopped
25g (1oz) flour
1 × 5ml tsp (1 tsp) mild mustard
1 × 5ml tsp (1 tsp) dried sage
½ × 5ml tsp (½tsp) ground bay leaves
275ml (½pt) cider
275ml (½pt) boiling chicken stock (page 64)
for serving: Cabbage with Mushrooms and Ham (page 155)

1 Remove the skin and bones from the chops. Place the meat in a single layer in a large dish. Cover and cook on 100% (full) setting for 6 min. Leave to stand.
2 Melt the butter and oil for 1 min, add the onion and celery and toss well. Cover and cook for 3 min, stir in the apple and continue to cook for another 4 min.
3 Stir in the flour, mustard, herbs, cider and boiling stock. Mix well together and bring to the boil in the microwave, about 4 min. Pour the sauce over the chops.
4 Reduce to 30% setting and cook for 50–60 min until tender. Stand for 10 min and serve hot with cabbage with mushrooms and ham.

Guard of honour *(serves 4)*
POWER LEVEL: 100% (FULL) OR 70% *(colour page 19)*

2 best ends of lamb (5–6 cutlets each)
double quantity Orange and Herb Stuffing (page 141)
for garnish: cutlet frills and bunches of parsley sprigs
for serving: Baked Onions (page 153)

1 Given sufficient notice, the butcher will prepare the best ends of lamb by trimming away any excess fat and paring off the meat from the tips of the bones.
2 Prepare the stuffing and spread it evenly on to the meat side of the best ends. Place the joints together so that the skin sides are outermost and the tips of the bones are crossed like swords. Insert any remaining stuffing and tie securely with string.
3 Protect the tips of the cutlet bones with small, smooth pieces of aluminium foil during the cooking time.
4 Place the meat on to a suitable cooking container and cook, uncovered, allowing 8–9 min per 450g (1lb) if using 100% (full) setting or 11–12 min per 450g (1lb) if using 70% setting. Allow the joint to stand for 15–20 min halfway through the cooking time and a further 5–10 min at the end.
5 Place cutlet frills over the bones before serving the guard of honour and garnish with bunches of parsley sprigs. Serve with baked onions.

Stuffed pork chops *(serves 4)*
POWER LEVEL: 100% (FULL)

4 pork chops
salt and freshly ground black pepper
Sage and Onion Stuffing (page 141)
slivers butter
for garnish: fresh sage leaves, optional
for serving: Apple Sauce (page 137)

1 Trim the rinds from the pork chops if preferred and place the meat into a dish with the thickest parts of

the chops to the outside of the dish. Season lightly.

2 Make up the stuffing and spread evenly over the chops. Cover and cook for 20 min, turning the dish halfway through.

3 Remove the cover from the dish and top the stuffing with slivers of butter. Continue to cook for a further 10–20 min, depending on the thickness of the chops.

4 Cover and leave to stand for 10 min. Garnish each chop with a sage leaf and serve with apple sauce.

Veal olives *(serves 4)*

POWER LEVEL: 100% (FULL)

4 veal escalopes, about 100g (4oz) each
ground black pepper
few drops lemon juice
50g (2oz) ham, finely chopped
2 anchovy fillets, rinsed and finely chopped
2 × 5ml tsp (2tsp) capers, finely chopped
1 clove garlic, finely chopped
2 × 5ml tsp (2tsp) chopped parsley
1 × 15ml tbsp (1tbsp) tomato purée
25g (1oz) dry breadcrumbs
salt and freshly ground black pepper
25–50g (1–2oz) butter, approximately
for garnish: chopped parsley and lemon wedges

1 Trim away any fat from the escalopes and beat into thin slices. Lay them out flat and sprinkle with black pepper and a few drops of lemon juice.

2 Place the remaining ingredients except the butter and garnish into a bowl and mix well. Stir in sufficient butter to make a fairly stiff paste, reserving about 25g (1oz).

3 Divide the stuffing between the escalopes, placing it in the middle of each slice. Roll up each escalope and fasten with 1 or 2 wooden cocktail sticks so that the stuffing will not come out.

4 Melt the remaining butter in a shallow dish for 30–60 sec; arrange the veal rolls in the dish and turn or brush them with the butter. Sprinkle with a little black pepper.

5 Cover and cook for 8–10 min, turning the dish halfway through or rearranging the veal if necessary. Stand for 5 min.

6 Serve hot garnished with chopped parsley and lemon wedges.

Note: *Parma ham, although a little more expensive, goes particularly well with the veal and could be used instead for special occasions.*

VARIATION

Beef olives: follow the above recipe using thinly sliced rump steak and sage and onion stuffing (page 141) instead of the veal and ham stuffing respectively.

Moroccan lamb stew *(serves 3–4)*

POWER LEVEL: 100% (FULL) AND 30% *(colour opposite)*

A mildly spiced casserole, served with toasted almonds and raisins, cooked slowly to bring out all the delicious flavours.

2 cloves garlic, finely chopped
1 onion, finely chopped
2 × 15ml tbsp (2tbsp) oil
$\frac{1}{4}$ × 5ml tsp ($\frac{1}{4}$tsp) each ground cinnamon and ginger
$\frac{1}{8}$ × 5ml tsp ($\frac{1}{8}$tsp) each ground turmeric and cloves
4 tomatoes, skinned and chopped *or*
200g (7oz) canned chopped tomatoes
675g (1$\frac{1}{2}$lb) lamb fillet, trimmed and cut into cubes
2 × 15ml tbsp (2tbsp) flour
1 beef stock cube
4 × 15ml tbsp (4tbsp) water
salt and freshly ground black pepper
40g (1$\frac{1}{2}$oz) split or flaked almonds
for garnish: stoned raisins or sultanas and sprigs of parsley
for serving: Spiced Busmati Rice (page 220) and pitta bread

1 Place the garlic, onion and oil into a casserole dish. Cover and cook on 100% (full) setting for 4 min. Stir in the spices and cook for 2 min, uncovered.

2 Stir in the tomatoes and meat and cook uncovered, for 5 min, stirring halfway through. Mix together the flour, stock cube, water and seasoning and stir into the dish.

3 Reduce to 30% setting, cover the dish and cook for about 1 hr until the meat is tender, stirring 2–3 times throughout. Allow to stand for 20 min.

4 Spread the almonds on to a glass ovenware plate and cook on 100% (full) setting for about 5–6 min until toasted, turning the almonds over halfway through.

5 Adjust the seasoning of the casserole and garnish with the almonds, raisins or sultanas and parsley. Serve with warmed pitta bread and spiced busmati rice.

Note: *The pitta bread may be warmed through in the microwave—4 will take about 1$\frac{1}{2}$ min.*

Moroccan Lamb Stew (above); Spiced Busmati Rice (page 220); Lentil Salad (page 221)

Beef fillet florentine *(serves 2)*

POWER LEVEL: 100% (FULL)

This very simple steak dish is marinated first, cooked in the browning dish and served with lemon.

2 × 15ml tbsp (2tbsp) oil
salt and freshly ground black pepper
2 × 200g (7oz) fillet steaks, about 2.5cm (1in) thick
2 × 5ml tsp (2tsp) lemon juice
for garnish: parsley sprigs
for serving: lemon wedges

1 Mix together the oil and seasoning and brush over the steaks on both sides. Leave to marinate in a cool place for 2 hr.
2 Preheat the browning dish for 6–8 min depending on size. Quickly add the steaks, press down against the hot base of the dish with a heatproof spatula and then cook, uncovered, for 1½ min. Turn the steaks over and again press down against the base of the dish. Cook for a further 1–1½ min.
3 Serve straightaway sprinkled with the lemon juice. Garnish with parsley sprigs and hand the lemon wedges separately.

Beef in red wine *(serves 3–4)*

POWER LEVEL: 100% (FULL) AND 50% (DEFROST)

450g (1lb) braising steak, trimmed and cut into
    cubes
25g (1oz) seasoned flour
50g (2oz) butter
1 onion, sliced
100g (4oz) lean bacon, derinded and cut into strips
150ml (¼pt) beef stock (page 64)
150ml (¼pt) red wine
100g (4oz) button mushrooms, sliced
salt and freshly ground black pepper
bouquet garni
for garnish: chopped fresh parsley

1 Toss the meat in the seasoned flour. Melt the butter in a large casserole dish for 1½–2 min and stir in the onion and the bacon.

2 Cover and cook for 3 min. Add the meat, mix well and continue to cook for a further 2 min.
3 Stir in the stock, red wine, mushrooms, seasoning and bouquet garni.
4 Cover and bring to the boil in the microwave, about 3–4 min; stir then reduce to 50% (defrost) setting and continue to cook for a further 45–50 min until the meat is tender.
5 Remove the bouquet garni and adjust the seasoning. Allow to stand for 20–25 min before serving garnished with chopped parsley.

Veal chops gruyère *(serves 4)*

POWER LEVEL: 70% *(colour page 159)*

4 veal chops or cutlets, cut from the loin about
    1.25cm (½in) thick
oil for brushing
freshly ground black pepper
few drops lemon juice
2 × 5ml tsp (2tsp) chopped fresh parsley
100g (4oz) gruyère cheese, finely grated
2–3 × 15ml tbsp (2–3tbsp) single cream
2–3 × 5ml tsp (2–3tsp) mild dijon mustard, to taste

1 Trim and wipe the chops. Brush them lightly with oil and sprinkle with pepper. Place into a large shallow dish with the meatiest parts of the chops towards the outside.
2 Sprinkle with lemon juice, cover with greaseproof paper or kitchen paper towel and cook for 12–15 min until the chops lose their pink colour. Turn the chops over and drain off the juices halfway through. Cover with foil and leave to stand 10 min.
3 Combine the remaining ingredients in a bowl and heat for 1–2 min until softened. Top the veal chops with the mixture and cook, uncovered for a further 2–3 min.

DO NOT FREEZE

Note: *The topping also goes well with pork or lamb chops.*

Poultry and game

When 'roasting' poultry by microwave, the results are really very good and, although the skin does not crisp as when cooking by conventional methods, the eating qualities are usually superior as the moist texture and excellent flavours are retained.

Although young, plump game birds are also suited to cooking by this method, tougher and older birds and those of uncertain age are better braised or casseroled. In the microwave this usually means cooking at a low 30% setting for $1\frac{1}{2}$–2 hours. This probably does not save much time over conventional methods but the advantage of cooking by microwave is that the dish really can be left unattended to cook at a constant setting, without the worry of food sticking to the pan and knowing that the microwave with switch itself off at the end of the set cooking period.

Similarly, rabbit and hare are generally more tender when braised or casseroled at a low setting for a longer time in the microwave. Joints and smaller cuts of venison can be cooked more quickly at a higher setting when the meat is from a young deer, but the flesh of an older animal is tougher and it is then preferable to marinate it before cooking.

Defrosting
All frozen poultry and game should be fully thawed before cooking to ensure more even results, and in the microwave cooker the total defrosting process can be easily and quickly carried out. However, depending on the time available, it is possible to commence the defrosting process in the microwave and then leave to thaw thoroughly in the refrigerator, larder or at room temperature.

When defrosting by microwave, the tips of wings and legs of poultry and game should be protected by covering with small, smooth pieces of aluminium foil, which prevent these outer parts from beginning to cook while the main section is still defrosting.

To ensure more even defrosting, turn whole poultry and game birds 2–3 times during the thawing process, and smaller cuts or portions should be separated and turned as quickly as possible after defrosting commences. In addition, the giblets from the cavity of an oven-ready prepared bird should be removed as soon as possible. Sometimes the giblets may be removed more easily if cold running water is poured into the cavity, helping to melt some of the remaining ice crystals surrounding the giblets.

As when defrosting meats, poultry and game require standing time, in addition to the off cycles in the defrosting setting, to ensure that the outer parts do not commence to cook while the inner section is still frozen. It is better to spread the recommended standing time at regular intervals throughout the given defrosting time to ensure the most even results. But if in doubt, when the food feels warm when touched, allow it to rest so that the heat equalises throughout as much as possible before continuing the defrosting cycle. Covering the food during defrosting will retain moisture and quicken the defrosting time—the lid of a dish, clingfilm or roasting bags are ideal.

Although the setting for defrosting given in the chart on page 116 is 50% power level for most poultry and game, it is recommended that a larger turkey or goose is defrosted using a lower 30% power level. (See page 27.)

Cooking
Most of the information given for cooking meat on page 96 is also applicable for poultry and game and I would recommend that you read that section for reference to some of the more general points.

113

Roasting

Poultry for roasting in the microwave should have the wings and legs tied closely to the body and any projecting parts should be protected by covering them with small, smooth pieces of aluminium foil. Seasonings may be sprinkled into the cavity and pieces of onion, garlic or bay leaves or stuffing may be added for extra flavour. The skin can be rubbed with paprika or other colouring spices but avoid salt as this draws moisture which can have a toughening effect on the outside of the food during cooking.

Roasting bags can be used but do not use the paper/metal ties—string or rubber bands are suitable alternatives. If 'open roasting' is preferred, the bird is placed on an inverted dish or plate which is used as a trivet inside the roasting dish; it is then covered with greaseproof paper or kitchen paper towel to prevent splatterings of fat on to the inside of the oven.

The cooking times given in the chart are when using 100% (full) and 70% power settings. If you have a microwave cooker with a 'roast' setting, it is advisable to check with the operating instructions as to the manufacturer's recommendation for timings when using this power level. Allow an extra 1–2 minutes per ½kg (1lb) when cooking stuffed poultry.

Larger chickens, ducklings and geese of 2½kg (5lb) weight require a standing time of 15–20 minutes halfway through the cooking time as well as the normal standing time at the end when using a 100% (full) setting. A meat thermometer may be used to test the final temperature of poultry and game birds which should be 80–85°C (175–180°F). On no account should the thermometer be left inside the microwave during cooking unless specially designed for this purpose, or when supplied as an integral part of the cooker.

If the total cooking time is 15 minutes or more on 100% (full) setting the skin will brown naturally, but for extra browning place the bird in a preheated conventional oven at a high temperature for 10–15 minutes, or place under a hot grill.

Tender joints of venison or saddle of hare may be roasted in the microwave following the recommendations for beef given in the previous section.

Casseroling or braising

Although more tender joints of poultry such as breasts of chicken may be cooked quickly using 100% (full) or 70% settings, the tougher game birds (rabbit, hare and venison) require cooking at a low 30% setting for a longer period to help tenderise them. The recipes in this section give details of the settings to use and cooking times.

When cooking by this method, it is important to ensure that the food is covered with the liquid ingredient otherwise the exposed meat may overcook. It is worth choosing the cooking container so that the poultry or game fits well into it without too much room to spare around the food, but of course allowing sufficient space for stirring the dish without spilling. Otherwise be prepared to adjust the liquid quantity given in the recipe to suit the size of the container.

Browning dish

Tender joints or cuts of poultry and game may be cooked in the browning dish which helps to give a browner appearance to the outside of the food. There are a few recipes within this section which use the browning dish but further information can be found on pages 17–18.

Defrosting and cooking turkey (5–6kg/10–12lb)

Place the wrapped turkey in a dish in the microwave or straight on to the oven shelf or turntable. It is unnecessary to remove the small metal clasp because of the large mass of food in the oven, although it must not be allowed to touch any part of the oven interior. Defrost the turkey on 30% setting for half the calculated cooking time, allowing 6–8 min per ½kg (1lb). Turn the turkey over halfway through. Take it out of the oven and allow to stand for 30 min.

Remove the wrapping and shield wing tips, legs and breastbone with small pieces of aluminium foil. Cover and continue to defrost for the remaining time, turning the turkey over once again halfway through. Remove the foil and any leg ties and allow to stand, covered, for another 30–45 min.

Run cold water into the cavity to remove the giblets and neck. This can be quite difficult, but continue to allow the water to run through until the ice crystals have melted sufficiently so that you can release the giblets. The neck is usually easier to get hold of if you wear rubber gloves or by using a clean cloth. Once the giblets and neck are removed, if the turkey still feels icy inside, either run more cold water through the cavity or allow to stand until completely thawed, 1½–2½ hours.

Before cooking, season the inside of the cavity with salt and pepper. A peeled onion may be placed inside the cavity to add flavour or the bird may be stuffed with up to 900g (2lb) stuffing. Place about three-quarters of the stuffing inside the cavity and the remaining quarter at the neck end of the turkey. Add an extra 1 minute per ½kg (1lb) for the stuffing when calculating the cooking time.

Brush the turkey with oil or melted butter and protect the tips of wings and legs as before. The bird may be cooked in a roasting bag which should be slit in order to allow the fat and juices to drain away into the dish during cooking. Alternatively, the turkey can

Tandoori Chicken (page 117); Spiced Aubergines (page 151); Bombay Potatoes (page 153); Mung Bean Dal (page 224)

Poultry and game defrosting and cooking chart

Poultry or game	Defrosting time 50% per $\frac{1}{2}$kg (1lb)	Cooking time 100% (full) per $\frac{1}{2}$kg (1lb)	Cooking time 70% per $\frac{1}{2}$kg (1lb)
capon, whole 3–4kg (6–8lb)	5–7 min Stand 50–60 min	7–9 min Stand 25–35 min	10–12 min Stand 10–15 min
chicken, joints 675–900g (1$\frac{1}{2}$–2lb)	5–6 min Stand 20–30 min	6–8 min Stand 5 min	8–10 min Stand 5 min
chicken, whole 1–2$\frac{1}{2}$kg (2–5lb)	6–7 min Stand 20–30 min	5–7 min Stand 15–25 min	9–10 min Stand 5 min
duckling, whole 2–2$\frac{1}{2}$kg (4–5lb)	6–7 min Stand 30–40 min	5–7 min Stand 15–25 min	9–11 min Stand 5 min
goose, whole 2$\frac{1}{2}$–3kg (5–6lb)	6–7 min Stand 30–40 min	6–8 min Stand 15–25 min	10–12 min Stand 5–10 min
hare, jointed 1$\frac{1}{2}$–2kg (3–4lb)	5–6 min Stand 30–35 min	See recipe	See recipe
hare, saddle 675–900g (1$\frac{1}{2}$–2lb)	5–6 min Stand 20–30 min	—	8–10 min Stand 15 min
partridge, whole 350g (12oz)	6–7 min Stand 20–30 min	—	11–12 min Stand 15 min
pheasant, whole $\frac{3}{4}$–1$\frac{1}{2}$kg (1$\frac{3}{4}$–3lb)	6–7 min Stand 20–30 min	—	11–12 min Stand 15 min
rabbit, boneless 900g (2lb)	7–8 min Stand 15 min	See recipe	See recipe
rabbit, jointed 900g (2lb)	5–6 min Stand 30–40 min	See recipe	See recipe
turkey, joint 1–2kg (2–4lb)	7–9 min Stand 50–60 min	8–10 min Stand 15 min	11–13 min Stand 10–15 min
turkey, jointed 1–1$\frac{1}{4}$kg (2–2$\frac{1}{2}$lb)	5–6 min Stand 20–30 min	7–9 min Stand 10 min	9–10 min Stand 5 min
turkey, whole 3–4kg (6–8lb)	5–7 min Stand 50–60 min	7–9 min Stand 25–35 min	10–12 min Stand 10–15 min
venison, joint 1$\frac{1}{2}$–2$\frac{1}{2}$kg (3–5lb)	7–9 min Stand 50–60	—	11–13 min Stand 15–20 min
venison, pieces 900g (2lb)	7–8 min Stand 15 min	See recipe	See recipe
wood pigeon, 2 whole 225g (8oz) each	6–7 min Stand 20–25 min	See recipe	See recipe

be 'open roasted' by placing it on a trivet or upturned plate in a dish and covered with greaseproof paper.

Place the turkey breast side down and cook on 70% setting, allowing 10–12 minutes per ½kg (1lb). Halfway through cooking, turn the turkey breast side up. Remove the foil pieces but if the breast meat near the bone appears to be cooking too quickly during the second half of the cooking time, protect it to prevent the microwave energy from reaching that part of the meat any longer. Drain off the fat and juices during cooking time as necessary. At the end of the cooking time, allow to stand covered for 10–15 min. The final temperature should be 85–90°C/180–185°F.

When time is important—such as a busy Christmas morning—the turkey may be cooked the day before and refrigerated overnight although any stuffing should be removed from the cavity and stored separately. On the day, cover the turkey and reheat for 15–20 minutes on 70% setting, and the stuffing for 4–6 minutes on 100% (full) setting. Alternatively, the turkey and stuffing can be sliced and placed on a plate in even layers. Cover and reheat on 70% setting allowing 5–6 min per ½kg (1lb).

Note: *a large goose should be defrosted and cooked following the above recommendations for turkey.*

Tandoori chicken *(serves 4)*
POWER LEVEL: 100% (FULL) *(colour page 115)*

The chicken is marinated for 24 hours before cooking. A food processor or blender would be useful to prepare the marinade.

900g (2lb) chicken portions, legs or breasts, skinned
1 × 5ml tsp (1tsp) salt
juice 1 lemon
425ml (¾pt) natural yoghurt
1 small onion, minced or finely chopped
1 clove garlic, crushed
2.5cm (1in) cube fresh ginger, peeled and minced or finely chopped
½ fresh green chilli, minced or finely chopped
2 × 5ml tsp (2tsp) garam masala
3 × 15ml tbsp (3tbsp) orange food colouring (or a mixture of red and yellow to make orange), optional
for garnish: shredded lettuce and lemon wedges

1 Cut the chicken legs into 2 pieces and the breasts into 4. Cut slits on each side of the chicken pieces well into the flesh to the bone.
2 Place the chicken on to plates or a large platter and sprinkle with the salt and lemon juice. Rub the salt and lemon juice into the flesh on both sides of the pieces, particularly between the slits. Leave to stand for 20–30 min.
3 Mix together the yoghurt, onion, garlic, ginger, chilli and garam masala. If preferred, the mixture may be puréed in a blender or food processor.
4 Drain any lemon juice from the chicken into the marinade. Brush the chicken pieces with orange food colouring.
5 Place the chicken into the marinade with any remaining food colouring. Turn the chicken over and rub the marinade well into the cuts in the flesh. Cover and refrigerate for at least 24 hr.
6 Remove the chicken from the marinade, shaking off as much of the liquid as possible. Arrange the pieces in a single layer in a shallow dish.
7 Cover and cook for 7 min, turn the pieces over and rearrange them in the dish. Cook, uncovered for a further 7 min.
8 Test the chicken with a skewer and, if not quite done, either cook for a further 1–2 min, or cover and leave to stand for 5 min.
9 Serve on a bed of shredded lettuce and garnish with lemon wedges.

Chicken with tarragon *(serves 4)*
(colour page 90)
POWER LEVEL: 100% (FULL) AND 50% (DEFROST)

25g (1oz) butter
2 rashers streaky bacon, derinded and cut into strips
2 onions, sliced
2 medium carrots, sliced
4 chicken joints, 900g (2lb) approximately, skin removed
75g (3oz) chicken livers
4 sprigs tarragon *or* 2 × 5ml tsp (2tsp) dried tarragon
550ml (1pt) hot chicken stock (page 64)
2 × 15ml tbsp (2tbsp) sherry or wine
salt and freshly ground black pepper
1 × 15ml tbsp (1tbsp) cornflour
for garnish: sprigs tarragon or dried tarragon

1 Melt the butter in a casserole dish on 100% (full) setting for 1 min. Add the bacon, onions and carrots, cover and cook for 6 min.
2 Add the chicken joints, placing the thickest parts towards the outside of the dish; add the chicken livers, tarragon, stock, sherry or wine and seasoning to taste. Stir well, reduce to 50% (defrost) setting, cover and cook for 35–40 min, turning the dish or rearranging the chicken halfway through. Allow to stand for 5 min.
3 Blend the cornflour with a little of the stock from the dish, stir into the rest of the liquid and cook for 2–3 min until thickened, stirring well halfway through.
4 Adjust the seasoning and garnish with fresh tarragon sprigs, but if not available sprinkle with a little dried tarragon.

Chicken with peanuts *(serves 4)*
POWER LEVEL: 100% (FULL) *(colour opposite)*

4 chicken joints
2 × 15ml tbsp (2tbsp) seasoned flour
2 × 15ml tbsp (2tbsp) oil
1 onion, chopped
150ml ($\frac{1}{4}$pt) milk
275ml ($\frac{1}{2}$pt) chicken stock (page 64)
1 × 15ml tbsp (1tbsp) peanut butter
1 × 15ml tbsp (1tbsp) cornflour
2 × 15ml tbsp (2tbsp) single cream
salt and pepper
50g (2oz) salted peanuts
for garnish: chopped parsley

1 Toss the chicken joints in the seasoned flour. Heat the oil in a large dish for 1 min, add the onion and cook, covered, for 3 min.
2 Add the chicken joints, flesh side downwards, and cook, uncovered, for 3 min. Turn the joints over and cook for 2 min.
3 Mix the milk, stock and peanut butter in a small bowl and heat for 2 min. Pour over the chicken joints, cover and cook for 15–18 min. Turn the dish every 5 min.
4 Remove the chicken pieces and blend the cornflour with a little of the sauce. Stir the cornflour into the liquid and cook for 4 min, stirring every minute. Add the cream and seasoning and mix well.
5 Return the chicken to the dish, spooning the sauce over the joints. Reheat in the microwave for 3 min. Sprinkle with the peanuts and chopped parsley and serve immediately.

DO NOT FREEZE

Duckling with sweet and sour cabbage
(serves 4–6)
POWER LEVEL: 70% AND 100% (FULL) *(colour opposite)*

The skin of the duck will not crisp in the microwave but the flesh will remain moist and succulent.

1 duckling, 2–2$\frac{1}{2}$kg (4–5lb) approximately
3 × 15ml tbsp (3tbsp) apricot jam
2 × 15ml tbsp (2tbsp) orange juice
225g (8oz) sausage meat
$\frac{1}{2}$ small onion, finely chopped
2 apples, peeled and chopped
450g (1lb) cabbage, shredded
4 × 15ml tbsp (4tbsp) salted water
3 × 15ml tbsp (3tbsp) wine vinegar
2 × 5ml tsp (2tsp) caraway seeds
for garnish: sliced apple and watercress or parsley

1 Prick the skin of the duck well with a fork. Place in a large dish, breast side up. Mix 1 × 15ml tbsp (1tbsp)
apricot jam with the orange juice and brush over the duck.
2 Cover and cook on 70% setting allowing 10 min per $\frac{1}{2}$kg (1lb). After 15 min cooking time, turn the duck over on to its breast. After a further 15 min, turn again breast side up; cover and allow the duck to stand for 20 min. Brush well with the juices and continue to cook, uncovered, for the remaining time. Test with a fork at the inside thigh; the juices should run clear and the flesh should be cooked at the bone. If not quite cooked, allow an extra few minutes' cooking time, although it should finish cooking during the final standing time. Leave to stand covered for 20 min. If preferred, the duck may be browned for a few minutes in a hot oven or under a hot grill.
3 Place the sausage meat into a bowl, break up with a fork and cook, covered, on 100% (full) setting for 1$\frac{1}{2}$–2 min until the meat loses its pink colour. Drain off the juices.
4 Add the remaining 2 × 15ml tbsp (2tbsp) apricot jam to the sausage meat with the rest of the ingredients (except the garnish).
5 Mix well together and cover and cook for 10–12 min until tender, stirring twice throughout. Allow to stand for 5 min.
6 Spoon the cabbage mixture on to a serving platter and place the duck on the cabbage. If preferred, the duckling may be jointed first and/or the skin removed.
7 Garnish with apple slices and watercress or parsley before serving.

Casserole of chicken *(serves 4)*
POWER LEVEL: 100% (FULL) AND 50% (DEFROST)

4 chicken joints, 900g (2lb) approximately
25g (1oz) seasoned flour
25g (1oz) butter
2–3 × 15ml tbsp (2–3tbsp) oil
1 large onion, finely chopped
1 carrot, diced
2 sticks celery, finely sliced
2 × 5ml tsp (2tsp) freshly chopped sage *or* 1 × 5ml tsp (1tsp) dried sage
550ml (1pt) boiling chicken stock (page 64)
salt and freshly ground black pepper
50g (2oz) mushrooms, sliced
for garnish: a little chopped sage or dried sage

1 Remove the skin from the chicken if preferred and coat the joints with some of the seasoned flour.

Chicken with Peanuts; Duckling with Sweet and Sour Cabbage

2 Place the butter and oil in a large casserole dish with the onion, carrot and celery. Cover and cook on 100% (full) setting for 8 min, stirring once halfway through.

3 Add the chicken to the dish, arranging the thicker parts to the outside of the dish. Brush with the butter and oil, cover and cook for 2 min. Turn the chicken over and cook for a further 2 min. Stir in the remaining seasoned flour.

4 Add the sage, stock and seasoning to taste. Stir well, cover and cook for 4 min, then reduce to 50% (defrost) setting and cook for 25 min, turning the chicken halfway through. Stir in the mushrooms and cook for a further 5 min. Stand for 10 min.

5 Adjust the seasoning and garnish with a little sage before serving.

Braised goose with peppers (serves 4)
POWER LEVEL: 70%

1 goose, 2½–3kg (5–6lb) approximately
1 onion, finely sliced
1 large red pepper, sliced
1 wineglass red wine
2 × 5ml tsp (2tsp) paprika pepper
275ml (½pt) chicken stock (page 64)
bouquet garni
salt and pepper
8 tomatoes, skinned or 425g (15oz) can tomatoes, drained
25g (1oz) flour
paprika pepper for sprinkling
for garnish: stuffed olives and fried or toasted croûtes

1 Wipe the goose and prick the skin well with a fork to allow the fat to drain away during the cooking process.

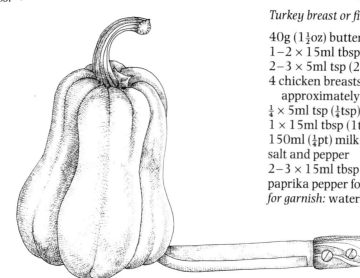

2 Place the goose, breast side down, in a large dish. Protect the wing tips and legs with small, smooth pieces of aluminium foil. Cover with greaseproof paper.

3 Allow 10 min cooking time per ½kg (1lb) weight. Cook for half the calculated time, turning the dish if necessary every 10 min. Pour off and reserve the fat and juices and remove all the pieces of foil.

4 Turn the goose over and continue to cook for the remaining time. Remove the goose from the dish and allow to stand for a few minutes, keeping it warm.

5 Place 2 × 15ml tbsp (2tbsp) of the goose fat into a bowl or dish and add the onion and pepper. Cover and cook for 10 min. Add the wine, paprika, stock, bouquet garni, seasoning, tomatoes and the juices (without fat) from the goose.

6 Test the goose with a skewer—the juices should run clear and the flesh near the bone should be cooked. Carve the goose into portions and place back into the casserole dish with the vegetable mixture, ensuring that the meat is covered with the liquid.

7 Cover and continue to cook for 30 min, turning the dish or rearranging the goose portions as required.

8 Allow to stand for 20 min. Mix 1 × 15ml tbsp (1tbsp) of the stock with the flour and stir into the casserole. Cook for 2–3 min until thickened, stirring once halfway through.

9 Sprinkle with a little paprika pepper. Garnish with the olives and fried or toasted croûtes before serving.

Chicken breasts with honey-mustard sauce (serves 4)
POWER LEVEL: 100% (FULL)

Turkey breast or fillet can be cooked in the same way.

40g (1½oz) butter
1–2 × 15ml tbsp (1–2tbsp) clear honey, to taste
2–3 × 5ml tsp (2–3tsp) mild mustard, to taste
4 chicken breasts, 175–225g (6–8oz) each, approximately
¼ × 5ml tsp (¼tsp) each dried rosemary and thyme
1 × 15ml tbsp (1tbsp) flour
150ml (¼pt) milk
salt and pepper
2–3 × 15ml tbsp (2–3tbsp) cream
paprika pepper for sprinkling
for garnish: watercress or sprigs parsley

1 Soften the butter in a small bowl for 10 sec and then blend with the honey and mustard.

2 Remove the skin from the chicken if preferred and, using half the butter mixture, coat the chicken breasts on both sides with a thin layer.

3 Place the chicken into a large casserole dish or on a plate, sprinkle with the herbs, cover and cook for 12–16 min. Turn the dish or rearrange the chicken pieces halfway through. Drain off the juices into a small bowl or jug. Cover the chicken, keep it warm and leave to stand for a few minutes.

4 Blend the flour with the remaining butter mixture. Stir in the juices and milk. Don't worry if the mixture curdles at this stage. Cook for 2–3 min until thickened, stirring halfway through; add the seasoning and stir in the cream.

5 Place the chicken on a serving plate and sprinkle with the paprika pepper. Coat with a little of the sauce and hand the rest separately. Garnish with watercress or parsley before serving.

Chicken with cream (serves 4–5)
POWER LEVEL: 100% (FULL)

1 × 15ml tbsp (1tbsp) oil
25g (1oz) butter
1 carrot, diced
8 spring onions, trimmed and sliced
1 × 1½kg (3lb) chicken
pinch saffron, optional
pinch ground ginger
150ml (¼pt) chicken stock (page 64)
1 glass sherry
50g (2oz) mushrooms, sliced
2 × 5ml tsp (2tsp) cornflour
1 × 15ml tbsp (1tbsp) water
salt and freshly ground black pepper
150ml (¼pt) cream
½ × 5ml tsp (½tsp) french mustard
for garnish: paprika pepper and chopped parsley

1 Place the oil and butter into a large casserole dish with the carrot. Mix well, cover and cook for 3 min. Add the spring onions and toss over in the butter and oil.

2 Add the chicken to the dish and spoon over some of the vegetables and juices. Sprinkle with the spices. Use small, smooth pieces of aluminium foil to protect wings, drumsticks and the narrow part of the breast.

3 Pour over the chicken stock and sherry. Cover and cook for 20 min, turning the dish and basting the chicken every 5 min.

4 Remove the foil pieces and add the mushrooms to the dish. Cover and continue to cook for a further 5–6 min. Test the chicken with a skewer or knife in

the thickest part of the meat between the thighs, and if not quite cooked allow another few minutes' cooking time. Leave to stand for 20 min.

5 Remove the chicken on to a serving plate or dish and keep warm. The skin of the chicken may be removed if preferred.

6 Blend the cornflour with the water and stir into the vegetables and juices. Add seasoning to taste. Cook for about 3 min until thickened, stirring every minute.

7 Mix in the cream and mustard and heat through for 1 min. Pour the sauce over the chicken and serve hot sprinkled with paprika pepper and chopped parsley.

Turkey escalopes with mushrooms (serves 2)
POWER LEVEL: 100% (FULL)

The commercially prepared turkey escalopes are cooked in the browning dish, coated with a creamy mushroom sauce and served with croquette potatoes.

2 turkey escalopes in breadcrumbs, about 175g (6oz) each
oil for brushing
225g (8oz) frozen potato croquettes
25g (1oz) butter
225g (8oz) button mushrooms, washed or wiped
15g (½oz) flour
salt and pepper
1 × 15ml tbsp (1tbsp) sherry
150ml (¼pt) double cream
for garnish: chopped parsley
for serving: lemon wedges

1 Brush each side of the escalopes with a little oil. Preheat a browning dish for 6–8 min, depending on its size.

2 Place the escalopes in the browning dish, pressing down well with a heatproof spatula, then cook for 1½ min; turn the escalopes over and cook for 1½–2 min on the second side. Remove and keep the escalopes warm.

3 Add the croquettes to the browning dish, turn them over in the oil and cook uncovered for 2 min. Turn the croquettes over and cook for a further 2–3 min. Drain on kitchen paper towel and keep warm.

4 Melt the butter in the dish for 1 min, add the mushrooms, toss over in the butter, cover and cook for 3 min. Blend in the flour, seasoning and sherry. Stir in the cream gradually.

5 Cook the sauce for 2–3 min until thickened and coat the turkey escalopes. Arrange the potatoes around the dish. Garnish with chopped parsley and serve hot with lemon wedges.

DO NOT FREEZE

121

Hare with chestnuts *(serves 4–6)*
POWER LEVEL: 100% (FULL) AND 30% *(colour opposite)*

The hare is marinated for 12–24 hours before cooking.

1 hare, jointed
3 × 15ml tbsp (3tbsp) oil
3 × 15ml tbsp (3tbsp) brandy or other spirit
1 small onion, sliced
freshly ground black pepper
25g (1oz) butter
1 × 15ml tbsp (1tbsp) flour
½ bottle red wine, approximately
salt
bouquet garni
1 clove garlic, finely chopped
225g (8oz) button onions
175g (6oz) button mushrooms
225g (8oz) peeled and cooked fresh chestnuts *or*
225g (8oz) canned chestnuts, drained
for garnish: chopped parsley
for serving: Creamed Potatoes (page 152)

1 Cut the joints of hare into small pieces, taking as much meat cleanly off the bone as possible. Wipe and place into a large bowl. Add the oil, brandy, onion and black pepper. Cover and refrigerate for 12–24 hr, turning the meat over occasionally in the marinade.
2 Remove the hare pieces from the marinade and pat dry with kitchen paper towel. Heat the butter for 1 min in a large casserole dish on 100% (full) setting; add the hare and brush with the butter. Cover and cook for 5 min, turning the pieces over halfway through.
3 Stir in the flour and wine just to cover. Season lightly and add the bouquet garni and garlic.
4 Cover and cook for 6 min, then reduce to 30% setting, cover and cook for 60 min. Stir in the button onions, continue to cook for 30 min. Add the mushrooms and chestnuts and continue to cook for a further 10 min. Stand for 15 min.
5 Adjust seasoning and remove the bouquet garni. Sprinkle with chopped parsley before serving.

Chestnuts
Skin the chestnuts by slitting the skins with a sharp knife and then heating 10–12 at a time in the microwave until hot, about 1–1½ min. Peel off the skins while hot. Place the peeled chestnuts in a bowl with 150ml (¼pt) stock, cover and cook on 100% (full) setting for 10–12 min until tender or add to the casserole dish 30 min before the end of the cooking period.

Hare with Chestnuts; Country Casserole of Rabbit; Stuffed Pheasant with Tomato Sauce

Stuffed pheasant with tomato sauce
(serves 2–4)
POWER LEVEL: 100% (FULL) AND 30% *(colour opposite)*

1 hen pheasant
freshly ground black pepper
15g (½oz) butter
1 small onion, finely chopped
75g (3oz) veal, pork or chicken, minced or finely chopped
75g (3oz) chicken livers, chopped
50g (2oz) fresh white breadcrumbs
1 × 5ml tsp (1tsp) dried thyme
salt
40g (1½oz) butter
1 sherry glass medium dry sherry
225g (8oz) can chopped tomatoes
for garnish: chopped parsley

1 Wipe the pheasant and sprinkle with a little black pepper. Melt the 15g (½oz) butter on 100% (full) setting for 30 sec in a bowl and add the onion; mix well, cover and cook for 3 min until soft. Add the veal and chicken livers, cover and cook for 5 min. Add the breadcrumbs and the thyme. Mix well together and season with salt and pepper. Fill the pheasant with the stuffing.
2 Melt the 40g (1½oz) butter in a casserole dish which is just large enough to take the pheasant. Add the pheasant and brush with the butter. Cover and cook for 2 min. Heat the sherry for 1 min until bubbling, pour over the pheasant and ignite. Do not ignite in the microwave.
3 Add the tomatoes to the dish around the pheasant; season with salt and freshly ground black pepper. Cover and cook for 55–65 min on 30% setting. Allow to stand for 15 min.
4 Remove the pheasant on to a serving dish and keep warm. Sieve the tomatoes and juices or purée in a food processor or blender. Add a little more sherry to the sauce if preferred and adjust the seasoning.
5 Pour the sauce over the pheasant and garnish with a little chopped parsley before serving.

Country casserole of rabbit *(serves 6)*
POWER LEVEL: 100% (FULL) AND 50% (DEFROST) *(colour opposite)*

The rabbit may be soaked overnight to remove its rather strong flavour.

1–2 rabbits, 2kg (4lb) approximately, jointed
225g (8oz) streaky bacon, derinded and cut into strips
100g (4oz) belly pork, derinded and cut into strips
2 onions, thinly sliced
25g (1oz) flour
275ml (½pt) chicken stock (page 64)

275ml (½pt) cider
salt and pepper
bouquet garni
3 × 15ml tbsp (3tbsp) chopped parsley

1 Soak the rabbit joints overnight in salted water. Rinse well in cold water and dry.
2 Place the bacon and belly of pork strips into a large casserole dish. Cover and cook on 100% (full) setting for 2 min, stirring once halfway through.
3 Add the onion slices, stir well, cover and cook for 5 min. With a draining spoon remove the onions, bacon and pork and add the rabbit joints to the dish. Spoon over the juices.
4 Cover and cook for 6 min, turning the rabbit joints over in the dish halfway through.
5 Return the onion mixture to the dish. Stir in the flour, stock, cider, seasoning and the bouquet garni. Cover and cook for 5 min.
6 Stir well, then reduce to 50% (defrost) setting and cook for 65–75 min until tender, stirring and rearranging the rabbit joints twice throughout. Stand for 25–35 min.
7 Adjust seasoning, stir in the chopped parsley and serve hot.

Mexican chicken (serves 4)
POWER LEVEL: 100% (FULL)

25g (1oz) butter
1 green pepper, deseeded and sliced
1 red pepper, deseeded and sliced
2 medium-sized onions, chopped
2 cloves garlic, crushed
salt and pepper
1 × 396g (14oz) can tomatoes
2 × 15ml tbsp (2tbsp) tomato purée
4 chicken portions
100g (4oz) sweetcorn
100g (4oz) mushrooms, washed and sliced
4 × 15ml tbsp (4tbsp) single cream
2 × 15ml tbsp (2tbsp) chopped parsley

1 Melt the butter in a large casserole dish for 1 min.
2 Add the peppers, onions, garlic and seasoning, then cover with clingfilm and cook for 3 min. Mix the tomatoes and tomato purée into the pepper mixture.
3 Season the chicken joints lightly and add to the pepper mixture. Cover and cook for 15 min.
4 Add the sweetcorn and mushrooms and cook, still covered, for a further 15–20 min.
5 Remove the chicken joints from the casserole. Stir the cream into the sauce and return the chicken to the casserole dish. Sprinkle with parsley before serving.

Turkey tetrazzini (serves 4)
POWER LEVEL: 100% (FULL)

A favourite use for leftover turkey, although in this microwave version the spaghetti is cooked separately. The turkey mixture can be made in advance and quickly reheated later.

25g (1oz) butter
1 onion, finely chopped
1 stick celery, finely sliced
2 rashers lean bacon, derinded and cut into strips
40g (1½oz) flour
275ml (½pt) turkey or chicken stock (page 64)
100g (4oz) mushrooms, sliced
1 green pepper, cut into strips
1 red pepper, cut into strips
350g (12oz) cooked turkey, chopped
1 × 15ml tbsp (1tbsp) dry sherry, optional
salt and freshly ground black pepper
pinch dry mustard
1–2 × 15ml tbsp (1–2tbsp) grated parmesan cheese
for garnish: chopped parsley
for serving: 175g (6oz) spaghetti, cooked (page 216)

1 Melt the butter in a large casserole dish for 1 min. Add the onion, celery and bacon, cover and cook for about 4 min until tender.
2 Stir in the flour and add the stock gradually. Mix well together and cook for 3–4 min until thickened and boiling, stirring every minute. Stir in the mushrooms.
3 Place the peppers in a separate bowl, cover and cook for 4–5 min until tender. Add to the sauce with the turkey, sherry, seasoning to taste and the mustard.
4 Cover and cook for 4–5 min, stirring well halfway through, until completely heated.
5 Cook the spaghetti and arrange around the edge of a warm serving dish or platter. Spoon the sauce into the centre of the dish and sprinkle with the parmesan cheese.
6 Garnish with chopped parsley before serving.

FREEZE THE SAUCE SEPARATELY

Turkey meat loaf
POWER LEVEL: 100% (FULL)

450g (1lb) cooked turkey
1 large onion
100g (4oz) breadcrumbs
3 × 15ml tbsp (3tbsp) tomato purée
4 eggs
½ × 5ml tsp (½tsp) allspice
pinch of nutmeg
salt and pepper

1 Mince the meat and onion together and place in a large mixing bowl. Add all the other ingredients and mix thoroughly.
2 Press the mixture into a rectangular loaf dish and cook in the microwave for 12–15 min. Turn the dish every 5 min and allow 5 min standing time halfway through cooking.
3 Serve hot with vegetables or cold with salad.

Note: *Cooked ham or chicken can be used as alternatives to the turkey.*

Braised hare with potatoes *(serves 4)*
POWER LEVEL: 100% (FULL) AND 30%

The hare is marinated for 12–24 hours before cooking to remove some of the strong flavour.

1 hare, jointed
275ml (½pt) brown ale
1 clove garlic, crushed
1 bay leaf
1 large onion, finely sliced
½ × 5ml tsp (½tsp) grated nutmeg
freshly ground black pepper
25g (1oz) flour
1 × 5ml tsp (1tsp) paprika pepper
2–3 × 15ml tbsp (2–3tbsp) oil
275ml (½pt) stock (page 64)
1 × 5ml tsp (1tsp) wine vinegar
salt
4 potatoes, thinly sliced
slivers butter
paprika pepper for sprinkling

1 Wipe the hare and place in a large bowl with the ale, garlic, bay leaf, onions, nutmeg and black pepper. Leave in the refrigerator or cool place for 12–24 hr.
2 Remove the joints of hare from the marinade and pat dry with kitchen paper towel. Toss the joints in the flour mixed with the paprika.
3 Heat the oil in a large casserole dish for 2 min on 100% (full) setting, add the hare and brush with the oil. Cover and cook for 4 min. Stir in the stock, wine vinegar, salt to taste and the marinade.
4 Cover and bring to the boil in the microwave, about 5–6 min. Reduce to 30% setting, cover the dish and cook for 1 hr, turning the hare joints halfway through.
5 Wash and dry the potato slices, arrange over the top of the casserole and brush with a little of the liquid from the casserole. Dot with slivers of butter and continue to cook for a further 30–45 min until tender.
6 Sprinkle with paprika pepper before serving hot.

Duck in orange and ginger sauce *(serves 4)*
POWER LEVEL: 100% (FULL)

1 × 15ml tbsp (1tbsp) oil
1 onion, chopped
4 portions of duckling
2 oranges
1 chicken stock cube
3 × 15ml tbsp (3tbsp) clear honey
1½ × 5ml tsp (1½tsp) ground ginger
salt and pepper
1 bay leaf
1 × 15ml tbsp (1tbsp) cornflour

1 Heat the oil in a large casserole dish for 1 min. Add the onions, cover and cook for 3 min.
2 Add the duck portions, cover and cook for 5 min.
3 Grate the rind from the oranges. Squeeze the juice from 1½ oranges. Add the stock cube and make the juice up to 550ml (1pt) with boiling water.
4 Add the honey, ginger and seasoning to the liquid, then pour over the duck. Sprinkle the orange rind over the duck and add the bay leaf.
5 Cover and cook for 20 min, stand for 10 min, cook for 10–15 min.
6 Blend the cornflour with a little water. Remove the duck portions from the casserole. Stir the cornflour into the sauce after skimming off the surplus fat and removing the bay leaf. Cook for 3 min or until boiling. Stir well.
7 Return the duck to the sauce and reheat for 2 min. Before serving, garnish with orange slices from the remaining half orange.

Blanquette of turkey *(serves 4–5)*
POWER LEVEL: 100% (FULL) AND 70%

A delicious way to use up the turkey after Christmas, made into a main course with the cold meat and stock from the carcass.

1 large onion, finely chopped
40g (1½oz) butter, melted
50g (2oz) flour
550ml (1pt) boiling turkey or chicken stock (page 64)
50g (2oz) button mushrooms, sliced
1 small can pimentos, drained and thinly sliced
1 clove garlic, crushed
pinch each of powdered nutmeg and mace
675g (1½lb) cooked turkey, finely sliced
2 egg yolks
4 × 15ml tbsp (4tbsp) double cream
1 × 15ml tbsp (1tbsp) lemon juice
salt and freshly ground black pepper

1 Add the onion to the butter in a large casserole dish, cover and cook for 5 min on 100% (full) setting until tender, stirring once halfway through.

2 Stir in the flour until well blended and then add the stock gradually, mixing well after each addition.

3 Cover and cook for 2–3 min until thickened and boiling, stirring every minute. Add the mushrooms, pimentos, garlic, spices and the turkey slices. Mix well together and heat through for 3–4 min, stirring well halfway through.

4 Beat together the egg yolks, cream and lemon juice and add this to the sauce with the seasoning. Reduce to 70% setting and cook, covered, for 3–4 min until heated through, but do not allow the mixture to boil. Stir well every minute.

5 Serve straightaway.

DO NOT FREEZE

Pigeons in red wine (serves 4)
POWER LEVEL: 100% (FULL) (colour opposite)

25g (1oz) butter
4 pigeons
1 spanish onion, finely chopped
75g (3oz) green bacon rashers, derinded and cut into strips
1 × 15ml tbsp (1tbsp) flour
275ml (½pt) red wine, approximately
2 × 5ml tsp (2tsp) tomato purée
1 × 15ml tbsp (1tbsp) sugar
salt and freshly ground black pepper
bay leaf
bouquet garni
225g (8oz) button mushrooms, wiped or washed
3 × 15ml tbsp (3tbsp) cream
for garnish: chopped parsley

1 Melt the butter in a large deep casserole dish on 100% (full) setting for 1 min. Add the pigeons to the dish and brush with the butter. Cover and cook for 2 min, turn the pigeons over and continue to cook for 2 min.

2 Remove the pigeons from the dish on to a plate. Stir the onion and bacon into the juices in the dish, cover and cook for 5 min.

3 Stir in the flour, wine, tomato purée, sugar, seasoning, bay leaf and bouquet garni. Cover and cook for 5 min, stirring once halfway through.

4 Add the pigeons to the dish, ensuring that they are covered with the sauce. If not, add a little more wine to the dish. Reduce to 30% setting, cover and cook for 1½–2 hr turning the dish, or rearranging the pigeons, halfway through if necessary.

5 Add the mushrooms to the dish, stirring them into the sauce. Cover and continue to cook for a further 10 min. Leave to stand for 20 min.

6 Stir in the cream, reheat the dish if necessary for 1–2 min and serve garnished with chopped parsley.

Braised stuffed partridge (serves 4)
POWER LEVEL: 100% (FULL) AND 30%

2 partridges
freshly ground black pepper
40g (1½oz) butter
1 shallot or small onion, finely chopped
65g (2½oz) fresh white breadcrumbs
50g (2oz) raisins, stoned
25g (1oz) walnuts, chopped
1 × 5ml tsp (1tsp) finely chopped parsley
½ lemon, grated rind
salt
1 small egg
1 onion, sliced
1 carrot, sliced
50g (2oz) lean bacon rashers, derinded and cut into strips
25g (1oz) flour
550ml (1pt) hot game or chicken stock (page 64)
bouquet garni
4 croûtes toasted or fried bread
for garnish: watercress

1 Wipe the partridges, sprinkle with a little black pepper and set to one side.

2 Melt 15g (½oz) butter for 30 sec on 100% (full) setting, mix in the shallot and cook for 2 min. Stir in the breadcrumbs, raisins, walnuts, parsley and lemon rind. Add salt and pepper and bind the stuffing together with the egg. Fill the partridges with the stuffing.

3 Melt the remaining butter for 1 min in a casserole dish, add the partridges and brush with the butter. Cover and cook for 3 min.

4 Remove the partridges from the dish, add the onion and carrot, stir well, cover and cook for 3 min. Stir in the bacon, continue to cook for 1 min.

5 Stir in the flour and add the stock, salt and pepper and the bouquet garni. Cover and cook for 3 min until boiling and thickened.

6 Add the partridges to the casserole dish. Reduce to 30% setting, cover and cook for 60–70 min until tender. Stand for 20 min.

7 Remove the partridges from the dish and keep warm. Take out the bouquet garni from the liquid and purée or blend the sauce in a food processor or blender. Adjust the seasoning.

8 Cut each partridge into 2 and place each half on to a toasted or fried croûte. Spoon a little of the sauce over each partridge.

9 Garnish the partridges with watercress before serving and hand the rest of the sauce separately.

Pigeons in Red Wine (above); Black Forest Gâteau (page 180); Salmon Mousse (page 52)

Pheasant normande *(serves 4)*

POWER LEVEL: 100% (FULL) AND 50% (DEFROST)

1 hen pheasant, jointed
25g (1oz) butter
2 × 15ml tbsp (2tbsp) oil
2 medium cooking apples, sliced
1 onion, finely sliced
2 sticks celery, finely sliced
salt and pepper
1 bay leaf
2 × 15ml tbsp (2tbsp) flour
150ml ($\frac{1}{4}$pt) cider
2 × 15ml tbsp (2tbsp) calvados, optional
75ml ($\frac{1}{8}$pt) double cream
for garnish: chopped parsley

1 Wipe the pheasant pieces and place with the butter and oil into a large casserole dish. Cover and cook on 100% (full) setting for 10 min, turning the joints over halfway through. Remove the pheasant from the dish, cover and keep warm.
2 Add the apples, onion and celery to the dish, toss over in the juices and add the seasoning and bay leaf. Cover and cook for 10 min, stirring twice throughout. Stir in the flour and add the cider.
3 Bring to the boil in the microwave, about 3 min, and add the calvados if used. Replace the pheasant in the dish and cover with the sauce.
4 Reduce to 50% (defrost) setting and cook, covered, for 25 min. Allow to stand for 15 min, remove the bay leaf and stir in the cream. Adjust the seasoning.
5 Garnish with chopped parsley before serving.

Rabbit with creamy mustard sauce

(serves 4−6)

POWER LEVEL: 100% (FULL) AND 50% (DEFROST)

15g ($\frac{1}{2}$oz) butter
100g (4oz) bacon rashers, derinded and cut into strips
2 onions, quartered
675g (1$\frac{1}{2}$lb) boneless rabbit, cut into 2.5cm (1in) pieces
15g ($\frac{1}{2}$oz) flour
salt and freshly ground black pepper
275ml ($\frac{1}{2}$pt) chicken stock (page 64)
bouquet garni
bay leaf
150ml ($\frac{1}{4}$pt) double cream
2 × 5ml tsp (2tsp) french or whole-grain mustard
for garnish: freshly chopped chives

1 Melt the butter in a large casserole dish for 30 sec on 100% (full) setting. Add the bacon and onions, stir well, cover and cook for 6 min, stirring well halfway through.
2 Stir in the rabbit, cover and cook for 4 min, stirring once throughout.
3 Mix in the flour and seasoning. Add the stock gradually, mix well together and add the bouquet garni and bay leaf.
4 Reduce to 50% (defrost) setting and cook for 50−60 min until tender, stirring 2−3 times throughout. Stand for 15 min.
5 Mix the cream with the mustard and stir into the casserole. Reheat for 2−3 min if necessary and sprinkle with the chopped chives before serving hot.

Chicken provençale *(serves 4)*
POWER LEVEL: 100% (FULL)

2 × 15ml tbsp (2tbsp) oil
1 onion, finely chopped
1–2 cloves garlic, crushed or finely chopped
4 chicken joints, about 900g (2lb)
8 tomatoes, skinned *or* 1 large can tomatoes, drained
2 × 15ml tbsp (2tbsp) tomato purée
2 × 5ml tsp (2tsp) sugar
½ × 5ml tsp (½tsp) each dried basil, tarragon and
    oregano leaves
pinch ground nutmeg
salt and freshly ground black pepper
100g (4oz) mushrooms, sliced
for garnish: 8 black olives and chopped parsley

1 Place the oil, onion and garlic in a large casserole dish, cover and cook for 4 min, stirring halfway through.
2 Add the chicken joints, placing the thickest parts of the meat towards the outside of the dish. Spoon over the onion and oil, cover and cook for 3 min.
3 Quarter the fresh tomatoes or roughly chop the canned tomatoes. Add these to the dish with the tomato purée, sugar, herbs, nutmeg and seasoning.
4 Cover and cook for 7 min. Turn the dish or re-arrange the chicken pieces and add the mushrooms to the dish. Continue to cook for a further 7–8 min. Test with a skewer and if not quite cooked allow an extra few minutes' cooking time.
5 Garnish with the olives and chopped parsley before serving.

Casserole of partridge *(serves 2–4)*
POWER LEVEL: 100% (FULL) AND 30%

175g (6oz) piece green streaky bacon
2 medium-sized carrots
4 shallots or small onions
100g (4oz) chipolata sausages
25g (1oz) butter
2 partridges
freshly ground black pepper
550ml (1pt) good stock, hot (page 64)
salt
bouquet garni
1 × 15ml tbsp (1tbsp) cornflour
for garnish: chopped parsley

1 Remove the rind from the bacon and cut into strips. Cut each carrot into thick slices and peel the shallots or onions. Twist the chipolata sausages in halves and cut into 2; prick the skins with a fork.
2 Melt the butter in a casserole dish on 100% (full) setting for 1 min, add the bacon and carrots and stir. Cover and cook for 3 min, stirring once

throughout. Add the onion and sausages, continue to cook for 3 min.
3 Sprinkle the partridges with a little ground black pepper. Remove the vegetable mixture from the dish with a draining spoon and put to one side.
4 Add the partridges to the casserole dish and spoon over the juices. Cover and cook for 2 min.
5 Stir in the stock with seasoning to taste and the bouquet garni. Cover and cook for 5 min, then reduce to 30% setting and cook for 45 min.
6 Stir in the vegetable mixture and continue to cook for 20–25 min. Allow to stand for 15 min.
7 Cut each partridge into 2 and place on a serving platter. Remove the vegetables, bacon and sausages and arrange them on the serving dish with the partridges and keep warm.
8 Mix 1 × 15ml tbsp (1tbsp) of the liquid with the cornflour and add to the rest of the juices. Cook for about 2 min on 100% (full) setting until thickened, stirring halfway through.
9 Remove the bouquet garni. Pour a little of the juices over the partridges and hand the rest separately. Sprinkle with chopped parsley before serving.

Casserole of venison *(serves 4–6)*
POWER LEVEL: 100% (FULL) AND 30%

The venison is left to soak in milk for 12–24 hours before cooking.

675g (1½lb) venison
¼ × 5ml tsp (¼tsp) each salt and freshly ground black
    pepper
1 bay leaf
sprig rosemary
275–425ml (½–¾pt) milk
225g (8oz) belly pork, derinded and cut into strips
25g (1oz) flour
1 × 5ml tsp (1tsp) paprika pepper
1 × 15ml tbsp (1tbsp) oil
25g (1oz) butter
2 onions, finely sliced
275–425ml (½–¾pt) good beef stock, hot (page 64)
2 wineglasses red wine, approximately
salt and freshly ground black pepper
bouquet garni
150ml (¼pt) soured cream
juice ½ lemon
for garnish: chopped parsley
for serving: Creamed Potatoes (page 152)

1 Cut the venison into 2.5cm (1in) cubes. Place in a bowl and sprinkle with the ¼tsp each of salt and pepper. Add the herbs and sufficient milk to cover. Refrigerate for 12–24 hr, turning the venison occasionally in the marinade.
2 Remove the meat and dry with kitchen paper

towel. Mix with the belly of pork and toss in the flour mixed with the paprika.

3 Heat the oil and butter for 2 min in a large covered casserole dish. Add the onions, cover and cook for 3 min. Add the venison and pork, toss well, cover and cook for 6 min. Stir once or twice throughout.

4 Stir in sufficient stock and wine to cover the meat. Add the herbs from the marinade, seasoning and bouquet garni. Cover and bring to the boil in the microwave, about 4 min. Stir well.

5 Reduce to 30% setting and continue to cook for $1\frac{1}{4}$–$1\frac{1}{2}$ hr until tender. Allow to stand for 20 min.

6 Adjust seasoning, stir in the cream and lemon juice. Reheat for 2–3 min if necessary before garnishing with chopped parsley and serving with creamed potatoes.

Venison steaks in wine sauce *(serves 4)*
POWER LEVEL: 100% (FULL) AND 50% (DEFROST)

The steaks are marinated overnight before cooking in the browning dish.

4 steaks cut from the haunch of venison, 675g ($1\frac{1}{2}$lb) approximately
3 × 15ml tbsp (3tbsp) oil
3 × 15ml tbsp (3tbsp) red wine
1–2 cloves garlic, finely chopped
salt and freshly ground black pepper
1 bay leaf
oil for brushing
150ml ($\frac{1}{4}$pt) red wine
150ml ($\frac{1}{4}$pt) stock (page 64)
2 × 5ml tsp (2tsp) lemon juice
2 × 15ml tbsp (2tbsp) redcurrant jelly
1 × 15ml tbsp (1tbsp) butter
1 × 15ml tbsp (1tbsp) flour
for garnish: chopped parsley
for serving: Braised Red Cabbage (page 44) and redcurrant jelly

1 Trim and wipe the venison steaks and place in a single layer in a shallow dish. Whisk together the oil, wine, garlic and seasoning. Pour over the venison and add the bay leaf. Refrigerate for 12–24 hr, turning the steaks over in the marinade occasionally.

2 Remove the steaks from the marinade and dry with kitchen paper towel. Brush them on both sides with a little oil.

3 Preheat a browning dish on 100% (full) setting for 6–8 min depending on its size.

4 Place the steaks quickly into the base of the dish and press the meat against the hot base with a heatproof spatula. While they are still sizzling, turn the steaks over and press down well again.

5 Reduce to 50% (defrost) setting and cook, un-covered for 18–22 min until tender. Remove them from the browning dish on to a serving dish and keep warm.

6 Pour the wine, stock, lemon juice into the browning dish with the redcurrant jelly and bring to the boil—about 4 min.

7 Blend the butter with the flour and stir this into the sauce. Adjust the seasoning and cook for 2–3 min until thickened.

8 Pour the sauce over the venison steaks and garnish with chopped parsley. Serve with braised red cabbage and hand the redcurrant jelly separately.

Spiced turkey with avocado *(serves 4)*
POWER LEVEL: 100% (FULL) *(colour opposite)*

350g (12oz) turkey fillet, sliced into thin strips
1 × 15ml tbsp (1tbsp) flour
1–2 × 5ml tsp (1–2tsp) ground cumin, to taste
1–2 × 5ml tsp (1–2tsp) ground ginger, to taste
1 ripe but firm avocado
1 × 15ml tbsp (1tbsp) lemon juice
3 × 15ml tbsp (3tbsp) oil
1 clove garlic, crushed or finely chopped
75g (3oz) spring onions, trimmed and sliced
1 × 225g (8oz) can bamboo shoots, drained
salt and freshly ground black pepper
paprika pepper for sprinkling, optional

1 Toss the strips of turkey in the flour, ground cumin and ginger.

2 Peel, halve and stone the avocado and cut into thick slices. Sprinkle with the lemon juice.

3 Heat the oil and the garlic in a large shallow dish for 3 min. Add the turkey, toss over in the oil and cook uncovered for $4\frac{1}{2}$–$5\frac{1}{2}$ min, turning the turkey over halfway through. Allow to stand, covered, for 3 min.

4 Add the spring onions and bamboo shoots and continue to cook for 2 min. Stir in the avocado and lemon juice and season to taste.

5 Serve straightaway sprinkled with a little paprika pepper.

DO NOT FREEZE

Glazed Mixed Vegetables (page 150); Sweet and Sour Beef (page 108); Spiced Turkey with Avocado (above)

Sauces, stuffings, gravies and dressings

A good sauce can be quite simple to make and will improve the flavour and appearance of many dishes. Initially you may consider that it is hardly worth cooking sauces in the microwave as the time saving is very little but, providing a sauce is stirred at intervals during the cooking process, the result is a very smooth sauce. The advantage is that other ingredients can be added for heating as the sauce is cooking and, of course, there will be only one dish or bowl to wash afterwards. When a sauce is to be handed separately at the table, it can be made in advance and then quickly reheated before serving—very often in the jug in which it is to be served thereby eliminating messy pans to clean afterwards.

Sauces can be defrosted and reheated in next to no time in the microwave but do beat or whisk thoroughly where necessary, especially if the ingredients have slightly separated. When reheating sauces which make part of the main dish—cauliflower au gratin for example—a 50–70% power level should be used to ensure that the sauce does not overheat and bubble too quickly before the main ingredient has heated through.

Recipes are included for both sweet and savoury sauces—some traditional as well as a few more unusual ones—so you can experiment and try out new flavours. I have also included in this section recipes for stuffings and a few gravies and dressings, some of which are referred to in the other various recipe sections throughout the book.

White sauce *(makes about 275ml/½pt)*
POWER LEVEL: 100% (FULL)

25g (1oz) butter
25g (1oz) plain flour
275ml (½pt) milk
salt and pepper

1 Melt the butter in a medium-sized glass bowl for 1–1½ min. Blend in the flour and gradually stir in the milk.
2 Add the seasonings and cook for 4–5 min, stirring every minutes. Use as required.

VARIATIONS
One of the following ingredients may be added to the sauce 2 min before the end of the cooking time:

Prawn sauce: 100g (4oz) peeled prawns
Cheese sauce: 50–75g (2–3oz) cheese, grated
Mushroom sauce: 50g (2oz) mushrooms, chopped
Onion sauce: 100g (4oz) cooked onion, chopped
Parsley sauce: 2 × 5ml tsp (2tsp) parsley, chopped
Egg sauce: 1 hard-boiled egg, chopped finely

White wine sauce: follow the recipe replacing a wineglass of dry white wine for the same measure of milk.
Quick white sauce: place all the ingredients into a bowl or serving jug and stir briskly or whisk. The ingredients will not combine at this stage. Heat for 3–4 min, stirring or whisking every 15 sec, until

cooked and thickened. As the butter or margarine melts it will absorb the flour and, providing the mixture is stirred or whisked frequently, a smooth sauce will be obtained. Adjust seasoning if necessary.

Velouté sauce: follow the recipe for white sauce, replacing the milk with the same quantity of light chicken or fish stock. When cooked, stir in 2 × 15ml tbsp (2tbsp) double cream.

Hollandaise sauce *(serves 4)*

POWER LEVEL: 50% (DEFROST)

Serve with freshly cooked asparagus, broccoli or globe artichokes as a starter to a meal.

100g (4oz) butter
2 × 15ml tbsp (2tbsp) wine vinegar
2 egg yolks
salt and pepper

1 Melt the butter on 50% (defrost) setting for 2 min, add the vinegar and egg yolks and whisk lightly.
2 Cook on 50% (defrost) setting for 1 min, whisk well, season and serve immediately.

DO NOT FREEZE

Béarnaise sauce

POWER LEVEL: 100% (FULL) AND 50% (DEFROST)

Use the above recipe for hollandaise sauce, but before blending the ingredients, cook 1 small chopped onion, 1 × 5ml tsp (1tsp) dried tarragon and freshly ground black pepper in the wine vinegar uncovered, for 3–4 min on 100% (full) setting. Continue as for hollandaise sauce.

DO NOT FREEZE

Béchamel sauce *(makes about 275ml/½pt)*

POWER LEVEL: 100% (FULL) OR 50% (DEFROST)

This is basic white sauce but with an excellent flavour.

1 small onion
6 cloves
1 bay leaf
6 peppercorns
1 blade mace
275ml (½pt) milk
25g (1oz) butter
25g (1oz) flour
salt and pepper

1 Peel the onion and stick with the cloves. Place in a bowl with the rest of the spices and milk.
2 Heat on 100% (full) setting without boiling: cook on 100% (full) setting for 3 min, stand for 3 min,

heat for 2 min, stand for 3 min. Alternatively heat at 50% (defrost) setting for 10–11 min. This allows the infusion of the flavours from the spices into the milk.
3 Melt the butter for 1 min and stir in the flour and the seasonings. Strain the milk and add a little at a time to the roux, stirring continuously.
4 Cook on 100% (full) setting for 1½–2 min, stirring every ½ min until thickened and bubbling. Adjust seasoning if necessary.

VARIATIONS

Mornay sauce: make 275ml (½pt) béchamel sauce and when it has thickened, stir in 50g (2oz) grated parmesan or gruyère cheese, paprika pepper and salt and pepper to taste. Beat until the cheese has blended and reheat for 30 sec if necessary. Serve with eggs, chicken or fish.

Soubise sauce: make 275g (½pt) béchamel sauce. Melt 25g (1oz) butter for 1 min, add 225g (8oz) chopped onions and a little stock or water. Cover and cook for 5–6 min until tender and then sieve or purée and add to the béchamel sauce. Adjust seasonings and reheat for 30 sec. Serve with meat *(colour page 135)*.

Bolognaise sauce *(serves 4)*

POWER LEVEL: 100% (FULL) AND 50% (DEFROST)

2 × 15ml tbsp (2tbsp) oil
1 onion, chopped
2 cloves garlic, finely chopped
2 sticks celery, finely chopped
1 carrot, diced
4 rashers streaky bacon, diced
450g (1lb) minced beef
½ green pepper, diced
4 tomatoes, skinned and chopped
275ml (½pt) boiling beef stock (page 64)
2 × 15ml tbsp (2tbsp) tomato purée
1 bay leaf
1 × 5ml tsp (1tsp) mixed herbs
pinch nutmeg
salt and pepper
for serving: freshly cooked spaghetti (page 216)
grated parmesan cheese

1 Heat the oil in a large bowl for 2 min on 100% full setting. Add the onion, garlic, celery and carrot, cover and cook on 100% (full) setting for 3 min.
2 Add the bacon and cook on 100% (full) setting for 2 min, then add the minced beef; stir well and cook for a further 2 min.
3 Stir in all the remaining ingredients and season well. Cook on 100% (full) setting for 10 min and stir, reduce to 50% (defrost) setting and cook for 20 min. Adjust seasoning to taste. Serve with spaghetti and grated parmesan cheese.

Curry sauce *(makes about 550ml/1pt)*
POWER LEVEL: 100% (FULL) AND 30%

150ml ($\frac{1}{4}$pt) milk
25g (1oz) desiccated coconut
50g (2oz) butter
1 onion, chopped
1 apple, peeled and diced
1–2 × 15ml tbsp (1–2tbsp) curry powder
2 × 15ml tbsp (2tbsp) plain flour
550ml (1pt) boiling stock (page 64)
2 × 15ml tbsp (2tbsp) chutney
25g (1oz) sultanas
salt and pepper
pinch cayenne pepper

1 Heat the milk and coconut together in a small dish for 1$\frac{1}{2}$ min on 100% (full) setting. Stir; leave for 10 min to infuse the flavours.
2 Melt the butter in a medium-sized bowl for 1$\frac{1}{2}$–2 min on 100% (full) setting. Add the onion and apple and cook on 100% (full) setting for 3 min.
3 Stir in curry powder and flour, mixing thoroughly. Cook for a further 1 min.
4 Add the boiling stock gradually, beating well after each addition.
5 Strain the coconut milk into the sauce through a sieve. Add the remaining ingredients.
6 Bring to the boil on 100% (full) setting, stirring every 2 min.
7 Cover and cook on 30% setting for 10–15 min to allow flavours to blend, stirring occasionally.

Tomato sauce *(makes about 275ml/$\frac{1}{2}$pt)*
POWER LEVEL: 100% (FULL) *(colour opposite)*

1 × 15ml tbsp (1tbsp) olive oil
1 large onion, peeled and finely chopped
1–2 cloves garlic, crushed or finely chopped
400g (14oz) can tomatoes, drained
1 × 15ml tbsp (1tbsp) tomato purée
1 wineglass red wine or juice from tomatoes
few sprigs fresh herbs *or*
1 × 5ml tsp (1tsp) dried herbs, eg thyme or rosemary
salt and freshly ground black pepper

1 Place olive oil, onion and garlic into a bowl and toss well. Cook for 4–5 min until soft.
2 Roughly chop the tomatoes and add to the bowl with the remaining ingredients.
3 Cook uncovered until soft and the liquid quantity is reduced giving a fairly thick sauce, stirring every 3 min.
4 Use when referred to in recipes or where a good, well-flavoured tomato sauce is required, ie as a topping for pizzas or to mix with plain boiled pasta.

Raisin sauce *(makes about 275ml/$\frac{1}{2}$pt)*
POWER LEVEL: 100% (FULL) AND 70% *(colour opposite)*

75g (3oz) stoned raisins
2 cloves
275ml ($\frac{1}{2}$pt) water
75g (3oz) brown sugar
2 × 5ml tsp (2tsp) cornflour blended with a little water
salt and pepper
25g (1oz) butter
2 × 5ml tsp (2tsp) lemon juice

1 Place the raisins and cloves into a bowl with the water. Cover and bring to the boil on 100% (full) setting, about 2 min, then reduce to 70% setting and continue to cook for 5 min.
2 Remove the cloves from the bowl and stir in the sugar, cornflour and seasonings. Blend well and continue to cook on 70% setting for 1$\frac{1}{2}$–2 min until thickened, stirring twice throughout.
3 Add the butter and lemon juice and adjust seasoning. Serve with gammon rashers or steaks.

Rich mushroom sauce
(makes approximately 425ml/$\frac{3}{4}$pt)
POWER LEVEL: 100% (FULL)

15g ($\frac{1}{2}$oz) butter
1 small onion, finely chopped
175g (6oz) mushrooms, finely chopped
1 sherry glass sherry or madeira
225ml (8fl oz) milk, approximately
salt and freshly ground black pepper
15g ($\frac{1}{2}$oz) butter, melted
15g ($\frac{1}{2}$oz) flour
1 egg yolk
2–3 × 15ml tbsp (2–3tbsp) single cream

1 Melt the butter in a bowl for 30 sec. Add the onion, cover and cook for 3 min, then stir in the mushrooms and continue to cook for a further 3 min.
2 Make up the sherry or madeira to 275ml ($\frac{1}{2}$pt) with milk and stir this into the mushroom mixture adding seasonings to taste.
3 Blend the melted butter with the flour and the egg yolk to make a paste. Stir into the sauce until blended and cook for 2$\frac{1}{2}$–3 min until thickened and cooked.
4 Purée or blend the sauce if preferred and stir in the cream. Serve hot with grilled or roasted meats or when a well-flavoured mushroom sauce is required.

Soubise Sauce (page 133) with steak; Raisin Sauce (above) with gammon; Tomato Sauce (above) with pasta

Barbecue sauce *(makes about 275ml/½pt)*
POWER LEVEL: 100% (FULL)

15g (½oz) butter
1 onion, finely chopped
2 × 5ml tsp (2tsp) worcestershire sauce
6 × 15ml tbsp (6tbsp) tomato ketchup
225ml (8fl oz) water
salt and pepper

1 Melt the butter in the microwave for 1 min. Add the onion, cover and cook for 3 min.
2 Add the remaining ingredients, stir well and cook for a further 3 min.
3 Serve the sauce with beefburgers, chicken or any barbecued food.

Fennel sauce *(serves 4)*
POWER LEVEL: 100% (FULL)

This sauce makes a good accompaniment to salmon or mackerel.

1 medium head fennel, washed and trimmed
2 × 15ml tbsp (2tbsp) salted water
for the sauce:
15g (½oz) butter
15g (½oz) flour
salt and pepper
275ml (½pt) milk and fennel juice, mixed
3 × 15ml tbsp (3tbsp) single cream

1 Cut the fennel into small pieces and cook with the salted water in a covered dish or boiling bag for 6–7 min. Drain off the juices and reserve.
2 Chop the fennel finely.
3 Melt the butter, add the flour and seasonings. Make

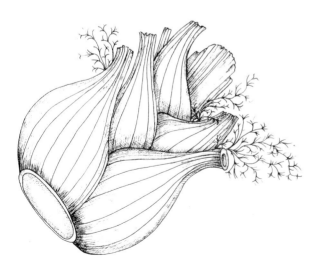

the reserved juices up to 275ml (½pt) with milk and add gradually to the roux, stirring continuously. Stir in the fennel. (If preferred, the sauce may be puréed in a blender at this stage.)
4 Heat the sauce for 4–5 min until thickened and bubbling, stirring every 30 sec.
5 Allow the sauce to cool slightly and stir in the cream. Serve hot with fish.

Gooseberry sauce *(makes about 275ml/½pt)*
POWER LEVEL: 100% (FULL)

This sauce is traditionally served with stuffed mackerel or herrings, but without the chopped fennel it goes very well with smoked mackerel instead of the more usual horse-radish sauce, and may also be served with cold turkey or chicken.

225g (8oz) gooseberries, topped and tailed
90ml (3fl oz) water
1–2 × 15ml tbsp (1–2tbsp) caster sugar
25g (1oz) butter
1 × 15ml tbsp (1tbsp) chopped fennel *or* 1 × 5ml tsp (1tsp) ground fennel (optional)

1 Place all the ingredients in a covered bowl or dish.
2 Cook for 3–4 min, shaking or stirring halfway through, or until the gooseberries pop open. Serve hot or cold.

Lemon foamy sauce *(makes about 275ml/½pt)*
POWER LEVEL: 100% (FULL)

This light sauce can be served with sweet puddings.

25g (1oz) butter or margarine
25g (1oz) caster sugar
1 lemon, grated rind and juice
1 egg, separated
25g (1oz) plain flour
150ml (¼pt) water

1 Cream the butter or margarine and caster sugar together until soft, beat in the lemon rind, egg yolk and flour.
2 Add the lemon juice to the water and gradually beat this into the creamed mixture. Do not worry if the mixture separates, as it will become smooth again as it cooks.
3 Heat for 2–3 min, stirring every 30 sec until thickened. If the sauce is too thick, add a little warm water and beat well.
4 Just before serving, whisk egg white until it holds its shape and fold into the sauce.
5 If required hot, heat slowly until warmed through by giving 15–30 sec cooking at a time.

DO NOT FREEZE

Quince and apple sauce
(makes about 275ml/½pt)
POWER LEVEL: 100% (FULL)

Serve with rich roast meats and poultry, ie pork, duck or goose.

2 small quinces, peeled, cored and thinly sliced
150ml (¼pt) cider or water
2 × 15ml tbsp (2tbsp) sugar
225g (8oz) red apples, cored and thinly sliced
strip lemon rind
salt and pepper
15g (½oz) butter

1 Place the sliced quinces in a bowl with half the cider or water and the sugar. Cover and cook for 6–7 min until tender.
2 Put the apples with the rest of the cider or water and rind into a bowl, cover and cook for 4–5 min until tender. Rub the apples through a sieve.
3 Combine the apple purée with the quinces and season lightly. Stir in the butter and cook uncovered until thick, 2–3 min.
4 Serve hot or cold with pork, duck or goose.

Chocolate sauce *(makes about 425ml/¾pt)*
POWER LEVEL: 100% (FULL)

175g (6oz) plain chocolate
1 × 5ml tsp (1tsp) butter
3–4 × 15ml tbsp (3–4tbsp) golden syrup
1 × 5ml tsp (1tsp) coffee essence
150ml (¼pt) single cream

1 Break up the chocolate and place in a bowl with the butter, golden syrup and coffee essence.
2 Heat until melted, 2–3 min, stirring once halfway through.
3 Stir in the single cream and heat without boiling.
4 Serve hot or cold.

Apple sauce *(makes about 275ml/½pt)*
POWER LEVEL: 100% (FULL)

450g (1lb) cooking apples
15g (½oz) butter
sugar to taste
1 strip lemon peel
1 × 15ml tbsp (1tbsp) water

1 Peel and core the apples and slice thinly. Cook with the other ingredients in a covered dish or roasting bag for 6 min.
2 When cooked, remove lemon peel, beat well or purée in a blender or sieve.
3 Serve hot or cold with rich meat or poultry, eg pork or duck.

Egg custard sauce *(makes about 275ml/½pt)*
POWER LEVEL: 100% (FULL) AND 50% (DEFROST)

2 egg yolks
25g (1oz) caster sugar
15g (½oz) cornflour
275ml (½pt) milk
few drops vanilla essence

1 Place the egg yolks in a bowl with the sugar and mix well.
2 Blend the cornflour smoothly with the milk and heat in the microwave for 2–3 min on 100% (full) setting, stirring every minute.
3 Pour the milk on to the egg and sugar mixture and stir well. Add the vanilla essence and stir again. Reduce to 50% (defrost) and cook for 4–4½ min, stirring every minute.

Jam sauce *(makes about 425ml/¾pt)*
POWER LEVEL: 100% (FULL)

275ml (½pt) water or fruit juice
225g (8oz) jam
1 × 15ml tbsp (1tbsp) cornflour or arrowroot
4 × 15ml tbsp (4tbsp) cold water
lemon juice

1 Warm the water or fruit juice for 2–2½ min and stir in the jam.
2 Blend the cornflour or arrowroot with the cold water and stir into the sauce. Cook for 2–3 min, stirring every minute.
3 Add lemon juice to taste.

VARIATION

Syrup sauce: follow the ingredients and method for jam sauce, substituting syrup for the jam.

Blender mayonnaise *(makes about 150ml/¼pt)*

1 egg or 2 egg yolks
2 × 15ml tbsp (2tbsp) wine vinegar or lemon juice
½ × 5ml tsp (½tsp) salt
¼ × 5ml tsp (¼tsp) each dry mustard and pepper
½ × 5ml tsp (½tsp) sugar
150ml (¼pt) salad oil

1 Place all the ingredients except the oil in a blender or food processor and blend on maximum speed for 1 min.
2 Gradually add the oil in a steady stream through the lid while the blender or food processor is running.
3 Store in the refrigerator.

DO NOT FREEZE

Rum or brandy butter *(makes about 225g/½lb)*
(colour opposite)

Also called hard sauce, this is traditionally served with Christmas pudding, but could also be served with any special hot dessert.

100g (4oz) unsalted butter
100g (4oz) caster sugar
2–3 × 15ml tbsp (2–3tbsp) rum or brandy

1 Cream the butter, add the sugar gradually, beating well together until the mixture is soft and fluffy.
2 Add the rum or brandy a little at a time, beating well after each addition.
3 Place in the serving bowl and chill in the refrigerator until hard. To make the sauce more decorative, pipe it into the serving bowl in swirls before chilling.

Cornflour sauce *(makes about 275ml/½pt)*
POWER LEVEL: 100% (FULL) *(colour opposite)*

1 × 15ml tbsp (1tbsp) sugar
1 × 15ml tbsp (1tbsp) cornflour
275ml (½pt) milk
few drops vanilla essence

1 Mix the sugar and cornflour together with a little of the milk. Gradually add the rest of the milk and the vanilla essence.
2 Cook for 3–4 min until thick, stirring every minute.

VARIATION

Custard sauce: follow the ingredients and method for cornflour sauce substituting custard powder for the cornflour.

Bread sauce *(makes about 425ml/¾pt)*
POWER LEVEL: 100% (FULL *(colour opposite)*)

1 medium-sized onion
2 cloves
425ml (¾pt) milk
pinch salt
6 peppercorns
1 bay leaf
25g (1oz) butter
75g (3oz) breadcrumbs

1 Peel the onion but leave it whole. Place in a bowl with the cloves, milk and salt. Heat for 3 min.
2 Add the other ingredients and cook for 5 min, stirring once during cooking.
3 Remove the onion, cloves, peppercorns and bay leaf, then beat well. Beat in an extra 15g (½oz) butter if required.

Cranberry sauce *(makes about 275ml/½pt)*
POWER LEVEL: 100% (FULL) *(colour opposite)*

450g (1lb) cranberries, washed
100g (4oz) sugar
1 × 15ml tbsp (1tbsp) water
25g (1oz) butter

1 Place the cranberries in a covered dish, roasting bag or boiling bag with the sugar and water.
2 Cook for 5–6 min or until the fruit is soft.
3 Add the butter, stir until melted, then cook uncovered for 1 min.
4 Serve hot or cold with roast turkey or chicken.

Meat or poultry gravy
POWER LEVEL: 100% (FULL) *(colour opposite)*

While the joint is in its final standing period, pour off the meat juices into a jug or gravy boat. Add the usual flavourings or thickening and stock. Heat until cooked, stirring every minute.

Sweetcorn stuffing
POWER LEVEL: 100% (FULL) *(colour opposite)*

25g (1oz) butter
1 onion, chopped
1 × 200g (7oz) can sweetcorn
salt and pepper
1 × 15ml tbsp (1tbsp) chopped parsley
1 lemon, grated rind and a few drops of juice
150g (5oz) fresh breadcrumbs
1 egg, beaten

1 Melt the butter in a bowl in the microwave for 1 min. Toss the onion in the butter and cover and cook for 4 min.
2 Add the sweetcorn and seasoning and cook for 2 min. Allow to cool.
3 Stir in the parsley, grated lemon rind, a little juice from the lemon and the breadcrumbs. Adjust the seasoning to taste and then bind with the egg. Use for fish or poultry.

Cornflour Sauce; Rum Butter; Cranberry Sauce; Bread Sauce; Poultry Gravy; Sweetcorn Stuffing with turkey

Sausage stuffing

POWER LEVEL: 100% (FULL)

25g (1oz) butter
1 onion, chopped
75g (3oz) fresh brown or white breadcrumbs
75g (3oz) mushrooms, chopped, optional
450g (1lb) pork sausage meat
2 turkey livers *or* 4 chicken livers, chopped, optional
2 × 15ml tbsp (2tbsp) dried mixed herbs
salt and freshly ground black pepper
1 egg, beaten

1 Melt the butter in a large bowl for 1 min. Toss in the onion, cover and cook for 4 min.
2 Stir in the breadcrumbs, mushrooms, if used, and the sausage meat. Mix well together.
3 Add the chopped livers from the poultry, if used, and the herbs, seasoning and egg to bind. This quantity makes enough for a 5–6kg (10–12lb) turkey; use half the amount for chicken.

Melba sauce *(makes about 275ml/½pt)*

POWER LEVEL: 100% (FULL)

4 × 15ml tbsp (4tbsp) redcurrant jelly
75g (3oz) sugar
150ml (¼pt) raspberry purée, made from 225g (8oz) fresh raspberries *or* 425g (15oz) can raspberries
2 × 5ml tsp (2tsp) cornflour blended with
1 × 15ml tbsp (1tbsp) cold water

1 Mix together the jelly, sugar and purée in a bowl. Heat for about 2 min, covered, until boiling.
2 Stir a little of the raspberry mixture into the blended cornflour and water. Mix well and then stir this into the remaining sauce.
3 Reheat for 1½–2 min until thickened and clear, stirring twice throughout. Serve with ice cream.

Walnut stuffing

POWER LEVEL: 100% (FULL)

100g (4oz) walnuts
1 medium-sized onion
40g (1½oz) butter
40g (1½oz) breadcrumbs
1 × 15ml tbsp (1tbsp) chopped parsley
1 × 5ml tsp (1tsp) dried marjoram
½ lemon, grated rind and juice
1 egg, beaten
salt and pepper

1 Finely chop the walnuts and onion. Melt the butter in the microwave for 1 min. Add the onion and cook for 3 min.
2 Mix in the rest of the ingredients, using just enough beaten egg to bind the stuffing. Season well.
3 The stuffing can also be made by melting the butter for 1 min and then liquidising all the ingredients together. This gives a finely textured stuffing.

Aïoli *(makes about 200ml/⅓pt)*

Aïoli is a very thick mayonnaise sauce with garlic, and this recipe is made quickly in a blender or liquidiser.

3–5 cloves garlic, peeled
salt and pepper
1 whole egg and 1 egg yolk *or* 3 egg yolks
few drops lemon juice
200ml (7½fl oz) olive oil, approximately

1 Place all the ingredients except the olive oil into a blender or liquidiser goblet. Blend for 1 min, then gradually pour in the olive oil while the blender is running. Add sufficient oil until the mixture is really thick.
2 Turn out into a bowl or dish and stir well before serving. Serve with fish, chicken, boiled or raw vegetables.

DO NOT FREEZE

Orange and herb stuffing

POWER LEVEL: 100% (FULL) *(colour page 19)*

50g (2oz) butter
50g (2oz) onion, chopped
100g (4oz) fresh white breadcrumbs
1 orange, grated rind and juice
2 × 15ml tbsp (2tbsp) fresh chopped herbs *or*
1 × 15ml tbsp (1tbsp) dried mixed herbs
seasoning
1 egg, beaten

1 Melt the butter for 1½ min in a bowl. Toss the onion in the butter, cover and cook for 3 min.
2 Add all the remaining ingredients and mix well together. Use with duck, pork or lamb.

Vinaigrette dressing

150ml (¼pt) oil
3 × 15ml tbsp (3tbsp) wine vinegar
½ × 5ml tsp (½tsp) dry mustard
salt and freshly ground black pepper
1 × 15ml tbsp (1tbsp) chopped fresh herbs (optional)

Blend the oil, vinegar, mustard and seasoning by whisking together in a bowl or placing in a screw-top jar and shaking vigorously. Alternatively, blend in a liquidiser. Beat in the chopped herbs if used.

VARIATION

French dressing: follow the ingredients and method for vinaigrette dressing, omitting the herbs.

DO NOT FREEZE THESE DRESSINGS

Sage and onion stuffing

POWER LEVEL: 100% (FULL)

50g (2oz) butter
450g (1lb) onions, chopped
1 × 15ml tbsp (1tbsp) fresh chopped sage *or*
2 × 5ml tsp (2tsp) dried sage
100g (4oz) fresh white or brown breadcrumbs
salt and pepper
1 egg, beaten

1 Melt the butter in a bowl for 1½ min. Toss the onions in the butter and cook for 4–5 min until soft.
2 Stir in the sage, breadcrumbs and seasoning, mixing well. Allow to cool slightly before binding with the egg. Use for pork or chicken.

Rice stuffing

POWER LEVEL: 100% (FULL)

25g (1oz) butter
1 small onion, finely chopped
50g (2oz) rice, cooked
1–2 chicken livers, chopped, optional
50g (2oz) raisins
50g (2oz) blanched almonds, chopped
2 × 15ml tbsp (2tbsp) chopped parsley
salt and pepper
1 egg, beaten, optional

1 Melt the butter in a bowl for 1 min. Toss in the onion, cover and cook for 2 min.
2 Add all the remaining ingredients and mix well together. Use for meat, fish, chicken or vegetables.

Port wine sauce *(makes 150ml/¼pt)*

Pour off 150ml (¼pt) gravy or juices from roast mutton or venison. Add 1–2 × 15ml tbsp (1–2tbsp) redcurrant jelly and 4 × 15ml tbsp (4tbsp) port wine. Cook uncovered on 100% (full) setting for 4–5 min until blended and syrupy. Serve with roast mutton or venison.

141

Vegetables

Vegetables which have been cooked by microwave are delicious—looking and tasting better than those cooked by any other method. Because they are cooked quickly, in their own juices with very little extra liquid or butter, their full flavour, colour and nutritional value are retained. Certain types of leafy vegetables—spinach and spring greens for example—may be cooked using only the water which clings to the leaves after washing although with some, curly kale for instance, this can result in a stronger-flavoured vegetable than perhaps you are used to. I would recommend, therefore, using a little more liquid until you adjust to the new, real flavour of vegetables when cooked by microwave. It is not always quicker to cook vegetables by microwave than cooking conventionally, particularly if larger quantities are required, but the results are well worth while.

Covered casserole dishes or mixing bowls which are suitable for use in the microwave may be used to cook the vegetables. Boiling bags and roasting bags are also ideal as the bag may easily be shaken or turned over to stir the contents during the cooking process. Remember though that the wire ties supplied with some makes must not be used—loosely tied string or rubber bands or simply twisting the neck of the bag are suitable alternatives. Vegetables carry on cooking during their standing time out of the microwave and will remain hot for a considerable time. It is therefore possible to cook several varieties of vegetables, one after another, and serve them together. Reheating too is most successful as there is no drying out or loss in quality, which means that vegetables may be cooked in advance to be reheated quickly after the main dish has been prepared.

Blanching vegetables

Vegetables for the freezer may be blanched in the microwave although some varieties are more successful and keep a better colour than others. For best results, only small quantities should be attempted at a time.

Prepare the vegetables for blanching in the usual way and place in a large, covered casserole dish with 75–100ml (3–4fl oz) water for 450g (1lb) of vegetables. Adjust the quantity of water to suit the type of vegetable, for example, sliced runner beans or peas would require slightly less water than cauliflower florets or brussels sprouts.

Heat the vegetables for half the time given in the vegetable cooking chart and shake or stir them at least once during this blanching period; then cool the vegetables in iced water—in the normal way—before packing, labelling and freezing.

An alternative, convenient method is to use boiling bags (instead of a casserole dish as described above) and less water is required—about the same amount as when cooking vegetables. To blanch them, cook in the microwave for half the recommended cooking time, shaking the bag frequently throughout. Chill them by plunging the whole package up to the opening in a bowl of iced water; this will reduce the temperature and expel the air at the same time, automatically creating a vacuum pack for the freezer. Seal the bag in the normal way and freeze.

Roast Beef (page 98); Potatoes Dauphinoise (page 152); Courgettes Gratinée (page 153)

Vegetable cooking chart

Vegetable and quantity	Preparation	Amount of salted water to be added	Cooking time in min 100% (full)
artichokes, jerusalem 450g (1lb)	peel and cut into even-sized pieces	4 × 15ml tbsp (4tbsp) or 25g (1oz) butter	8–10
asparagus 225g (8oz)	trim and leave whole	2 × 15ml tbsp (2tbsp)	thin spears 6–8 thick spears 8–10
aubergines 450g (1lb)	wash, slice, sprinkle with salt and leave for 30 min, rinse	2 × 15ml tbsp (2tbsp)	8–10
beans, broad 450g (1lb)	remove from pods	3 × 15ml tbsp (3tbsp)	8–10
beans, french 450g (1lb)	wash and cut	2 × 15ml tbsp (2tbsp)	8–10
beans, runner 450g (1lb)	string and slice	2 × 15ml tbsp (2tbsp)	8–10
beetroot 450g (1lb) 225g (8oz) whole	peel and slice, prick skin, wrap in clingfilm	2 × 15ml tbsp (2tbsp)	7–8 12–15
broccoli 450g (1lb)	trim, cut into spears	2 × 15ml tbsp (2tbsp)	8–12
brussels sprouts 450g (1lb)	wash, remove outer leaves and trim	2 × 15ml tbsp (2tbsp)	8–10
cabbage 450g (1lb)	wash and shred finely	2 × 15ml tbsp (2tbsp)	8–10
carrots 225g (8oz)	new—wash, scrape and cut into strips or leave whole, depending on size old—scrape or peel and slice	2 × 15ml tbsp (2tbsp)	7–10
cauliflower 675g (1½lb) 450g (1lb) whole	wash and cut into florets trim outside leaves, wash	4 × 15ml tbsp (4tbsp)	10–11
celery 350g (12oz)	wash, trim and slice	3 × 15ml tbsp (3tbsp)	10–12
corn on the cob 2 × 225g (8oz)	Wash and trim	4 × 15ml tbsp (4tbsp) or 40g (1½oz) butter	6–8
courgettes 450g (1lb)	wash, trim and slice	—	8–10
curly kale 225g (8oz)	remove thicker stalks, wash thoroughly	4 × 15ml tbsp (4tbsp)	10–12
leeks 450g (1lb)	wash, trim and slice	2 × 15ml tbsp (2tbsp)	7–10
marrow 450g (1lb)	peel, cut into 2cm (¾in) rings, remove seeds and quarter the rings	2 × 15ml tbsp (2tbsp)	8–10
mushrooms 225g (8oz)	peel, wipe or wash	2 × 15ml tbsp (2tbsp) stock or 25g (1oz) butter	5–6

Vegetable and quantity	Preparation	Amount of salted water to be added	Cooking time in min 100% (full)
okra 450g (1lb)	wash, trim, sprinkle with salt, leave for 30 min, rinse	2 × 15ml tbsp (2tbsp) or 25g (1oz) butter or oil	8–10
onions 225g (8oz)	peel and slice	2 × 15ml tbsp (2tbsp) or 25g (1oz) butter or oil	5–7
parsnips 450g (1lb)	peel and slice	2 × 15ml tbsp (2 tbsp)	8–10
peas 225g (8oz)	remove from pods	2 × 15ml tbsp (2tbsp)	8–10
potatoes 450g (1lb)	peel and cut into even-sized pieces	4 × 15ml tbsp (4tbsp) or 25g (1oz) butter	8–10
potatoes, new, in their jackets 450g (1lb)	wash thoroughly	2 × 15ml tbsp (2tbsp)	10–12
potatoes, old, in their jackets 450g (1lb)	wash and scrub thoroughly, dry and prick skins	—	10–12
spinach 450g (1lb)	break up thicker stalks, wash thoroughly	—	6–8
spring greens 450g (1lb)	break up thicker stalks, wash and shred	2 × 15ml tbsp (2tbsp)	8–10
swedes 450g (1lb)	peel and dice	2 × 15ml tbsp (2tbsp)	6–7
tomatoes 450g (1lb)	wash and halve, place in shallow dish and cover with lid or clingfilm	—	6–8
turnips 450g (1lb)	peel and dice	2 × 15ml tbsp (2tbsp)	8–10

Home-frozen vegetables when required for use should be cooked for the full time recommended for fresh vegetables, but allow an extra 1–3 min if using them straight from the freezer, when no extra water will be required.

Frozen vegetables

Home-frozen vegetables may take longer to thaw and cook than commercially frozen ones. This is due to the fact that the initial freezing time is relatively much longer in a home freezer. Commercial freezing takes place at very high speed and consequently the ice crystals are smaller and melt more quickly during the defrosting process. The cooking times given on the right are approximate, as the type and size of the container and the freezing method used will affect the cooking time required. Also the degree of cooking is a personal choice—some may prefer crisper vegetables,

Vegetable	Cooking time	
	225g (½lb)	450g (1lb)
asparagus	6–7 min	10–11 min
beans, broad	7–8 min	10–11 min
beans, french or runner	7–8 min	10–11 min
broccoli	6–8 min	8–10 min
cabbage	6–7 min	10–11 min
carrots	6–8 min	9–10 min
cauliflower florets	4–6 min	7–9 min
corn kernels	3–4 min	7–8 min
corn on the cob	4–5 min (1 cob)	7–8 min (2 cobs)
courgettes	4–5 min	6–8 min
peas	4–5 min	8–9 min
spinach, chopped or leaf	7–8 min	10–11 min
stewpack	6–8 min	9–11 min
swedes or turnips	7–8 min	10–12 min
vegetables mixed, diced	5–6 min	7–9 min

while others prefer them cooked a little longer. Adjust the cooking times to suit your own requirements.

Frozen vegetables are defrosted and cooked in one operation, using 100% (full) setting:

Canned vegetables

Most canned vegetables are cooked during the processing and, therefore, only need reheating in the microwave. The food must be removed from the can and placed in a suitable covered container. Heat on 100% (full) setting for 3–4 min for the 400–425g (14–15oz) size and for 2–2½ min for the 200–225g (7–8oz) size. Stir the contents of the dish halfway through the cooking time to ensure even heating.

Drying herbs

Many varieties of herbs are annual plants and, when near to the end of their season, it is possible to dry them by microwave to last through the winter months. Compared with conventional methods, preserving herbs by drying in the microwave is extremely fast and small quantities can be quickly and easily dried most successfully. The method is simple and the results are excellent, retaining better colours and aromas than conventionally dried herbs.

Preferably the herbs should be clean and dry when picked, otherwise wash them thoroughly and pat them dry between pieces of kitchen paper towel. Gently squeeze as much moisture as possible from them after washing as this will give better results. Remove the leaves from the stems (where applicable) and measure about 1 cupful of the leaves. Spread the herbs out evenly on two thicknesses of kitchen paper towel. This helps to absorb moisture during the heating process. Cover with two more pieces of kitchen paper towel.

Heat on 100% (full) setting for 4–6 min, turning over the kitchen paper towel (with the herbs) once throughout. Check after the minimum time—when dry, the herbs will be brittle and break very easily. Leave to cool between the kitchen paper towels before crushing and storing in an airtight jar which should be kept in a cool, dry place.

Points to remember

1 Do not over-season the vegetables as it can have a toughening effect. If in doubt, adjust the seasoning after cooking.
2 The times given are approximate as the age and the thickness of the vegetables will affect cooking time. Therefore, test regularly during cooking.
3 If the quantity given on the chart is altered, the time should be adjusted accordingly. Allow about a third to half extra time if doubling the quantity of vegetables to be cooked.
4 Do not overcook as the vegetables will continue to

cook for a short while after they are removed from the oven due to the heat retained.
5 Vegetables cooked in their skins, ie jacket potatoes and whole tomatoes, should be pricked well to prevent them bursting during the cooking process.
6 When 'boiling' potatoes it is usually better to cook them in their skins with a little added water as described previously and to remove the skins, if required, after cooking. Some kinds of potatoes cook extremely well either scraped or peeled, but others tend to turn black during cooking in the microwave; a few drops of lemon juice added to the water when cooking will help to overcome this.
7 When cooking an item such as a jacket potato, 1 potato weighing 100–150g (4–5oz) will take 5–6 min, 2 will take 7–9 min and 3 will take 10–11 min and so on.

Orange glazed carrots (serves 4)
POWER LEVEL: 100% (FULL) (colour opposite)

450g (1lb) carrots
4 × 15ml tbsp (4tbsp) orange juice
25g (1oz) butter
freshly ground black pepper
1 × 5ml tsp (1tsp) brown sugar
1 × 15ml tbsp (1tbsp) grated orange rind
for garnish: 1 × 5ml tsp (1tsp) chopped parsley

1 Wash and peel or scrape the carrots. If the carrots are young, cut into quarters or leave whole; if they are large, cut into thin slices.
2 Place the carrots in a casserole dish with the orange juice, butter, pepper and sugar.
3 Cover with a tightly fitting lid or clingfilm and cook for 9–10 min until tender, shaking or stirring 3 times throughout.
4 Remove the lid from the dish and cook uncovered for about 2 min until some of the liquid quantity has reduced.
5 Stir in the grated orange rind and serve hot sprinkled with the chopped parsley.

Mushrooms in cream (serves 4)
POWER LEVEL: 100% (FULL) (colour opposite)

25g (1oz) butter
450g (1lb) button mushrooms
1 clove garlic, crushed
salt and freshly ground black pepper
3 × 15ml tbsp (3tbsp) dry sherry or white wine
150ml (¼pt) double cream
grated nutmeg for sprinkling

Orange Glazed Carrots (above); Mushrooms in Cream (above); Leeks Provençale (page 148)

1 Melt the butter for 1 min in a serving dish. Add the mushrooms and garlic, season lightly and add the sherry or wine.
2 Cook, covered, for $4\frac{1}{2}$–5 min, stirring once halfway through.
3 Remove the mushrooms with a slotted spoon and keep warm. Boil the juices in the microwave for about 5 min until slightly reduced, leaving the dish uncovered.
4 Add the mushrooms and the cream to the dish, adjust seasoning and reheat if necessary for 1–$1\frac{1}{2}$ min.
5 Sprinkle with a little grated nutmeg before serving hot.

Leeks provençale *(serves 4)*
POWER LEVEL: 100% (FULL) *(colour page 147)*

2×15ml tbsp (2tbsp) oil
450g (1lb) leeks, washed, trimmed and thinly sliced
2×15ml tbsp (2tbsp) finely chopped onion
2–3 cloves garlic, crushed
425g (15oz) can tomatoes, drained and roughly chopped
salt and freshly ground black pepper
1×15ml tbsp (1tbsp) tomato purée
1 bay leaf
1 wineglass white wine
2×15ml tbsp (2tbsp) chopped parsley

1 Place the oil, leeks, onion and garlic into a large casserole dish, toss well in the oil; cover and cook for 8–9 min, stirring twice throughout.
2 Add the tomatoes, salt and freshly ground black pepper, tomato purée, bay leaf and the wine. Cover and cook for 4 min. Stir well and continue to cook uncovered for a further 2 min.
3 Stir in the chopped parsley before serving hot, although this dish is also very good served chilled with cold meats.

Broccoli in soured cream
POWER LEVEL: 100% (FULL)

450g (1lb) green broccoli, washed and trimmed into sprigs
4×15ml tbsp (4tbsp) salted water
juice half lemon
150ml ($\frac{1}{4}$pt) double cream
$\frac{1}{2} \times 5$ml tsp ($\frac{1}{2}$tsp) grated nutmeg

1 Place the broccoli in a casserole dish with the salted water.
2 Cover and cook for 8–12 min—this will depend on the size of the sprigs. Allow to stand for a few minutes, then drain and place on to a serving dish.

3 Mix the lemon juice with the double cream to produce soured cream, add nutmeg and heat in the microwave for 30–45 sec, stirring once halfway through.
4 Coat the broccoli with the soured cream and serve hot.

DO NOT FREEZE

Potatoes parisienne *(serves 3–4)*
POWER LEVEL: 100% (FULL) *(colour page 159)*

These potato balls can be plainly boiled in the microwave or cooked in butter.

675g ($1\frac{1}{2}$lb) potatoes, peeled
4×15ml tbsp (4tbsp) salted water *or*
40g ($1\frac{1}{2}$oz) butter
for garnish: chopped parsley

1 Scoop out potato balls with a cutter. This should produce about 450g (1lb) potato balls. Wash well and dry.
2 Place them into a casserole dish with the salted water or melt the butter first in the dish for 1–$1\frac{1}{2}$ min, then add the potato balls to the dish. Toss the potatoes well in the butter.
3 Cover and cook for 10–12 min, tossing or stirring well twice throughout. Sprinkle with chopped parsley before serving.

Creamed parsnips *(serves 4)*
POWER LEVEL: 100% (FULL)

450g (1lb) parsnips
2×15ml tbsp (2tbsp) salted water
40g ($1\frac{1}{2}$oz) butter
2–3×15ml tbsp (2–3tbsp) single cream or top of the milk
freshly ground black pepper
grated nutmeg for sprinkling

1 Peel the parsnips and cut into slices or quarters, depending on their size. If very large, cut into dice. Cut out and discard the core if woody.
2 Place the parsnips with the salted water into a casserole dish. Cover and cook for 8–10 min until tender. Drain well.
3 Add the butter to the hot parsnips, toss over until the butter is melted then mash with a fork or potato masher. Alternatively, the parsnips may be puréed in a blender or food processor.
4 Stir in the single cream or top of the milk and the freshly ground black pepper. Sprinkle with grated nutmeg before serving hot.

Note: *The above recipe is also suitable for swedes.*

Turnips with onions *(serves 4–6)*

POWER LEVEL: 100% (FULL)

450g (1lb) small turnips, peeled
2 × 15ml tbsp (2tbsp) salted water
450g (1lb) medium onions, peeled
40g (1½oz) butter
salt and freshly ground black pepper

1 Cut the turnips into 6mm (¼in) slices. Place in a roasting bag or casserole dish with the salted water, cover and cook for 8–10 min until tender, shaking or stirring halfway through. Drain the turnips well.
2 Slice the onions into thin rings. Melt the butter for 1–1½ min, add the onions and toss over well. Cover and cook for 8–9 min, stirring twice throughout.
3 Mix together the turnips and onions, adjust seasoning and serve hot, sprinkled with a little extra ground black pepper.

Sauté cucumber with mint *(serves 4)*

POWER LEVEL: 100% (FULL)

450g (1lb) cucumber
salt for sprinkling
25g (1oz) butter
1 × 15ml tbsp (1tbsp) freshly chopped mint

1 Wash the cucumber, trim off the ends and discard. Peel the cucumber if preferred and cut the flesh into dice.

2 Place the cucumber into a plate or a dish, and sprinkle with salt. Allow to stand for about 30 min; this will extract some of the moisture from the cucumber.
3 Wash and drain well. Dry the cucumber in kitchen paper towel.
4 Melt the butter in a dish for 1 min, add the cucumber and toss well in the butter. Cover and cook for 3½–4½ min, shaking or tossing well halfway through. Take care not to overcook as the cucumber should remain crispy.
5 Drain the cucumber and stir in the mint. Serve hot.

DO NOT FREEZE

Braised celery with ham *(serves 4)*

POWER LEVEL: 100% (FULL)

25g (1oz) butter
1 small onion, finely chopped
350g (12oz) celery, cut into 5cm (2in) strips
275ml (½pt) boiling chicken stock (page 64)
salt and freshly ground black pepper
15g (½oz) butter, softened
15g (½oz) flour
50g (2oz) cooked ham, cut into 5cm (2in) strips
for garnish: chopped parsley

1 Melt the 25g (1oz) butter for 1 min in a shallow dish. Add the chopped onion, toss well, cover and cook for 2 min.
2 Add the celery to the onion, cover and cook for 5 min. Pour on the stock and season to taste. Cover and cook for about 15 min until the celery is tender.
3 Blend the butter with the flour and add to the celery. Stir until blended and add the ham strips. Cook uncovered for 2½–3 min until thickened and heated through.
4 Sprinkle with chopped parsley before serving hot.

The following two stir-fry-style recipes are cooked in the microwave instead of a wok or large fry-pan. The vegetables should be crisp when cooked but the cooking times can be extended to cook the vegetables to a softer texture if preferred.

Glazed mixed vegetables *(serves 4)*
POWER LEVEL: 100% (FULL) *(colour page 131)*

100g (4oz) carrots
100g (4oz) leeks
100g (4oz) celery
100g (4oz) cauliflower
175g (6oz) frozen cut green beans, thawed
50g (2oz) frozen peas, thawed
50g (2oz) frozen sweetcorn, thawed
3–6 × 15ml tbsp (3–6tbsp) oil
small piece fresh root ginger, peeled and grated
50g (2oz) demerera sugar
3 × 15ml tbsp (3tbsp) lemon juice
salt and freshly ground black pepper
for garnish: a little grated root ginger

1 Wash and prepare the vegetables. Cut the carrots, leeks and celery into fine slices and the cauilflower into small florets. Mix together with the beans, peas and sweetcorn.
2 Place 3 × 15ml tbsp (3tbsp) oil into a large mixing bowl or casserole dish, cover and cook for 3 min. Add all the vegetables and the ginger. Stir well, cover and cook for 4–5 min, stirring halfway through and adding more oil if necessary.
3 Add the sugar and lemon juice; continue to cook for 5–6 min until the vegetables are tender but crisp, stirring every minute.
4 Add seasoning to taste and serve immediately garnished with a little root ginger.

DO NOT FREEZE

Red cabbage with beetroot *(serves 4)*
POWER LEVEL: 100% (FULL)

3–6 × 15ml tbsp (3–6tbsp) oil
225g (8oz) red cabbage, finely shredded
1 small onion, finely sliced
175g (6oz) cooked beetroot, skinned and coarsely grated
2 × 15ml tbsp (2tbsp) creamed horseradish
salt and freshly ground black pepper
2 × 15ml tbsp (2tbsp) natural yoghurt

1 Place 3 × 15ml tbsp (3tbsp) oil in a large mixing bowl or casserole dish, cover with a lid or clingfilm and heat in the microwave for 3 min.
2 Add the cabbage and onion, toss well in the oil, cover and cook for 5–6 min, stirring every minute and adding more oil if required. The cabbage should soften but retain its crispness.
3 Stir in the beetroot, horseradish and seasoning. Cover and cook for a further 2–3 min to heat through.
4 Serve straightaway with the yoghurt drizzled over the top.

DO NOT FREEZE

Jacket potatoes *(serves 2–4)*
POWER LEVEL: 100% (FULL)

2 potatoes, each 225–250g/8–9oz
knob of butter
salt and pepper

1 Scrub the potatoes then dry and prick them with a fork or score them.
2 Cook for 10–12 min, or until soft. Cut the potatoes in half and scoop out the soft potato.
3 Mix with the butter and seasoning, then pile the filling back into the potato skins. Reheat for 1½ min before serving.

VARIATIONS

Add the following to the cooked potato and reheat as above:
Cheese: 50g (2oz) cheese, grated
15g (½oz) butter
½ × 5ml tsp (½tsp) milk
Bacon: 50g (2oz) cooked bacon, chopped
1 × 5ml tsp (1tsp) milk
Soured cream and chives: When the potatoes are cooked, score a cross on top, open by pushing in the corners, and top with
2 × 15ml tbsp (2tbsp) soured cream
1 × 5ml tsp (1tsp) chopped chives
(colour page 26)

DO NOT FREEZE

Brussels sprouts with mushrooms *(serves 4)*
POWER LEVEL: 100% (FULL)

450g (1lb) brussels sprouts, trimmed and washed
4 × 15ml tbsp (4tbsp) salted water
for the sauce:
15g (½oz) butter
2 × 5ml tsp (2tsp) finely chopped onion
100g (4oz) mushrooms, washed and finely chopped
15g (½oz) flour
175ml (6fl oz) chicken stock (page 64)
salt and pepper
1 bay leaf
for garnish: chopped parsley

1 Place the brussels sprouts and salted water in a covered casserole dish and cook for 8–10 min. Leave to stand for a few minutes.
2 Melt the butter in a bowl or jug for 30 sec. Stir in the onion, cover and cook for 1 min. Add the mushrooms and toss well in the onion and butter. Cover and cook for 3 min.
3 Stir in the flour, then pour on the stock, seasonings and bay leaf. Bring to the boil in the microwave, stirring every minute until thickened; continue to cook for 1 min.
4 Drain the sprouts and place back into the dish. Remove the bay leaf from the sauce and stir the sauce into the sprouts.
5 Serve hot sprinkled with chopped parsley.

Green beans in yoghurt sauce *(serves 4–6)*
POWER LEVEL: 100% (FULL) AND 50% (DEFROST)

450g (1lb) french green beans
2 × 15ml tbsp (2tbsp) salted water
for the sauce:
3 egg yolks
225ml (8fl oz) natural yoghurt
2 × 5ml tsp (2tsp) lemon juice
salt and pepper
½–1 × 5ml tsp (½–1tsp) mild mustard
for garnish: chopped parsley

1 Wash and trim the beans and place with the salted water into a serving dish. Cover and cook on 100% (full) setting for 8–10 min and allow to stand for a few minutes.
2 Beat the egg yolks into the yoghurt with the lemon juice, seasoning and mustard to taste. Reduce to 50% (defrost) setting and cook the sauce for 6–8 min, stirring every 2 min until thickened. Do not allow the sauce to boil.
3 Drain the liquid from the beans and pour the sauce over the top. Garnish with the chopped parsley before serving hot.

DO NOT FREEZE

Cauliflower au gratin *(serves 4)*
POWER LEVEL: 100% (FULL)

1 cauliflower, about 675g (1½lb)
4 × 15ml tbsp (4tbsp) salted water
for the sauce:
25g (1oz) butter
25g (1oz) flour
salt and pepper
150ml (¼pt) chicken stock (page 64)
150ml (¼pt) milk
3 × 15ml tbsp (3tbsp) cream
2 × 5ml tsp (2tsp) french mustard
few drops of lemon juice
3 × 15ml tbsp (3tbsp) browned breadcrumbs
3 × 15ml tbsp (3tbsp) grated cheese

1 Trim the cauliflower and wash. Place into a large casserole dish with the salted water. Cover and cook for 10–11 min. Leave to stand for a few minutes.
2 Melt the butter for 1 min, add the flour and seasoning, stir well until blended, then gradually add the stock and milk, stirring well after each addition.
3 Heat for 3–4 min until thickened, whisking every 30 sec. Allow to cool slightly then beat in the cream, mustard and lemon juice.
4 Drain the cauliflower and arrange in a serving dish. Spoon the sauce over the cauliflower.
5 Mix the browned breadcrumbs and cheese together and sprinkle over the sauce. Heat for 2 min until the cheese has melted, or brown under a hot grill. Serve hot.

FREEZE THE SAUCE SEPARATELY

Spiced aubergines *(serves 8)*
POWER LEVEL: 100% (FULL) *(colour page 115)*

This dish can be served with curries but goes just as well with grilled or roast meats. In addition, it may be served cold—as a starter or with cold meats.

2.5cm (1in) cube fresh ginger, peeled and chopped
4–6 large cloves garlic, peeled and chopped
4 × 15ml tbsp (4tbsp) water
800g (1¾lb) aubergines
150ml (¼pt) oil, approximately
1 × 5ml tsp (1tsp) fennel seeds
½ × 5ml tsp (½tsp) cumin seeds
400g (14oz) can chopped tomatoes
1 × 15ml tbsp (1tbsp) ground coriander seeds
¼ × 5ml tsp (¼tsp) ground turmeric
¼ × 5ml tsp (¼tsp) cayenne pepper
1¼ × 5ml tsp (1¼tsp) salt

1 Blend together the ginger, garlic and water. If preferred they may be puréed in a food processor or liquidiser.

2 Wash and dry the aubergines and cut them into thick slices about 1.25cm ($\frac{1}{2}$in) thick. Cut the slices into halves.

3 Place the aubergines into a large mixing bowl or casserole dish with about three-quarters of the oil. Mix well so that the aubergine slices are coated with the oil as much as possible.

4 Cover and cook for 12–14 min, stirring well 3 times throughout and adding more oil if required. Stir in the ginger, garlic and water mixture.

5 Mix the rest of the ingredients together and stir into the aubergines. Cover and cook for 5 min, stirring once halfway through. Stand for 5 min. Serve hot or cold.

Potatoes dauphinoise (serves 3–4)
POWER LEVEL: 100% (FULL) AND 70% (colour page 143)

An excellent potato dish to serve with plain meats but it is also delicious enough to serve on its own as a starter or vegetable course.

15g ($\frac{1}{2}$oz) butter
450g (1lb) peeled potatoes
salt and freshly ground black pepper
1–2 cloves garlic, finely chopped
275ml ($\frac{1}{2}$pt) cream, single and double mixed
slivers butter
for garnish: a little chopped parsley

1 Melt the butter in a 17.5–20cm (7–8in) shallow, round dish, for 30 sec. Brush the butter around the sides of the dish.

2 Cut the potatoes into very thin slices; this is easier if using a mandoline or food processor or slicer attachment to a food mixer. Wash the potato slices well and dry.

3 Layer the potato slices in the dish, sprinkling each layer with salt, pepper and garlic. Pour on the cream and top with slivers of butter.

4 Reduce to 70% setting and cook, covered, for 20 min. Stand for 5 min before garnishing with a little chopped parsley and serving hot.

DO NOT FREEZE

Creamed potatoes (serves 3–4)
POWER LEVEL: 100% (FULL)

Boil about 450g (1lb) peeled potatoes which have been cut into even-sized pieces in a covered container with 4 × 15ml tbsp (4tbsp) salted water for 10–12 min. Toss over or stir well twice throughout. Drain well and mash with a fork or potato masher. Beat in a knob of butter and a little milk or cream, adding salt and pepper to taste.

Potato salad (serves 4–6)
POWER LEVEL: 100% (FULL)

450g (1lb) peeled potatoes
few drops lemon juice
salt and pepper
1 small onion, finely chopped
1 clove garlic, crushed
1 × 15ml tbsp (1tbsp) oil
3 × 15ml tbsp (3tbsp) Blender Mayonnaise (page 137)
2 × 15ml tbsp (2tbsp) soured cream
2 × 15ml tbsp (2tbsp) chopped chives

1 Cut the peeled potatoes into 6mm ($\frac{1}{4}$in) dice. Rinse well in cold water and place into a 17.5cm (7in) round dish or a boiling bag. Sprinkle with a few drops of lemon juice and very little salt.

2 Cover and cook for 8–10 min, shaking or tossing twice throughout. Leave to stand for a few minutes while preparing the dressing.

3 Place the onion, garlic and oil into a bowl, cover and cook for 3 min. Stir into the potatoes and leave to cool slightly.

4 Add the mayonnaise, soured cream and 1 × 15ml (1tbsp) of the chives. Adjust seasoning before serving warm or cold sprinkled with the remaining chives.

DO NOT FREEZE

Ratatouille (serves 4–6)
POWER LEVEL: 100% (FULL)

Ideal for the freezer made in quantity.

2 medium aubergines, sliced
225g (8oz) courgettes, sliced
salt
4 × 15ml tbsp (4tbsp) oil
1 large onion, sliced
2 cloves garlic, finely chopped
1 red pepper, deseeded and finely sliced
1 green pepper, deseeded and finely sliced
225g (8oz) tomatoes, canned or fresh, skinned and roughly chopped
freshly ground black pepper

1 Sprinkle the prepared aubergines and courgettes with the salt. Allow to stand for 30 min then wash thoroughly.

2 Heat the oil in a large casserole for 3–4 min, add the onion and garlic and cook for 3 min.

3 Add the aubergines and courgettes and cook for 3 min. Add the peppers, tomatoes and seasoning to taste.

4 Cover and cook for 20–22 min, stirring 2–3 times throughout.

5 Serve hot or cold.

Baked onions *(serves 4)*
POWER LEVEL: 70% *(colour page 19)*

4 large spanish onions, washed but unpeeled
50–75g (2–3oz) butter
freshly ground salt and pepper
for garnish: sprigs parsley

1 Cut a slice from the root ends of the whole onions so that they stand upright and cut a cross in the tops to a depth of about 6mm ($\frac{1}{4}$in). Place the onions into a dish which has been lightly greased.
2 Cover the dish and cook for 18–22 min, turning the dish or rearranging the onions halfway through. The onions should be tender when tested with a skewer. Allow to stand for 5 min.
3 Carefully peel away the skins and place the onions on a hot serving dish. With a skewer or sharp knife, open the tops of the onions slightly and top with a knob of butter.
4 Sprinkle with salt and pepper and garnish with parsley sprigs before serving.

Note: *Cook 2 onions for 12–15 min.*

Bombay potatoes *(serves 4)*
POWER LEVEL: 100% (FULL) *(colour page 115)*

This potato dish goes well with curries instead of the more usual rice accompaniment.

675g (1$\frac{1}{2}$lb) potatoes, peeled and cut into 2.5cm (1in) cubes
6 × 15ml tbsp (6tbsp) salted water
1 clove garlic, finely chopped
$\frac{1}{2}$ green chilli, finely chopped
$\frac{1}{2}$ small onion, finely chopped
4 × 15ml tbsp (4tbsp) oil
1 × 5ml tsp (1tsp) mustard seeds
1 × 5ml tsp (1tsp) ground turmeric
$\frac{1}{2}$ × 5ml tsp ($\frac{1}{2}$tsp) ground cumin seeds
1 × 5ml tsp (1tsp) sugar
few drops lemon juice

1 Wash the potato cubes in cold water. Place into a dish with the salted water, cover and cook for 12 min until tender stirring well 2–3 times throughout. Allow to stand for a few minutes and then drain.
2 Mix together the garlic, chilli, onion and oil. Cover and cook for 4 min. Add the mustard seeds, ground turmeric and cumin. Continue to cook for 1 min.
3 Stir in the sugar, lemon juice and drained potatoes to the spice mixture. Mix well together and heat for a further 1 min if necessary. Stand for 5 min before serving.

Courgettes gratinée *(serves 4)*
POWER LEVEL: 100% (FULL) AND 70% *(colour page 143)*

450g (1lb) courgettes, washed or wiped and trimmed
salt
freshly ground black pepper
1 egg
75ml ($\frac{1}{8}$pt) double cream
3 × 15ml tbsp (3tbsp) grated gruyère cheese
slivers butter
paprika pepper for sprinkling

1 Cut the courgettes into 1.25cm ($\frac{1}{2}$in) thick slices, cutting diagonally across each courgette. Place into a dish or bowl with a tight fitting lid or use clingfilm.
2 Cook for 8–10 min until tender, leave to stand for a few minutes and then drain. Add salt and pepper to taste.
3 Beat together lightly the egg, cream and 2 × 5ml tbsp (2tbsp) of the cheese. Season with a little black pepper.
4 Pour the egg and cream mixture over the courgettes in a serving dish and sprinkle with the remaining cheese. Top with slivers of butter and cook, uncovered, on 70% setting for about 4–5 min until set and heated through.
6 Sprinkle with paprika pepper before serving or alternatively brown the top under a medium hot grill.

DO NOT FREEZE

Tomatoes with cheese *(serves 3–4)*
POWER LEVEL: 100% (FULL)

450g (1lb) tomatoes, skinned
salt and freshly ground black pepper
1 onion, finely chopped
1 × 15ml tbsp (1tbsp) oil
75g (3oz) cheese, gruyère and parmesan mixed
3 × 15ml tbsp (3tbsp) browned breadcrumbs
slivers butter
for garnish: 1 × 15ml tbsp (1tbsp) chopped parsley

1 Slice the tomatoes and sprinkle with salt and freshly ground black pepper.
2 Mix the onion with the oil in a small bowl, cover and cook for 4 min until tender.
3 Layer the tomatoes, onion and cheese in a dish, ending with a layer of the cheese. Cover and cook for 4–5 min, turning the dish halfway through.
4 Sprinkle with the browned breadcrumbs and top with slivers of butter. Cook uncovered, for 1–1$\frac{1}{2}$ min until the butter has melted.
5 Sprinkle with chopped parsley before serving.

Vegetable crumble *(serves 4–6)*
POWER LEVEL: 100% (FULL) *(colour opposite)*

425ml (¾pt) Tomato Sauce (page 134)
450g (1lb) mixed cooked vegetables
50g (2oz) cooked butter or haricot beans, optional
75g (3oz) wholemeal flour
75g (3oz) plain flour
½ × 5ml tsp (½tsp) salt
½ × 5ml tsp (½tsp) dry mustard
75g (3oz) butter or margarine
75g (3oz) cheese, finely grated
for garnish: tomato slices

1 Mix the tomato sauce with the mixed vegetables and the cooked butter or haricot beans. Place the mixture into a large pie dish.
2 Sift the flours with the salt and mustard and rub in the butter or margarine finely. Stir in the grated cheese.
3 Sprinkle the crumble topping lightly over the vegetable mixture and smooth the top.
4 Cook for 9–10 min until hot through and the crumble is cooked, giving a quarter turn every 2 min.
5 Serve hot garnished with tomato slices.

Cabbage with mushrooms and ham *(serves 4)*
POWER LEVEL: 100% (FULL) *(colour opposite)*

25g (1oz) butter
1 × 15ml tbsp (1tbsp) oil
2 sticks celery, sliced
1 small onion, sliced
350g (12oz) cabbage, shredded
1 × 15ml tbsp (1tbsp) water
1 × 15ml tbsp (1tbsp) sherry, optional
salt and pepper
50g (2oz) mushrooms, sliced
50g (2oz) ham, cut into strips
50g (2oz) cheddar cheese, grated

1 Melt the butter in a large bowl for 1 min, add the oil. Stir in the celery and onion, cover and cook for 6 min.
2 Add the cabbage, water and sherry with salt and pepper to taste. Mix thoroughly.
3 Cover and cook for 9 min, stirring 3 times throughout. Stir in the mushrooms and ham, mix well, cover and cook for 3 min.
4 Stir in the grated cheese until melted, cover and allow to stand for 3 min before serving.

Peperoni *(serves 4)*
POWER LEVEL: 100% (FULL) *(colour opposite)*

25g (1oz) butter
2 × 15ml tbsp (2tbsp) olive oil
2 large red peppers, deseeded and cut into thin strips
2 large green peppers, deseeded and cut into thin strips
1 onion, finely chopped
8 tomatoes, skinned and roughly chopped
1–2 cloves garlic, crushed
salt and freshly ground black pepper
1–2 × 5ml tsp (1–2tsp) sugar to taste

1 Heat the butter and oil in a large casserole dish for 1½–2 min. Add the peppers and onion, cover and cook for 6–8 min, until the vegetables are tender, stirring 2–3 times throughout.
2 Add the tomatoes, garlic, seasoning and sugar to taste. Cook, uncovered for a further 5–6 min when the mixture should be quite soft and the juices slightly evaporated.
3 Serve hot with grilled meat or fish, or cold as a salad or starter.

Vegetable Crumble; Cabbage with Mushrooms and Ham; Peperoni

Fruits and puddings

With a good selection of fruits available, the range of desserts which can be quickly prepared or cooked by microwave is almost never ending. Jellies and gelatin for trifles or mousses can be melted in seconds, and fresh fruit in wine or liqueur can be easily prepared for a simple, really delicious sweet course; and the advantage of this fast cooking method is that all the colour, vitamins and fresh flavours are retained with very little loss of the natural juices from the fruits.

Those almost-forgotton sponge or suet puddings which took hours to cook over the steamer can be yours again with the help of the microwave—producing delicious, light textured results—in just a fraction of the time. The advantage here is that they may be made in advance and reheated quickly when required, either as a whole pudding or in individual portions if necessary, according to your family's preference.

Traditional pies cooked in the microwave are normally not so successful as the filling tends to boil out before the pastry is cooked. But conventionally cooked pies can be reheated most successfully in the microwave. Crumbles and charlottes, however, can be cooked extremely well and you will find in this section some of these together with a few more unusual dessert recipes for you to try. Many of the mixtures for puddings require similar techniques and methods to those given in the Cakes section and I would suggest you read the introductory pages to that section as a useful guide (page 169).

Most puddings freeze extremely well, perhaps with the exception of egg-custard-based ones, and with a selection available in the freezer, you have an instant sweet trolley for the family. The advantage with the microwave is that individual portions can be chosen, defrosted and then reheated while the dishes from the main course are being cleared away.

Cooking
Fresh fruit should be prepared in the usual way and sprinkled with sugar to taste. Cook in a roasting or boiling bag in a similar way to fresh vegetables although, when it is important that the fruit pieces do not break, cook them in a covered casserole when the liquid quantity should be increased and the cooking time adjusted accordingly. The fruit should be checked and stirred or turned regularly to make sure it does not overcook. Fruits cooked in their skins, such as baked apples, should first be pricked or scored to prevent the fruit from bursting during the cooking process. As most fruits may be cooked with no additional liquid, they can be sieved or puréed to make delicious sauces to pour over ice cream, natural yoghurt or puddings.

Defrosting
Frozen fruits should be partially defrosted by microwave and then allowed to stand at room temperature until completely thawed. This ensures that the delicate textures do not start to cook on the outside before the inside of the fruit is thawed. When defrosting frozen desserts, use a low 30% power level to ensure that a good even result is obtained. This is most important for cream-based sweets, otherwise the cream will quickly melt before the rest of the ingredients.

Frozen fruit defrosting chart

Fruit and quantity	50% (defrost)	100% (full)
in dry sugar 450g (1lb)	—	4–8 min stand until thawed
in sugar syrup 450g (1lb)	—	8–12 min stand until thawed
in dry pack (free flow or open frozen) 450g (1lb)	4–8 min stand until thawed	—

Dried fruits

For best results, dried fruits should be soaked overnight before cooking conventionally or by microwave. Although dried fruits can be cooked without soaking first the results will not give such tender, plump fruits. The exceptions of course are date and figs, and dried fruits used in cake making—currants, sultanas and raisins—unless specified in the recipe.

After soaking 225g (8oz) dried fruits for 6–8 hours, or overnight if possible, they should be drained and placed in a suitable container. Add sugar, syrup or honey to taste with some grated lemon rind or juice and about 275ml ($\frac{1}{2}$pt) water, or water and wine or port mixed. Cook on 100% (full) setting for approximately 15 minutes, stirring or turning the dish if necessary halfway through. Leave to stand for a few minutes before serving.

Fruit cooking chart

Fruit and quantity	Preparation	Cooking time 100% (full)	50% (defrost)
cooking apples 450g (1lb)	Peel, core and slice. Sprinkle with sugar to taste	6–8 min	11–15 min
apricots 450g (1lb)	Stone and wash. Sprinkle with sugar to taste	6–8 min	11–15 min
peaches 4 medium sized	Stone and wash. Sprinkle with sugar	4–5 min	7–8 min
pears 6 medium sized	Peel, halve and core. Dissolve 75g (3oz) sugar and a pinch of cinnamon in a little hot water. Pour over the pears	8–10 min	15–20 min
plums, cherries, damsons, greengages 450g (1lb)	Stone and wash. Sprinkle with sugar to taste and add grated rind of $\frac{1}{2}$ lemon	4–5 min	7–8 min
rhubarb 450g (1lb)	Trim, wash and cut into short lengths. Add 100g (4oz) sugar and grated rind of 1 lemon	7–10 min	14–20 min
soft fruits 450g (1lb)	Top and tail currants, hull the berries. Wash well and add sugar to taste	3–5 min	6–10 min

Strawberry flan (serves 6–8)

POWER LEVEL: 100% (FULL)

1 × 20cm (8in) baked flan case (page 248)
1 × 15ml tbsp (1tbsp) custard powder
2 × 5ml tsp (2tsp) caster sugar
150ml ($\frac{1}{4}$pt) milk
150ml ($\frac{1}{4}$pt) double cream, whipped
450g (1lb) strawberries, washed and dried
2–3 × 15ml tbsp (2–3tbsp) redcurrant jelly

1 Place the cooked flan case on a large serving plate or in its flan dish.
2 Make a custard with the custard powder, caster sugar and milk, cook for 2–3 min, stirring every minute until thick. Beat well and then leave to cool.
3 When cold, whisk the custard and fold in the whipped cream. Place the mixture in the base of the flan case and smooth the top.
4 Arrange the strawberries over the top of the custard, piling them up in the centre if necessary.
5 Heat the redcurrant jelly for 30–60 sec until melted and brush over the strawberries to make a glaze.
6 Serve when the glaze is cooled and set.

DO NOT FREEZE

Dark chocolate ice cream *(serves 4–6)*
POWER LEVEL: 100% (FULL) *(colour opposite)*

This ice cream is very quick to make. There is no need to stir it during the freezing time—you just make it with the aid of a food processor or blender and then freeze it.

50g (2oz) caster sugar
4 × 15ml tbsp (4tbsp) water
175g (6oz) plain chocolate
3 egg yolks
275ml ($\frac{1}{2}$pt) double cream
for serving: extra whipped cream and a few chopped hazelnuts for sprinkling

1 Place the sugar and water into a mixing bowl and heat in the microwave for $1–1\frac{1}{2}$ min until hot without boiling. Stir until the sugar has dissolved.
2 Replace into the microwave and bring to the boil, about 1 min and then continue to cook for $1\frac{1}{2}$ min.
3 Break the chocolate into a bowl or goblet of a food processor or blender and add the hot syrup. Blend on high speed until the chocolate is smooth.
4 Add the egg yolks and blend again for a few seconds.
5 Whip the double cream and then gently fold in the chocolate mixture until well blended.
6 Pour the mixture into a freezer container—a large polythene ice-cream container is ideal—cover with a lid and freeze until firm, about 24 hr.
7 Serve scoopfuls in individual serving glasses or dishes with extra whipped cream and a sprinkling of chopped hazelnuts. Small dessert biscuits may also be served.

Chocolate pots *(serves 4)*
POWER LEVEL: 100% (FULL) *(colour page 19)*

100g (4oz) plain chocolate
25g (1oz) butter
4 egg yolks
2 × 15ml tbsp (2tbsp) brandy or rum
2 egg whites
for decoration: whipped cream and a few chopped walnuts or almonds or grated chocolate

1 Break up the chocolate and place into a heatproof mixing bowl. Cover and cook for 2–3 min until softened and then add the butter to the dish. Cover and cook for another 1–2 min until the chocolate and the butter are melted. Mix well until smooth.
2 Beat in the egg yolks and brandy or rum. Whisk the egg whites until stiff and fold into the chocolate mixture until evenly blended together.
3 Divide the mixture between 4–5 individual dishes and chill. Before serving, decorate the tops with whipped cream and a sprinkling of chopped walnuts or almonds or grated chocolate.

Christmas pudding *(makes about 3.5 1itres/6pt)*
POWER LEVEL: 50% (DEFROST)

225g (8oz) plain flour
450g (1lb) fresh breadcrumbs
1 × 5ml tsp (1tsp) salt
2 × 5ml tsp (2tsp) mixed spice
1 orange, juice and grated rind
1 lemon, juice and grated rind
675g ($1\frac{1}{2}$lb) shredded suet
450g (1lb) brown sugar
450g (1lb) currants
450g (1lb) sultanas
225g (8oz) glacé cherries, quartered
50g (2oz) almonds, chopped
450g (1lb) raisins, stoned
100g (4oz) mixed peel
50g (2oz) ground almonds
675g ($1\frac{1}{2}$lb) cooking apples, chopped
1 medium carrot, grated
8 eggs, beaten
1 wineglass brandy or milk, beer, stout or barley wine to mix
for serving: Cornflour Sauce (page 138) and/or Rum or Brandy Butter (page 138)

1 Place the flour, breadcrumbs, salt, mixed spice, grated rinds of the orange and lemon, and the suet and sugar in a large bowl. Mix thoroughly together.
2 Add all the fruit, nuts and grated carrot and mix well. Stir in the eggs, orange and lemon juice. Stir in the brandy and/or sufficient of the milk or beer to mix to a soft dropping consistency. If time allows, leave the mixture to stand for 12–24 hr in a cool place.
3 Lightly grease or line with clingfilm some 850ml ($1\frac{1}{2}$pt) and/or 1.1 litre (2pt) pudding basins to the total capacity of 3.5 1itres (6pt). Fill the pudding basins to within about 1.25–2.5cm ($\frac{1}{2}$–1in) of the top. Cover each pudding basin with clingfilm and slit with the pointed end of a sharp knife.
4 Cook the smaller puddings for 17–20 min and the larger ones for 26–30 min. Allow them to stand for 15–20 min before removing the clingfilm and inverting on to a plate.
5 Serve hot with cornflour sauce and/or rum or brandy butter.

Note: *The puddings may be cooked and then left to mature wrapped in greaseproof paper and then in aluminium foil. On the day, they can be reheated in the microwave for $2\frac{1}{2}$–$3\frac{1}{2}$ min, depending on the size, using 100% (full) setting, or in individual portions for about 1 min each.*

Dark Chocolate Ice Cream (above); Veal Chops Gruyère (page 112); Potatoes Parisienne (page 148)

Frosted grapes *(serves 6–8)*

POWER LEVEL: 100% (FULL)

Frosted fruits make a refreshing, unusual end to a dinner party and children love them. This recipe uses grapes but redcurrants, blackcurrants or cherries are also ideal.

450–675g (1–1½lb) black or white grapes or a
  mixture
100g (4oz) granulated sugar
275ml (½pt) hot water
225g (8oz) caster sugar, approximately

1 Pick over the grapes, wash them if necessary and dry very well. Cut the stems of the bunch of grapes so that small bunches of 4–6 grapes are on each bunch.
2 Place the granulated sugar into an ovenproof mixing bowl and pour on the hot water. Stir to dissolve the sugar slightly and then heat for 1 min and stir until completely dissolved.
3 Bring to the boil, uncovered, about 2 min and then continue to cook for 7 min. Place the caster sugar into a bowl.
4 Quickly dip the grapes into the syrup, holding them by the stems or use a fork to get hold of them. Shake off the excess syrup and then dip the grapes into the caster sugar, using a spoon or fingers to toss the sugar over the grapes.
5 Place the grapes on to a tray or plate. When all the grapes have been coated, place them in a single layer on the tray and leave in a warm, airy place to dry which will take about 2–3 hr. If you have a conventional fan oven, this can be done without heat (with the fan only operating) or on a very low heat setting for ¾–1 hr.
6 Chill before serving. The frosted fruits may be stored in the refrigerator.

DO NOT FREEZE

Peach and ginger crème brûlée *(serves 6–8)*

POWER LEVEL: 100% (FULL) AND 70% *(colour page 39)*

425g (15oz) can sliced peaches, drained
50g (2oz) crystallized or stem ginger, finely chopped
4 egg yolks
25g (1oz) caster sugar
550ml (1pt) double cream
100–175g (4–6oz) granulated sugar
3–4 × 15ml tbsp (3–4tbsp) boiling water

1 Place the peaches and ginger into the base of a 1.1 litre (2pt) ovenproof glass dish.
2 Whisk the egg yolks with the caster sugar until thick and creamy.
3 Pour the cream into a bowl or jug and heat, uncovered, on 100% (full) setting for 5–6 min, stirring every minute until just on boiling point.
4 Pour the cream in a steady stream on to the egg yolks and sugar mixture, whisking until well blended. Return to the microwave and continue to cook for 1–2 min, stirring every 30 sec until thickened.
5 Carefully pour the cream over the peaches and ginger. Cook uncovered on 70% setting for 5–6 min until firm to touch and the mixture has set. Leave to cool and then chill overnight.
6 To make the topping, place the granulated sugar into a bowl and add the boiling water. Stir well and then heat for 30 sec on 100% (full) setting. Stir well again and heat for another 30 sec. Stir until all the sugar has dissolved.
7 Cook on 100% (full) setting for 5–6 min until a golden brown colour. Leave to cook slightly and then pour over the chilled cream. When set, return to the refrigerator. Crack the top of the caramel before serving.

DO NOT FREEZE

Plum pie *(serves 4–6)*
POWER LEVEL: 100% (FULL)

675g (1½lb) plums
75–100g (3–4oz) sugar
½ × 5ml tsp (½tsp) ground cinnamon
100g (4oz) plain flour
pinch salt
50g (2oz) rolled oats
75g (3oz) butter or margarine
100g (4oz) demerara sugar
for serving: whipped cream

1 Halve and stone the plums. Cover and cook them with the sugar and cinnamon for 4–5 min or until just soft, stirring once halfway through. Leave to cool. Place the fruit in a 20–22.5cm (8–9in) dish. If there is too much juice, drain some off and reserve.
2 Sift the flour with the salt, stir in the rolled oats and rub in the butter or margarine. Stir in the demerara sugar. This will make a coarse crumb mixture.
3 Sprinkle the mixture over the plums and cook for 8–10 min until the topping is cooked. Turn 2–3 times throughout.
4 Serve hot or cold with whipped cream and serve the rest of the juice separately.

Roly poly pudding *(serves 6)*
POWER LEVEL: 100% (FULL)

225g (8oz) self-raising flour
pinch salt
100g (4oz) shredded suet
150ml (¼pt) water, approximately
100g (4oz) jam or mincemeat
1 × 15ml tbsp (1tbsp) caster sugar
½ × 5ml tsp (½tsp) cinnamon
for serving: Jam Sauce (page 137) and/or Custard Sauce (page 138)

1 Sift the flour and salt together, stir in the shredded suet. Mix in sufficient cold water to form a soft, manageable dough.
2 Knead the dough lightly and roll out the pastry on a floured surface into a 22.5cm (9in) square, about 6mm (¼in) thick.
3 Warm the jam or mincemeat for 30 sec and spread over the pastry leaving a border 1.25cm (½in) all round. Roll up like a swiss roll, sealing the top and edges.
4 Place with the top edge down on a large piece of greased greaseproof paper. Roll up the paper loosely around the pastry, allowing sufficient room for it to rise.
5 Tie the ends with string or rubber bands and cover loosely with clingfilm. Place on the microwave shelf and cook for 7½–8½ min, until well risen and

cooked through. Test with a fine skewer pierced through the coverings.
6 Mix the sugar and cinnamon together. Remove the clingfilm and the greaseproof from the roly poly and sprinkle with the cinnamon sugar.
7 Serve hot with jam sauce and/or custard sauce.

Grapefruit sherbet ice *(serves 4)*
POWER LEVEL: 100% (FULL)

175g (6oz) caster sugar
1 large grapefruit
200ml (7½fl oz) water
1 × 15ml tbsp (1tbsp) lemon juice
1 egg white
pinch salt

1 Place the caster sugar into a heatproof bowl. Grate half the rind of the grapefruit and squeeze out the juice from the whole grapefruit.
2 Add the water to the caster sugar and the grated rind. Stir and heat for 3 min, then stir until the sugar has dissolved.
3 Replace into the microwave, bring to the boil and then boil for 5 min. Allow to cool.
4 Stir in the grapefruit and lemon juice. Pour the mixture into a freezer tray and freeze until icy but not solid.
5 Beat the egg white to soft peaks with the salt. Fold it into the grapefruit ice and continue to freeze for ½ hr.
6 Whip the mixture so that the egg white is well blended and then continue to freeze for 2½–3 hr.

Apple and raspberry pudding *(serves 6)*
POWER LEVEL: 70%

225g (8oz) self-raising flour
175g (6oz) shredded suet
150ml (¼pt) water, approximately
450–675g (1–1½lb) cooking apples, sliced
100g (4oz) caster sugar
1 × 425g (15oz) can raspberries, drained

1 Place the flour and the suet into a mixing bowl and mix to a soft manageable dough with water.
2 Grease an 850ml (1½pt) pudding basin and line with two-thirds of the suet pastry.
3 Layer the filling into the lined basin and roll out the remaining pastry to a circle to fit the top of the pudding. Damp and seal the edges.
4 Cover the top of the pudding with clingfilm and make a slit with the pointed end of a sharp knife.
5 Cook for 10 min and then cover the top of the pudding with aluminium foil to prevent the top from overcooking. Cook for a further 5–6 min and then allow to stand for 15 min before serving.

Cherries with chestnut cream *(serves 4)*
POWER LEVEL: 100% (FULL) *(colour opposite)*

275g (10oz) stoned frozen black cherries, thawed
2 × 15ml tbsp (2tbsp) caster sugar
4 × 15ml tbsp (4tbsp) brandy or cherry brandy
2 × 5ml tsp (2tsp) arrowroot, blended with a little
　cold water
4 × 15ml tbsp (4tbsp) chestnut purée
275ml (½pt) double or whipping cream
2 egg whites
for decoration: 2 marrons glacés or canned chestnuts

1 Place the cherries, 1 × 15ml tbsp (1tbsp) caster
　sugar and 2 × 15ml tbsp (2tbsp) of the brandy or
　cherry brandy into a bowl or dish. Cover and cook
　for 3–4 min, stirring once throughout.
2 Stir in the arrowroot blended with the water and
　heat for a further 1 min, stirring halfway through,
　until thickened. Leave to cool, then chill.
3 Mix the remaining sugar and liqueur with the
　chestnut purée. Whip the cream until stiff and fold
　three-quarters into the chestnut mixture.
4 Beat the egg whites until stiff and fold them into the
　chestnut mixture until well blended. Spoon the
　chestnut cream and cherries in layers in tall glasses
　and chill for a further ½ hr.
5 Pipe the remaining cream in whirls on the top of
　each serving and decorate with halves of marron
　glacé or canned chestnuts.

Chocolate fondue *(serves 8–10)* *(colour opposite)*
POWER LEVEL: 100% (FULL) AND 50% (DEFROST)

1 large can evaporated milk
3 × 5ml tsp (3tsp) soft dark brown sugar
175g (6oz) plain chocolate, grated
few drops vanilla essence
2 × 15ml tbsp (2tbsp) rum or brandy
for serving: grapes, marshmallows, pieces of banana
　and melon cut into bite-sized pieces

1 Place the evaporated milk, sugar and chocolate in a
　bowl, cover and cook on 100% (full) setting for
　2–3 min until the chocolate has melted; stir once
　or twice throughout.
2 Cover and bring to the boil in the microwave then
　reduce to 50% (defrost) setting and continue to
　cook for 3 min. Add the vanilla essence and rum or
　brandy. Stir well and cook uncovered, for a further
　3–4 min until the mixture thickens.
3 Serve at once, using forks or fondue spears to dip
　the fruit and marshmallows into the chocolate.

Cherries with Chestnut Cream; Highland Syllabub; Chocolate Fondue

Highland syllabub *(serves 4–6)* *(colour opposite)*
POWER LEVEL: 50% (DEFROST) AND 100% (FULL)

2 × 15ml tbsp (2tbsp) clear honey
3 × 15ml tbsp (3tbsp) whisky
1 × 15ml tbsp (1tbsp) lemon juice
275ml (½pt) double cream
1–1½ × 15ml tbsp (1–1½tbsp) fine oatmeal

1 Place the honey into a mixing bowl and heat in the
　microwave for 1–1½ min on 50% (defrost) setting
　until just warm and runny.
2 Beat in the whisky and lemon juice until well
　blended. Add the double cream and whisk the
　ingredients together until light and fluffy and the
　mixture has thickened.
3 Spoon the mixture into 4–6 individual serving
　glasses and chill for 2–3 hr.
4 'Toast' the oats by placing on a plate and cooking
　on 100% (full) setting for 4–5 min in the micro-
　wave, stirring or tossing them over every minute.
　Leave to cool.
5 Sprinkle the toasted oats over the top of the
　syllabubs before serving.

Note: *Tiny sprigs of heather with the stalks wrapped in
foil make an attractive and decorative garnish for the
syllabubs.*

Orange cheese flan *(serves 6–8)*
POWER LEVEL: 50% (DEFROST) *(colour page 90)*

175g (6oz) digestive biscuits, crushed
2 × 5ml tsp (2tsp) caster sugar
75g (3oz) butter, melted
for the filling:
450g (1lb) cream cheese
75g (3oz) caster sugar
2 eggs, beaten
1 orange, grated rind
1 × 15ml tbsp (1tbsp) orange juice
for decoration: thinly sliced orange and whipped
　cream

1 Mix the biscuit crumbs, caster sugar and butter
　until well blended. Press the mixture into the base
　and around the sides of a 20cm (8in) flan dish. Chill
　in the refrigerator.
2 For the filling, beat the cheese until smooth, then
　beat in the sugar and the eggs gradually. When
　well blended, beat in the orange rind and juice.
3 Pour the filling on to the prepared flan base and
　cook for 15–20 min until set, turning the dish if
　necessary 3–4 times.
4 Leave to cool and then chill for 1 hr. Decorate with
　thinly sliced orange and pipe with whipped cream
　before serving.

Strawberry flambé *(serves 4–6)*
POWER LEVEL: 100% (FULL)

100g (4oz) light brown sugar
150ml (¼pt) orange juice
1 × 15ml tbsp (1tbsp) lemon juice
2 × 15ml tbsp (2tbsp) grated orange peel
1 × 15ml tbsp (1tbsp) grated lemon peel
675g (1½lb) strawberries, washed and hulled
3–4 × 15ml tbsp (3–4tbsp) brandy
for serving: ice cream

1 Place the sugar, fruit juices and peel into a large microwave heatproof serving dish. Cover and cook for 2–3 min until bubbling, stirring once or twice to dissolve the sugar.
2 Add the strawberries to the dish and turn over so that the fruit is evenly coated with the syrup.
3 Place the brandy in a small bowl or mug and heat for 15–30 sec until hot.
4 Quickly pour the brandy over the strawberries and ignite. Do not ignite in the microwave.
5 Spoon the juices over the strawberries and serve with ice cream.

DO NOT FREEZE

Pears in red wine *(serves 4)*
POWER LEVEL: 100% (FULL) *(colour page 15)*

275ml (½pt) red wine
demerara sugar to taste
1 orange, grated rind
2.5cm (1in) cinnamon stick
½ × 5ml tsp (½tsp) grated nutmeg
4 cooking pears
for serving: cream

1 Place the red wine, sugar, orange rind and spices in a large dish, cover and bring to the boil in the microwave and then cook for 2 min, uncovered.
2 Peel the pears and cut in half lengthways. Remove the cores and place the pear halves, cut side down, into the wine.
3 Cover and cook for about 5 min or until tender. Remove the pears and boil the wine in the microwave until slightly reduced.
4 Replace the pears into the hot wine and leave to cool.
5 Serve cool or chilled with whipped cream.

Rice pudding *(serves 3–4)*
POWER LEVEL: 100% (FULL) 50% (DEFROST)

50g (2oz) pudding rice
25g (1oz) caster sugar
25g (1oz) butter
550ml (1pt) milk
for serving: 1 × 5ml tsp (1tsp) ground nutmeg, optional

1 Place all ingredients for the pudding in a 1.1 litre (2pt) dish or bowl and stir.
2 Leave the dish uncovered and bring to boiling point on 100% (full), 7–10 minutes, stirring every 5 min.
3 Reduce to 50% (defrost) setting and cook for 25–30 minutes stirring every 5 min.
4 Sprinkle with ground nutmeg before serving hot or cold.

Baked stuffed apples

POWER LEVEL: 100% (FULL)

4 medium cooking apples
40g (1½oz) butter
50g (2oz) demerara sugar
25g (1oz) sultanas, currants or seedless raisins
2 × 15ml tbsp (2tbsp) chopped almonds
2 × 15ml tbsp (2tbsp) water
1 × 15ml tbsp (1tbsp) lemon juice
1½ × 15ml tbsp (1½tbsp) golden syrup
for serving: cream or Egg Custard Sauce (page 137)

1 Core the apples but do not peel. Score them around the middle and place them in a suitable serving dish.
2 Mix together the butter, sugar, fruit and nuts. Fill the centre of each apple with the mixture.
3 Blend the water, lemon juice and syrup together and spoon over the apples.
4 Cover the apples with greaseproof paper and cook for 6–8 min.
5 Serve hot or cold with cream or custard.

Note: *Cook 1 apple for 2–3 min; cook 2 apples for 4–5 min.*

Creamed rice caramel *(serves 4–6)*

POWER LEVEL: 100% (FULL)

550ml (1pt) quantity Rice Pudding (page 164)
150ml (¼pt) whipping or single cream
1 egg, beaten
6 × 15ml tbsp (6tbsp) caster sugar
3 × 15ml tbsp (3tbsp) hot water

1 Make up and cook the rice pudding as given on page 164 and leave until cool.
2 Beat together the cream and egg in a small bowl. Cook, uncovered, for 2½–3 min, stirring every 30 sec until the cream has thickened but do not allow the mixture to boil.
3 In a food processor or blender, purée the rice pudding and then add the cream mixture. Divide this between 4–6 small individual serving dishes or ramekin dishes. Chill in the refrigerator until firm.
4 Mix together the sugar and water in a heatproof jug or bowl. Heat, uncovered for 1 min and then stir until the sugar has dissolved.
5 Replace into the microwave and heat and allow to boil for 5–6 min until the caramel has turned to a pale straw colour.
6 Quickly pour the caramel over the top of the creamed rice and allow to set.
7 Before serving chilled, crack the set caramel with the bowl of a spoon.

DO NOT FREEZE WITH THE CARAMEL TOPPING

Lemon honey pudding *(serves 5–6)*

POWER LEVEL: 100% (FULL)

100g (4oz) butter or margarine
100g (4oz) caster sugar
2 eggs, beaten
75g (3oz) self-raising flour
pinch salt
25g (1oz) fresh white breadcrumbs
1 lemon, grated rind and juice
1–2 × 15ml tbsp (1–2tbsp) hot water
3 × 15ml tbsp (3tbsp) clear honey
for serving: Lemon Foamy Sauce (page 136) and warmed honey

1 Lightly grease a 850ml (1½pt) pudding basin.
2 Cream the butter or margarine and caster sugar together until light.
3 Add the eggs gradually, beating well after each addition.
4 Sift the flour and salt together and fold into the creamed mixture. Stir in the breadcrumbs and grated lemon rind.
5 Fold in the lemon juice and sufficient hot water to make a soft mixture.
6 Place the honey in the bottom of the prepared basin and place the sponge mixture on top. Press down and smooth the top.
7 Cover with clingfilm, slit with the pointed end of a sharp knife. Cook for 6–7 min.
8 Leave to stand for 5 min before inverting on to a serving plate.
9 Serve hot with lemon foamy sauce and a little extra warmed honey.

Raspberry mousse *(serves 4)*

POWER LEVEL: 100% (FULL) *(colour page 95)*

275ml (½pt) raspberry purée (page 166)
2–3 × 15ml tbsp (2–3tbsp) caster sugar
150ml (¼pt) double cream
3 × 15ml tbsp (3tbsp) raspberry juice or water
15g (½oz) gelatin
2 egg whites, whisked
for decoration: whipped cream

1 Place the raspberry purée into a mixing bowl and stir in the caster sugar to taste.
2 Whip the double cream and fold into the raspberry purée.
3 Place the raspberry juice or water into a small bowl or jug and sprinkle on the gelatin.
4 Heat for 15–30 sec and stir until the gelatin is dissolved completely and then allow to cool slightly.
5 Pour the gelatin into the raspberry mixture in a steady stream, stirring the mixture all the time.

6 Fold in the whisked egg whites carefully with a metal spoon, cutting and turning until smooth.
7 Pour into a serving dish or into individual serving glasses.
8 Chill before serving piped with whipped cream.

Note: *2 × 425g (15oz) cans raspberries, drained or 450g (1lb) fresh or frozen raspberries are sieved or blended into a liquidiser or food processor to make 275ml (½pt) purée.*

Raisin pudding *(serves 6)*
POWER LEVEL: 70% *(colour opposite)*

75g (3oz) self-raising flour
75g (3oz) fresh brown breadcrumbs
75g (3oz) shredded suet
25g (1oz) soft brown sugar
pinch salt
225g (8oz) raisins, stoned
25g (1oz) walnuts, chopped
1 lemon, grated rind and juice
2 eggs, beaten
milk for mixing
for serving: warmed honey or syrup and cream

1 Lightly grease an 850ml (1½pt) pudding basin.
2 Sift the flour into a mixing bowl and add all the dry ingredients, fruit, nuts and lemon rind. Mix well together.
3 Add the lemon juice, eggs and sufficient milk to make a soft mixture. Mix well together.
4 Place the mixture into the prepared pudding basin, smooth the top and cover with clingfilm. Make a slit with the pointed end of a sharp knife.
5 Cook for 11 min, turning once halfway through. Leave to stand for 5 min.
6 Invert on to a serving plate and serve hot with a little warmed honey or syrup and cream.

Bananas hawaiian *(serves 4)*
POWER LEVEL: 100% (FULL) *(colour opposite)*

4 firm bananas
1 lemon, juice and grated rind
50g (2oz) demerara sugar
50g (2oz) desiccated coconut
25g (1oz) raisins
25g (1oz) butter
for serving: cream or Egg Custard Sauce (page 137)

1 Peel the bananas, cut in half lengthways and place in a serving dish. Sprinkle with lemon juice.
2 Mix the grated lemon rind with the sugar, coconut and raisins. Melt the butter for 1 min and stir into the mixture.

3 Cover the bananas with the topping and cook, uncovered, for 6 min.
4 Serve hot or cold with cream or custard.

DO NOT FREEZE

Prune compôte *(serves 4–6)*
POWER LEVEL: 100% (FULL) *(colour opposite)*

350g (12oz) large prunes, soaked overnight
4 × 15ml tbsp (4tbsp) clear honey
275ml (½pt) boiling water
275ml (½pt) port or red wine
1 orange, grated rind
25g (1oz) flaked almonds
for serving: cream

1 Drain the prunes and place in a casserole dish with the honey, boiling water and port or red wine. Stir in the grated orange rind.
2 Cover and cook for about 15 min until the fruit is tender, stirring once or twice throughout. Leave to stand for 15 min.
3 Serve hot or cold with the flaked almonds scattered on the top.

Apple crumble *(serves 6)*
POWER LEVEL: 100% (FULL)

675g (1½lb) cooking apples
75–100g (3–4oz) caster sugar
75g (3oz) plain flour
75g (3oz) wholemeal flour
pinch salt
75g (3oz) butter or margarine
50g (2oz) demerara sugar
2 × 15ml tbsp (2tbsp) finely chopped walnuts
for serving: cream

1 Lightly grease a 1.1 litre (2pt) pie dish or large soufflé dish.
2 Peel, core and slice the apples and place in the bottom of the prepared dish. Sprinkle with the caster sugar.
3 Mix together the flours and salt, and rub in the butter or margarine finely. Reserving 1 × 15ml tbsp (1tbsp) demerara sugar, stir the rest into the crumb mixture with the walnuts.
4 Sprinkle the crumb mixture lightly over the fruit and cook for 10–12 min, giving the dish a quarter turn every 3 min.
5 Sprinkle with the remaining demerara sugar and serve hot or cold with cream.

Prune Compôte; Raisin Pudding; Bananas Hawaiian

Trifle *(serves 8–10)*

POWER LEVEL: 100% (FULL) *(colour page 11 and front cover)*

A trifle can be as basic or as exotic as you care to make it and although the precise ingredients may be varied according to the foods you have in store, the basic requirements are sponge cake, biscuits, jam, nuts, fruit, custard and cream, at best displayed in layers in a clear glass bowl. I used fresh exotic fruits to obtain the special effect I wanted for the trifle pictured on the front cover, but almost any dessert or cooked fruits could be used.

for the custard:
3 eggs, separated
75g (3oz) caster sugar
25g (1oz) cornflour
20g (¾oz) plain flour
425ml (¾pt) milk
150ml (¼pt) double cream, lightly whipped

2 egg quantity whisked sponge cake see Jam Sponge (page 170)
675g (1½lb) fruit, cooked (page 157) *or* fresh fruit, ie 2 kiwi fruits, 2 star fruits, 2 mangoes, stoned
225g (8oz) red jam
2–3 × 15ml tbsp (2–3tbsp) water
275ml (½pt) white wine, approximately
8 macaroons
16 ratafia biscuits
50g (2oz) flaked almonds, toasted
for decoration: sliced kiwi fruit, whipped cream, chocolate triangles, Chocolate Caraque (page 180) or toasted flaked almonds

1 To make the basic custard, mix the egg yolks with 40g (1½oz) of the sugar. Add the cornflour and the flour, mix well together and stir in 150ml (¼pt) of the milk. Heat the remaining milk in a jug for 2½–3 min to boiling point and pour into the egg mixture, stirring well. Return the mixture to the microwave and cook for 2½–3 min, stirring every 30 sec until thickened and cooked. Beat well, then cover with wet greaseproof paper and leave until cold.
2 Make up the whisked sponge mixture and cook for 2–3 min. Leave to stand for a few minutes before turning onto a wire rack to cool.
3 Prepare and cook the fruit if necessary, referring to the chart on page 157. Drain off the juice and leave until cold. (Some of the fruit juice may be reserved and mixed with some wine for soaking the cake if preferred, see point 5 below.) Cut dessert fruits into slices.
4 Heat the jam and water together for 30–45 sec, stir well and heat for another 30 sec. Leave until cold.

5 When the cake is cold, cut into 2.5cm (1in) cubes. Sprinkle the cake, macaroons and ratafias with the white wine (or white wine and fruit juice mixed).
6 Whisk the egg whites until stiff, add the remaining 40g (1½oz) caster sugar and whisk again until stiff and glossy. Beat into the cold custard and then fold in the whipped cream.
7 To layer the trifle, place the sponge cake into the bottom of a deep glass bowl and drizzle with the jam sauce. Sprinkle with half the almonds and place the macaroons on top; arrange the ratafias around the edge.
8 Arrange any sliced dessert fruit (ie kiwi and star fruit slices) around the outside edge of the bowl. Place the cooked fruit or sliced dessert fruit (ie mangoes) over the top of the macaroons and ratafias. Sprinkle with the rest of the almonds.
9 Carefully pour the custard over the fruit and smooth the top. Refrigerate for 2–3 hr until well chilled.
10 Decorate with swirls of whipped cream, sliced kiwi fruit and chocolate or flaked almonds.

DO NOT FREEZE

Rhubarb charlotte *(serves 6–8)*

POWER LEVEL: 100% (FULL)

450g (1lb) rhubarb, trimmed and cut into 2.5cm (1in) lengths
100g (4oz) butter or margarine
2 lemons, grated rind and juice
100g (4oz) caster sugar
450g (1lb) cake crumbs or brown breadcrumbs
1 × 5ml tsp (1tsp) ground mixed spice
1 × 15ml tbsp (1tbsp) demerara sugar
for serving: whipped cream

1 Place the rhubarb into a bowl with 25g (1oz) butter or margarine. Add the lemon rind and juice and the caster sugar. Cover and cook 7–10 min until tender.
2 Melt the rest of the butter for 2–3 min and stir in the cake or breadcrumbs and the mixed spice. Stir well so that the crumbs are evenly coated in the butter.
3 Layer the crumb mixture with the rhubarb in a 17.5–20cm (7–8in) cake dish or soufflé dish, starting and finishing with a layer of crumbs.
4 Sprinkle the top with demerara sugar and cook uncovered for 5–6 min.
5 Serve hot or cold with whipped cream.

Cakes, biscuits and scones

Although a microwave-cooked cake does not brown as when baking in a conventional oven, there is much to be said for the fact that it can be cooked in next to no time resulting in a good, light texture and a delicious flavour usually associated with a home-baked one. Many cakes are self-coloured anyway—chocolate or coffee cakes and gingerbreads—and for those that are not, a variety or toppings, icings and frostings or simply a dusting of icing sugar can be used to cleverly disguise the paler result and make them virtually indistinguishable from conventionally cooked cakes.

Most containers, including paper, can be used for cooking the cakes, but those with straight sides generally give a better shape. If a container needs lining, lightly greased greaseproof paper or clingfilm may be used, although with the latter a slightly moist base to the cake may result. Do not sprinkle the container with flour as this forms a doughy crust on the outside of the cake.

Cooking
Wetter cake mixtures are the most successful in the microwave and therefore the liquid quantities given in the recipes may seem greater than those you normally use. As cakes rise extremely well, the container should not be more than half filled with the uncooked mixture to allow for rising during cooking. If a cake starts to rise unevenly, simply give it a turn every $1\frac{1}{2}$–2 minutes during a 6 minute cooking period, although this may be unnecessary in those microwave cookers with turntables. During cooking, the centre cooks more slowly than the outside of the cake, therefore it may be necessary to hollow out the middle of stiffer or richer mixtures before cooking to prevent the top surface from doming. A trussing needle or fine skewer can be inserted into the cake to test whether it is cooked. If the skewer comes out clean and dry, the cake is cooked. However, it is always better to remove the cake when it is very slightly moist on top as it will finish setting during its standing time. Do not be impatient and invert the cake too soon on to a cooling rack; it should be left to cool for 5–15 minutes depending on its texture before turning out. To avoid the edges of the cake sticking when it is left to stand and cool in its container, roll it around gently in the container after cooking. This will bring the cake away from the edges and ensure a neat result.

Not all biscuit mixtures can be baked in the microwave cooker but those recipes given in this section will enable you to achieve success with 'cookie' types and a few specialities. As biscuits are best made in small quantities and eaten quickly, the microwave is ideal. After cooking, allow them to set before removing to a cooling rack. When cool, store them immediately on their own (never with cakes) in an airtight tin.

Scones are very quickly cooked and can be made while preparing the rest of the tea. Alternatively, they can be cooked in advance and just reheated in the microwave to serve warm or hot with cream and jam—1 or 2 minutes is usually sufficient for a plateful of scones. When cooking several scones, biscuits or small cakes together in the microwave, they should be arranged in a circle where possible; if some are cooked before others, remove them from the oven, then rearrange and leave the remainder to carry on cooking.

Defrosting
In order to ensure that cream does not melt before the rest of the cake is completely thawed, it is best to give a large, frozen cream cake only $\frac{1}{2}$–$\frac{3}{4}$ minute exposure to

microwave energy and then let it stand until completely thawed. I normally find that it is preferable to allow individual cream cakes to thaw naturally. Other large cakes may be given 2–3 minutes in the microwave and then allowed to stand for 5–10 minutes before serving. An individual cake, scone or slice of cake requires only 15–30 seconds in the microwave depending on size and type and is then allowed to stand for 2 minutes before serving. Do not allow frozen cakes to get hot when thawing as this may result in a dry cake. As soon as it feels warm, remove the cake from the cooker and allow it to stand and heat equalise before serving. If it is not then completely thawed, put it back into the microwave for another minute.

Most biscuits will thaw out very quickly at room temperature; one or two should be heated in the microwave for not longer than 10–25 seconds and a plate of biscuits for no longer than 1 minute. Leave them to stand for a few minutes before serving. Any biscuits or pastries will remain crispier if placed on and covered with kitchen paper towel or paper serviette while defrosting. If they are left to stand, still covered, for a few minutes, moisture will be absorbed by the paper and not by the biscuit or pastry.

Jam sponge *(cuts into 8)*
POWER LEVEL: 100% (FULL)

4 eggs
100g (4oz) caster sugar
100g (4oz) plain flour
pinch salt
jam
whipped cream, optional
icing sugar for dusting

A light sponge cake which relies on the whisking of air into the eggs as the raising agent, best eaten on the day it is made.

1 Line an 18.75–20cm (7½–8in) cake dish with clingfilm, or lightly grease and line the base with greaseproof paper.
2 Whisk the eggs and sugar together until trebled in volume and really thick and creamy.
3 Sift the flour and salt and sprinkle over the mixture, very carefully folding in with a metal spoon and turning the mixture over from the base of the bowl to ensure all the flour is mixed in.
4 Pour into the prepared container and cook for 4½–5 min. Leave for 5–10 min before placing on a cooling rack.
5 When cold, cut in half horizontally and sandwich the two halves together with jam and cream. Dust the top with icing sugar.

VARIATION

Genoese sponge sandwich *(cuts into 8)*
(colour opposite)

This cake has better keeping qualities than the jam sponge and makes a good base for various fillings and toppings for richer gâteaux.

Follow the ingredients and method for Jam Sponge. Melt 50g (2oz) butter for 1–1½ min and add to the thickened mixture with the flour by pouring the melted butter in a thin stream down the side of the bowl while folding in the flour and butter with a metal spoon. Fold in very carefully, ensuring that the spoon cuts across the base of the bowl so that all the flour and butter are well mixed in. Cook and decorate as for jam sponge.

Frosted walnut gâteau *(cuts into 8)*
POWER LEVEL: 100% (FULL) *(colour opposite)*

The basic cake is cut into 3 or 4 thin layers and is usually better made one or two days in advance.

4 egg quantity Genoese Sponge (preceding recipe)
3 × 15ml tbsp (3tbsp) chopped walnuts
150ml (½pt) double cream, whipped
Quick American Frosting (page 172)
8 walnut halves for decoration

1 Follow the ingredients, method and cooking for genoese sponge.
2 When cooked and cold, carefully cut the cake horizontally into 3 or 4 thin circles. (Often it is easier to cut if the cake is made 1 or 2 days before and kept well wrapped or in an airtight tin.)
3 Fold the chopped walnuts into the whipped cream and use to sandwich the layers together.
4 Cover the sides and top of the cake with the quick american frosting, using a palette knife to give a swirled effect. Decorate the top with 8 halves of walnut.

VARIATIONS

Frosted cherry gâteau *(cuts into 8)*

Follow the ingredients and method for the frosted walnut gâteau, substituting a small bottle of maraschino cherries for the walnuts. Drain and halve the cherries and add the whipped cream. Sandwich the layers together and cover with quick american frosting, tinted pale pink with a few drops of cochineal added during the whisking. Decorate the top with small pieces of glacé cherry.

Frosted Walnut Gâteau (above); Genoese Sponge Sandwich (above); Farmhouse Fruit Cake (page 172)

Frosted pineapple gâteau (*cuts into 8*)

Follow the ingredients and method for the frosted walnut gâteau substituting 3 × 15ml tbsp (3tbsp) chopped, drained canned or fresh pineapple for the walnuts. Sandwich the layers together and cover with quick american frosting, tinted pale yellow with a few drops of yellow food colouring. Decorate the top with glacé or crystallized pineapple.

Note: *If freezing these cakes, freeze the basic cake on its own or in layers with the whipped cream filling. Just before serving, coat with the quick american frosting and decorate.*

Quick american frosting

2 egg whites
400g (14oz) caster sugar
pinch salt
4 × 15ml tbsp (4tbsp) water
2 × 5ml tsp (2tsp) cream of tartar

1 If using an electric table mixer, place all ingredients except the cream of tartar into the bowl and whisk on full speed. When stiff add the cream of tartar.
2 If using a hand mixer or rotary whisk, place all ingredients into a bowl over a bowl or pan of hot water and whisk for 5 min. Remove from the heat and allow to cool for 4–5 min. Whisk again until thick and shiny and holding shape.
3 This quantity is sufficient to coat the outside of a 20–22.5cm (8–9in) cake. Half quantity would be sufficient to coat the outside of a 15–17.5cm (6–7in) cake.

DO NOT FREEZE

Farmhouse fruit cake (*cuts into 8–10*)
POWER LEVEL: 100% (FULL) (*colour page 171*)

100g (4oz) butter
100g (4oz) light soft brown sugar
2 eggs, beaten
175g (6oz) self-raising flour
1 × 5ml tsp (1tsp) mixed spice
100g (4oz) mixed dried fruit
few drops vanilla essence
milk for mixing
Apricot Glaze (page 180) *or* icing sugar for dusting, optional

1 Lightly grease a 20cm (8in) microwave ring mould.
2 Cream the butter, add the sugar and beat together until light and fluffy. Add the eggs gradually, beating well after each addition.
3 Sift the flour and mixed spice and fold into the creamed mixture alternately with the fruit, using a metal spoon. Stir in the vanilla essence and sufficient milk to make a soft mixture.
4 Place into the prepared ring mould and cook for 5–6 min, turning every 2 min. Leave for 10–15 min before turning on to a cooling rack.
5 When cold, brush with apricot glaze or dust with icing sugar.

Christmas cake (*makes 1*)
POWER LEVEL: 30%

175g (6oz) sultanas
175g (6oz) raisins
225g (8oz) currants
75g (3oz) glacé cherries, halved
75g (3oz) mixed peel, chopped
25g (1oz) ground almonds
25g (1oz) almonds, chopped
2 × 15ml tbsp (2tbsp) beer, ale or milk
3–4 × 15ml tbsp (3–4tbsp) lemon or orange juice
$\frac{1}{4}$ × 5ml tsp ($\frac{1}{4}$tsp) coffee essence
few drops each almond, vanilla and rum essence
65g (2$\frac{1}{2}$oz) caster sugar
75g (3oz) soft brown sugar
165g (5$\frac{1}{2}$oz) butter
grated rind $\frac{1}{2}$ orange and $\frac{1}{2}$ lemon
3 eggs, beaten
175g (6oz) plain flour
$\frac{1}{2}$ × 5ml tsp ($\frac{1}{2}$tsp) nutmeg
1 × 5ml tsp (1tsp) mixed spice
$\frac{1}{4}$ × 5ml tsp ($\frac{1}{4}$tsp) salt
few drops gravy browning, optional

1 Place all the prepared fruits and nuts into a bowl and mix well together. Stir in the liquid ingredients and essences and leave to stand for about 1 hr.
2 Cream the sugars with the butter and grated rinds until light and fluffy. Beat in the eggs.
3 Sift the flour with the spices and salt and stir into the creamed mixture alternately with the fruits. Add extra liquid if required to give a medium dropping consistency. Add a few drops of gravy browning if a darker mixture is preferred.
4 Turn the mixture into an 18.75cm (7$\frac{1}{2}$in) cake dish which has been lightly greased and the base lined with a circle of greaseproof paper. Smooth the top and slightly hollow out the centre.
5 Cook for about 50 min, turning the dish 3–4 times throughout, although this may be unnecessary if the microwave has a turntable.
6 Leave the cake to cool before turning out of the dish. To store, wrap the cake in fresh greaseproof paper and then completely in foil. A small amount of brandy or sherry can be brushed over the top and sides of the cake at regular intervals during storage.

Chocolate fudge cake *(cuts into 8)*
POWER LEVEL: 100% (FULL)

100g (4oz) white shortening
275g (10oz) light soft brown sugar
2 eggs, beaten
225g (8oz) plain flour
½ × 5ml tsp (½tsp) baking powder
1 × 5ml tsp (1tsp) bicarbonate of soda
pinch salt
50g (2oz) cocoa
150ml (¼pt) cold water
Chocolate Fudge Icing (following recipe)

1 Lightly grease an 18.75cm (7½in) cake dish and line the base with a circle of greaseproof paper.
2 Cream the fat, add the sugar and beat together until light and fluffy.
3 Add the eggs gradually, beating well after each addition.
4 Sift the flour with the baking powder, bicarbonate of soda and salt. Blend the cocoa with the water.
5 Stir the flour into the creamed mixture alternately with the cocoa and water, using a metal spoon.
6 Place the mixture into the prepared container and cook for 7–8 min, turning every 2 min. (The mixture will rise up well during cooking, but will sink back a little towards the end of the cooking.)
7 Leave until cool before turning on to a wire rack.
8 When cold, cover top and sides with chocolate fudge icing.

DO NOT FREEZE WITH THE ICING

Chocolate fudge icing
POWER LEVEL: 100% (FULL)

25g (1oz) butter
50g (2oz) soft brown or demerara sugar
2 × 15ml tbsp (2tbsp) cocoa
3 × 15ml tbsp (3tbsp) cold water
2 × 5ml tsp (2tsp) milk
225g (8oz) icing sugar, sifted
2 × 15ml tbsp (2tbsp) warm water
few drops vanilla essence

1 Place the butter and sugar into a large bowl. Blend the cocoa with the cold water and add to the bowl with the milk.
2 Heat for 1–2 min, stir until the sugar is dissolved.
3 Heat until boiling, then allow to boil for 2–2½ min.
4 Add icing sugar, warm water and vanilla essence. Mix well together then beat well for 5 min.
5 Pour over the cake while still warm as this icing sets when cold.

DO NOT FREEZE

Marble cake *(cuts into 8)*
POWER LEVEL: 100% (FULL)

175g (6oz) butter or margarine
175g (6oz) caster sugar
3 eggs, beaten
225g (8oz) self-raising flour
pinch salt
1 × 15ml tbsp (1tbsp) cocoa blended with a little hot water
few drops cochineal
½ × 5ml tsp (½tsp) vanilla essence
Feathered Glacé Icing or Buttercream (following recipes below) and hundreds and thousands

1 Line a 21.25–22.5cm (8½–9in) cake dish with clingfilm or grease and line the base with greaseproof paper.
2 Cream the butter or margarine until soft, add the sugar and beat together until light and fluffy.
3 Add the eggs gradually, beating well after each addition.
4 Sift flour and salt, fold into the creamed mixture with a metal spoon. Divide between 3 bowls.
5 To one bowl add and mix the cocoa and water; to the second add a few drops of cochineal to give a good colour; to the third add the vanilla essence.
6 Place spoonfuls of the mixtures into the prepared dish, alternating the colours then lightly swirl them together.
7 Cook for 7–8 min, turning the dish every 2 min.
8 Leave to cool 10–15 min before removing cake to a wire rack.
9 When cold, decorate with feathered glacé icing, or buttercream tinted pale pink, and hundreds and thousands.

Glacé icing: mix 175g (6oz) sifted icing sugar with sufficient hot water to make a soft paste, thick enough to coat the back of a spoon. Mix well and use immediately.

DO NOT FREEZE

Feathered icing: make up glacé icing and coat the top of the cake. With a fine paintbrush, draw lines with two food colourings alternately across the surface of the icing or in graduated circles from the centre to the outside edge. Alternatively, pipe tinted glacé icing in lines using a fine writing nozzle. Draw a fine skewer through the lines of colouring, alternating the direction to give a feathered effect. Leave to set before cutting the cake.

DO NOT FREEZE

Buttercream: soften 75g (3oz) butter and gradually add 175g (6oz) sifted icing sugar. Beat well after each addition and then beat until light and fluffy. Flavour and colour as required.

Buttercream flavourings

Chocolate: melted plain chocolate or a little cocoa powder dissolved in warm water.

Coffee: coffee essence or a little instant coffee dissolved in warm water.

Orange: finely grated rind of orange.

Lemon: finely grated rind of lemon.

Chocolate layer gâteau *(cuts into 8)*
POWER LEVEL: 100% (FULL) *(colour opposite)*

4 egg quantity Genoese Sponge (page 170)
225g (8oz) Chocolate Buttercream (above)
100g (4oz) plain chocolate, grated
Chocolate Caraque, optional (page 180)
icing sugar for dusting

1 Follow the ingredients, method and cooking for genoese sponge.
2 When cooked and cold, cut into 3 horizontally and sandwich together with some of the buttercream. Reserve some buttercream for piping.
3 Spread the remaining buttercream around the sides and over the top of the cake and dip into the grated chocolate.
4 Pipe the reserved buttercream around the top of the cake and dust with sifted icing sugar.

Iced scone round *(cuts into 6)*
POWER LEVEL: 100% (FULL) *(colour opposite)*

225g (8oz) self-raising flour
pinch salt
$\frac{1}{2}$ × 5ml tsp ($\frac{1}{2}$tsp) mixed spice
$\frac{1}{2}$ × 5ml tsp ($\frac{1}{2}$tsp) baking powder
50g (2oz) butter or margarine
2 × 5ml tsp (2tsp) sugar
75g (3oz) mixed dried fruits
milk for mixing
for decoration: Glacé Icing (page 173) quartered glacé cherries, few chopped almonds or walnuts

1 Lightly grease an 18.75cm (7$\frac{1}{2}$in) round flan dish and line the base with greaseproof paper.
2 Sift flour, salt, mixed spice and baking powder into a bowl. Cut up the butter or margarine and rub into the flour finely.
3 Stir in the sugar with the fruit and sufficient milk to make a soft manageable dough. Knead lightly on a floured surface.
4 Roll out to about 1.25cm ($\frac{1}{2}$in) thick. Using a 6.25cm (2$\frac{1}{2}$in) cutter, cut into 7 rounds, rerolling the dough if necessary. Place 6 around the outside edge of the prepared container and 1 in the centre. Alternatively, roll into a round and mark into 8 triangles.

5 Cook uncovered for 3–4 min, turning the dish halfway through if necessary. Leave to cool on a wire rack.
6 When cold, decorate the top of the scone round with glacé icing, quartered glacé cherries and a sprinkling of chopped almonds or walnuts.

DO NOT FREEZE WITH GLACÉ ICING

Lemon cup cakes *(makes about 36)*
POWER LEVEL: 100% (FULL) *(colour opposite)*

24 paper cake cases, approximately
225g (8oz) self-raising flour
pinch salt
100g (4oz) butter or margarine
100g (4oz) soft brown sugar
2 eggs, beaten
2 lemons, grated rind and juice
milk for mixing
Lemon Glacé Icing (page 173)

1 Place 6 paper cake cases into a microwave muffin pan or bun tray.
2 Sift the flour and salt, rub in the butter or margarine finely and stir in the sugar. Mix in the eggs, lemon rind and juice and sufficient milk to form a soft dropping consistency.
3 Place spoonfuls of the mixture into the cake cases, filling them each about one-third full.
4 Cook for about 1$\frac{1}{2}$ min, turning the dish once halfway through. Place on to a cooling rack and cook the remaining mixture in batches of 6.
5 When cold, coat the tops with lemon glacé icing.

DO NOT FREEZE WITH THE ICING

Melting moments *(makes 12)*
POWER LEVEL: 100% (FULL) *(colour opposite)*

100g (4oz) butter
50g (2oz) soft brown sugar
few drops vanilla essence
100g (4oz) plain flour
25g (1oz) cocoa powder
pinch salt
25g (1oz) porridge oats
6 glacé cherries

1 Cream together the butter and sugar thoroughly. Add the vanilla essence and beat in to the creamed mixture.
2 Sieve the flour, cocoa powder and the salt and stir

Iced Scone Round; Melting Moments; Chocolate Layer Gâteau; Lemon Cup Cakes

in to the creamed mixture mixing well together.

3 Lightly flour your fingers and form the mixture into a sausage shape. Cut into 12 pieces and roll each piece into a ball.

4 Dip each ball into the porridge oats, pressing the oats well on to the surface of the biscuits. Place 6 on to the microwave oven shelf arranging them in a circle, and press each biscuit down lightly with a palette-knife or a fork.

5 Cut the cherries in halves and place a half on to each biscuit. Cook uncovered, for $2-2\frac{1}{4}$ min. Allow to stand for a few minutes before removing to a cooling rack. Repeat with the remaining biscuits.

VARIATION

Chocolate and walnut slices: follow the recipe given above, omitting the oats and cherries. Form the mixture into a 25cm (10in) sausage and brush with egg white before rolling in 50g (2oz) chopped walnuts. Cut into 24 slices and cook 12 at a time for $2-2\frac{1}{4}$ min. Remove to a wire rack and repeat with the remaining biscuits.

Lemon and honey cake *(cuts into 6)*
POWER LEVEL: 100% (FULL)

100g (4oz) self-raising flour
65g ($2\frac{1}{2}$oz) caster sugar
2 × 15ml tbsp (2tbsp) clear honey
1 egg, beaten
60ml (2fl oz) milk
75ml ($2\frac{1}{2}$fl oz) oil
1 lemon, grated rind and juice
clear honey and Lemon Buttercream (page 174)

1 Sieve the flour if necessary and stir in the sugar. Beat in the honey and egg.

2 Whisk together the milk and the oil and beat this into the mixture. Finally beat in the lemon rind and juice. This will produce a batter type of mixture.

3 Pour into a 20cm (8in) round dish, which has been lined with lightly greased greaseproof paper or clingfilm. Cook for 3–4 min.

4 Allow to cool before turning out. Spread the top of the cake with clear honey and pipe with lemon buttercream.

Note: *This cake does not keep well and is best eaten on the day it is made.*

Victoria sandwich *(cuts into 8)*
POWER LEVEL: 100% (FULL)

175g (6oz) butter or margarine
175g (6oz) caster sugar
3 eggs, beaten
175g (6oz) plain flour
pinch salt
2 × 5ml tsp (2tsp) baking powder
2 × 15ml tbsp (2tbsp) hot water
jam or Buttercream (page 173)
icing sugar for dusting

1 Line an 18.75–20cm ($7\frac{1}{2}$–8in) cake dish with clingfilm or lightly grease and line the base with greaseproof paper.

2 Cream the butter or margarine until soft, add the sugar and beat well together until light and fluffy.

3 Add the eggs gradually, beating well after each addition.

4 Sift the flour, salt and baking powder and fold into

the creamed mixture carefully with a metal spoon. Add the hot water and fold into the mixture.
5 Turn the mixture into the prepared dish and cook for $6\frac{1}{2}$–$7\frac{1}{2}$ min. Leave for 5–10 min before placing on a cooling rack.
6 When cold, cut in half horizontally and sandwich the two halves together with jam or buttercream. Dust the top with icing sugar.

Ginger glacé icing: sift 175g (6oz) icing sugar together with 1×5ml tsp (1tsp) ground ginger. Mix with sufficient hot water to make a soft paste, thick enough to coat the back of a spoon. Mix well and use immediately.

DO NOT FREEZE

Orange or lemon glacé icing: mix together 175g (6oz) sifted icing sugar with sufficient strained orange or lemon juice to give a thick icing. A few drops of orange or lemon colouring may be added to give a little more colour.

DO NOT FREEZE

Coffee or chocolate glacé icing: sift 175g (6oz) icing sugar into a bowl. Dissolve a little instant coffee or cocoa powder in hot water and add to the icing sugar to make a soft paste, thick enough to coat the back of a spoon.

DO NOT FREEZE

Marmalade cake *(cuts into 8)*
POWER LEVEL: 70%

225g (8oz) self-raising flour
pinch salt
100g (4oz) butter or margarine
100g (4oz) soft brown sugar
2 eggs, beaten
2 oranges, grated rind
2×15ml tbsp (2tbsp) orange marmalade
milk for mixing
few drops orange colouring, optional
Apricot Glaze (page 180)

1 Line an 18.75–20cm ($7\frac{1}{2}$–8in) cake dish with clingfilm or lightly grease and line the base with greaseproof paper.
2 Sift the flour and salt, rub in the butter or margarine finely and stir in the sugar.
3 Mix in the eggs, orange rind, marmalade and sufficient milk to form a soft dropping consistency; add a few drops of orange colouring if required.
4 Turn the mixture into the prepared dish and cook for 8–10 min. Allow to cool slightly before removing from the dish on to a cooling rack.
5 When cold, brush with apricot glaze.

Chocolate and biscuit cake *(cuts into 8)*
POWER LEVEL: 100% (FULL) *(colour page 23)*

This is a very easy no-bake cake that children will love.

100g (4oz) chocolate cake covering, plain flavour
75g (3oz) butter or margarine
1 egg, size 3
175g (6oz) icing sugar, sieved
200g (7oz) rich tea biscuits, crushed
50g (2oz) unsalted toasted peanuts, skins removed
50g (2oz) seedless raisins

1 Break up the chocolate cake covering and place into a bowl with the butter. Cook for 3–4 min until melted and beat well until blended.
2 Beat the egg and add to the chocolate mixture mixing well together; stir in the icing sugar.
3 Reserve 2×15ml tbsp (2tbsp) of the mixture and add all the remaining ingredients to the rest. Mix well.
4 Spread the cake mixture into a 20cm (8in) sandwich tin which should be lined with greased greaseproof paper.
5 Level the top of the cake with the back of a metal spoon, pressing down well. Pour over the reserved icing and spread evenly over the surface of the cake with a palette-knife.
6 Leave the cake to set in a cool place. Loosen the edge of the cake from the tin with a knife and turn out. Remove the greaseproof paper and place the cake on to a plate. Serve cut into wedges.

Crystallized ginger cake *(cuts into 12–16 wedges)*
POWER LEVEL: 100% (FULL) AND 70%

100g (4oz) butter
225g (8oz) black treacle
75g (3oz) soft brown sugar
2×15ml tbsp (2tbsp) orange marmalade
150ml ($\frac{1}{4}$pt) milk
$\frac{1}{2} \times 5$ml tsp ($\frac{1}{2}$tsp) bicarbonate of soda
100g (4oz) self-raising flour
2×5ml tsp (2tsp) ground ginger
1×5ml tsp (1tsp) mixed spice
100g (4oz) wholemeal flour
75g (3oz) crystallized ginger
2 eggs, beaten

1 Line a 22.5cm (9in) cake dish with clingfilm or a circle of greased greaseproof paper.
2 Place the butter, treacle, sugar and marmalade into a bowl and heat on 100% (full) setting for 2–3 min until melted and then stir until blended.
3 Warm the milk for 30 sec on 100% (full) and stir in the bicarbonate of soda.

4 Sift the self-raising flour with the spices and stir in the wholemeal flour. Add 50g (2oz) of the ginger to the dry ingredients.

5 Add the treacle mixture, milk and eggs to the dry ingredients and mix thoroughly until smooth.

6 Pour the mixture into the prepared dish and cook on 70% setting for 12–15 min, turning every 3 min. Remove from the microwave while still slightly moist on top and sprinkle with the remaining ginger. Allow to stand until set and serve warm or cold cut into wedges.

One stage coffee cake *(cuts into 8)*
POWER LEVEL: 100% (FULL) *(colour opposite)*

175g (6oz) soft margarine
175g (6oz) caster sugar
3 eggs, beaten
175g (6oz) self-raising flour
pinch salt
1 × 15ml tbsp (1tbsp) instant coffee granules dissolved in 2 × 15ml tbsp (2tbsp) hot water
Coffee Buttercream (page 174)
Coffee Glacé Icing (page 173) *or* icing sugar for dusting

1 Line an 18.5–20cm (7½–8in) cake dish with cling-film or lightly grease and line the base with grease-proof paper.

2 Place all the ingredients except the buttercream and glacé icing or icing sugar into a bowl and mix until combined, then beat well until smooth.

3 Place mixture into prepared dish, smooth the top and cook for 6½–7½ min. Leave for about 10 min before placing on cooling rack.

4 When cold, cut in half horizontally and sandwich together with buttercream. On the top, coat with glacé icing or dust with icing sugar.

DO NOT FREEZE WITH GLACÉ ICING

Date fudge fingers *(makes 16)*
POWER LEVEL: 100% (FULL) *(colour opposite)*

200g (7oz) Marie or semi-sweet biscuits, crumbled
50g (2oz) walnuts, chopped
100g (4oz) dates, stoned and chopped
½ × 5ml tsp (½tsp) vanilla essence
2 × 5ml tsp (2tsp) cocoa powder
2 × 5ml tsp (2tsp) instant coffee powder
175g (6oz) plain chocolate
250g (9oz) condensed milk

1 Lightly grease a 20cm (8in) square or equivalent size oblong dish or tin.

2 Mix the biscuit crumbs, walnuts and dates together.

3 Place the rest of the ingredients into a bowl and melt in the microwave for 2–3 min. Stir well until blended.

4 Pour the melted mixture on to the dry ingredients and mix thoroughly.

5 Turn into the prepared container and press down well, smooth the top and mark into fingers.

6 Place in the refrigerator until set. Cut into fingers before serving.

Sultana girdle scones *(makes 8–10)*
POWER LEVEL: 100% (FULL) *(colour opposite)*

Traditionally cooked on a girdle, these microwave 'girdle' scones are cooked in a browning dish.

225g (8oz) plain flour
pinch salt
1 × 15ml tbsp (1tbsp) baking powder
50g (2oz) butter or margarine
1 × 5ml tsp (1tsp) sugar
2 × 15ml heaped tbsp (2 heaped tbsp) sultanas
150ml (¼pt) milk or milk and water mixed
oil

1 Sift flour, salt and baking powder into a bowl. Rub in the butter or margarine finely. Stir in the sugar with the sultanas and mix to a manageable soft dough with the milk or milk and water.

2 Knead lightly on a floured surface and roll into a round, approximately 6mm (¼in) thick. Cut into rounds with a 5cm (2in) cutter or cut the large round into 8 triangles.

3 Preheat the browning dish for 4–5 min, depending on size. Lightly brush the base with oil.

4 Quickly place the scones into the browning dish, arranging the triangles with the pointed ends towards the centre.

5 Cook for 1 min, turn the scones over and the dish round, cook for a further 1½–2 min.

6 Leave to cool on wire rack. Serve hot or cold, split and buttered.

VARIATION

Cheese girdle scones: follow the ingredients and method for sultana girdle scones omitting the sugar and sultanas, and add 50g (2oz) grated cheese to the dry ingredients.

One Stage Coffee Cake (above); Date Fudge Fingers (above); Light Wholemeal Loaf (page 205); Strawberry Jam (page 188); Sultana Girdle Scones (above); Devilled Sardines on Toast (page 91)

Cinnamon streusel cake (makes 1)

POWER LEVEL: 100% (FULL)

This goes well served warm with coffee.

225g (8oz) self-raising flour
$\frac{1}{2}$ × 5ml tsp ($\frac{1}{2}$tsp) salt
$\frac{1}{2}$ × 5ml ($\frac{1}{2}$tsp) baking powder
75g (3oz) white shortening or lard
175g (6oz) caster sugar
1 egg, beaten
150ml ($\frac{1}{4}$pt) milk, approximately
Cinnamon Streusel Topping (below)

1 Lightly grease an 18.75cm ($7\frac{1}{2}$in) cake dish and line the base with greaseproof paper.
2 Sift the flour, salt and baking powder into a bowl, rub in the fat finely and stir in the sugar.
3 Add the egg with sufficient milk to make a very soft mixture. Beat thoroughly.
4 Turn the mixture into the prepared container and cook until the mixture is risen and the top is just set, approximately 4 min. Sprinkle with the prepared topping and continue to cook for $1\frac{1}{2}$–2 min.
5 Leave until nearly cold before removing from the dish. Serve warm cut into wedges.

Cinnamon streusel topping

25g (1oz) butter
75g (3oz) soft brown sugar
25g (1oz) plain flour
1 × 5ml tsp (1tsp) cinnamon
50g (2oz) walnuts, chopped

Heat the butter for 1 min, add the remaining ingredients and mix well together with a fork. The mixture should resemble coarse breadcrumbs.

Black Forest gâteau

POWER LEVEL: 100% (FULL) *(colour page 127)*

4 egg quantity chocolate-flavoured Genoese Sponge (page 170)
2 × 425g (15oz) cans black cherries
2 × 15ml tbsp (2tbsp) kirsch or cherry brandy
425ml ($\frac{3}{4}$pt) double or whipping cream
75g (3oz) plain chocolate
Chocolate Caraque, optional (following recipe)

1 Follow the ingredients and method for the genoese sponge substituting 25g (1oz) cocoa for 25g (1oz) flour. When cooked, allow to cool and cut in half horizontally.
2 Drain the cherries, reserving 150ml ($\frac{1}{4}$pt) of the juice. Add the kirsch or cherry brandy to the reserved juice and use to moisten the cake halves. Stone the cherries.

3 Whip the cream until it is just holding its shape. Spread some over the bottom cake layer, and top with half the cherries. Place the top cake layer over the cherries.
4 Cover the sides and top of the cake with cream, reserving a little for decoration.
5 Grate the chocolate and press into the sides of the cake, reserving a little for decoration.
6 Place the cake on to its serving plate or dish and arrange the remaining cherries on the top. Pipe the remaining cream around the top edge and sprinkle with the remaining grated chocolate. Alternatively, arrange chocolate caraque over the top of the cherries and cream.

Note: *One can of cherry pie filling can be used instead of one can of the black cherries to fill the middle of the cake.*

Chocolate caraque

POWER LEVEL: 100% (FULL)

Melt about 75g (3oz) plain chocolate for 2–3 min. Stir until smooth and spread the chocolate thinly on to a flat, smooth surface such as a worktop, marble slab or laminate chopping board. When nearly set, using a long, sharp knife and a slight sawing movement, shave the chocolate off the top surface holding the knife almost upright. Long rolls or flakes will form which are best chilled in the refrigerator before using to decorate a cake.

Apricot glaze

POWER LEVEL: 100% (FULL)

Place 450g (1lb) apricot jam in a bowl with 2 × 15ml tbsp (2tbsp) lemon juice and 4 × 15ml tbsp (4tbsp) water. Mix well together and then bring to the boil in the microwave. Allow to boil for 2–3 min, stirring frequently. Sieve and allow to cool and thicken slightly before use. This keeps very well in a covered jar so can be made in large quantities.

Chocolate chip cakes (makes about 24)

POWER LEVEL: 100% (FULL)

24 paper cake cases, approximately
175g (6oz) butter or margarine
175g (6oz) caster sugar
3 eggs, beaten
175g (6oz) self-raising flour
pinch salt
75g (3oz) polka dots (chocolate chips)
milk for mixing

1 Place 6 paper cake cases into a 6 ring microwave muffin pan or bun tray.

2 Cream the butter or margarine, add the sugar and beat well together until light and fluffy.

3 Add the eggs gradually, beating well after each addition. Sift the flour and salt and gradually fold into the creamed mixture with the polka dots. Mix in a little milk to give a soft consistency.

4 Place spoonfuls of the mixture into the paper cases filling them no more than two-thirds full. Cook for $2-2\frac{1}{2}$ min, turning the dish once halfway through.

5 Remove on to a cooling rack and cook the remainder in batches of 6.

Note: *The cakes may be placed directly on to the oven shelf in the paper cases although not such a good shape will result. Arrange them in a circle and cook as above.*

Cherry strudel *(serves 6−8)*
POWER LEVEL: 100% (FULL)

Thinly rolled puff pastry makes a good substitute for strudel paste when in a hurry.

50g (2oz) butter or margarine
75g (3oz) white breadcrumbs
175g (6oz) frozen puff pastry, thawed
25g (1oz) butter, melted
450g (1lb) cherries, stoned and halved
1 × 15ml tbsp (1tbsp) soft brown sugar
1 × 5ml tsp (1tsp) cinnamon
$\frac{1}{2}$ lemon, grated rind
icing sugar for dredging

1 Preheat a browning dish for 5−6 min, add the butter or margarine and, when melted, toss the breadcrumbs in the butter and cook until lightly browned for about 2 min.

2 Roll out the pastry very thinly into a large rectangle on a lightly floured surface. Spread with the melted butter.

3 Scatter the breadcrumbs over the butter then scatter on the halved cherries.

4 Mix the sugar and cinnamon and sprinkle over the cherries; sprinkle with the grated lemon rind.

5 Fold over about 2.5cm (1in) of the pastry over the mixture on both of the shorter sides and brush with water.

6 Roll up the strudel, starting from one of the longer sides. Dampen the other long side and seal. Curve the strudel to form the shape of the letter C.

7 Carefully place the strudel on kitchen paper and slide on to a microwave baking tray or, if preferred, directly on the cooker shelf.

8 Cook for 6−7 min, turning halfway through the cooking time.

9 Leave to cool on a cooling rack. Sprinkle heavily with icing sugar. Serve in slices, hot or cold.

Strawberry shortcake *(serves 6−8)*
POWER LEVEL: 100% (FULL)

40g ($1\frac{1}{2}$oz) strawberry-flavoured blancmange powder
175g (6oz) plain flour
1 × 5ml tsp (1tsp) cream of tartar
$\frac{1}{2}$ × 5ml tsp ($\frac{1}{2}$tsp) bicarbonate of soda
pinch of salt
50g (2oz) butter or margarine
50g (2oz) caster sugar
1 egg, beaten
milk for mixing

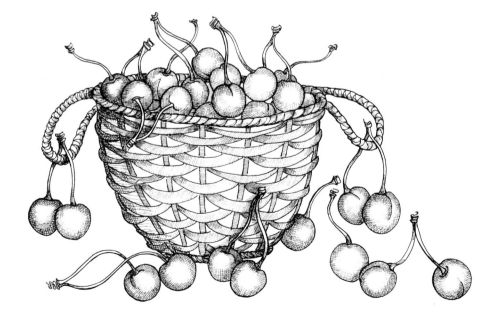

for serving:
225g (8oz) strawberries
275ml (½pt) double cream
caster sugar to taste
butter for spreading

1 Line a 15–17.5cm (6–7in) flan dish with clingfilm.
2 Sift together the blancmange powder, flour, raising agents and salt. Rub in the butter or margarine finely and stir in the sugar.
3 Add the egg and sufficient milk to make a soft manageable dough. Knead lightly and roll out on a floured surface into a circle to fit the flan dish.
4 Place the dough into the prepared dish and cook for about 6 min turning once halfway through.
5 Leave for 5–10 min before removing on to a wire rack to cool.
6 Hull, wash and dry the strawberries. Reserving a few whole ones for decoration, cut the rest into slices.
7 Whip the double cream and stir in the caster sugar to taste.
8 Cut the cold shortcake in half horizontally. Spread the bottom half with a little softened butter and then the whipped cream, piling it up in the centre and reserving some for piping.
9 Place the sliced strawberries on the cream and top with remaining shortcake layer and cut into wedges.
10 Pipe the remaining cream on the top and decorate with the whole strawberries.

Potato girdle scones *(makes 12–16)*
POWER LEVEL: 100% (FULL)

1–2 × 5ml tsp (1–2tsp) salt
450g (1lb) potatoes, cooked and mashed
50g (2oz) butter
100g (4oz) flour
oil

1 Add salt to taste to the potatoes with the butter. Work in sufficient flour to give a stiff mixture.
2 Knead lightly on a floured surface and roll out to a thickness of 6mm (¼in). Cut into rounds with a 5cm (2in) cutter or into triangles.
3 Preheat the browning dish for 4–5 min depending on size and lightly brush the base with oil.
4 Quickly place half the scones in the browning dish, cook for 1 min, turn the scones over and the dish round, cook for 1½–2 min.
5 Reheat the browning dish for 1–2 min and cook the second batch as before.
6 Serve hot, spread with butter.

Note: *If using leftover cold potatoes, heat them through after mashing, as hot potatoes give lighter scones.*

Devonshire wholemeal scone round *(cuts into 6 or 8 wedges)*
POWER LEVEL: 100% (FULL)

100g (4oz) plain flour
pinch salt
1 × 5ml tsp (1tsp) bicarbonate of soda
1 × 5ml tsp (1tsp) cream of tartar
100g (4oz) wholemeal flour
2 × 5ml tsp (2tsp) sugar
50g (2oz) butter or margarine
150ml (¼pt) buttermilk or fresh milk with
    1½ × 5ml tsp (1½tsp) baking powder
for serving: butter, jam and whipped cream

1 Lightly grease a 17.5cm (7in) round flan dish and line the base with greaseproof paper.
2 Sift the flour, salt, bicarbonate of soda and cream of tartar into a bowl; stir in the wholemeal flour and sugar. Rub in the butter or margarine finely.
3 Stir in the buttermilk or fresh milk with baking powder and mix to a soft dough. Knead lightly on a floured surface.
4 Roll out or shape into a round about 17.5cm (7in) in diameter and place in prepared container. Score to half the depth into 6 or 8 wedges. Dust with wholemeal flour.
5 Cook for 4½–5 min. Serve hot or cold split into wedges, with butter, jam and cream.

Oatmeal scone round *(cuts into 10 wedges)*
POWER LEVEL: 100% (FULL) *(colour page 15)*

rolled oats for sprinkling
275g (10oz) plain flour
175g (6oz) rolled oats
1 × 5ml tsp (1tsp) salt
1 × 5ml tsp (1tsp) bicarbonate of soda
1 × 5ml tsp (1tsp) cream of tartar
100g (4oz) butter or margarine
1 × 15ml tbsp (1tbsp) caster sugar
275ml (½pt) buttermilk or sour milk, approximately

1 Lightly grease a 22.5cm (9in) round dish and line the base with greaseproof paper; sprinkle with oats.
2 Sift the flour, mix in the oats, salt and raising agents. Rub in the butter or margarine finely and mix in the sugar.
3 Add sufficient of the milk to mix to a light scone dough. Knead lightly on a floured surface and shape into a round about 2.5cm (1in) thick.
4 Place into the prepared container. Score or cut into 10 wedges and sprinkle the top with oats.
5 Cook for 5 min, turning once halfway through. If necessary, test with a skewer and give an extra minute if not quite cooked.
6 Leave for 10–15 min before turning on to a wire rack to cool.

Treacle girdle scones *(makes 8)*
POWER LEVEL: 100% (FULL)

275g (10oz) plain flour
½ × 5ml tsp (½tsp) salt
1 × 5ml tsp (1tsp) bicarbonate of soda
1 × 5ml tsp (1tsp) cream of tartar
50g (2oz) butter or margarine
2 × 15ml tbsp (2tbsp) black treacle
150ml (¼pt) sour or fresh milk
oil

1 Sift flour, salt and raising agents. Rub in the butter or margarine finely.
2 Mix the treacle with the milk and stir into the dry ingredients.
3 Knead lightly on a floured surface and roll or shape into a round about 1.25cm (½in) thick. Cut across making 8 triangles.
4 Preheat the browning dish for 4–5 min depending on size and lightly brush the base with oil.
5 Quickly place the scones in the dish, arranging the triangles with the pointed ends towards the centre.
6 Cook for 1 min, turn the scones over and the dish round, and cook for 1½–2 min.
7 Serve hot or cold, split and spread with butter.

Chocolate oat cookies *(makes approximately 60)*
POWER LEVEL: 100% (FULL)

100g (4oz) plain chocolate
100g (4oz) butter
175g (6oz) brown sugar
2 eggs, beaten
100g (4oz) plain flour
1 × 5ml tsp (1tsp) baking powder
1 × 5ml tsp (1tsp) salt
75g (3oz) walnuts, chopped
175g (6oz) rolled oats
2 × 5ml tsp (2tsp) vanilla essence

1 Break up the chocolate and place into a bowl. Heat for 2–3 min until melted and then beat. Leave to cool.
2 Cream the butter and sugar, beat in the eggs and cooled chocolate.
3 Sieve the flour, baking powder and salt together and then add to the creamed mixture. Stir in the walnuts, oats and vanilla essence and beat well.
4 Place in walnut-sized pieces on to the microwave oven shelf; cook 6–7 at a time and make sure there is sufficient room for them to spread during cooking. Cook each batch for 2 min; remove them from the oven and leave to cool on a wire rack.

Florentine fingers *(makes about 16)*
POWER LEVEL: 100% (FULL) AND 70%

75g (3oz) butter
3 × 15ml tbsp (3tbsp) golden syrup
100g (4oz) rolled oats
25g (1oz) soft brown sugar
25g (1oz) peel, finely chopped
25g (1oz) glacé cherries, finely chopped
25g (1oz) walnuts, finely chopped
100g (4oz) plain chocolate

1 Lightly grease a 20cm (8in) square dish or equivalent size oblong dish and line the base with rice paper.
2 Melt the butter and golden syrup for 1½ min on 100% (full) setting. Stir until blended and stir in all the other ingredients except the chocolate.
3 Spoon the mixture into the prepared dish and press over the base.
4 Reduce to 70% and cook for about 6 min, turning every 2 min. Allow to cool slightly, cut into squares and place on a cooling rack until cold.
5 Melt the chocolate for 2–3 min and spread over the base of the florentines. When nearly set, make ripples in the chocolate with the prongs of a fork.

Tea-time cookies *(cuts into 24)*
POWER LEVEL: 100% (FULL)

100g (4oz) butter or margarine
150g (5oz) soft brown sugar
2 large eggs, beaten
175g (6oz) self-raising flour
100g (4oz) chocolate buttons
100g (4oz) sultanas
50g (2oz) walnuts, chopped
few drops vanilla essence

1 Cream together the butter or margarine with the sugar and beat in the eggs.
2 Stir in the remaining ingredients and mix well together. Place the mixture into a lightly greased dish approximately 27.5 × 17.5cm (11 × 7in).
3 Smooth the top. Cook uncovered for 7–8 min until firm. Allow to stand for 10 min before marking into fingers. Remove from the dish on to a cooling rack.

Preserves

Preserve making in the microwave simplifies what can sometimes be a long, laborious process. Small quantities can be made with such little fuss or bother that it is very easy to build up a stock of different varieties of microwave-cooked preserves without that feeling that you have to give some away to friends and relatives because you just wouldn't have the room to store them all, let alone eat them!

One important advantage is that very good, clear colours are achieved, just what is needed for jams and marmalades; and for chutneys the ingredients can be cooked quickly and to the preferred degree of softness, without the worry of overcooking or the foods sticking to the base of the cooking container—the kitchen remains cooler and free of smells too which is an important consideration when cooking chutneys!

Fruits such as gooseberries, blackcurrants, red-currants, damsons and citrus fruits all have a high pectin content and will achieve very good sets. Strawberries, apricots and cherries are lower in pectin and therefore better results are obtained with these fruits if citric acid, lemon juice or commercial pectin is added. For some jams, blackcurrant for example, the liquid quantity is reduced compared with conventional recipes, as there is very little evaporation from the surface during cooking in the microwave oven. At the same time, however, it is important to soften the fruit and release the pectin during the initial cooking stage, therefore the balance of water to fruit needs to be correct. As a general rule, cut the quantity of water by one-third when converting your own jam recipes.

On the other hand, in marmalade making, about the same quantity of water to fruit is required as for conventional methods to ensure that the peel is softened sufficiently before adding the sugar and boiling for the final set. Sugar may be warmed for a few minutes in the microwave before adding to the cooked fruit. This will cut down on the length of time required to dissolve the sugar.

Use a large heat-resistant bowl or dish for cooking the preserves—approximately 3 litre (6pt)—ensuring that there is enough room for expansion when the preserves are boiling. For larger quantities, conventional preserving is probably faster, unless you are prepared to divide into smaller amounts and cook one at a time in the microwave.

Test your jams and marmalades for setting point in the usual way, by pouring a little on to a saucer and leaving it to cool for a few minutes. Setting point is reached if the skin formed on the top wrinkles when touched. Alternatively, a sugar thermometer can be used when the temperature should reach 105°C (220°F), although some fruits require a degree or two higher than this to obtain a satisfactory set. The thermometer should not be left in the oven when cooking unless specially designed for use in the microwave. The glass jars can be sterilized by adding water to each and heating in the microwave until the water is boiling rapidly. Drain the jars and pour in the preserve. Top with waxed discs and when completely cold, cover the jars with cellophane tops and label clearly.

184

Quince jelly *(makes about 1¾kg/3½lb)*
POWER LEVEL: 100% (FULL)

1½kg (3lb) unripe quinces, washed
850ml (1½pt) hot water, approximately
675g (1½lb) preserving sugar, approximately
1 lemon, pared rind and juice

1 Cut the quinces into small pieces and place in a large bowl with sufficient hot water barely to cover the fruit. Cover and cook for 12–15 min until tender.
2 Put the fruit and water through a jelly bag or cloth and measure the extract. You will need 450g (1lb) sugar for every 550ml (1pt) juice.
3 Stir the sugar into the extract and continue to stir until dissolved. If necessary, heat for 2–3 min at a time to boost the temperature of the extract.
4 Add the pared lemon rind and the lemon juice and cook uncovered in the microwave until setting point is reached, about 35–40 min.
5 Remove the lemon rind, pour into warm jars, seal and label.

Note: *If ripe quinces are used, commercial pectin or 6g (¼oz) citric acid may be required to assist with the setting of the jelly.*

Spiced cranberry preserve *(makes about 275ml/½pt)*
POWER LEVEL: 100% (FULL)

225g (8oz) cranberries, washed
small piece each of root ginger and cinnamon stick
6 cloves
½ × 5ml tsp (½tsp) ground allspice
150ml (¼pt) cider vinegar
100g (4oz) demerara sugar

1 Place the cranberries in a covered dish with the spices and cider vinegar.
2 Cook for 5–6 min or until the fruit is soft.
3 Add the demerara sugar and cook for a further 3 min.
4 Remove root ginger, cinnamon stick and cloves.
5 Pot and seal in small jars.
6 Serve cold with roast turkey or chicken.

Apple jelly *(makes about 1kg/2¼lb)*
POWER LEVEL: 100% (FULL)

Windfall cooking apples may be used for this jelly but not dessert apples.

1½kg (3lb) cooking apples, washed
1 lemon, juice
850ml (1½pt) water
675g (1½lb) preserving sugar, approximately

1 Cut the apples into thick slices without peeling or coring. Place in a large bowl with the lemon juice and water.
2 Cover and cook for about 30–35 min until the apples are soft, stirring every 10 min.
3 Strain the pulp through a jelly cloth and measure the extract. There should be approximately 850ml (1½pt). (If it is more or less than this quantity, the sugar should be adjusted accordingly. You will need 450g/1lb sugar for every 550ml/1pt extract.)
4 Return the extract to the bowl and stir in the sugar until it has dissolved.
5 Cook uncovered for 30–35 min until setting point is reached, stirring every 10 min.
6 Pot, seal and label.

Note: *The jelly is a very pale colour—just tinged with pink. Add a few redcurrants or raspberries to the apples when cooking to give a slightly deeper colour if preferred.*

Blackcurrant jam *(makes about 1kg/2¼lb)*
POWER LEVEL: 100% (FULL)

550g (1¼lb) blackcurrants
425ml (¾pt) boiling water
675g (1½lb) preserving sugar

1 Remove stalks, wash the fruit, drain well and place into a large bowl with the boiling water.
2 Bring to the boil in the microwave then cook for about 5 min until the fruit is tender.
3 Stir in the sugar until dissolved. Cook uncovered for 25–30 min or until setting point is reached, stirring every 5 min.
4 Allow to stand for 20 min and then pour into warmed jars. Seal and label.

Apricot jam *(makes about 2½kg/5lb)*
POWER LEVEL: 100% (FULL)

1¾kg (3½lb) apricots
225ml (8fl oz) water
6g (¼oz) citric acid
2kg (4lb) preserving sugar
25g (1oz) blanched almonds, split and cut into slivers

1 Wash, halve and stone the apricots. Place in a large glass bowl with the water and citric acid.
2 Cover with a lid or clingfilm slit with the pointed end of a sharp knife. Cook for 15–20 min, stirring 2–3 times throughout.
3 Add the sugar and stir well. Cook uncovered for 45–50 min, or until setting point is reached, stirring every 5–10 min.
4 Stir in the almonds and allow to cool before potting the jam so that the almonds do not float to the surface. Seal and label.

Sweet piccalilli *(makes 1¼–1½kg/2½–3lb)*
POWER LEVEL: 100% (FULL) *(colour opposite)*

900g (2lb) mixed vegetables, ie cauliflower, onion,
   cucumber, courgettes, peppers
175g (6oz) salt
425ml (¾pt) distilled malt vinegar
75g (3oz) demerara sugar
2 × 5ml tsp (2tsp) turmeric
1½ × 5ml tsp (1½tsp) dry mustard
1½ × 5ml tsp (1½tsp) ground ginger
20g (¾oz) cornflour

1 Cut the cauliflower into small florets and chop the
   onions; cut all the other vegetables into small dice.
2 Layer the prepared vegetables in a bowl with the
   salt, cover and leave for 24 hr. Rinse thoroughly
   and drain.
3 Reserve 2 × 15ml tbsp (2tbsp) vinegar. Place the
   rest in a large bowl with the sugar and spices and
   mix well.
4 Add the vegetables, cover and cook for 10–15 min
   depending on the required crispness. Stir once
   halfway through.
5 Blend the cornflour with the reserved vinegar. Stir
   into the pickle and cook, uncovered, for 5–6 min
   until thick, stirring every 2 min.
6 Pour into warmed jars, seal and label.

Note: *The piccalilli is best made about 6 weeks before
required to allow the flavours to blend.*

Diabetic marmalade *(makes about 2½kg/5lb)*
POWER LEVEL: 100% (FULL)

4 large oranges
550ml (1pt) boiling water
1½kg (3lb) sorbitol
1 × 225ml (8fl oz) bottle of commercial pectin

1 Wash and dry the fruit, then place in the microwave and heat for 2 min. Squeeze the juice and
   place in a large bowl. Remove and discard the pith
   and pips.
2 Shred the orange peel finely and add to the juice
   with the boiling water. Cover and cook for
   15–20 min, stirring once.
3 Add the sorbitol and stir well. Cook, uncovered for
   25 min stirring every 5 min.
4 Remove the marmalade from the microwave and
   add the pectin. Allow to stand for 10 min then pour
   into small warmed jars and seal immediately.
5 Diabetic marmalade is best if sterilized. This may be
   done conventionally on a trivet in a saucepan on
   the hob, or in the microwave using a temperature
   probe. If no temperature probe is fitted to your
   model, a thermometer may be used instead, but this
   should not be left in the microwave during the

heating process unless specially designed. For steri-
lizing by microwave, stand the jars in a deep bowl
so that they do not touch and cover the jars with
cold water. Heat for approximately 1 hr on 50%
(defrost) setting, to a temperature of 72°C (164°F).
Hold at this temperature for 10 min.

Note: *Use small jars with metal screw-tops for the
diabetic marmalade.*

Sweet orange marmalade
(makes about 2¾kg/5½lb)
POWER LEVEL: 100% (FULL) *(colour opposite)*

5 large oranges
juice of 2 lemons
850ml (1½pt) boiling water
1.8kg (4lb) granulated sugar

1 Wash and dry the fruit, then heat in the microwave
   for 2 min. Squeeze the juice from the fruit and place
   in a large bowl.
2 Remove the pith and pips from the fruit, tie in a
   clean J-cloth or muslin and place in a bowl with the
   juice.
3 Finely shred the orange peel and add to the bowl
   with the boiling water. Cover and cook for
   25–30 min, depending on the thickness of the peel.
   Stir once during cooking.
4 Remove the muslin bag, add the sugar and stir well.
   Cook for 20–25 min until setting point is reached,
   stirring every 5 min.
5 Allow to stand for 30-40 min, then pour into
   warmed jars, seal and label.

Note: *If a softer peel is required, allow to stand in the
water for 1 hr before cooking.*

Dried fruits jam *(makes 1¾kg/3½lb)*
POWER LEVEL: 100% (FULL)

450g (1lb) semi-dried prunes
100g (4oz) split almonds, roughly chopped
450g (1lb) seedless raisins
550ml (1pt) water
450g (1lb) demerara sugar

1 Chop the prunes, almonds and raisins and place
   them in a large bowl with the water. Cover and
   cook for 15 min, stirring once halfway through.
2 Add the sugar and stir well. Cook, uncovered, for
   15 min or until setting point is reached, stirring
   every 5 min.
3 Pour into warmed jars, seal and label.

Sweet Orange Marmalade; Sweet Piccalilli

Strawberry jam *(makes about 1½kg/3lb)*
POWER LEVEL: 100% (FULL) *(colour page 179)*

1¾kg (3½lb) strawberries, hulled and washed
15g (½oz) citric acid
1¼kg (2¾lb) preserving sugar

1 Place the strawberries in a large bowl. Sprinkle with the citric acid and cook for about 15 min until soft, stirring 2–3 times throughout.
2 Add the sugar and stir well. Cook the jam, un-covered, for 40 min or until setting point is reached. Stir the jam every 10 min at the beginning of cooking and every 5 min towards the end.
3 Allow the jam to stand for 20–30 min. Pour into warmed jars, seal and label.

Red tomato chutney *(makes about 1¼kg/2½lb)*
POWER LEVEL: 100% (FULL)

225g (8oz) onions, finely chopped
1½kg (3lb) ripe tomatoes, skinned and chopped
15g (½oz) salt
1 × 5ml tsp (1tsp) paprika
good pinch of cayenne pepper
150ml (¼pt) distilled malt vinegar
175g (6oz) granulated sugar

1 Place the onions in a large bowl, cover and cook for 5 min, stirring once.
2 Add the tomatoes and cook for a further 8 min, uncovered, until the vegetables are soft and pulpy. Stir once during cooking.
3 Add the salt, spices and vinegar. Cook for 5 min, stir; continue to cook for a further 5 min.
4 Add the sugar and stir well. Cook uncovered for 35–40 min, until thick, stirring occasionally.
5 Pour into warmed jars, seal and label.

Sweet damson pickle *(makes about 1kg/2¼lb)*
POWER LEVEL: 50% (DEFROST) AND 100% (FULL)

900g (2lb) damsons, washed
rind ½ lemon
6 cloves
6 allspice seeds
small piece each root ginger and cinnamon stick
450g (1lb) brown sugar
275ml (½pt) vinegar

1 Place the whole damsons into a large bowl. Tie the lemon rind and spices in a muslin bag.
2 Dissolve the sugar in the vinegar and pour over the damsons.
3 Cover with a lid or clingfilm slit with the pointed end of a knife and cook for 12–15 min on 50% (defrost) setting until the damsons are tender.
4 Drain and reserve the vinegar; pack the fruit neatly into warmed jars.
5 Boil the vinegar in the microwave on 100% (full) setting until it is reduced to a thin syrup.
6 Pour over the fruit in the jars, seal and label immediately.

Cucumber relish *(makes 1¼–1½kg/2½–3lb)*
POWER LEVEL: 100% (FULL)

2 cucumbers, weighing approximately 900g (2lb)
2 onions, chopped
25g (1oz) salt
275ml (½pt) distilled malt vinegar
75g (3oz) granulated sugar
½ × 5ml tsp (½tsp) celery seeds
½ × 5ml tsp (½tsp) mustard seeds

1 Wash and trim the cucumbers (but do not peel) and cut into small dice. Layer the cucumber in a bowl

with the onion and salt, and allow to stand for
$1\frac{1}{2}$–2 hr.
2 Turn the vegetables into a colander, wash and
drain well. Pack the vegetables into warm jars.
3 Heat the remaining ingredients in a jug for 2 min
and stir; cook for a further 5 min.
4 Pour the liquid over the cucumber. Seal and label
and keep for 4 weeks before using to allow the
flavours to blend.

Ginger marmalade (makes about 675g/1½lb)

POWER LEVEL: 100% (FULL)

450g (1lb) cooking apples, washed
1 × 15ml tbsp (1tbsp) lemon juice
6g ($\frac{1}{4}$oz) root ginger
275ml ($\frac{1}{2}$pt) water
450g (1lb) preserving sugar
100g (4oz) preserved ginger, finely chopped

1 Slice the apples without peeling and place in a large
glass bowl with the lemon juice.
2 Bruise the ginger by hitting it with a rolling pin,
then add it to the apples.
3 Add the water, cover with clingfilm and cook for
10 min. Remove the ginger.
4 Press the apples through a jelly cloth to extract all
the juice. This should produce 550ml (1pt) of
extract.
5 Add the sugar and preserved ginger to the extract.
Stir until the sugar is dissolved. Cook uncovered for
25 min or until setting point is reached, stirring
every 5 min.
6 Cool for 20–30 min, stir, then pot, seal and label.

Pineapple and apricot conserve

(makes about 2kg/4lb)
POWER LEVEL: 100% (FULL)

175g (6oz) dried apricots
550ml (1pt) water
1 medium pineapple, weighing approximately
$1\frac{1}{4}$kg ($2\frac{1}{2}$lb)
900g (2lb) sugar

1 Place the apricots in a bowl with the water, cover
with clingfilm and heat for 8 min. Allow to stand
for 10 min.
2 Peel and dice the pineapple into small pieces. If the
stalk is hard, remove and discard.
3 Drain the apricots, reserving 150ml ($\frac{1}{4}$pt) of liquid.
Place the pineapple and apricots in a large bowl
with the apricot liquid.
4 Add the sugar and stir—the sugar may not dissolve
completely at this stage. Cook for 5 min, stir. Cook
for a further 20 min, stirring about every 5 min.
5 Pour into warmed jars, seal and label.

Orange curd (makes about 900g/2lb)

POWER LEVEL: 100% (FULL)

3 medium oranges
175g (6oz) butter, cut into pieces
4 eggs and 2 yolks
275g (10oz) caster sugar

1 Carefully grate the zest from the oranges and
reserve it. Heat the oranges for 1 min, then
squeeze out the juice.
2 Melt the butter for 2–3 min. Mix the orange rind
and juice with the eggs then beat into the melted
butter.
3 Cook for 6–7 min, stirring every minute, until the
mixture coats the back of a wooden spoon.
4 Pour into warm jars, seal and label. Use within 1
month.

Pickled beetroot (makes 450g/1lb)

POWER LEVEL: 100% (FULL)

$\frac{1}{2}$ × 5ml tsp ($\frac{1}{2}$tsp) pickling spice
275ml ($\frac{1}{2}$pt) malt vinegar
450g (1lb) fresh beetroot
3 × 15ml tbsp (3tbsp) water

1 Place the pickling spice into a bowl or jug, pour the
vinegar on to the spice and allow to stand.
2 Wash the beetroot to remove any earth from the
skins. Place in a bowl with the water, cover and
cook for 8–12 min depending on size until tender.
Remove cover, allow to cool then remove the skins
of the beetroot.
3 If the beetroot are large, cut them into 6mm ($\frac{1}{4}$in)
slices. Baby beets may be left whole.
4 Pack the prepared beetroot into warmed jars. Heat
the vinegar and spice for 2 min then strain over the
beetroot.
5 Cover and label.

Note: In testing, 450g (1lb) of beetroot and 275ml ($\frac{1}{2}$pt)
vinegar filled a 900g (2lb) jar.

Apple and walnut chutney

(makes about 675g/1½lb)
POWER LEVEL: 100% (FULL)

450g (1lb) cooking apples
1 orange
1 small lemon
40g ($1\frac{1}{2}$oz) walnuts, chopped
100g (4oz) sultanas
225g (8oz) soft brown sugar
150ml ($\frac{1}{4}$pt) vinegar

1 Peel, core and chop the apples. Grate the rinds from
the citrus fruits. Heat the orange and lemon for

1 min then squeeze out the juices.

2 Place the apples in a large bowl with the fruit rinds and juices. Add all the remaining ingredients and cook for 20–25 min, until thick, stirring occasionally.

3 Pour into warmed jars, seal and label.

Carrot and lemon marmalade

(makes about 900g/2lb)
POWER LEVEL: 100% (FULL)

2 large lemons, washed, halved lengthwise and thinly sliced
225g (8oz) carrots, peeled and shredded
550ml (1pt) boiling water
450g (1lb) preserving or granulated sugar

1 Remove any pips from the lemon slices and place in a large bowl with the carrots. Add the boiling water, cover with a lid or clingfilm and leave to stand for 1 hr.

2 Make a slit in the clingfilm, if used, and cook the carrots and lemon in the water for 10 min, until tender.

3 Remove the lid or clingfilm, add the sugar and stir well. Cook uncovered for 30–35 min, until setting point is reached, stirring every 5 min.

4 Allow the marmalade to stand for 30 min, then pot, seal and label. Eat within 3 months.

Apple and tomato cheese

(makes about 1½kg/3lb)
POWER LEVEL: 100% (FULL)

This is delicious served with any white meat or poultry.

900g (2lb) green cooking apples
450g (1lb) green tomatoes
150ml (¼pt) boiling water
450g (1lb) preserving or granulated sugar

1 Wash the apples but do not peel them. Cut the apples into quarters, core and slice. Wash and roughly chop the tomatoes.

2 Place the prepared apples and tomatoes in a large bowl, add the boiling water, cover the bowl with a lid or clingfilm (slit the film) and cook the fruits for 10 min. Stir thoroughly, recover and continue to cook for a further 5 min, until the fruit becomes pulpy.

3 Remove the lid or clingfilm. Allow the mixture to cool slightly, then purée in a food processor or liquidiser or rub through a sieve.

4 Rinse the bowl and replace the purée. Add the sugar, stirring well. Cook uncovered for a further 20 min, stirring every 5 min.

5 Pot, seal and label.

Plum jam *(makes about 2½kg/5lb)*
POWER LEVEL: 100% (FULL)

1½kg (3lb) plums, washed and stoned
150ml (¼pt) boiling water
1½kg (3lb) sugar, granulated or preserving

1 Place the prepared plums in a large bowl with the boiling water. Cover with a lid or clingfilm (slit the film), then cook for 10 min. Stir the plums, recover and cook for a further 5 min.

2 Add the sugar and stir well. Cook, uncovered, for 25 min or until setting point is reached, stirring every 5 min.

3 Pot, seal and label.

Pear chutney *(makes 1¼kg/2½lb)*
POWER LEVEL: 100% (FULL)

225g (8oz) onions, chopped
225g (8oz) celery, chopped
900g (2lb) cooking pears, peeled, cored and chopped
225g (8oz) tomatoes, skinned and sliced
100g (4oz) stoned dates, chopped
150ml (¼pt) malt vinegar
½ × 5ml tsp (½tsp) cayenne pepper
½ × 5ml tsp (½tsp) ground ginger
1 × 5ml tsp (1tsp) salt
350g (12oz) soft brown sugar

1 Place the onion and celery in a large bowl. Cover and cook for 6 min, stirring once halfway through.

2 Stir in the chopped pears and continue to cook for a further 5 min.

3 Add all the remaining ingredients and cook, uncovered, for 40–45 min until thick, stirring occasionally.

4 Pour into warm jars, seal and label.

Mango chutney *(makes about 900g/2lb)*
POWER LEVEL: 100% (FULL)

450g (1lb) fresh mangoes *or*
500g (1lb 2oz) drained canned mangoes
225g (8oz) cooking apples, peeled, cored and sliced
1 × 5ml tsp (1tsp) salt
175g (6oz) onions, finely chopped
150ml (¼pt) distilled or light malt vinegar
1 × 5ml tsp (1tsp) ground ginger
1 × 5ml tsp (1tsp) chilli powder, optional
300g (10oz) demerara sugar

Selection of preserves

1 Peel and slice the fresh mangoes or slice the canned mangoes and place in a bowl with the apples. Sprinkle with salt and allow to stand for 2–3 hr.

2 Rinse and drain the fruit and place in a large bowl, with the onion. Cover and cook for 6 min, stirring after 3 min.

3 Add the vinegar, spices and sugar, mix well and cook, uncovered, for a further 20 min, stirring every 5 min, until the chutney is thick.

4 Pour into warmed jars, seal and label.

Pumpkin chutney *(makes about 675g/1½lb)*
POWER LEVEL: 100% (FULL)

500g (1¼lb) prepared pumpkin, cut into small dice
1 medium onion, peeled and chopped
15g (½oz) salt
225g (8oz) tomatoes, skinned and chopped
25g (1oz) sultanas
175g (6oz) soft brown sugar
1 × 5ml tsp (1tsp) salt
1 × 5ml tsp (1tsp) ground ginger
1 × 5ml tsp (1tsp) allspice
1 clove garlic, crushed
150ml (¼pt) tarragon vinegar

1 Place the pumpkin and onion in a bowl. Sprinkle with the salt and allow to stand for 2 hr. Rinse and drain well.

2 Add all the remaining ingredients and stir well. Cook uncovered for 40 min, stirring occasionally, until thick.

3 Pour into warm jars, seal and label.

Pumpkin marmalade *(makes about 1½kg/3lb)*
POWER LEVEL: 100% (FULL) *(colour page 35)*

900g (2lb) prepared pumpkin flesh
900g (2lb) sugar
2 oranges, thinly sliced

1 Cut the pumpkin into small cubes, layer with the sugar in a large bowl and allow to stand for 8 hr.

2 Add the sliced oranges. Cook, uncovered, for 45–50 min, stirring every 5 min until setting point is reached.

3 Pour into warm jars, seal and label.

Note: *Keep the whole pumpkin until the end of October/beginning November to allow the flesh to dry slightly before making the marmalade. Turn once a day to ensure even drying.*

Sweets and candies

The advantage of making sweets and candies in the microwave is that they are quick and easy to do, particularly important as many of them do not keep for long—in more than one sense! Children will enjoy cooking some for their friends—under parental supervision of course. Let them try Cherry Fondants, Fruit 'n' nut Clusters or Coconut Ice. Most of the recipes are uncomplicated and simple to follow, using basic methods, although the use of a sugar thermometer will be an advantage for some. (Do not leave the thermometer in the microwave during cooking unless specially designed.)

I have, however, also included one or two more sophisticated recipes which you may find suitable for serving after a lunch or dinner party.

Coconut ice *(makes about 550g/1¼lb)*
(colour page 195)
POWER LEVEL: 50% (DEFROST) AND 100% (FULL)

450g (1lb) granulated sugar
150ml (¼pt) milk
150g (5oz) desiccated coconut
cochineal or red colouring

1 Lightly grease a tin approximately 20 × 15cm (8 × 6in)
2 Heat together the sugar and milk in a large bowl for 7 min on 50% (defrost) setting until the sugar has dissolved. Stir occasionally.
3 Heat the mixture for 2 min on 100% (full) setting and stir well. Continue to heat for a further 7 min on 100% (full) setting or until the mixture reaches 116°C (240°F) measured on a sugar thermometer.
4 Stir in the coconut and quickly pour half the mixture into the prepared tin. Colour the remaining mixture and pour it over the first layer.
5 Allow the coconut ice to cool. When half set, mark into bars. Cut or break the bars when completely cool.

Chocolate stuffed dates *(makes 12)*
POWER LEVEL: 100% (FULL)

12 dates
50g (2oz) marzipan
100g (4oz) plain chocolate
broken brazil nuts to decorate

1 Using a sharp knife, carefully slit one side of each date and remove the stone. Keep the dates whole.
2 Lightly knead the marzipan until soft. Divide it into 12, and roll each piece to a small sausage shape. Carefully fill each date with a piece of marzipan.
3 Break the chocolate into squares and heat in a bowl in the microwave for 3 min until melted. Beat well.
4 Using two lightly oiled forks, dip the stuffed dates into the chocolate until coated. Leave to set on a tray lined with waxed or non-stick paper. Before the chocolate is completely set decorate each stuffed date with a piece of brazil nut.
5 Serve in small paper cases.

DO NOT FREEZE

Quick chocolate peppermint creams
(makes 18)
POWER LEVEL: 100% (FULL)

1 × 225g (8oz) packet prepared fondant
peppermint essence
green colouring
75g (3oz) plain chocolate

1 Work the fondant until soft, adding a few drops of peppermint essence and green colouring. Continue to knead lightly until the fondant is evenly coloured.
2 Divide into 18 pieces, then roll each into a small ball and flatten to give a round peppermint cream.
3 Leave the peppermint creams overnight to dry on a sheet of waxed or non-stick paper.
4 Break the chocolate into squares, place in a bowl and heat for 2 min until melted. Beat well.
5 Half dip each peppermint cream into the melted chocolate, then return the creams to the paper and allow the chocolate to set. Serve in small paper cases.

FREEZE BEFORE DIPPING

Colettes *(makes about 18)*
POWER LEVEL: 100% (FULL)

100g (4oz) plain or milk chocolate
150g (5oz) plain chocolate
50g (2oz) unsalted butter
4 × 15ml tbsp (4tbsp) strong black coffee
2 egg yolks
rum to taste
blanched hazelnuts

1 Break 100g (4oz) of chocolate into squares and heat in a bowl for 3 min until melted. Beat well.
2 Place 1 × 5ml tsp (1tsp) of the chocolate into a small paper case, press another case over the chocolate and use it to squeeze it into a cup shape up the sides of the case. Leave overnight to set, then carefully remove the inner paper case. 100g (4oz) of chocolate should make about 18 cups.
3 Break the remaining chocolate into squares and heat for 3½ min in a bowl until melted. Add the butter and beat well until the butter has melted. Add the coffee and allow the mixture to cool slightly.
4 Beat in the egg yolks and rum to taste. Allow the mixture to cool until thick and almost set.
5 Place the mixture in a piping bag fitted with a large star nozzle and pipe a little of the mixture into each chocolate case. Top with a hazelnut and leave until completely set.

DO NOT FREEZE

Sesame snaps *(makes approximately 450g/1lb)*
POWER LEVEL: 100% (FULL) *(colour opposite)*

225g (8oz) sesame seeds
225g (8oz) caster sugar

1 Lightly oil a baking sheet.
2 Place the sesame seeds in a medium-sized bowl and heat for 3 min. Add the sugar and stir well. Heat for 6 min stirring thoroughly after every 2 min.
3 Heat for a further 2–3 min until the mixture is golden brown in colour. Stir every minute until the required colour is reached.
4 Spread the mixture on to the prepared tin and mark into squares. Allow to cool.
5 When cold, break the sesame mixture into small pieces. Store in an airtight tin.

DO NOT FREEZE

Selection of sweets and candies

1 *Orange and Lemon Jellies (page 200)*
2 *Vanilla and Almond Truffles (page 200)*
3 *Fruit 'n Nut Clusters (page 198)*
4 *Fig Bonbons (page 200)*
5 *Coconut Ice (page 193)*
6 *Coffee Fudge (page 200)*
7 *Triple Treats (page 198)*
8 *Sesame Snaps (above)*
9 *Chocolate and Chestnut Nougat (page 198)*

Lemon pastilles *(makes 800g/1¾lb)*
POWER LEVEL: 100% (FULL)

These pastilles are very refreshing, especially in hot weather. They do not, however, keep well and should be eaten within two or three days of making.

900g (2lb) cooking apples
150ml (¼pt) water
350g (12oz) caster sugar
150ml (¼pt) water
40g (1½oz) or 4 envelopes gelatin
2 × 15ml tbsp (2tbsp) lemon juice
yellow colouring
caster sugar to serve (optional)

1 Peel, core and slice the apples. Place in a covered dish, boiling bag or roasting bag with the water and cook for 10 min, stirring after 5 min. Cool slightly then purée.
2 Place the purée and sugar in a large bowl and cook for 10 min. Meanwhile, grease and line a tin approximately 27.5 × 17.5 × 2.5cm (11 × 7 × 1in) deep.
3 Place the water in a bowl and sprinkle the gelatin on to the surface. Leave to soften for 3 min. Heat for 1 min then stir gently until the gelatin is dissolved.
4 Add the gelatin to the apple purée, together with the lemon juice and yellow colouring. Mix well and pour the mixture into the prepared tin.
5 Leave to set in a cool place for approximately 12 hr. When set, cut into squares using a sharp knife dipped in hot water.
6 Serve the pastilles in small paper cases. If liked, the pastilles may be tossed in caster sugar before serving.

DO NOT FREEZE

Rum truffles *(makes 12)*
POWER LEVEL: 100% (FULL) *(colour page 39)*

75g (3oz) plain chocolate
1 egg yolk
15g (½oz) unsalted butter
1 × 5ml tsp (1tsp) rum
1 × 5ml tsp (1tsp) single cream or top of the milk
for serving: drinking chocolate or chocolate vermicelli

1 Break the chocolate into squares, place in a medium-sized bowl and heat for 2½ min until melted.
2 Add the egg yolk, butter, rum and cream. Beat well until thick. Chill in the refrigerator until firm enough to handle.
3 Shape the mixture into 12 balls and toss each in drinking chocolate or vermicelli. Serve the truffles in small paper cases.

VARIATION

Try flavouring the truffles with ginger wine instead of rum.

Jujubes *(makes approximately 900g/2lb)*
POWER LEVEL: 100% (FULL)

Jujubes are very popular with children but do not keep well and should be eaten within a few days of making, which normally presents no problem!

175g (6oz) dried apricots
275ml (½pt) water
450g (1lb) caster sugar
150ml (¼pt) water
50g (2oz) gelatin
2 × 5ml tsp (2tsp) lemon juice

1 Place the dried apricots in a bowl, cover them with water then cover the bowl with clingfilm, making a small slit in the film. Heat in the microwave for 5 min, then allow to stand for 10 min before straining the apricots.

2 Return the apricots to the bowl, add 275ml ($\frac{1}{2}$pt) of water, cover with clingfilm and make a small slit in the film. Cook the apricots for 5 min until soft. Allow to cool slightly then purée the fruit and water or rub the mixture through a sieve. This should yield approximately 275ml ($\frac{1}{2}$pt) of thick purée.

3 Place the purée in a large bowl, add the sugar and stir well. Heat for 3 min then stir until the sugar is completely dissolved.

4 Place 150ml ($\frac{1}{4}$pt) water in a small bowl and heat for 2 min. Sprinkle the gelatin on to the surface and stir briskly until it has dissolved.

5 Add the gelatin with the lemon juice to the apricot purée.

6 Rinse a 17.5cm (7in) square tin in cold water and pour the mixture into the tin. Leave to set overnight.

7 Cut the jelly into squares using a knife dipped in hot water. Serve the jujubes in small paper cases.

DO NOT FREEZE

Honeyed fruit 'n' nut caramels

(makes approximately 550g/1$\frac{1}{4}$lb)
POWER LEVEL: 100% (FULL)

75g (3oz) unsalted butter
150g (5oz) golden syrup
175g (6oz) clear honey
100g (4oz) broken walnuts
100g (4oz) sultanas

1 Lightly grease a shallow tin approximately 20 × 15cm (8 × 6in) and line it with non-stick baking parchment.

2 Place the butter, syrup and honey in a large bowl and heat for 3 min until the butter has melted. Cook for a further 6 min or until the mixture reaches 126°C (270°F) measured with a sugar thermometer.

3 While the syrup is boiling, finely chop the nuts and fruit, then add them to the syrup and beat thoroughly with a wooden spoon until opaque in colour.

4 Pour the caramel into the prepared tin and leave to cool. When almost set, mark into squares with a knife.

5 Leave to set for about 24 hr then break into squares. Wrap in waxed paper and store in an airtight jar.

DO NOT FREEZE

Devilled almonds *(makes 100g/4oz)*
POWER LEVEL: 100% (FULL) *(colour page 11)*

3 × 15ml tbsp (3tbsp) olive oil
100g (4oz) blanched almonds
salt
cayenne pepper

1 Heat the oil on a dinner plate for 3 min. Add the almonds, toss over in the oil and cook for 5 min, stirring occasionally.

2 Remove the almonds from the oil using a slotted spoon and drain them on some crumpled kitchen paper.

3 Sprinkle some salt mixed with a little cayenne pepper on to a sheet of greaseproof paper. While the almonds are still warm, place them on the prepared paper and sprinkle with a little extra salt and cayenne.

4 Continue to toss the almonds occasionally in the seasonings until they are quite cold.

5 Store the devilled almonds in a screw-top jar.

DO NOT FREEZE

Orange fondant cups *(makes 18)*
POWER LEVEL: 50% (DEFROST) AND 100% (FULL)

100g (4oz) plain chocolate
1 × 225g (8oz) packet of prepared fondant
1 small orange, peeled, with pips and membrane removed, and flesh chopped
few drops of orange colouring, optional
75g (3oz) plain chocolate

1 Break 100g (4oz) of chocolate into squares, place in a bowl and heat for 3 min until melted. Beat well.

2 Place 1 × 5ml tsp (1tsp) of the melted chocolate into a small paper case; press a second paper case over the chocolate, gently squeeze up the sides to form a cup. Leave overnight in a cool place to set, then remove the inner paper case. This mixture makes approximately 18 cases.

3 Cut the fondant into squares and heat in a bowl for 3 min on 50% (defrost) setting until melted. Beat well, then add the chopped orange and colouring, if used.

4 Divide the fondant mixture between the 18 cases and leave for 2–3 hr in a cool place to allow the fondant to start to set.

5 Break the remaining chocolate into squares and heat for 2$\frac{1}{2}$ min in a small bowl on 100% (full) setting. Spoon a little of the melted chocolate over the fondant to complete the sweets.

6 Allow the chocolate top to set for at least 4 hr in a cool place before serving.

DO NOT FREEZE

Chocolate and chestnut nougat

(makes 450g/1lb)
POWER LEVEL: 100% (FULL) *(colour page 195)*

This soft, spanish nougat should be kept in the refrigerator and eaten within 1 week.

75g (3oz) plain chocolate
75g (3oz) unsalted butter
75g (3oz) caster sugar
few drops vanilla essence
1 × 440g (15½oz) can whole chestnuts, drained

1 Lightly grease and line a tin approximately 17.5cm (7in) square.
2 Break the chocolate into squares, place in a large bowl and heat for 3 min until melted. Stir well. Add the butter, sugar and vanilla essence. Mix well.
3 Place the drained chestnuts in a bowl, cover with clingfilm and make a small slit in the film. Cook for 5 min.
4 Pass the chestnuts through a sieve into the chocolate mixture to produce a finely textured sweet. Chopping the nuts in a food processor or blender will produce a coarser-textured sweet.
5 Spread the nougat in the prepared tin and leave for 24 hr before serving. Mark into small bars or squares after 12 hr.

DO NOT FREEZE

Fruit 'n' nut clusters *(makes approximately 450g/1lb)*

POWER LEVEL: 100% (FULL) *(colour page 195)*

275g (10oz) plain chocolate
75g (3oz) seedless raisins, roughly chopped
75g (3oz) hazelnuts, roughly chopped
50g (2oz) mixed peel, finely chopped

1 Break 100g (4oz) chocolate into squares, place in a large bowl and heat for 3 min until melted. Beat well.
2 Add the raisins, hazelnuts and peel to the chocolate and mix well.
3 Line a tray with non-stick or waxed paper. Place teaspoonfuls of the mixture on to the tray and leave to set in a cool place for at least 1 hr.
4 Break the remaining 175g (6oz) chocolate into squares and heat in a bowl for 4 min until melted. Beat well.
5 Lightly oil two forks and use them to dip the clusters in the melted chocolate. Return the dipped sweets to the lined tray and leave in a cool place until set.
6 Serve the fruit and nut clusters in small paper cases.

DO NOT FREEZE

Triple treats *(makes approximately 675g/1½lb)*

POWER LEVEL: 100% (FULL) *(colour page 195)*

icing sugar for dredging
225g (8oz) marzipan
100g (4oz) crystallized fruit, eg pineapple or ginger
50g (2oz) unsalted butter
50g (2oz) icing sugar, sieved
100g (4oz) plain chocolate
few drops vanilla essence
175–225g (6–8oz) plain chocolate for dipping, optional

1 Lightly dredge a board with icing sugar. Knead the marzipan until pliable then roll into a square on the sugared board, leaving the marzipan approximately 6mm (¼in) thick.
2 Cut the crystallized fruit into slivers and press the pieces all over the surface of the marzipan.
3 Beat the butter and the icing sugar together until light and fluffy. Break the 100g (4oz) of chocolate into squares and heat in a small bowl for 3 min until melted. Beat the chocolate then allow it to cool slightly before adding it to the butter and icing sugar. Mix well, adding vanilla essence to taste.
4 Carefully spread the chocolate cream over the crystallized fruit. Place the board in a cool place for about 1 hr to allow the cream to set.
5 Using a sharp knife, cut the layered treats into evenly sized pieces. These could be squares, diamonds or triangles. Leave the separated pieces on a tray for approximately 1 hr to allow the cut surfaces to harden.
6 Break the remaining chocolate into squares and heat in a bowl for 4–5 min until melted. Beat well. Using two lightly oiled forks coat the treats in the melted chocolate. Place on to non-stick paper and allow to set. Serve in small paper cases.

DO NOT FREEZE

Caramel surprises *(makes 18)*

POWER LEVEL: 100% (FULL)

These sweets should be eaten on the day that they are made, otherwise the caramel will become soft.

100g (4oz) marzipan
few drops green colouring
36 walnut halves
150ml (¼pt) water
175g (6oz) caster sugar

1 Lightly knead the marzipan until pliable, working a few drops of food colouring into the paste to give it an even green colour.
2 Divide the marzipan and form into 18 small balls, then sandwich each ball between 2 small walnut halves.

3 Place the water and sugar in a bowl and heat for 4 min, stirring every minute, until the sugar is completely dissolved. Heat for a further 11 min without stirring, until the syrup is thick and light golden brown in colour.

4 While the caramel is boiling, lightly oil a baking sheet and two forks.

5 Working quickly, use the forks to dip each sweet into the caramel, making sure that they are completely coated. Place the caramels on the oiled baking sheet and allow to set. Serve in paper cases.

DO NOT FREEZE

Indian coconut barfi *(makes approximately 225g/8oz)*
POWER LEVEL: 100% (FULL)

Coconut barfi is similar to coconut ice but produces a less firm set.

butter
225ml (½pt) creamy milk
100g (4oz) desiccated coconut
75g (3oz) caster sugar
cochineal
vanilla essence
6 green cardamoms, seeds removed and crushed

1 Butter a shallow 15cm (6in) square tin.

2 Heat the milk in a large bowl for 4 min until boiling; stir after 3 min. Continue to cook for a further 10 min, stirring every 2 min to prevent boiling over.

3 Add the coconut and stir well. Add the sugar and continue to stir.

4 Cook for 2 min, stir, then cook for a further 2 min.

5 Remove the barfi from the microwave. Colour with a few drops of cochineal and add a little vanilla essence and the crushed cardamom seeds. Mix well.

6 Transfer the barfi to the prepared tin and smooth the surface with the back of a spoon. Leave to cool. Mark into bars before completely set. Store in the refrigerator.

Chocolate brazils *(makes 18)*
POWER LEVEL: 100% (FULL)

18 blanched brazil nuts
100g (4oz) plain or milk chocolate

1 Ensure that there is no skin left on the brazil nuts—remove any brown skin that you may find with a sharp knife.

2 Break the chocolate into squares and heat in a bowl in the microwave for 3 min until the chocolate is melted. Beat well.

3 Using two lightly oiled forks dip the brazils into the chocolate until they are completely coated. Place on a tray lined with waxed or non-stick paper until they are set.

4 Serve the chocolate brazils in small paper cases.

DO NOT FREEZE

Fondant dipped fruits *(makes 12–15)*
POWER LEVEL: 50% (DEFROST)

These fruits are a delicious way of finishing a summer dinner party, but they should be eaten on the same day that they are made.

12–15 pieces of fruit of your choice, eg strawberries, cherries, orange segments, etc
100g (4oz) prepared fondant
2 × 5ml tsp (2tsp) warm water
caster sugar

1 Choose perfectly ripe fruit, to be eaten on the day that these sweets are made. Wash the fruits, leaving stalks on strawberries and cherries.

2 Cut the fondant into pieces and heat for 2 min in a bowl in the microwave, on 50% (defrost) setting. Add warm water and beat well.

3 Carefully half dip the fruits in the melted fondant, then coat them in a little caster sugar.

4 Place the fruits in paper cases and allow the fondant to set for at least 1 hr before serving.

DO NOT FREEZE

199

Orange and lemon jellies *(makes 550g/1¼lb)*
POWER LEVEL: 100% (FULL) *(colour page 195)*

To measure liquid glucose easily by the spoonful, heat the pot of glucose for 1 min in the microwave and then measure.

2–3 oranges
50g (2oz) gelatin
8 × 15ml tbsp (8tbsp) water
175g (6oz) sugar
8 × 15ml tbsp (8tbsp) liquid glucose
orange and lemon colourings, optional
3–4 lemons

1 Heat the oranges for 1 min to ensure maximum juiciness. Squeeze the oranges to yield 150ml (¼pt) of juice.
2 Sprinkle 25g (1oz) of gelatin on 4 × 15ml tbsp (4tbsp) water and leave to soften for 2 min.
3 Place the orange juice, 75g (3oz) sugar and 4 × 15ml tbsp (4tbsp) liquid glucose in a large bowl and heat for 1½–2 min until the sugar has dissolved.
4 Add the gelatin to the orange liquid and stir well. Heat for 1 min until the gelatin is dissolved. Add colouring if required.
5 Wet a tin, approximately 15–17.5cm (6–7in) square, under the cold water tap. Pour the jelly mixture into the tin, and allow it to set in a cool place for approximately 6 hr.
6 Repeat steps 1–5 using lemons instead of oranges. Pour the lemon jelly on to the orange jelly and allow to set to give a two coloured sweet.
7 Cut into shapes and eat as soon as possible after making as these jellies do not keep well.

DO NOT FREEZE

Vanilla and almond truffles *(makes 12–15)*
POWER LEVEL: 100% (FULL) *(colour page 195)*

150g (5oz) white chocolate
50g (2oz) unsalted butter, cut into small pieces
½ × 5ml tsp (½tsp) vanilla essence
2 egg yolks
25g (1oz) almonds, finely chopped
icing sugar, sieved

1 Break the chocolate into squares, place in a bowl and heat for 1–1½ min until melted. Beat well.
2 Add the pieces of butter and the essence, mix well. Allow to cool slightly.
3 Add the egg yolks and finely chopped almonds and beat thoroughly. Refrigerate the mixture until it is firm enough to handle.
4 Form the truffle mixture into 12–15 balls. Turn the truffles in sieved icing sugar and serve in paper cases.

Cherry fondants *(makes 18)*
POWER LEVEL: 100% (FULL)

1 × 225g (8oz) packet of prepared fondant
6–8 maraschino cherries, drained and chopped
cherry brandy, to taste
icing sugar
175g (6oz) plain chocolate

1 Knead the fondant to a workable consistency, add the chopped cherries and the brandy and work them evenly into the fondant.
2 Dredge your hands with icing sugar and form the mixture into 18 walnut-sized balls. Leave overnight on a tray lined with waxed or non-stick paper to dry.
3 Break the chocolate into squares and heat in a bowl for 4 min until melted. Beat well. Using two lightly oiled forks dip the fondants in the chocolate until coated. Return them to the waxed paper and leave until the chocolate has set.
4 Serve the fondants in paper cases.

FREEZE BEFORE DIPPING

Fig bonbons *(makes 18)*
POWER LEVEL: 100% (FULL) *(colour page 195)*

3 × 15ml tbsp (3tbsp) olive oil
75g (3oz) blanched hazelnuts
225g (8oz) figs in honey or moist dried figs, minced
100g (4oz) granulated sugar, approximately

1 Heat the oil on a plate for 3 min. Add the hazelnuts and cook for 6 min, stirring occasionally.
2 Remove the hazelnuts with a slotted spoon, drain them on kitchen paper then chop them finely.
3 Mix together the minced figs and chopped nuts. Divide the mixture and form it into 18 small balls.
4 Roll the sweets in sugar, leave for 15 min then roll them in sugar again.
5 Serve the fig sweets in small paper cases.

Coffee fudge *(makes approximately 450g/1lb)*
POWER LEVEL: 100% (FULL) *(colour page 195)*

50g (2oz) butter
150ml (¼pt) evaporated milk
150ml (¼pt) milk
450g (1lb) granulated sugar
2 × 15ml tbsp (2tbsp) coffee essence

1 Grease a tin 15 × 15cm (6 × 6in).
2 Place the butter and the milks in a large bowl and heat for 3½ min until the butter has melted.
3 Add the sugar and stir well to allow the sugar granules to dissolve. Heat for 1–2 min until the

sugar is completely dissolved.

4 Heat for 15 min, stirring every 2 min, until the mixture reaches 116°C (240°F) measured on a sugar thermometer. The mixture will thicken during cooking.

5 Remove the bowl to the work surface, add the coffee essence and beat thoroughly until the fudge becomes grainy. Pour immediately into the prepared tin.

6 Leave the fudge until cool then mark into squares. When completely cold, cut into squares using a sharp knife. Store in an airtight tin.

Honeycomb *(makes approximately 175g/6oz)*
POWER LEVEL: 100% (FULL)

150ml ($\frac{1}{4}$pt) water
225g (8oz) caster sugar
1 × 15ml tbsp (1tbsp) golden syrup
$\frac{1}{4}$ × 5ml tsp ($\frac{1}{4}$tsp) cream of tartar
$\frac{1}{2}$ × 5ml tsp ($\frac{1}{2}$tsp) bicarbonate of soda
1 × 5ml tsp (1tsp) hot water

1 Place the 150ml ($\frac{1}{4}$pt) water in a large bowl and heat for 2 min. Add the sugar, syrup and cream of tartar and stir well until the sugar is dissolved. If necessary, heat the mixture for 1–2 min, stirring after every minute, to dissolve the sugar completely.

2 Heat the syrup for 10 min or until it reaches 154°C (310°F) measured on a sugar thermometer. The syrup should be a golden colour, and not too dark.

3 While the syrup is boiling, grease a 17.5cm (7in) square tin with butter.

4 As soon as the sugar syrup reaches the required colour remove the bowl from the microwave cooker. Quickly mix together the bicarbonate of soda and the hot water and immediately add this mixture to the syrup, stirring gently.

5 Pour the honeycomb into the prepared tin and leave it to cool. Mark it into bars with a buttered knife before it has completely set.

6 Eat quickly! Honeycomb is best eaten on the day that it is made as it will become soft when exposed to air.

DO NOT FREEZE

Butterscotch *(makes 450g/1lb)*
POWER LEVEL: 70% AND 100% (FULL)

150ml ($\frac{1}{4}$pt) water
450g (1lb) caster sugar
$\frac{1}{4}$ × 5ml tsp ($\frac{1}{4}$tsp) cream of tartar
75g (3oz) unsalted butter
$\frac{1}{4}$ × 5ml tsp ($\frac{1}{4}$tsp) vanilla essence

1 Grease a tin 27.5 × 17.5cm (11 × 7in).

2 Heat the water in a large bowl on 70% setting for 1$\frac{1}{2}$ min. Add the sugar and stir thoroughly. Heat for 6 min on 70% setting, stirring every minute, until the sugar is dissolved.

3 Add the cream of tartar and cook for 8 min on 100% (full) setting, or until the mixture reaches 116°C (240°F) measured on a sugar thermometer.

4 Cut the butter into small pieces, add to the mixture and heat for a further 5 min to a temperature of 138°C (280°F) without stirring.

5 Remove the bowl from the microwave, add the vanilla essence and pour the mixture into the prepared tin.

6 When the butterscotch has almost set, mark it into small bars. When completely cold, break it into bars.

7 Store in an airtight tin.

DO NOT FREEZE

Breads and yeast

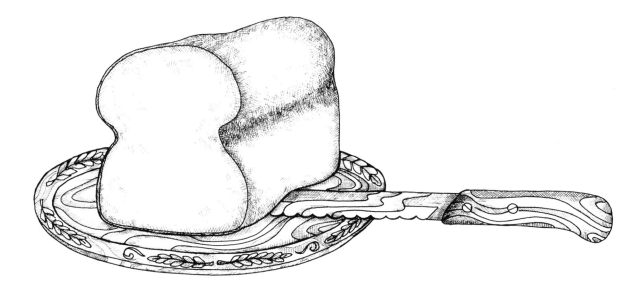

The taste and aroma of freshly home-baked bread are delicious and yet one of the detractions from making your own is the lengthy time required for proving the dough. Normally a warm place—like an airing cupboard—must be found for the slow rising process to take place, but with a microwave cooker the proving time can be halved, by giving the dough combinations of short bursts of microwave energy alternated with standing or rest periods. This allows an even distribution of warmth through the dough, ensuring a steady rise and, together with the quick cooking times, gives the housewife a fast, trouble-free method of bread making.

Proving the dough
Once the ingredients for basic breads have been mixed together and kneaded, the dough will become smooth and leave the sides of the bowl clean. Richer mixtures with the addition of milk, eggs or butter are usually wetter, resembling a heavy batter and are ready for proving when the mixture is smooth with many tiny air bubbles visible just under the surface.

After kneading, the dough is covered with clingfilm and then proved in the microwave. There are two methods available for proving the dough, depending on the type of microwave cooker and the time available; either give the dough 3–4 minutes on a 10% (very low or keep warm) setting followed by standing periods of 10 minutes *or*, the method I prefer, 15 seconds on 100% (full) setting followed by resting periods of 5–10 minutes. Repeat this process until the dough has doubled in size.

On no account during the proving stage allow the dough to be subjected to too much heat otherwise it may begin to cook around the edges. This has the effect of killing the yeast which in turn stops its growth, resulting in a hard, unrisen loaf. If you feel at any stage that the dough has been overheated, allow it to continue to rise naturally and just remove that part of the dough which has started to cook at the edges before rekneading and shaping.

When the dough has risen sufficiently for the first time, it is 'knocked back' or kneaded again to distribute the air bubbles evenly through the dough. Most breads are then shaped and put into their containers and given a second rising as before until double their size. Some richer doughs are given a second proving before shaping, and then proved for a third time before baking. Loaves of bread and rolls which are to be proved and cooked in the microwave cooker must, of course, be placed in suitable microwave containers. If the shaped bread dough is to be baked conventionally in a loaf tin or other metal container, it must *not* be proved for the second time in the microwave, but should be allowed to rise naturally in a warm place.

Shaping
Large round loaves should be placed as evenly as possible in the cooking container to ensure that the outside edges do not overcook before the centres. Ring-shaped loaves with hollow centres avoid this

Selection of Breads

202

and tend to give the most even results. You may find that loaves cooked in a microwave loaf dish are inclined to overcook at the two ends before the middle is cooked; small, smooth pieces of aluminium foil placed over the ends of the dough for half the cooking time will assist in protecting the loaf from over-cooking at these ends, but do check with your manufacturer's instructions with regard to the use of foil in your particular model.

Baking

After shaping and proving for the second time, the dough should spring back when lightly touched with the fingertips. It is then ready for baking. The top of the dough may be sprinkled with nibbed wheat, poppy seeds or sesame seeds for a more decorative finish. It can then be cooked by microwave on 100% (full) setting which will produce a good-textured loaf with a soft crust. Of course it will not be browned as when baking conventionally, but if a crisper crust is preferred, the dough can be partly cooked for 3–4 minutes in the microwave and then finished in a conventional oven preheated to a high temperature for 8–10 minutes. Alternatively, the dough can be prepared and proved by microwave and afterwards completely cooked conventionally, and there are a few recipes included in this section which give this method of proving and baking.

Defrosting

Remember that textures of food affect defrosting times and so a light-textured vienna or french bread will thaw more quickly then the heavier kinds. One roll or slice of bread or croissant may be thawed in 10–15 seconds, two would take 15–30 seconds, and three 20–35 seconds. Crumpets and slices of bread to be toasted may be cooked from the frozen state, whereas muffins and tea-cakes need to be defrosted in the microwave for 10–20 seconds before being cut and toasted or, if not to be toasted, leave them to stand for 2 minutes before serving. Loaves of bread should be given short cooking periods of 1–2 minutes followed by rest periods repeated until the bread is thawed.

Included in this section are sweet yeast mixtures, some richer, continental-style doughs, a few recipes for breads which are leavened with soda rather than yeast and a couple of 'one-stage' bread doughs which have the addition of vitamin C capsules, helping to give a good rise and dispensing with the second proving stage. Most of the recipes use fresh yeast which may be stored in the refrigerator for up to two weeks. There are a few recipes using dried yeast which is normally left to soak and activate in some of the liquid from the recipe, although there are dried yeasts available which are mixed directly into the flour.

Basic white bread *(makes 1 loaf or 16 rolls)*
POWER LEVEL: 100% (FULL)

450g (1lb) strong plain white flour
1 × 5ml tsp (1tsp) salt
40g (1½oz) margarine or lard
15g (½oz) fresh yeast
275ml (½pt) water

1 Sieve the flour and salt into a large bowl and rub in the fat. Make a well in the centre of the flour.
2 Heat the water for 30 sec. Cream the yeast with a little of the water and pour into the centre of the flour. Add sufficient of the warm water to make a workable dough.
3 Knead on a lightly floured surface until smooth and elastic. Clean the bowl and return the dough to it, covering with either a lid or clingfilm.
4 Heat for 15 sec then allow to stand for 5–10 min. Repeat 3–4 times until double in size. Knead again and shape as required.
5 **For a loaf:** shape the dough to fit a 15–17.5cm (6–7in) round dish or an 11.25 × 17.5 × 5cm (4½ × 7 × 2in) microwave loaf dish. Cover with clingfilm and prove again as before until well risen. Remove the clingfilm, sprinkle with a little flour and cook for 5 min. Allow to stand for 5 min before turning on to a wire rack to cool.
6 **For rolls:** divide and shape the dough into 16 even-sized rolls. Arrange on a large lightly oiled plate. Cover loosely with clingfilm and prove again as before until well risen. Cook 8 at a time for 2–2½ min, turning the rolls if necessary during cooking. Cool on a wire rack.

Quick white bread *(makes 1 loaf or 16 rolls)*
POWER LEVEL: 100% (FULL)

This recipe is only suitable for fresh yeast and, together with the ascorbic acid/vitamin C tablet, cuts out the first rising process completely.

450g (1lb) strong plain white flour
1 × 5ml tsp (1tsp) salt
40g (1½oz) lard
15g (½oz) fresh yeast
1 × 50mg ascorbic acid/vitamin C tablet, crushed
275ml (½pt) milk or water

1 Sieve the flour and salt into a large bowl, rub in the fat and make a well in the centre of the mixture.
2 Place the yeast in a small dish and add the ascorbic acid/vitamin C tablet (this can be easily crushed between 2 teaspoons).
3 Heat the liquid for 30 sec. Use a little of the liquid to cream the yeast and tablet. Add the yeast liquid to the flour with sufficient of the remaining liquid to give a manageable dough.

4 Knead thoroughly on a lightly floured surface until smooth and elastic. Shape immediately as required into a loaf or rolls and prove and cook as for basic white bread (see preceding recipe).

Light wholemeal bread *(makes 1 large loaf)*
POWER LEVEL: 100% (FULL) *(colour page 179)*

225g (8oz) wholemeal flour
225g (8oz) strong white flour
1 × 5ml tsp (1tsp) salt
25g (1oz) lard or margarine
275ml ($\frac{1}{2}$pt) milk or water
15g ($\frac{1}{2}$oz) fresh yeast
for garnish: oil for brushing and a few poppy seeds, optional

1 Place the flours in a large bowl with the salt and rub in the fat. Make a well in the centre of the flour.
2 Heat the liquid for 30 sec. Cream the yeast with a little of the liquid and add it to the flour with sufficient of the remaining liquid to give a workable dough.
3 Turn on to a floured surface and knead thoroughly until smooth and elastic. Clean the bowl and return the dough to it, covering with a lid or clingfilm. Heat for 15 sec and allow to stand for 5–10 min. Repeat 3–4 times until double in size.
4 Knead again and shape to fit a 17.5cm (7in) round dish or a microwave loaf dish. Cover loosely with clingfilm and prove again as before until the dough is well risen.
5 Remove the clingfilm and, if required, brush the loaf with oil and sprinkle with poppy seeds. Cook for 5 min then stand for 5–10 min before turning out on to a wire rack to cool.

Granary bread *(makes 1 loaf)*
POWER LEVEL: 100% (FULL)

1$\frac{1}{2}$ × 5ml tsp (1$\frac{1}{2}$tsp) soft brown sugar
425ml ($\frac{3}{4}$pt) water, approximately
1 × 5ml tsp (1tsp) dried yeast
450g (1lb) granary meal
100g (4oz) wheatmeal or strong plain flour
1$\frac{1}{2}$ × 5ml tsp (1$\frac{1}{2}$tsp) salt
2 × 15ml tbsp (2tbsp) oil
nibbed wheat for sprinkling

1 Lightly grease a 22.5cm (9in) round dish or 900g (2lb) microwave loaf dish and line the base with greaseproof paper.
2 Add the sugar to a third of the water and warm for 30 sec. Stir in the yeast and leave for 8–12 min to activate.
3 Mix the flours and salt well and warm for 30 sec. Warm the remaining liquid for 45 sec.

4 Add the yeast, oil and sufficient of the remaining liquid to the flour to form a soft dough. Mix well—very little kneading is required—and form into a ball.
5 Place the dough into a bowl covered with clingfilm and prove by heating for 15 sec and leaving to stand for 5–10 min. Repeat this 3–4 times until double in size.
6 Turn the dough on to a lightly floured surface, knead well until smooth. Shape the dough and place in the prepared container and prove as described previously until double in size.
7 Lightly oil the surface of the dough and sprinkle with nibbed wheat. Cut two deep cuts crossways over the top.
8 Cook for 5$\frac{1}{2}$–6$\frac{1}{2}$ min, turning once if necessary. Leave to stand for 10 min and then turn out on to a wire rack to cool.

Gannat *(makes 1 loaf)*
POWER LEVEL: 100% (FULL) *(colour page 23)*

A rich cheese bread which makes delicious sandwiches.

1 × 5ml tsp (1tsp) sugar
150ml ($\frac{1}{4}$pt) milk
2 × 5ml tsp (2tsp) dried yeast
275g (10oz) plain flour
$\frac{1}{4}$ × 5ml tsp ($\frac{1}{4}$tsp) salt and pinch pepper
50g (2oz) butter
2 eggs, beaten
100g (4oz) emmenthal or gruyère cheese, finely grated
paprika pepper for sprinkling

1 Lightly butter a 17.5–20cm (7–8in) microwave flan dish.
2 Add the sugar to the milk and warm for 30 sec. Stir in the yeast and leave for 8–12 min to activate.
3 Sift the flour and seasoning and warm for 30 sec. Melt the butter for 1–1$\frac{1}{4}$ min.
4 Add the yeast, butter and eggs to the flour and beat well to form a soft sticky dough.
5 Cover with clingfilm and prove by heating for 15 sec and leaving for 5–10 min. Repeat until the dough has doubled in size.
6 Knead the dough and work in most of the cheese, reserving 1 × 15ml tbsp (1tbsp). Shape the dough and place in the prepared container.
7 Cover with clingfilm and prove until double in size. Remove clingfilm and sprinkle the top of the dough with the remaining cheese and paprika pepper.
8 Cook for about 5 min, turning once halfway through. Leave to cool for a few minutes before removing on to a cooling rack.
9 Serve hot with butter or leave to cool and split in half and sandwich together with cream cheese.

Onion bread *(makes 1 loaf)*
POWER LEVEL: 100% (FULL) *(colour opposite)*

Delicious when eaten with salad or hot soup.

1 × 5ml tsp (1tsp) sugar
375ml (12fl oz) water
2 × 5ml tsp (2tsp) dried yeast
450g (1lb) plain flour
1 × 5ml tsp (1tsp) salt
40g (1½oz) butter or margarine
3 × 15ml tbsp (3tbsp) dried onion soup mix

1 Lightly grease a 15cm (6in) soufflé dish or micro-wave loaf dish and line the base with greaseproof paper.
2 Add sugar to half the water and warm for 30 sec. Stir in the yeast and leave to activate for 8–12 min.
3 Sift the flour and salt and warm for 30 sec. Rub in the butter or margarine finely and stir in the onion soup mix, reserving 2 × 5ml tsp (2tsp). Warm the rest of the water for 30 sec.
4 Add the yeast and warm water to the flour. Mix well and knead until smooth.
5 Place the dough in a bowl and cover with clingfilm. Prove by heating for 15 sec and leaving to rest for 5–10 min. Repeat 3–4 times until double in size.
6 Knead on a floured surface, shape the dough and place in the prepared container. Prove as described previously and when double in size lightly oil the top and sprinkle with the remaining soup mix.
7 Cook for 5 min, turning once halfway through if necessary. Leave for 10–15 min before removing on to a wire rack to cool.

Kugelhopf *(cuts into about 16 slices)*
POWER LEVEL: 100% (FULL) *(colour opposite)*

This is a rich, light-textured yeast cake, usually eaten with coffee.

1 × 5ml tsp (1tsp) sugar
225ml (8fl oz) milk, approximately
2 × 5ml tsp (2tsp) dried yeast
350g (12oz) plain flour
pinch salt
25g (1oz) caster sugar
100g (4oz) butter
2 eggs, beaten
100g (4oz) currants and seedless raisins
25–50g (1–2oz) flaked or split almonds
icing sugar for dusting

1 Well butter a 20cm (8in) microwave ring mould.
2 Add 1 × 5ml tsp (1tsp) sugar to the milk and warm for 45 sec. Stir in the dried yeast and leave for 8–12 min to activate.
3 Sift the flour and salt, add the caster sugar and warm for 30 sec. Melt the butter for 2 min.
4 Add the yeast, butter and eggs to the flour and beat well to form a soft sticky batter, adding a little more milk if necessary. Stir in the dried fruit.
5 Press the almonds around the base and sides of the prepared container and carefully pour in the dough mixture.
6 Cover with clingfilm and prove by heating for 15 sec and leaving for 5–10 min. Prove until risen to within 2.5cm (1in) of the top of the container. This richer dough may take longer to rise.
7 Remove the clingfilm and cook for 8–9 min, turning the dish every 3 min.
8 Leave for a few minutes before turning on to a cooling rack. Dust heavily with icing sugar before serving.

Mincemeat tea-ring *(serves about 10–12)*
POWER LEVEL: 100% (FULL) *(colour opposite)*

1 quantity of Light Wholemeal Dough (page 205), using milk and margarine
50g (2oz) caster sugar
75g (3oz) butter
50g (2oz) soft brown sugar
1 × 5ml tsp (1tsp) mixed spice
8 × 15ml tbsp (8tbsp) mincemeat
for decoration: Glacé Icing (page 173) and walnut halves

1 Make up the wholemeal dough as directed, adding the caster sugar to the flour after rubbing in the margarine.
2 Knead the dough on a lightly floured surface until smooth and elastic. Clean the bowl and return the dough to it, covering with a lid or clingfilm. Heat for 15 sec then allow to stand for 5–10 min. Repeat 3–4 times until doubled in size.
3 Knead the dough again and roll out into a rectangle 60 × 25cm (24 × 10in). Heat the butter for 1½–2 min until melted then brush over the dough. Sprinkle with the soft brown sugar and spice and spread with the mincemeat.
4 Roll the dough into a long sausage starting at one long side. Dampen the final edge with water to seal.
5 Lightly oil a 25cm (10in) dinner plate and place the dough in a ring on the plate. Dampen the ends of the roll with water to seal it into a ring. Cover with clingfilm and prove again as described above. Remove the clingfilm.
6 Using a sharp knife, make slits across the dough. Cook uncovered for 16 min. Stand for 5 min and then transfer to a wire rack to cool.
7 Decorate with glacé icing and walnut halves. Serve cut into wedges.

Onion Bread; Mincemeat Tea-ring; Kugelhopf

Polish sausage loaf *(serves 4)*
POWER LEVEL: 100% (FULL)
OVEN TEMPERATURE: 230°C (450°F), MARK 8

This is a microwave/conventional recipe.

225g (8oz) strong plain flour
$\frac{1}{2}$ × 5ml tsp ($\frac{1}{2}$tsp) salt
100ml (4fl oz) milk
15g ($\frac{1}{2}$oz) fresh yeast
2 × 15ml tbsp (2tbsp) oil
1 egg, beaten
1 spicy smoked sausage, weighing approximately
    225g (8oz)
a little flour
beaten egg for glaze

1 Sieve the flour into a bowl and add the salt. Make a
  well in the centre. Heat the milk for 20 sec. Cream
  the yeast with a little of the warm liquid.
2 Add the oil, egg and yeast liquid to the flour and
  mix well, adding sufficient of the remaining warm
  milk to give a workable dough.
3 Turn on to a floured surface and knead thoroughly
  until smooth and elastic.
4 Clean the bowl and return the dough to it. Cover
  with a lid or clingfilm and heat for 15 sec. Allow to
  stand for 5–10 min. Repeat 3–4 times until the
  dough has doubled in size.
5 Prick the sausage thoroughly with a fork. Heat the
  sausage (placed on kitchen paper towel) for
  3–4 min. Using a sharp knife, slit and remove the
  skin of the sausage. Roll the skinless sausage in a
  little flour.
6 Knead the dough again and roll out until just large
  enough to wrap around the sausage. Enclose the
  sausage in the dough and seal the edges with

water. Place on a greased baking sheet.
7 Cover with clingfilm and leave in a warm place for
  30 min until risen. Preheat the oven.
8 Remove the clingfilm and brush the loaf with
  beaten egg. Bake for 30 min until rich golden
  brown. Serve sliced, hot or cold.

Bread sticks *(makes about 24 sticks)*
POWER LEVEL: 100% (FULL) *(colour page 203)*
OVEN TEMPERATURE: 200°C (400°F), MARK 6

This is a microwave/conventional recipe.

350g (12oz) strong plain flour
1 × 5ml tsp (1tsp) salt
200ml (7fl oz) milk
15g ($\frac{1}{2}$oz) fresh yeast

1 Sieve the flour and salt into a large bowl. Heat the
  milk for 20–30 sec until tepid. Cream the yeast
  with a little of the liquid.
2 Add the yeast liquid to the flour with sufficient of
  the remaining milk to give a manageable dough.
  Knead the dough on a lightly floured surface until
  smooth and elastic.
3 Clean the bowl and return the dough to it, covering
  with a lid or clingfilm. Heat for 15 sec then allow to
  stand for 5–10 min. Repeat 3–4 times until
  doubled in size.
4 Grease 2–3 baking sheets and put the oven on to
  preheat. Knead the dough again and divide into 24
  pieces. Roll out to the thickness of a pencil approximately 22.5cm (9in) long. Cover the trays and
  leave in a warm place for 10 min.
5 Bake for 15–20 min until crisp and the sticks break
  cleanly in half when snapped. Cool on a wire rack.

Soda bread *(makes 1 loaf)*
POWER LEVEL: 100% (FULL)

This bread is leavened with soda rather than yeast.

450g (1lb) plain flour
1 × 5ml tsp (1tsp) salt
1 × 5ml tsp (1tsp) bicarbonate of soda
1 × 5ml tsp (1tsp) cream of tartar
50g (2oz) butter or margarine
350ml (12 fl oz) buttermilk or sour milk

1 Lightly grease and flour a 22.5cm (9in) round dish and line the base with floured, greaseproof paper.
2 Sift the flour, salt and raising agents into a bowl. Rub in the butter finely.
3 Add the milk and mix to a soft dough. Knead lightly on a floured surface and shape or roll into a large round about 2.5cm (1in) thick.
4 Place the dough into the prepared dish and sprinkle the top with flour. Score or cut into 8 wedges.
5 Cook for 5 min, turn the dish, cook for 1–2 min. Leave for 10–15 min before turning out to cool on a wire rack.

VARIATIONS

Brown soda bread: follow the ingredients and method for soda bread substituting 225g ($\frac{1}{2}$lb) of wholemeal flour for white flour.

Fly bread: follow the ingredients and method for soda bread adding 50g (2oz) currants and 25g (1oz) caster sugar to the dry ingredients.

Salted pretzels *(makes 16 large pretzels)*
POWER LEVEL: 100% (FULL) *(colour page 203)*
OVEN TEMPERATURE: 230°C (450°F), MARK 8

This is a microwave/conventional recipe.

450g (1lb) strong plain flour
1 × 5ml tsp (1tsp) salt
200ml (7fl oz) water
15g ($\frac{1}{2}$oz) fresh yeast
20g ($\frac{3}{4}$oz) butter
150ml ($\frac{1}{4}$pt) milk
1 egg, beaten
salt

1 Sieve the flour and 1 × 5ml tsp (1tsp) salt into a large bowl and make a well in the centre.
2 Heat the water for 20 sec and cream the yeast with a little of the water. Pour the yeast and remaining water into the centre of the flour. Draw a little of the flour over the liquid. Cover the bowl with a lid or clingfilm and heat for 15 sec in the microwave. Allow to stand for 5 min and then repeat once if necessary until the liquid foams.
3 Heat the butter for 30–60 sec until melted. Heat

the milk for 30 sec and add the butter and milk to the yeast mixture. Beat well until a dough is formed and leaves the sides of the bowl. Knead the dough well on a floured surface until smooth and elastic.
4 Clean the bowl and return the dough to it. Cover with a lid or clingfilm and heat for 15 sec in the microwave. Allow to stand for 5–10 min. Repeat 3–4 times until the dough has doubled in size.
5 Lightly grease 2–3 baking sheets, and turn on the oven to preheat. Knead the dough again and divide into 16 pieces. Roll each piece into the thickness of a pencil approximately 30cm (12in) long.
6 Form into pretzel shapes and place on the baking sheet. Cover and leave in a warm place for 10 min.
7 Glaze the pretzels with beaten egg and sprinkle with salt. Bake in a preheated oven for 15 min until golden.
8 Leave to cool on a wire tray.

Pretzel shapes

Light rye bread *(makes 1 loaf)*
POWER LEVEL: 100% (FULL)

This closer-textured bread has good keeping qualities and is delicious with smoked fish and cheese.

$1\frac{1}{2}$ × 5ml tsp ($1\frac{1}{2}$tsp) brown sugar
425ml ($\frac{3}{4}$pt) water, approximately
1 × 5ml tsp (1tsp) dried yeast
450g (1lb) strong plain flour
100g (4oz) rye flour
$1\frac{1}{2}$ × 5ml tsp ($1\frac{1}{2}$tsp) salt
rye meal, caraway seeds or cumin seeds for sprinkling, optional

1 Lightly grease a 22.5cm (9in) round dish or 900g (2lb) microwave loaf dish and line the base with greaseproof paper.
2 Add the sugar to a third of the water and warm for 30 sec. Stir in the yeast and leave for 8–12 min to activate.
3 Mix the flours and salt well and warm for 30 sec. Warm the remaining liquid for 45 sec.
4 Add the yeast and sufficient of the remaining water to the flours to form a soft dough. Mix well, knead lightly and form into a ball.
5 Place the dough into a bowl covered with clingfilm and prove by heating for 15 sec and leaving to stand for 5–10 min. Repeat this 3–4 times until double in size. If you have the time, knead and prove again.

6 Turn the dough on to a floured surface, knead well until smooth. Shape the dough and place into the prepared container.

7 With a sharp knife, make a cut across the top of the dough and widen this by pressing into it with the blade of the knife. Brush the top with oil, sprinkle with rye meal and a few caraway seeds or cumin seeds.

8 Prove as described previously until double in size. Cook for $5\frac{1}{2}$–$6\frac{1}{2}$ min, turning once halfway through if necessary. Leave for 10 min before turning out on to a wire rack to cool.

Note: *$1\frac{1}{2} \times 5ml$ tsp ($1\frac{1}{2}$tsp) caraway or cumin seeds may be added to the flours before mixing for a characteristic flavour of rye bread.*

VARIATION

Dark rye bread: Follow the ingredients and method for light rye bread using all rye flour.

Wholemeal lardy cake *(serves 12–16)*
POWER LEVEL: 100% (FULL) *(colour page 203)*
OVEN TEMPERATURE: 220°C (425°F), MARK 7

This is a microwave/conventional recipe.

225g (8oz) plain flour
225g (8oz) wholemeal flour
1 × 5ml tsp (1tsp) salt
275ml ($\frac{1}{2}$pt) milk
15g ($\frac{1}{2}$oz) fresh yeast
1 × 15ml tbsp (1tbsp) oil
50g (2oz) butter, cut into slivers
50g (2oz) lard, cut into slivers
100g (4oz) light soft brown sugar
100g (4oz) currants and sultanas, mixed
$\frac{1}{2}$ × 5ml tsp ($\frac{1}{2}$ tsp) mixed spice
1 × 15ml tbsp (1tbsp) oil
25g (1oz) demerara sugar

1 Place the flours and salt into a bowl, making a well in the centre. Heat the milk for 30 sec and use a little of the warm liquid to cream the yeast.

2 Add the yeast liquid to the flour with the oil and sufficient of the warm milk to make a workable dough.

3 Knead the dough on a floured surface until smooth and elastic. Clean the bowl and return the dough to it, covering with a lid or clingfilm. Heat for 15 sec, leave to stand for 5–10 min. Repeat 3–4 times until doubled in size.

4 Knead the dough again on a lightly floured surface. Roll out into a rectangle approximately 37.5 × 22.5cm (15 × 9in). Dot two-thirds of the surface with half the slivers of fat and sprinkle with 50g (2oz) of the sugar. Mix together the fruit and spice and sprinkle half the mixture on to the fat.

5 Fold the one-third of uncovered dough over the fruit (to the centre), then fold the remaining third over to make a parcel. Seal the edges with a rolling pin and give the dough a half turn.

6 Roll the dough into another rectangle and repeat the above process with the remaining fat, sugar, spice and fruit. Repeat the folding and roll out to fit an ovenproof glass dish approximately 30 × 17.5cm (12 × 7in).

7 Cover the dish with clingfilm and heat for 15 sec. Allow to stand for 5–10 min. Repeat this process twice, and meanwhile preheat the oven.

8 Remove the clingfilm and brush the top of the lardy cake with oil. Mark the top of the cake into diamond shapes with a sharp knife and sprinkle the cake with the demerara sugar.

9 Bake in the preheated oven for approximately 30 min. Cool on a wire tray.

Walnut bread *(makes 1 small loaf)*
POWER LEVEL: 100% (FULL) *(colour page 203)*

15g ($\frac{1}{2}$oz) fresh yeast
1 × 5ml tsp (1tsp) sugar
150g (5oz) strong plain white flour
150ml ($\frac{1}{4}$pt) milk
100g (4oz) wholemeal flour
1 × 5ml tsp (1tsp) salt
25g (1oz) butter
20g ($\frac{3}{4}$oz) sugar
50g (2oz) walnuts, chopped
100g (4oz) dried dates, chopped

1 Add the yeast, 1 × 5ml tsp (1tsp) sugar and 25g (1oz) of the strong plain white flour to the milk and whisk thoroughly with a fork until blended. Cover with clingfilm and heat for 15 sec. Allow to stand for 5–10 min until foamy.

2 Place the remaining flours and salt in a bowl, rub in the butter and make a well in the centre. Add the sugar and yeast liquid and mix to a manageable dough. Knead on a lightly floured surface until smooth and elastic.

3 Clean the bowl and return the dough to it, covering with a lid or clingfilm. Heat for 15 sec then allow to stand for 5–10 min. Repeat 3–4 times until doubled in size.

4 Knead the dough again, working in the sugar, walnuts and dates until evenly distributed. Shape the dough and place in a small microwave loaf dish approximately 10 × 17.5 × 3.75cm (4 × 7 × 1$\frac{1}{2}$in).

5 Cover loosely with clingfilm and heat for 15 sec. Allow to stand for 5–10 min. Repeat 2–3 times until well risen.

6 Remove the clingfilm and cook for 3$\frac{1}{2}$–4 min. Leave to stand for 5 min then turn on to a wire rack to cool. Serve sliced and buttered.

Chelsea buns *(makes 8)*
POWER LEVEL: 100% (FULL)

450g (1lb) Basic White Bread Dough (page 204)
25g (1oz) butter
150g (5oz) currants
50g (2oz) soft brown sugar
soft brown sugar for sprinkling
pinch cinnamon or mixed spice
Apricot Glaze for top (page 180)

1 Lightly grease a large shallow dish.
2 Follow the instructions and method for the basic white bread dough until the end of the first proving.
3 Knead the dough on a floured surface. Roll out to a rectangle approximately 30 × 22.5cm (12 × 9in).
4 Melt the butter for 1 min and brush over the dough. Sprinkle over the currants and sugar. Roll up from one of the long sides like a swiss roll.
5 Cut into 8 slices and place side by side around the edges and middle of the prepared container. Prove as before until double in size. Sprinkle with the sugar and cinnamon or mixed spice.
6 Cook for 6−8 min, turning once halfway through if necessary. Leave to stand for 5−10 min before removing to cooling rack.
7 Brush with hot apricot glaze.

Savarin *(serves 8)*
POWER LEVEL: 100% (FULL)

1 × 5ml tsp (1tsp) sugar
150ml ($\frac{1}{4}$pt) water, approximately
2 × 5ml tsp (2tsp) dried yeast
225g (8oz) plain flour
$\frac{1}{2}$ × 5ml tsp ($\frac{1}{2}$tsp) salt
50g (2oz) butter or margarine
2 eggs, beaten
25g (1oz) flaked almonds
for serving: Syrup (below), Apricot Glaze (page 180), whipped cream, fruit salad

1 Lightly grease a 20cm (8in) microwave ring mould.
2 Add the sugar to the water and warm for 30 sec. Stir in the yeast and leave for 8−12 min to activate.
3 Sift the flour and salt and warm for 15 sec. Add the yeast mixture and a little more water if necessary. Mix and knead well; the dough should be fairly soft.
4 Cover and prove by heating for 10 sec and leaving for 5 min. Repeat until double in size.
5 Melt the butter or margarine for 1$\frac{1}{2}$ min. Beat the butter and eggs into the dough until it resembles a thick batter. Beat well.
6 Arrange the flaked almonds in the base of the container and carefully pour in the batter.

7 Cover with clingfilm and prove as described earlier until the mixture is well risen in the mould.
8 Remove the clingfilm and cook for 6$\frac{1}{2}$−7 min, turning once halfway through.
9 Leave to cool for a few minutes before turning on to a cooling rack.
10 While still warm, pour the syrup over the savarin and when cool, brush with apricot glaze.
11 To serve, fill the centre with mixed fruit salad and decorate with swirls of whipped cream.

Syrup
POWER LEVEL: 100% (FULL)

100g (4oz) caster sugar
150ml ($\frac{1}{4}$pt) water
1 × 5ml tsp (1tsp) lemon juice
2 × 15ml tbsp (2tbsp) kirsch

1 Add the sugar to the water and heat for 1 min. Stir until the sugar is dissolved. Bring to the boil in the microwave and keep boiling until a thick syrup is formed.
2 Stir in the lemon juice and kirsch and pour over the savarin while warm.

Pitka *(makes 1 large loaf, about 16 servings)*
POWER LEVEL: 100% (FULL) *(colour page 203)*

450g (1lb) strong plain white flour
1$\frac{1}{2}$ × 5ml tsp (1$\frac{1}{2}$tsp) salt
225ml (8fl oz) milk
15g ($\frac{1}{2}$oz) fresh yeast
1 egg, beaten
1 × 15ml tbsp (1tbsp) oil
50g (2oz) cottage or goat's cheese

1 Sieve together the flour and salt into a large bowl. Heat the milk for 20−30 sec until tepid, then cream the yeast with a little of the warm liquid.
2 Add the creamed yeast to the flour with the beaten egg and oil and sufficient of the remaining liquid to give a manageable dough.
3 Turn on to a floured surface and knead thoroughly until smooth. Clean the bowl and return the dough to it, covering with a lid or clingfilm. Heat for 15 sec then allow to stand for 5−10 min. Repeat 3−4 times until doubled in size.
4 Knead again, working in the cheese; shape into a round to fit a lightly oiled 25cm (10in) plate. Loosely cover with clingfilm and heat for 15 sec. Allow to stand for 5−10 min. Repeat 2−3 times until well risen.
5 Remove the film and cook for 4$\frac{1}{2}$−5 min. Stand for 5 min then turn on to a wire rack. Eat warm, liberally buttered.

Brioche ring *(serves 6–8)*
POWER LEVEL: 100% (FULL)

This rich moist brioche can be served hot in slices with butter for a continental-style breakfast or may be decorated with glacé fruits and glacé icing to serve with coffee or tea.

1 × 5ml tsp (1tsp) sugar
3 × 15ml tbsp (3tbsp) water
1 × 5ml tsp (1tsp) dried yeast
225g (8oz) plain flour
½ × 5ml tsp (½tsp) salt
1 × 15ml tbsp (1tbsp) sugar
175g (6oz) butter
2 eggs, beaten
for decoration, optional: Glacé Icing (page 173) glacé fruits

1 Lightly butter a 20cm (8in) microwave ring mould.
2 Add 1 × 5ml tsp (1tsp) sugar to the water and warm for 15 sec. Stir in the yeast and leave for 8–12 min to activate.
3 Sift the flour with the salt, add the 1 × 15ml tbsp (1tbsp) sugar and warm for 30 sec. Melt the butter for 2 min.
4 Add the yeast, eggs and butter to the flour and beat well to form a soft, smooth sticky dough.
5 Cover with clingfilm and prove by heating for 15 sec and leaving for 5–10 min. Repeat until well risen.
6 Knead lightly and pour into the prepared container. Cover with clingfilm and prove again as described previously until it rises to within 2.5cm (1in) of the top of the container. The rich dough may take longer to rise.
7 Remove the clingfilm and cook for 3½–4 min, turning once halfway through if necessary. Leave for a few minutes before turning on to a cooling rack.
8 Serve hot in slices with butter, or leave until nearly cold, brush with glacé icing and decorate with a few slices of glacé fruit.

Carrot bread *(makes 1 large loaf)*
POWER LEVEL: 100% (FULL) *(colour page 203)*

This bread has an interesting orange colour.

1 quantity Basic White Bread dough ingredients (page 204)
225g (8oz) carrots, finely shredded

1 Sieve the flour and salt into a bowl and rub in the fat.
2 Squeeze as much liquid as possible from the carrots with your hands and add the carrot to the flour, mixing well.
3 Heat the liquid for 30 sec and use a little to cream the yeast to a paste. Add the yeast to the flour and carrot, with sufficient of the remaining liquid to give a workable dough.
4 Turn on to a floured surface and knead thoroughly until smooth and elastic.
5 Clean the bowl and return the dough to it, covering with a lid or clingfilm. Heat for 15 sec then allow to stand for 5–10 min. Repeat 3–4 times until doubled in size.
6 Knead again and shape to fit a deep 17.5–20cm (7–8in) round dish. Loosely cover with clingfilm and heat for 15 sec. Allow to stand for 5–10 min. Repeat 3–4 times until well risen.
7 Remove the clingfilm and cook for 5–6 min. Stand for 5 min before turning on to a wire rack to cool.

Garlic or herb loaf *(makes 1 loaf)*
POWER LEVEL: 100% (FULL)

Delicious to serve as a snack or as an accompaniment to a meal.

1 short, crusty french stick
150g (5oz) butter, softened
3–4 cloves garlic, crushed or finely chopped *or*
1–1½ × 5ml tsp (1–1½tsp) garlic powder *or*
1–2 × 15ml tbsp (1–2tbsp) chopped fresh mixed
 herbs

1 Cut the loaf, not quite through, into slices 2.5cm (1in) thick.
2 Cream the butter and beat in the garlic or herbs.
3 Spread a large knob of butter between the slices.
4 Protect the thin ends of the loaf with small, smooth pieces of aluminium foil.
5 Place on kitchen paper towel in the microwave cooker and cover with a piece of damp kitchen paper towel.
6 Cook for 1½ min or until the butter has just melted and the bread is warmed through.

Family sardine pizza *(serves 4)*
POWER LEVEL: 100% (FULL)

This recipe uses the quick white dough method with the ascorbic acid/vitamin C tablet.

1 × 50g (2oz) can anchovy fillets
milk
225g (8oz) strong plain flour
½ × 5ml tsp (½tsp) salt
20g (¾oz) lard
15g (½oz) yeast
50mg tablet ascorbic acid/vitamin C, crushed
150ml (¼pt) water
4 × 15ml tbsp (4tbsp) oil
4 tomatoes, skinned and sliced
1 small red pepper, diced
1 onion, finely sliced
½ × 5ml tsp (½tsp) oregano
salt and pepper
2 × 115g (4½oz) cans sardines, drained
100g (4oz) dolcelatte cheese, sliced
parmesan cheese, grated for sprinkling
for garnish: olives

1 Soak the anchovy fillets in the milk to remove excess saltiness.
2 Sieve the flour and salt into a bowl, rub in the fat and make a well in the centre. Place the yeast and crushed vitamin C tablet in a small dish. Heat the water for 15–20 sec and use a little of the liquid to cream the yeast.
3 Add the yeast liquid to the flour with half the oil and

sufficient of the remaining liquid to give a manageable dough.
4 Knead the dough thoroughly on a lightly floured surface until smooth and elastic. Roll out to fit a dish 17.5 × 27.5cm (7 × 11in). Cover with clingfilm and heat for 15 sec, allow to stand 5–10 min. Repeat 2–3 times until well risen. Remove the clingfilm.
5 During a resting period, heat the remaining oil in a bowl for 2 min. Add the tomatoes, pepper and onion, cover and cook for 6 min, stirring once. Season with oregano and salt and pepper.
6 Spread the tomato mixture on top of the proved dough. Arrange the drained sardines on the top and cover with the cheese.
7 Drain the anchovy and use to garnish the pizza, then sprinkle with the parmesan cheese.
8 Cook for 10 min, turning the dish halfway through if necessary. Allow to stand for 2 min before serving garnished with olives.

Traditional herb bread *(makes 1 large loaf)*
POWER LEVEL: 100% (FULL)

This bread is delicious with ploughman's lunches.

1 egg
225ml (8fl oz) milk
20g (¾oz) fresh yeast
1 × 15ml tbsp (1tbsp) oil
3 × 5ml tsp (3tsp) caster sugar
1 × 5ml tsp (1tsp) dried tarragon
350g (12oz) strong plain white flour
1½ × 5ml tsp (1½tsp) salt
oil for brushing
dill or fennel seed for sprinkling

1 Beat the egg in a large bowl. Heat the milk for 20–30 sec until tepid. Cream the yeast with a little of the warm milk then add the yeast and remaining milk to the egg with the oil, sugar and tarragon.
2 Mix together the flour and salt. Sieve three-quarters of the flour into the liquid and beat well for 4–5 min to give a creamy soft dough. Stir in the remaining flour.
3 Turn the dough into a large microwave loaf dish, 11.25 × 17.5 × 5cm (4½ × 7 × 2in). Lightly flour your knuckles and gently press the dough into shape.
4 Cover loosely with clingfilm and heat for 15 sec, then allow to stand for 5–10 min. Repeat 3–4 times.
5 Remove the clingfilm and brush the top of the dough with oil and sprinkle with dill or fennel seeds.
6 Cook for 5 min then allow to stand for 5 min before turning out on to a wire cooling tray.

Light german pumpernickel
(*makes 1 small loaf*)
POWER LEVEL: 100% (FULL) (*colour page 203*)

175g (6oz) wholewheat flour
50g (2oz) rye flour
1 × 5ml tsp (1tsp) salt
15g ($\frac{1}{2}$oz) bran
15g ($\frac{1}{2}$oz) maize meal
65g ($2\frac{1}{2}$oz) cold mashed potato
40g ($1\frac{1}{2}$oz) margarine
150ml ($\frac{1}{4}$pt) water
15g ($\frac{1}{2}$oz) fresh yeast
1 × 5ml tsp (1tsp) soft brown sugar

1 Place the flours and salt in a large bowl together with the bran, maize meal and cold mashed potato. Make a well in the centre.
2 Heat the margarine until melted, about 30 sec. Heat the water for 20 sec. Cream the yeast and sugar with a little of the liquid.
3 Add the margarine and yeast liquid to the dry ingredients with sufficient of the remaining liquid to give a workable dough.
4 Turn out on to a floured surface and knead until smooth. Clean the bowl and return the dough to it, covering with a lid or clingfilm. Heat for 15 sec then allow to stand for 5–10 min. Repeat 4–5 times until doubled in size.
5 Knead again and shape to fit a small microwave loaf dish measuring 10 × 17.5 × 3.75cm (4 × 7 × $1\frac{1}{2}$in). Loosely cover with clingfilm and prove again as above until the dough has risen to the top of the dish. Remove the clingfilm.
6 Cook for $3\frac{1}{2}$–4 min, stand for 5 min then turn on to a wire rack to cool. Serve thinly sliced and buttered, with cheese or cold meat.

Christmas loaf (*makes 1 small loaf*)
POWER LEVEL: 100% (FULL) (*colour page 203*)

2 eggs
milk
15g ($\frac{1}{2}$oz) fresh yeast
15g ($\frac{1}{2}$oz) sugar
100g (4oz) strong plain flour
50g (2oz) lard
50g (2oz) soft brown sugar
2 × 5ml tsp (2tsp) black treacle
75g (3oz) wholemeal flour
$\frac{1}{2}$ × 5ml tsp ($\frac{1}{2}$tsp) salt
1 × 5ml tsp (1tsp) baking powder
$\frac{1}{2}$ × 5ml tsp ($\frac{1}{2}$tsp) grated nutmeg
1 × 5ml tsp (1tsp) mixed spice
100g (4oz) currants
50g (2oz) sultanas
25g (1oz) mixed peel

1 Beat 1 egg in a measuring jug, add sufficient milk to give 75ml ($\frac{1}{8}$pt). Beat the yeast, sugar and 25g (1oz) flour into the liquid until thoroughly blended.
2 Cover the jug with clingfilm and heat for 15 sec then allow to stand for 10 min.
3 Cream together the lard, brown sugar and treacle until pale and fluffy. Beat in the remaining egg then add the flour, salt, baking powder and spices.
4 Add the yeast mixture to the dough and mix to a smooth consistency. Add the fruits and work in until evenly distributed. The mixture should be a stiff dropping consistency.
5 Lightly oil a microwave loaf dish and transfer the dough to it, shaping the dough with the back of a spoon. Cover loosely with clingfilm and heat for 15 sec. Allow to stand for 5–10 min. Repeat 4–5 times until risen. (This is more like cake than bread and will not rise very much.) Remove clingfilm.
6 Cook for 4 min. Stand for 2–3 min then turn on to a wire cooling rack.

Moravian bread (*makes 1 large loaf*)
POWER LEVEL: 100% (FULL) (*colour page 203*)

350g (12oz) strong plain flour
$\frac{1}{2}$ × 5ml tsp ($\frac{1}{2}$tsp) salt
$\frac{1}{2}$ × 5ml tsp ($\frac{1}{2}$tsp) cinnamon
65g ($2\frac{1}{2}$oz) caster sugar
65g ($2\frac{1}{2}$oz) margarine
100g (4oz) cold mashed potato
150ml ($\frac{1}{4}$pt) water
15g ($\frac{1}{2}$oz) fresh yeast
1 × 5ml tsp (1tsp) grated nutmeg
pinch ground mace

1 Sift the flour into a bowl with the salt, cinnamon and sugar. Rub in 50g (2oz) of the margarine, add the mashed potato and mix well.
2 Heat the water for 20 sec and cream the yeast with a little of the warm liquid. Add the yeast liquid to the bowl with sufficient of the remaining liquid to give a workable dough.
3 Knead on a lightly floured surface until smooth and elastic. Clean the bowl and return the dough to it; cover with a lid or clingfilm.
4 Heat for 15 sec, stand for 5–10 min. Repeat 3–4 times or until doubled in size.
5 Knead the dough again and shape to fit an oiled microwave loaf dish, 11.25 × 17.5 × 5cm ($4\frac{1}{2}$ × 7 × 2in). Cover loosely with clingfilm and prove again as above. Remove the clingfilm.
6 Melt the remaining margarine for 30 sec and brush over the top of the loaf. Make 3 deep slits in the loaf with a sharp knife and fill with the nutmeg and mace. Sprinkle any remaining spices over the loaf.
7 Cook for 5–6 min, stand for 5 min. Turn on to a wire rack to cool before serving sliced and buttered.

Rice, pasta and pulses

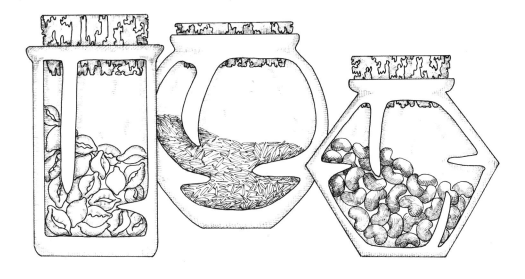

Rice, pasta and pulses cook extremely well in the microwave—probably better than most other conventional methods—and this is true also for defrosting and reheating after freezing. The main advantage though, is the fact that little or no attention is required during the cooking time and the kitchen remains relatively free of steam. Make sure that the cooking container is large enough to allow for the water to boil and the expansion of the food. All dishes should be covered either with a lid or clingfilm during the defrosting, reheating or cooking period.

Rice
Long grain rice may be boiled using lots of salted water and drained afterwards or by carefully measuring the quantity of salted water so that the rice absorbs all the liquid during cooking, thereby retaining more B vitamins. If the latter method is used, the ratio of rice to water is 1:2, ie 1 cup of rice to 2 cups of water, allowing about 1×5ml tsp (1tsp) salt for this quantity.

Easy-cook rice absorbs more water than the normal long-grain rice and takes about 1–2 minutes longer to cook. Brown rice has a 'nuttier' texture and a delicious flavour, which compensates for the fact that it takes approximately double the amount of cooking time than for white rice.

Rice may be defrosted and reheated in one operation. Simply place it in a covered container and cook for 2 minutes, breaking down any lumps with a fork and stirring halfway through. Depending of course on the quantity, continue to cook for a further 2–3 min until hot through. If preferred, add a knob of butter before defrosting plain rice or top with slivers of butter just before serving. Risottos, pilafs or dishes which contain other ingredients as well as the rice should be defrosted on 50% (defrost) setting for 4–5 minutes, stirring gently halfway through. Any unthawed portion may be returned to the microwave for another minute or two. Alternatively, after the defrosting time, allow to stand for a few minutes until completely thawed. Reheat on 100% (full) setting for 3–4 minutes, stirring halfway through. Allow to stand for 1–2 minutes and then fork over before serving.

Pasta
Pasta should be cooked in a large, covered container with plenty of boiling, salted water and a little oil to avoid sticking. When cooking quantities larger than 450g (1lb) you may find that conventional cooking methods are more convenient. When cooking pasta in the microwave, ensure that it is completely covered with water—any pieces that protrude above the water will become hard and brittle. To help prevent this, hold the pasta under the boiling water with a spoon or fork until it softens before covering and placing in the microwave to cook.

Pasta may be boiled in the microwave until it is cooked (see the chart on page 216) or it may be cooked for half the recommended time and then allowed to stand for 10–15 minutes before draining.

Defrost and reheat pasta in a covered dish. Add a knob of butter and use 50% (defrost) setting until thawed, stirring frequently. Any pieces of plain cooked pasta which are sticking together may be rinsed under cold running water before reheating.

Rice, pasta and pulses cooking chart

Rice/pasta/ pulses	Preparation	Cooking time 100% (full)
easy-cook rice (american) 225g (8oz)	Add 550ml (1pt) boiling salted water	12 min stand 5 min
long-grain rice (patna) 225g (8oz)	Add 550ml (1pt) boiling salted water and 1 × 15ml tbsp (1 tbsp) oil	10 min stand 5 min
brown rice 225g (8oz)	Add 550ml (1pt) boiling salted water	20–25 min stand 5 min
pasta whirls, egg noodles and tagliatelle 225g (8oz)	Add 550ml (1pt) boiling salted water and 1 × 15ml tbsp (1 tbsp) oil	5–6 min stand 3 min
macaroni 225g (8oz)	Add 550ml (1pt) boiling salted water and 1 × 15ml tbsp (1 tbsp) oil	8 min stand 3 min
pasta shells 225g (8oz)	Add 850ml (1½pt) boiling salted water and 1 × 15ml tbsp (1 tbsp) oil	15–18 min stand 2 min
spaghetti 225g (8oz)	Break spaghetti in half if necessary; add 850ml (1½pt) boiling salted water and 1 × 15ml tbsp (1 tbsp) oil	12 min stand 2 min
lasagne 225g (8oz)	Add 1 litre (1¾pt) boiling salted water and 1 × 15ml tbsp (1 tbsp) oil	10 min stand 2 min
lentils, split peas 225g (8oz), soaked	Add 550ml (1pt) boiling water	20–25 min stand 5 min
beans, whole peas 225g (8oz) soaked	Add 850ml (1½pt) boiling water	40–60 min stand 5 min

Pulses

Pulses—dried peas, beans and lentils—require soaking before cooking conventionally or by microwave. They should be soaked in cold water for 8–12 hours, or overnight if possible. Alternatively, cover them with cold water and bring to the boil in the microwave, cook for 2–3 minutes then allow them to stand for 1–1½ hours to swell and soften. Drain and rinse well.

To cook, place the pulses in a large container, ensuring that there is sufficient room for the water to boil during the cooking time. Cover with boiling water from the kettle and bring the dish to the boil in the microwave cooker. Do not add any salt to the water as this prevents the pulses from softening and therefore lengthens the cooking time. Once boiling—this will take about 3–4 minutes—lentils will take approximately 20–25 minutes to cook and larger pulses 40–60 minutes. All pulses should be covered during the cooking period. Be prepared to top up the cooking liquid with extra boiling water from the kettle when necessary.

Defrost and reheat pulses in a similar way to rice; using a 100% (full) setting, cook for 2–3 minutes, breaking down any lumps with a fork before continuing to cook until heated through. Pulses in a sauce should be defrosted using a 50% (defrost) setting and stirred frequently. When thawed, reheat for 3–4 minutes and allow to stand for 1–2 minutes before serving.

Chilli con carne *(serves 4–6)*

POWER LEVEL: 100% (FULL)

2 × 15ml tbsp (2tbsp) oil
2 large onions, finely chopped
450g (1lb) minced beef
2 × 15ml tbsp (2tbsp) tomato purée
1–2 × 15ml tbsp (1–2tbsp) chilli powder
1 × 5ml tsp (1tsp) paprika
salt and pepper
1 × 397g (14oz) can red kidney beans
for serving: boiled rice (see chart)

1 Heat the oil in a large bowl for 2 min. Add the onions and cook for 3 min. Add the meat and mix well.
2 Cover and cook for 2 min, stir, cook for 2 min. Add the tomato purée, chilli powder, paprika and seasoning, mixing well.
3 Drain the kidney beans, reserving the juice and making up to 225ml (8fl oz) with water. Add the liquid to the meat.
4 Cover and cook for 10 min, stand for 5 min. Stir in the kidney beans, then cook for 5–10 min. Skim off the surplus fat and adjust the seasoning before serving.

Rice pilaf (serves 4)
POWER LEVEL: 100% (FULL)

40g (1½oz) butter
1 small onion, chopped
1 small stick celery, chopped
225g (8oz) long-grain rice
425ml (¾pt) boiling chicken stock (page 64), approx
pinch saffron, optional
salt and pepper
50–75g (2–3oz) currants, optional
50–75g (2–3oz) pistachio nuts or almonds, blanched and shredded, optional

1 Melt the butter in a large shallow dish for 2 min. Add the onion and celery and cook for 3 min. Stir in the rice and cook for 1 min.
2 Soak the saffron in 2 × 15ml tbsp (2tbsp) boiling water. Add the stock, saffron and seasoning and cook, uncovered, for 12–15 min, adding extra stock if necessary.
3 Carefully stir in the currants and nuts if used, and fork over the pilaf before serving.

Macaroni with mushrooms (serves 4)
POWER LEVEL: 100% (FULL)

75g (3oz) butter
100g (4oz) button mushrooms, thinly sliced
225ml (8fl oz) single cream
275g (10oz) short cut macaroni
1 × 15ml tbsp (1tbsp) oil
1 × 5ml tsp (1tsp) salt
550ml (1pt) boiling water, approximately
salt and freshly ground black pepper
100g (4oz) cooked ham, cut into strips
50g (2oz) parmesan cheese, grated
275ml (½pt) White Sauce (page 132)
paprika pepper for sprinkling

1 Melt 25g (1oz) of the butter in a small bowl or dish for 1 min. Add the mushrooms, stir well, cover and cook for 2–2½ min. Stir in the cream.
2 Place the macaroni in a bowl with the oil and salt and pour on sufficient boiling water to cover. Stir, cover and cook for 8–10 min until plump and tender. Drain thoroughly.
3 Add the ham to the macaroni with 25g (1oz) of the cheese and 25g (1oz) of the remaining butter. Stir well and then mix in the mushrooms and cream.
4 Cover and reheat for 2–3 min. Heat the sauce if necessary and pour over the macaroni. Sprinkle with the remaining cheese, paprika pepper and dot with the remaining butter. Heat, uncovered for about 2 min to melt the butter. Alternatively, brown the top under a hot grill.

DO NOT FREEZE

Wholewheat spaghetti pie (serves 4)
POWER LEVEL: 100% (FULL)

2 × 15ml tbsp (2tbsp) oil
1 large onion, chopped
2 medium carrots, chopped
2 sticks celery, chopped
350g (12oz) minced beef
1 × 15ml tbsp (1tbsp) flour
1 × 225g (8oz) can tomatoes
2 × 15ml tbsp (2tbsp) tomato purée
salt and freshly ground black pepper
1 × 5ml tsp (1tsp) dried mixed herbs
75ml (⅛pt) beef stock (page 64)
225g (8oz) wholewheat spaghetti, cooked (page 216)
100g (4oz) cheddar cheese, grated
for garnish: tomato slices, sprigs parsley
for serving: green salad and crusty bread

1 Place oil, onion, carrots and celery in a large bowl. Mix well together, cover and cook for 5½ min.
2 Add the beef, stir well into the vegetables, cover and cook for 5 min, stirring twice throughout and breaking down any lumps with a fork.
3 Stir in the flour, tomatoes, tomato purée, seasoning, mixed herbs and beef stock. Cover and cook for 10–15 min until tender, stirring every 5 min.
4 Place half the spaghetti in the base of a buttered casserole dish, add the meat mixture and top with the remaining spaghetti.
5 Sprinkle with the grated cheese and cook uncovered, for 3–4 min to heat through and melt the cheese. Alternatively, brown the top under a hot grill.
6 Garnish with tomato slices and sprigs of parsley and serve with green salad and crusty bread.

Flageolets with ham (serves 4–6)
POWER LEVEL: 100% (FULL)

225g (8oz) flageolet beans, cooked or
1 × 425g (15oz) can flageolet beans
275ml (½pt) Béchamel Sauce (page 134)
2–3 × 15ml tbsp (2–3tbsp) cream
225g (8oz) lean ham, shredded
salt and freshly ground black pepper
1 × 15ml tbsp (1tbsp) chopped parsley

1 Soak and cook the dried flageolet beans as for haricot beans. Drain the cooked or canned beans thoroughly.
2 Heat the béchamel sauce if necessary for 2–3 min and stir in the cream.
3 Mix the beans and ham into the sauce and season to taste with salt and freshly ground black pepper. Reheat for 1½–2 min.
4 Serve sprinkled with chopped parsley.

Noodles with cream and herbs *(serves 4–6)*
POWER LEVEL: 100% (FULL) *(colour opposite)*

450g (1lb) egg noodles
1.1 litre (2pt) boiling water, approximately
salt
1 × 15ml tbsp (1tbsp) oil
150ml ($\frac{1}{4}$pt) cream
1 × 15ml tbsp (1tbsp) each chopped parsley, chives
   and rosemary
2 cloves garlic, crushed
100g (4oz) butter
freshly ground black pepper
parmesan cheese, grated, to taste

1 Place the noodles in a large mixing bowl or casserole dish. Cover with boiling water, add salt to
taste and the oil. Cover and cook for 5–6 min until
tender but with a 'bite'. Stand for 2 min then drain
thoroughly.
2 Warm the cream in a jug or small bowl for
1–1$\frac{1}{2}$ min. Mix the herbs with the garlic and soften
50g (2oz) of the butter for 30 sec.
3 Mix the noodles with the cream, herbs, garlic and
softened butter. Add salt and freshly ground black
pepper to taste.
4 Serve the noodles on warm plates and sprinkle with
grated parmesan cheese. Add a knob of butter to
the centre of each plate and serve hot.

Note: *spaghetti or tagliatelle or other fine stranded pasta
can be served in the same sauce.*

Spaghetti with seafood *(serves 4–6)*
POWER LEVEL: 100% (FULL) *(colour opposite)*

350g (12oz) spaghetti, cooked (page 216)
3 × 15ml tbsp (3tbsp) oil
1 clove garlic, finely chopped
225g (8oz) peeled prawns, fresh or frozen, thawed
200g (7oz) can tuna fish, drained and flaked
225g (8oz) can tomatoes
salt and freshly ground black pepper
2 × 15ml tbsp (2tbsp) chopped parsley

1 When the spaghetti is cooked, drain well and rinse
in hot water. Drain thoroughly.
2 Mix the oil with the garlic, prawns, flaked tuna and
the tomatoes. Cover and cook for 5 min, add salt
and pepper to taste.
3 Add the mixture to the spaghetti and stir over
lightly. Cover and reheat if necessary for 1–2 min.
Add the parsley and toss over well before serving.

DO NOT FREEZE

Lentils with bacon *(serves 4)*
POWER LEVEL: 100% (FULL) *(colour opposite)*

225g (8oz) beige or brown lentils, soaked for 2 hours
3 × 15ml tbsp (3tbsp) oil
1 large onion, finely chopped
225g (8oz) smoked streaky bacon, derinded and cut
   into strips
3 × 15ml tbsp (3tbsp) tomato purée
850ml (1$\frac{1}{2}$pt) boiling chicken stock (page 64)
salt to taste
for serving: toasted croûtes of french bread and salad

1 Drain the lentils after soaking.
2 Place the oil and onion into a large casserole dish,
toss over well, cover and cook for 2 min, stirring
once halfway through.
3 Stir in the bacon and continue to cook for a further
4 min. Add the lentils and cook, covered for 3 min,
stirring halfway through.
4 Mix in the tomato purée, boiling chicken stock and
a little salt to taste. Cover and cook for 20–25 min
until the lentils are tender. The consistency should
be quite thick, but if necessary remove the lid (or
cover) and continue to cook for a further 3–5 min
to reduce the liquid slightly. Stand for 5 min.
5 Taste and adjust the seasoning. Serve with toasted
croûtes of french bread and a salad.

*Lentils with Bacon; Noodles with Cream and Herbs; Spaghetti
with Seafood*

Risotto with lentils and chicken *(serves 4–6)*
POWER LEVEL: 100% (FULL)

50g (2oz) dried apricots
50g (2oz) butter
1 onion, finely chopped
2 chicken breasts, boned and cut into strips or dice
salt and freshly ground black pepper
225g (8oz) long grain rice
boiling water
100g (4oz) lentils, soaked for 2 hr and drained
1 × 15ml tbsp (1tbsp) chopped parsley or dill
50g (2oz) flaked almonds, toasted
slivers butter

1 Chop the apricots and place into a bowl and cover with warm water. Leave to soak for 30 min.
2 Melt 25g (1oz) butter in a small casserole dish for 1 min, stir in the onion, cover and cook for 3–4 min until tender. Add the chicken, stir well and continue to cook for 5–6 min; leave to stand and keep warm. Season with salt and pepper.
3 Cook the rice in a large covered bowl with boiling salted water for 10–12 min until tender. Drain and rinse in warm water.
4 Cover and cook the drained lentils in boiling salted water for about 25 min until tender. Drain and rinse in warm water.
5 Mix the rice and lentils and stir in the chicken mixture. Taste and adjust the seasoning. Stir in the softened apricots, the parsley or dill and the almonds.
6 Place the mixture into a serving dish and top with slivers of butter. Cover and heat through for 3–4 min before serving hot.

Cannelloni with spinach and cheese
(serves 2–4)
POWER LEVEL: 100% (FULL)

8 cannelloni tubes
boiling water
salt
1 × 15ml tbsp (1tbsp) oil
225g (8oz) frozen leaf spinach, thawed
150g (5oz) ricotta cheese
75g (3oz) grated parmesan cheese
75g (3oz) cream cheese
freshly ground pepper
freshly ground nutmeg
275ml (½pt) White Sauce (page 132)

1 Cook the cannelloni in a large, covered bowl of boiling, salted water with the oil for 5–6 min. Drain and rinse the pasta and pat dry with kitchen paper towel.
2 Drain the thawed spinach and mix with the ricotta cheese, about half the parmesan cheese and the

cream cheese. Add a little pepper and nutmeg.
3 Fill the cannelloni with the spinach and cheese mixture and place in a single layer in a casserole dish.
4 Cover and heat for 4 min and then allow to stand. Heat the sauce, if necessary, for 3–4 min and pour over the cannelloni.
5 Sprinkle with the remaining parmesan cheese and heat, uncovered, for 3–4 min until the top is bubbling and the dish is heated through. Alternatively, the top may be browned under a hot grill.

Spiced busmati rice *(serves 4) (colour page 111)*
POWER LEVEL: 100% (FULL) AND 50% (DEFROST)

This lightly spiced rice dish goes extremely well with curries but is also delicious with plainly cooked hot or cold meats.

225g (8oz) busmati rice, soaked for ½ hr
50g (2oz) onion, finely chopped
3 × 15ml tbsp (3tbsp) oil
½ green chilli, finely chopped
½ × 5ml tsp (½tsp) garam masala
1 × 5ml tsp (1tsp) turmeric
1–2 cloves garlic, finely chopped
425ml (¾pt) boiling chicken stock (page 64), approx

1 Drain the busmati rice in a sieve and leave to drain for 15–20 min.
2 Place the onion and the oil into a dish, cover and cook for 3 min. Add the chilli, garam masala, turmeric, garlic and the drained rice and continue to cook for 2 min.
3 Pour on 275ml (½pt) of the stock, mix well and cover the dish. Reduce to 50% (defrost) setting and continue to cook for 20–25 min, stirring 2–3 times throughout and adding more stock as necessary.
4 Allow to stand for 5 min, fork over the rice and serve hot.

Black eye beans with vegetables in cream sauce *(serves 4–6)*
POWER LEVEL: 100% (FULL) AND 50% (DEFROST)

175g (6oz) black eye beans
550ml (1pt) cold water
2 large carrots, cut into 20mm (¾in) slices
8 button onions
425ml (¾pt) White Sauce (page 132)
2–3 × 15ml tbsp (2–3tbsp) double cream
salt and freshly ground black pepper
3 × 15ml tbsp (3tbsp) chopped parsley

1 Place the beans and cold water into a large dish or bowl, cover and bring to the boil in the microwave

on 100% (full) setting, about 6 min; leave to stand for 1 hr.

2 Drain the beans and rinse in cold water. Place into the dish with the carrots and onions. Pour on sufficient cold water to cover.

3 Cover and bring to the boil, about 12–14 min, then reduce to 50% (defrost) setting and continue to cook for 25–30 min until the vegetables and beans are tender.

4 Drain well in a colander or sieve. Make the sauce and stir in the cream. Mix the sauce with the vegetables and beans and adjust the seasoning.

5 Stir in the chopped parsley and reheat if necessary before serving hot.

Cassoulet (serves 4–6)

POWER LEVEL: 100% (FULL) OR 50% (DEFROST)

Cassoulet is a French dish from the region of Languedoc. There are several local variations of the recipe but nearly all include lamb or goose with pork or bacon and garlic or smoked sausage. Haricot beans are the principal ingredient and this recipe is strongly flavoured with tomatoes and garlic. Normally the dish is cooked very slowly for anything up to 5 hours, but this microwave version is cooked much more quickly. Flavours will infuse and improve if the dish is allowed to cool, then placed in a refrigerator overnight and reheated the next day. It is a rather substantial dish and excellent for a cold winter's day.

225g (8oz) haricot beans, soaked
boiling water
1 small onion, peeled and finely chopped
4–5 cloves garlic
2 × 5ml tsp (2tsp) salt
225g (8oz) streaky pork, cut into small pieces
175g (6oz) lean lamb or mutton, cut into small pieces
2 × 5ml tsp (2tsp) french mustard
ground black pepper
425g (15oz) can tomatoes
3–4 × 15ml tbsp (3–4tbsp) tomato purée
275ml (½pt) boiling chicken stock (page 64), approximately
bouquet garni
225g (8oz) garlic or smoked sausage
browned breadcrumbs

1 After the haricot beans have been soaked (see page 00), drain and rinse. Pour on boiling water from the kettle to cover the beans. Allow to stand for 5 min, then drain and place the beans in a 2 litre (3½pt) dish.

2 Add the onion, garlic, salt, pork, lamb, mustard, pepper, tomatoes and tomato purée. Mix well together then pour on half the boiling chicken stock. Stir well and add the bouquet garni.

3 Cover and cook for either 1 hr on 100% (full) setting *or* 2 hrs on 50% (defrost); stir 2–3 times throughout and add more boiling stock as and when necessary. At the end of the cooking time the mixture should be fairly thick as the liquids are absorbed.

4 Add the garlic or smoked sausage and continue cooking for 15 min on 100% (full) setting *or* 20–30 min on 50% (defrost). At the end of the cooking time, the beans should be tender. Remove the bouquet garni.

5 If to be served the same day, sprinkle the top of the dish with browned breadcrumbs and cook for 4–5 min on 100% (full) setting *or* 8–10 min on 50% (defrost). Allow to stand for 15 min before serving.

6 If to be served the next day, allow to cool and refrigerate overnight. Before serving, heat for 8–10 min on 100% (full) setting, stirring 2–3 times throughout. Sprinkle with the browned breadcrumbs and heat for 4–5 min. Allow to stand for a few minutes before serving.

Note: *The choice of power settings and cooking times are dependent upon the time you have available.*

Lentil salad (serves 4–6)

POWER LEVEL: 100% (FULL) *(colour page 111)*

Serve as an accompaniment to cold poultry or pork.

225g (8oz) lentils, soaked for 2 hrs
1 small onion, peeled
6 cloves
1 bay leaf
1 bouquet garni
1 carrot, peeled and sliced
boiling, salted water
stock, optional (page 64)
French Dressing (page 141) to taste
1 clove garlic, crushed
for garnish: tomato slices and onion rings

1 Drain the lentils and place in a large bowl or casserole dish.

2 Stick the cloves into the onion and add to the lentils with the bay leaf, bouquet garni and carrot slices. Pour on boiling, salted water to cover.

3 Cover the dish and cook for 20–25 min until the lentils are tender. Drain and remove the onion, bay leaf and bouquet garni.

4 Sieve or purée the lentil mixture, adding a little stock if it is too thick. Allow to cool.

5 Beat in french dressing to taste and the garlic.

6 Serve cold, garnished with tomato slices and onion rings.

221

Seafood ring *(serves 6)*
POWER LEVEL: 100% (FULL)

225g (8oz) long-grain, easy-cook rice
1 small onion, finely chopped
1 green pepper, deseeded and finely chopped
1 × 5ml tsp (1tsp) turmeric
550ml (1pt) boiling water
1 × 15ml tbsp (1tbsp) oil
salt and freshly ground black pepper
350g (12oz) white fish fillets, cooked
100g (4oz) peeled prawns
4 × 15ml tbsp (4tbsp) mayonnaise
1 × 5ml tsp (1tsp) curry paste, optional
paprika pepper for sprinkling
for garnish: lemon twists and a few prawns

1 Place the rice, onion and pepper into a large bowl. Stir in the turmeric, boiling water, oil and seasoning.
2 Cook for 10–12 min until the rice is tender. Allow to stand for 5 min.
3 Drain off any excess water then press the rice firmly into a lightly greased ring mould, leave to cool then chill in the refrigerator.
4 Flake the fish and mix with the prawns. Blend the mayonnaise and curry paste (if used) together and stir into the fish mixture.
5 When the rice mould is firm and cold, turn out on to a serving plate. Pile the fish mixture into the centre and sprinkle with paprika pepper.
6 Serve cold, garnished with lemon twists and a few prawns.

DO NOT FREEZE

Catalan-style rice *(serves 4) (colour opposite)*
POWER LEVEL: 100% (FULL) AND 50% (DEFROST)

2 × 15ml tbsp (2tbsp) oil
1 onion, finely chopped
350g (12oz) pork fillet, cut into strips or cubes
2 tomatoes, skinned and finely chopped
100g (4oz) chorizo sausage, sliced
2 cloves garlic, finely chopped
¼ × 5ml tsp (¼tsp) turmeric or powdered saffron
225g (8oz) long grain rice
550ml (1pt) chicken stock (page 64), approximately
salt and pepper
25g (1oz) frozen peas, thawed

1 Place the oil and onion in a large casserole dish; mix well, cover and cook on 100% (full) setting for 3 min. Stir in the pork and continue to cook for 5 min, stirring once halfway through.
2 Add the tomatoes, chorizo sausage, garlic, turmeric or saffron and the rice. Cover and cook for 2 min.
3 Pour over half the stock, bring to the boil and then reduce to 50% (defrost) setting. Continue to cook, covered, for 15–20 min, stirring every 5 min and adding more stock as necessary.
4 Add seasoning to taste and the peas. Cook uncovered, for 2–3 min. Fork over the rice before serving hot.

Haricot beans à la grecque *(serves 6–8)*
POWER LEVEL: 100% (FULL) AND 50% (DEFROST)
(colour opposite)

This recipe uses haricot beans but almost any dried bean can be cooked and served the same way. When time is short, drained, canned beans may be substituted and mixed in the sauce. The dish can be served hot or cold.

225g (8oz) haricot beans
boiling water
1 small carrot
1 small onion
4 cloves
2 bay leaves
2 cloves garlic
bouquet garni
for the sauce:
1 onion, finely chopped
2–3 cloves garlic, crushed
3 × 15ml tbsp (3tbsp) oil
200g (7oz) canned chopped tomatoes
2–3 × 15ml tbsp (2–3tbsp) chopped fresh herbs
salt and freshly ground black pepper
150ml (¼pt) soured cream, optional

1 Place the beans into a large casserole dish with sufficient boiling water to cover. Cover and cook for 3 min on 100% (full) setting and then allow to soak for 1–1½ hr.
2 Drain and rinse the beans and replace in the dish with the whole carrot, the small onion stuck with the cloves, bay leaves, cloves of garlic and the bouquet garni.
3 Cover with boiling water, cover the dish and bring to the boil in the microwave. Reduce to 50% (defrost) setting and continue to cook for 35–40 min until the beans are tender.
4 To make the sauce, place the onion, garlic and oil in a bowl or dish, cover and cook on 100% (full) setting for 3 min. Add the tomatoes and continue to cook for a further 1½ min.
5 Stir in the herbs and add seasoning to taste. Drain the beans, remove the vegetables and discard. Stir the beans into the tomato sauce.
6 Reheat for 1–2 min if to be served hot or leave to cool if to be served cold.

Haricot Beans à la Grecque; Catalan-style Rice

Mung bean dal *(serves 6–8) (colour page 115)*
POWER LEVEL: 100% (FULL) AND 50% (DEFROST)

The small, green mung bean is perhaps more familiar to those who grow their own bean sprouts. In this Indian-style recipe, they are cooked whole with mild spices to give an excellent dish to serve with meats or vegetables.

225g (8oz) mung beans
550ml (1pt) cold water
1 × 5ml tsp (1tsp) each of ground cumin and
  coriander
$\frac{1}{4}$ × 5ml tsp ($\frac{1}{4}$tsp) turmeric
$\frac{1}{8}$ × 5ml tsp ($\frac{1}{8}$tsp) cayenne pepper
1 × 15ml tbsp (1tbsp) cold water
2 × 15ml tbsp (2tbsp) oil
275ml ($\frac{1}{2}$pt) boiling water
salt
15g ($\frac{1}{2}$oz) butter
$\frac{1}{2}$ × 5ml tsp ($\frac{1}{2}$tsp) whole cumin seeds

1 Place the beans in a bowl or dish with the water. Cover and bring to the boil on 100% (full) setting in the microwave, about 6 min. Leave to stand for $1–1\frac{1}{2}$ hr, and then drain and rinse in cold water.
2 Mix together the ground cumin, coriander, turmeric and cayenne with the cold water. Heat the oil for 1 min, stir in the spices and water and cook for 1 min.
3 Add the drained beans to the dish with the boiling water. Cover and bring to the boil, about 3–4 min. Reduce to 50% (defrost) setting and continue to cook for 25 min until tender.
4 Stir in sufficient salt to taste. Melt the butter for 30 sec in a small bowl or cup, stir in the whole cumin seeds and cook, uncovered, for 1 min.
5 Stir the butter and cumin into the beans and serve hot or cold.

Quick jambalaya *(serves 6)*
POWER LEVEL: 100% (FULL) AND 70%

2–3 × 15ml tbsp (2–3tbsp) oil
1 large onion, finely chopped
1 green pepper, deseeded and finely chopped
1 clove garlic, finely chopped
150ml ($\frac{1}{4}$pt) dry white wine
425g (15oz) can tomatoes
$\frac{1}{2}$ × 5ml tsp ($\frac{1}{2}$tsp) thyme
$\frac{1}{4}$ × 5ml tsp ($\frac{1}{4}$tsp) oregano or basil
1 bay leaf
$\frac{1}{4}$ × 5ml tsp ($\frac{1}{4}$tsp) tabasco sauce
225g (8oz) long-grain rice
salt and freshly ground black pepper
225g (8oz) peeled prawns
225g (8oz) cooked ham or sausage, diced
for garnish: 2 × 15ml tbsp (2tbsp) chopped parsley

1 Mix the oil, onion, pepper and garlic in a large bowl or casserole dish. Cover and cook on 100% (full) setting for 5–6 min until tender.
2 Add the wine, tomatoes, herbs, tabasco sauce and the rice. Season to taste, cover and cook for 5 min.
3 Reduce to 70% setting and cook for a further 15 min. Add the prawns and ham or sausage, continue to cook for another 5 min, adding more liquid if necessary.
4 Allow to stand for 10 min. Remove the bay leaf before garnishing with chopped parsley. Serve hot.

Lasagne bolognaise *(serves 6)*
POWER LEVEL: 50% (DEFROST)

This lasagne is made with the pasta which requires no precooking, making this a simple, easily prepared version for the microwave.

850ml ($1\frac{1}{2}$pt) Bolognaise Sauce, using 450g (1lb)
  minced beef (page 133)
550ml (1pt) Cheese Sauce (page 132)
225g (8oz) barilla lasagne
50g (2oz) cheese, grated
grated parmesan cheese for sprinkling
paprika for sprinkling

1 Make up and cook the bolognaise and cheese sauces.
2 Fill a large oblong dish with alternate layers of cheese sauce, bolognaise sauce and lasagne, beginning and ending with cheese sauce. Sprinkle with the grated cheeses and paprika pepper.
3 Cover and cook for 20–25 min, turning the dish twice throughout. Stand for 5 min before serving hot. The top of the dish may be browned under a hot grill if required.

Layered rice pudding *(serves 4–6)*
POWER LEVEL: 70% *(colour page 26)*

675g ($1\frac{1}{2}$lb) spinach, cooked and drained (page 145)
25g (1oz) butter, softened
225g (8oz) long-grain rice, cooked (page 216)
225g (8oz) cooked ham, finely shredded
100g (4oz) gruyère cheese, finely grated
for garnish: sprigs parsley
for serving: Tomato Sauce (page 134)

1 While the spinach is still warm, stir in the butter. Grease a 1.1 litre (2pt) pudding basin and fill it with layers of rice, ham and spinach, starting and finishing with a layer of rice.
2 Sprinkle with half the grated cheese. Cover the basin with clingfilm, slit with the pointed end of a sharp knife. Cover and cook for 8–10 min until heated through.

3 Allow the pudding to stand for 5 min, then invert it on to a serving plate. Sprinkle with the remaining cheese and garnish with parsley. Serve hot with tomato sauce handed separately.

Tagliatelle with shrimp sauce *(serves 4)*
POWER LEVEL: 100% (FULL)

350g (12oz) tagliatelle (or noodles)
25g (1oz) butter
1 clove garlic, crushed
1 stick celery, finely chopped
1 small green pepper, deseeded and finely chopped
25g (1oz) flour
salt and pepper
275ml ($\frac{1}{2}$pt) milk, or milk and white wine mixed
350g (12oz) peeled shrimps (or prawns), fresh or
   canned
for garnish: few shrimps (or prawns)
for serving: grated parmesan cheese

1 Cook the tagliatelle as described on page 216.
2 Melt the butter in a large bowl for 1 min, stir in the garlic, celery and green pepper, cover and cook for 4–5 min until tender.
3 Stir in the flour and seasoning. Gradually add the milk or milk and wine. Cook for 3–4 min until thickened, stirring every minute.
4 Stir in the shrimps (or prawns) and cook for a further 1–2 min until heated through.
5 Drain the tagliatelle and arrange in a serving dish or on a platter. Pour over the sauce and garnish with a few shrimps (or prawns). Serve hot, handing the cheese separately.

FREEZE THE SAUCE SEPARATELY

Pease pudding *(serves 4)*
POWER LEVEL: 100% (FULL)

Traditionally served with boiled ham.

225g (8oz) dried split peas, soaked overnight
15g ($\frac{1}{2}$oz) butter
1 egg, optional
salt and pepper

1 After soaking, cook the peas in a covered bowl or dish in plenty of water for 45–50 min until tender.
2 Drain well, then mash, sieve or blend in a liquidiser or food processor with the butter, egg if used, and the seasoning.
3 Place the mixture in a cloth or muslin and cook with the ham for the last 5 min of microwave cooking time.
4 Turn the pudding out of the cloth before serving.

Cockles with noodles *(serves 4)*
POWER LEVEL: 100% (FULL)

3 × 15ml tbsp (3tbsp) oil
1 onion, chopped
1 clove garlic, chopped
450g (1lb) tomatoes, skinned, deseeded and chopped
1 × 15ml tbsp (1tbsp) chopped parsley
salt and freshly ground black pepper
550ml (1pt) fresh, shelled cockles
350–450g (12–16oz) noodles, freshly cooked (page 216)
for garnish: slivers of butter and chopped parsley, optional

1 Put the oil into a large bowl with the onion and garlic. Cover and cook for 4–5 min.

2 Add tomatoes, parsley and seasoning to taste, cover and cook for 2–3 min. The tomatoes should not be overcooked.
3 Wash the cockles very well in cold running water. Drain and add to the dish. Stir, cover and cook for 2–3 min until just heated through.
4 Pour the sauce over a bed of noodles and serve hot, garnished with slivers of butter and chopped parsley.

DO NOT FREEZE

Seafood pilaf *(serves 4–6)*
POWER LEVEL: 100% (FULL)

50g (2oz) butter
1 medium onion, finely chopped
225g (8oz) long-grain rice
550ml (1pt) boiling chicken or fish stock (page 64)
salt and pepper
1 × 5ml tsp (1tsp) turmeric
100g (4oz) mushrooms, sliced
100g (4oz) peeled prawns, fresh or frozen, thawed
225g (8oz) peeled scampi, fresh or frozen, thawed
225g (8oz) mussels, canned or frozen, thawed
15g ($\frac{1}{2}$oz) butter, melted
for garnish: few prawns in their shells and lemon wedges

1 Melt 25g (1oz) butter for 1 min in a large casserole dish, stir in the onion, cover and cook for 3–4 min. Stir in the rice, cover and cook for 1 min.
2 Add about half the stock to the rice, stir well and add the seasoning and turmeric. Cover and cook for about 12 min, adding extra stock as necessary and stirring 2–3 times throughout. Leave to stand.
3 Melt the remaining 25g (1oz) butter for 1 min, add the mushrooms, cover and cook for 1 min. Stir in the prawns, scampi and the mussels, cover and cook for 4–5 min. Leave to stand for 2 min.
4 Fork over the rice and stir in the melted butter. Add the mushroom and shellfish mixture. Serve hot, garnished with a few prawns in their shells and lemon wedges.

DO NOT FREEZE

Spaghetti in tomato sauce *(serves 4)*
POWER LEVEL: 100% (FULL)

550–675g (1$\frac{1}{4}$–1$\frac{1}{2}$lb) tomatoes, skinned, deseeded and diced
4–6 cloves garlic, crushed
1–2 × 15ml tbsp (1–2tbsp) chopped fresh basil *or*
  1–2 × 5ml tsp (1–2tsp) dried basil
150ml ($\frac{1}{4}$pt) olive oil
225g (8oz) spaghetti, cooked (method 1 and page 216)
salt and freshly ground black pepper

1 Mix together the tomatoes, garlic, basil and olive oil and leave to stand for a few minutes while the spaghetti is cooking.
2 Drain the spaghetti thoroughly and toss straight-away in the tomato sauce. Add seasoning to taste.
3 Serve immediately.

Snacks and suppers

The recipes included in this section provide a perfect answer when there is not time to prepare a full-scale meal or when you just don't feel like eating one. Many of the dishes use simple ingredients and most are quick to prepare so are also ideal as a 'trial run' for those of you who are new to microwave cooking. Obviously there are many recipes throughout the book which can be served as snack or supper dishes but the selection here includes a variety of recipes for your easy reference and guidance.

Bacon sandwich *(serves 1)*
POWER LEVEL: 100% (FULL)

3 rashers bacon, trimmed
2 large slices bread
butter, optional

1 Place the bacon rashers on a plate, cover with kitchen paper and cook for 2½–3 min.
2 Butter the bread slices or brush with the bacon fat.
3 Make up the sandwich and reheat for 30 sec; cut and serve.

Tomatoes on toast *(serves 1–2)*
POWER LEVEL: 100% (FULL)

4 tomatoes, cut in halves
salt and pepper
slivers of butter
2 slices hot buttered toast

1 Place the tomato halves in a circle on a plate. Sprinkle with salt and pepper and add a sliver of butter to each half.
2 Cook for 3–4 min, turning the plate halfway through.
3 Serve on slices of hot buttered toast.

DO NOT FREEZE

Porridge *(serves 1–2)*
POWER LEVEL: 100% (FULL)

4 × 15ml tbsp (4tbsp) porridge oats
150ml (¼pt) water or milk and water
pinch salt
for serving: sugar and milk or cream

1 Mix the porridge with the water and salt in a serving bowl or dish.
2 Cook for 1¾ min, stirring twice throughout.
3 Allow to stand for 1–2 min.
4 Serve hot with sugar and milk or cream.

DO NOT FREEZE

Baked beans or spaghetti on toast
(serves 1)
POWER LEVEL: 100% (FULL)

1 slice hot buttered toast
3–4 × 15ml tbsp (3–4tbsp) canned baked beans or spaghetti

1 Place the toast on a plate. Add the topping.
2 Heat through uncovered for $1\frac{1}{2}$–2 min. Serve immediately.

Note: *Alternatively, the topping can be heated separately in a dish or bowl for 1–$1\frac{1}{4}$ min before adding to the toast.*

DO NOT FREEZE

Cheese on toast *(serves 1)*
POWER LEVEL: 100% (FULL)

1 slice toast
thin slices of cheese
chutney, sweet pickle or tomato slices, optional

1 Put the toast on a plate and cover with thin slices of cheese, making sure the layer of cheese is even.
2 Cook for 1–$1\frac{1}{4}$ min until the cheese is soft. Do not overheat otherwise the cheese will melt and run off the toast.
3 Top with chutney, sweet pickle or tomato slices and serve immediately.

DO NOT FREEZE

Mushrooms on toast *(serves 1–2)*
POWER LEVEL: 100% (FULL)

25g (1oz) butter
100g (4oz) button mushrooms, washed
salt and pepper
2 slices hot buttered toast

1 Melt the butter in a small bowl for 1 min. Add the mushrooms, tossing well in the butter.
2 Cover and cook for 2–$2\frac{1}{2}$ min. Serve on hot buttered toast.

DO NOT FREEZE

Hot dogs *(makes 4)*
POWER LEVEL: 100% (FULL)

4 frankfurter sausages
50g (2oz) butter, approximately
1 small onion, finely sliced
4 soft finger rolls

1 Place the frankfurters on a piece of paper towel on a plate.
2 Melt 15g ($\frac{1}{2}$oz) butter for 30 sec, stir in the onion, cover and cook for 3–4 min until tender. Heat the frankfurters for 1–$1\frac{1}{2}$ min.
3 Cut the rolls down one side and spread with the remaining butter. Place the onions and sausages inside the rolls and reheat for 1–$1\frac{1}{2}$ min.

DO NOT FREEZE

Bacon and egg sandwich *(serves 2)*
POWER LEVEL: 100% (FULL) AND 50% (DEFROST)

The sandwiches are lightly 'fried' in the browning dish.

4 rashers lean bacon, derinded
4 slices bread
butter
2 eggs

1 Place the bacon rashers on a plate, cover with kitchen paper and cook on 100% (full) setting for $2\frac{1}{2}$–3 min. Allow a little longer if the bacon is preferred more crispy.
2 Preheat the browning dish for 6–8 min, depending on size.
3 Brush the slices of bread with the bacon fat or use butter. Make up the sandwiches with the greased side outwards.
4 When the browning dish is preheated, quickly place the sandwiches on to the hot base of the dish and press down well with a heatproof spatula to brown the first side lightly.
5 Turn the sandwich over, press down again and place in the microwave; cook, uncovered for $1\frac{1}{2}$–2 min. Drain on kitchen paper towel and keep warm.
6 Place the eggs in 2 lightly buttered small dishes and prick the yolks. Cook on 50% (defrost) setting for 2–$2\frac{1}{2}$ min, turning the dishes halfway through.
7 Top each sandwich with an egg and serve straightaway.

DO NOT FREEZE

Beefburgers *(makes 4 large burgers)*
POWER LEVEL: 100% (FULL)

450g (1lb) lean beef, minced
$\frac{1}{2}$ onion, finely chopped
salt and freshly ground black pepper
1 egg
50g (2oz) cheese, finely grated, optional
50g (2oz) mushrooms, finely chopped, optional
1–2×5ml tsp (1–2tsp) dried mixed herbs, optional
2×15ml tbsp (2tbsp) melted butter or oil

1 Mix the beef and onion together and add the seasoning. Stir in the egg and, if preferred, add either the cheese, mushrooms or herbs or a mixture of these.
2 Knead the mixture together and divide into 4. Shape each portion into a flat round cake and brush with the melted butter or oil.
3 Place in a circle on a large plate or dish and cook uncovered for 5–6 min, turning the beefburgers over once halfway through.
4 Allow to stand, covered, for 3–4 min before serving hot.

Soufflé rarebit *(serves 2)*
POWER LEVEL: 100% (FULL)

1 egg, separated
75g (3oz) cheese, finely grated
25g (1oz) butter, softened
salt and pepper
pinch dried mustard
2 thick slices toasted bread
paprika pepper for sprinkling

1 Mix together the egg yolk, 50g (2oz) of the cheese and the butter until blended. Stir in the seasoning and mustard.
2 Whisk the egg white until stiff and fold into the cheese mixture. Pour over the slices of toast and sprinkle with the remaining cheese and paprika pepper.
3 Cook uncovered, for $1\frac{1}{2}$–2 min until hot through and lightly risen. Serve straightaway.

DO NOT FREEZE

Chicken and peanut burgers
(makes 4 large burgers)
POWER LEVEL: 100% (FULL)

450g (1lb) lean chicken, finely minced
$\frac{1}{2}$ onion, finely chopped
50g (2oz) peanuts, finely chopped (or peanut butter)
salt and freshly ground black pepper
1 egg
2 × 15ml tbsp (2tbsp) melted butter or oil

1 Combine the chicken, onion, peanuts, seasoning and egg together and divide the mixture into 4.
2 Knead each portion and shape into a flat round cake and brush with the melted butter or oil.
3 Place in a circle on a large plate or dish and cook uncovered for 5–6 min, turning the burgers over once halfway through. Cover and allow to stand for 5 min before serving hot.

TO SERVE IN BAPS
Warm 4 split baps in the microwave for 45–60 sec. Place the burgers into the split baps and reheat for 30 sec if necessary before serving topped with a little sliced tomato and accompanied by a salad.

Tuna stuffed rolls *(serves 4)*
POWER LEVEL: 100% (FULL)

4 crispy rolls
25g (1oz) butter
200g (7oz) canned tuna fish, flaked
50g (2oz) cheese, finely grated
salt and pepper

1 Slice the tops from the rolls, remove the centres from the rolls and crumb.
2 Melt the butter in a bowl for 1 min, add the breadcrumbs, tuna fish, cheese and seasoning. Mix well together and heat through for $1-1\frac{1}{2}$ min.
3 Fill the rolls with the mixture, replace tops and heat through for $1-1\frac{1}{2}$ min.
4 Serve warm.

Vienna roll *(serves 4–6)*
POWER LEVEL: 100% (FULL)

1 small vienna loaf
8 lean bacon rashers, derinded and chopped
75g (3oz) butter
100g (4oz) mushrooms, chopped
1 green pepper, deseeded and diced
8–10 stuffed olives, sliced
1 clove garlic, crushed
salt and freshly ground black pepper

1 Cut the loaf lengthways through the centre, leaving a 1.25cm ($\frac{1}{2}$in) crust. Carefully remove and crumb the soft bread.
2 Cook the bacon for 5–6 min until crisp, stirring once halfway through. Add the breadcrumbs, 25g (1oz) of the butter and the remaining ingredients. Cover and cook for 3 min.
3 Butter the inside of the loaf with the remaining butter and fill with the bacon mixture.
4 Place the loaf on kitchen paper towel and then directly on to the oven shelf or a plate. Cook, uncovered for about 3 min until heated through. Serve hot cut into slices.

Curried chicken and rice salad *(serves 4)*
POWER LEVEL: 100% (FULL) *(colour page 11)*

15g ($\frac{1}{2}$oz) butter
1 small onion, chopped
1 × 5ml tsp (1tsp) curry powder
225g (8oz) long-grain rice
550ml (1pt) boiling salted water
150ml ($\frac{1}{4}$pt) Blender Mayonnaise (page 137)
1 × 15ml tbsp (1tbsp) chopped chives
2 × 15ml tbsp (2tbsp) lemon juice
1 red eating apple, cored and sliced
1 green pepper, deseeded and chopped
75g (3oz) raisins
225g (8oz) cooked chicken, diced
salt and freshly ground black pepper
50g (2oz) flaked almonds, toasted
for garnish: watercress

1 Melt the butter in a small bowl for 30 sec, stir in the onion, cover and cook for 2 min. Stir in the curry

powder and continue to cook for a further 1 min. Leave to cool.

2 Cook the rice in the salted water for 10–12 min, drain and rinse under cold running water. Combine the rice with the onion and curry mixture.

3 Mix the mayonnaise with the chives and 1 × 15ml tbsp (1tbsp) of the lemon juice. Dip the apple slices into the remaining juice and add to the mayonnaise.

4 Stir in the pepper, raisins, cooked chicken and seasoning to taste. Add the rice mixture and place into a serving dish or plate. Fork over the salad before topping with the flaked almonds and garnishing with watercress. Serve cold.

DO NOT FREEZE

Sausage and bacon hotpot *(serves 4)*

POWER LEVEL: 100% (FULL) AND 50% (DEFROST)
(colour opposite)

450g (1lb) pork or beef sausages
225g (8oz) lean bacon rashers, derinded and cut into strips
1 large onion, finely chopped
1 clove garlic, finely chopped
225g (8oz) can tomatoes
100g (4oz) mushrooms, sliced
450g (1lb) potatoes, thinly sliced or cut into dice
550ml (1pt) boiling stock (page 64)
2 × 5ml tsp (2tsp) paprika pepper
$\frac{1}{2}$ × 5ml tsp ($\frac{1}{2}$tsp) worcestershire sauce
salt and pepper
for garnish: chopped parsley
for serving: crusty bread and butter

1 Place all the ingredients except the salt and pepper into a large casserole dish and stir well. Cover and bring to the boil on 100% (full) setting, about 5 min.

2 Reduce to 50% (defrost) setting and continue to cook for 50–60 min until tender, stirring 2–3 times throughout.

3 Taste for seasoning and adjust if necessary. Sprinkle with chopped parsley and serve hot, with lots of crusty bread and butter.

Quick pizza napolitana *(serves 1–2)*

POWER LEVEL: 100% (FULL) *(colour opposite)*

The pizza base is made from a simple scone dough.

175g (6oz) self-raising flour
pinch each salt and pepper and dry mustard
$\frac{1}{2}$ × 5ml tsp ($\frac{1}{2}$tsp) baking powder
40g (1$\frac{1}{2}$oz) butter or margarine
75ml ($\frac{1}{8}$pt) milk or milk and water mixed, approximately

275ml ($\frac{1}{2}$pt) Tomato Sauce (page 134)
175g (6oz) mozzarella cheese, thinly sliced
50g (2oz) can anchovy fillets, drained and cut into halves lengthways
50g (2oz) black olives
1 × 5ml tsp (1tsp) dried herbs, eg oregano, basil or marjoram
1 × 15ml tbsp (1tbsp) olive oil

1 Lightly grease a 20–22.5cm (8–9in) microwave pizza or flan dish.

2 Sift the flour, seasonings and baking powder into a bowl and rub in the butter or margarine finely. Stir in sufficient milk to form a soft scone dough.

3 Knead the dough lightly until smooth and pat or roll into a round to fit the dish. Cook uncovered for 3–4 min, turning the dish if necessary halfway through.

4 Spread the tomato sauce over the dough. Cover with the mozzarella cheese and arrange the anchovies and olives on the top.

5 Sprinkle with the herbs and olive oil and cook the pizza uncovered, for 3–4 min, turning after 2 min. Allow to stand for 5 min.

6 Serve hot or warm.

Beans au gratin *(serves 6)*

POWER LEVEL: 100% (FULL)

450g (1lb) runner or french beans, freshly cooked (page 144)
40g (1$\frac{1}{2}$oz) butter, softened
1 clove garlic, crushed
2 × 5ml tsp (2tsp) finely chopped parsley
salt and freshly ground black pepper
425ml ($\frac{3}{4}$pt) Cheese Sauce (page 132)
2 × 15ml tbsp (2tbsp) finely grated cheese
2 × 15ml tbsp (2tbsp) browned breadcrumbs
for garnish: chopped parsley

1 Mix together the beans, butter, garlic, parsley and seasoning. Toss over gently so that the beans are well coated.

2 Place into a suitable microwave gratin dish and coat with the cheese sauce. Cover and cook for 5 min until hot through, turning the dish twice throughout.

3 Sprinkle with the grated cheese and breadcrumbs and cook, uncovered, for 2–3 min until the cheese is melted.

4 Garnish with chopped parsley before serving hot.

Sausage and Bacon Hotpot; Quick Pizza Napolitana

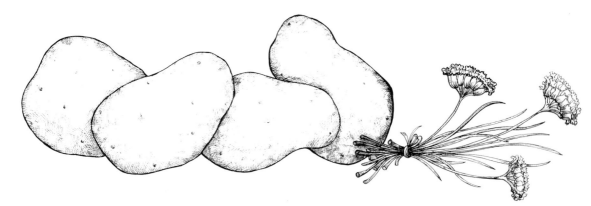

Egg-baked potatoes *(serves 4)*
POWER LEVEL: 100% (FULL) AND 50% (DEFROST)

4 large potatoes, scrubbed
50g (2oz) butter
salt and pepper
50g (2oz) cheese, grated
4 small eggs
4 × 15ml tbsp (4tbsp) double cream, optional
2 × 5ml tsp (2tsp) chopped chives

1 Prick the potato skins with a fork. Weigh them and then cook uncovered on 100% (full) setting, allowing 10–12 min per $\frac{1}{2}$kg (1lb). Turn the potatoes over halfway through.
2 Cut a slice lengthways from each potato and scoop out the insides but leave a shell about 1.25cm ($\frac{1}{2}$in) thick.
3 Mix the soft potato with the butter, seasoning and the cheese. Beat well and then replace back into the potato shells, pressing down well to allow room for the egg.
4 Carefully break an egg into each potato, prick the yolks and spoon over the cream. Reduce to 50% (defrost) setting and cook for about 5–6 min until the eggs are lightly set. If not quite set, allow to stand for a few minutes.
5 Serve straightaway, sprinkled with the chopped chives.

DO NOT FREEZE

Cod's roe sauté *(serves 4)*
POWER LEVEL: 100% (FULL)

The cod's roe slices are lightly fried in a browning dish.

450g (1lb) cod's roe
1 × 15ml tbsp (1tbsp) seasoned flour
2 × 15ml tbsp (2tbsp) oil
freshly ground black pepper
for garnish: lemon wedges
for serving: hot buttered toast

1 Cut the cod's roe into 2.5cm (1in) thick slices and dip into the seasoned flour.
2 Preheat the browning dish for 6–8 min, add the oil and heat for a further minute.
3 Lay the slices of cod's roe on the base of the dish, pressing down well with a heatproof spatula. Cover and cook for 1 min.
4 Turn the slices over, press down well again, cover and cook for 2–3 min.
5 Serve straightaway, sprinkled with freshly ground black pepper, garnish with lemon wedges and serve with hot buttered toast.

Hot potato and frankfurter salad *(serves 4)*
POWER LEVEL: 100% (FULL)

450g (1lb) potatoes, peeled and diced
4 × 15ml tbsp (4tbsp) salted water
1 large onion, sliced
4–6 anchovy fillets, chopped
4–6 gherkins, chopped
3 × 15ml tbsp (3tbsp) oil
1$\frac{1}{2}$ × 15ml tbsp (1$\frac{1}{2}$tbsp) wine vinegar
salt and freshly ground black pepper
4 frankfurter sausages

1 Place the potatoes in a bowl or dish with the salted water. Cover and cook for 8–10 min until tender.
2 While the potatoes are cooking, push the onion slices through into rings, combine the anchovies and gherkins and beat the oil and vinegar together with the seasoning.
3 When the potatoes are cooked, allow to stand for a few minutes. Heat the frankfurters for 2–3 min until hot and then cut into slices.
4 Toss together the drained potatoes and the frankfurters. Arrange the onion rings over the top and sprinkle with the oil and vinegar.
5 Stir the salad to combine the ingredients and allow to stand for 5 min before topping with the anchovy and gherkin mixture and serving warm.

DO NOT FREEZE

Country soup *(serves 6)*

POWER LEVEL: 100% (FULL)

This substantial main-course soup is very welcoming on a cold day served on its own with plenty of fresh crusty bread.

40g (1½oz) butter
1 × 15ml tbsp (1tbsp) oil
2 large onions, finely sliced
2 cloves garlic, finely chopped
2 × 5ml tsp (2tsp) paprika pepper
225g (8oz) minced veal
100g (4oz) minced pork
1.1 litre (2pt) boiling chicken stock (page 64)
salt and freshly ground black pepper
2 medium potatoes, peeled and sliced
3 tomatoes, skinned and quartered
for garnish: chopped parsley
for serving: crusty bread and butter

1 Heat the butter and oil in a large bowl for 1½ min. Stir in the onions and the garlic, cover and cook for 3 min.
2 Add the paprika pepper and the minced meats, cover and cook for 3 min, stirring twice throughout and breaking down any lumps with a fork.
3 Add the stock and the seasoning, stir well together, cover and cook for 5 min. Add the potatoes and continue to cook for a further 8 min. Add the tomatoes and cook for 2–3 min or until the vegetables are tender.
4 Adjust seasoning and serve hot with crusty bread and butter.

Potato and ham au gratin *(serves 4)*

POWER LEVEL: 100% (FULL) AND 50% (DEFROST)

50g (2oz) butter
2 large onions, finely sliced
4 large potatoes, cut into very thin matchsticks or grated
100g (4oz) cooked ham slices, cut into strips
salt and freshly ground black pepper
150ml (¼pt) single cream
3 × 15ml tbsp (3tbsp) browned breadcrumbs

1 Melt the butter in a large bowl on 100% (full) setting for 1½ min. Add the onions, toss well in the butter, cover and cook for 6 min until transparent.
2 Add the potatoes, stir well, cover and cook for 8–10 min until the vegetables are tender.
3 Place half the potatoes and onions into a serving dish and scatter with the ham. Season with salt and freshly ground black pepper.
4 Cover with the remaining potato and onion and press well down into the dish. Season again and pour over the cream.

5 Reduce to 50% (defrost) setting, cover and cook for 4–5 min until heated through. Sprinkle with the brown breadcrumbs and cook, uncovered, for 2 min. Serve hot.

DO NOT FREEZE

Prawns creole *(serves 4)*

POWER LEVEL: 100% (FULL)

25g (1oz) butter
1 small onion, finely chopped
1 green pepper, deseeded and finely chopped
2–3 × 15ml tbsp (2–3tbsp) flour
675g (1½lb) canned tomatoes, roughly chopped
1 × 5ml tsp (1tsp) each dried rosemary, thyme and oregano
salt and pepper
2 × 5ml tsp (2tsp) sugar
225g (8oz) peeled prawns
for serving: boiled rice (page 216)

1 Melt the butter in a large casserole dish for 1 min. Add the onion and pepper, toss well in the butter, cover and cook for 4–5 min until tender.
2 Stir in the flour until smooth and gradually add the tomatoes; add the herbs, seasoning and sugar.
3 Cover and cook for 5 min, stirring frequently until the sauce has thickened. Allow to stand for 5 min.
4 Stir in the prawns, cover and cook for 1–2 min until heated through. Serve with boiled rice.

Leek and ham rolls *(serves 2 or 4)*

POWER LEVEL: 100% (FULL)

450g (1lb) leeks, washed and trimmed
2 × 15ml tbsp (2tbsp) salted water
4 large, thin slices of ham
275ml (½pt) Mornay Sauce (page 133)
3 × 15ml tbsp (3tbsp) grated cheese
paprika pepper for sprinkling

1 Cut the leeks in half lengthways, or if they are very large, cut into quarters.
2 Place the leek halves or quarters in a casserole dish with the salted water. Cover and cook for 7–10 min until tender. Drain well.
3 Keeping the leeks in strips, divide between the slices of ham. Roll up each slice and place back into the dish.
4 Cover and cook for 2 min until the ham is heated through.
5 Heat the mornay sauce, if necessary, and pour over the rolls.
6 Sprinkle with the grated cheese and paprika pepper and cook uncovered for 2–3 min until the cheese is melted. Alternatively, brown under a hot grill.

Mushroom pudding (serves 4)
POWER LEVEL: 100% (FULL)

450g (1lb) button mushrooms
75g (3oz) butter
75g (3oz) fresh white breadcrumbs
1 × 15ml tbsp (1tbsp) chopped parsley
1 × 15ml tbsp (1tbsp) double cream
salt and freshly ground black pepper
2 eggs, beaten
for serving: Mushroom Sauce (page 132), optional, and crusty bread and butter

1 Thinly slice 2–3 of the mushrooms to give about 8–10 even pieces. Chop the rest.
2 Melt 25g (1oz) of the butter for 1 min in a bowl or dish and add the sliced mushrooms. Cover and cook for ½–1 min until softened but not overcooked.
3 Remove the slices from the dish, drain on kitchen paper towel and reserve. Add the chopped mushrooms to the dish, toss well in the butter, cover and cook for 4–4½ min, stirring halfway through. Drain off the juices.
4 Melt the remaining butter for 1½ min and add to the chopped mushrooms with the breadcrumbs, parsley, cream and seasoning.
5 Stir well and add the beaten eggs. Place the mixture into a lightly greased 850ml (1½pt) pudding basin and cover with clingfilm slit with the pointed end of a sharp knife.
6 Cook for 4–5 min, turning once halfway through. Allow to stand for a few minutes before inverting on to a serving platter.
7 Arrange the reserved mushroom slices around the top of the pudding and serve hot with the mushroom sauce handed separately.

Special omelette (serves 3–4) (colour opposite)
POWER LEVEL: 100% (FULL) AND 50% (DEFROST)

100g (4oz) chinese egg noodles
275–425ml (½–¾pt) boiling water
salt
50g (2oz) butter
100g (4oz) button mushrooms, sliced
225g (8oz) frozen peas, thawed
100g (4oz) frozen peeled prawns, shrimps or seafood sticks, thawed
6 × 15ml tbsp (6tbsp) milk or water
6 size 3 eggs
pepper
50g (2oz) cheddar cheese, grated
for serving: green salad and french bread

1 Place the noodles into a large bowl or casserole dish and add sufficient boiling water to cover. Add salt to taste, cover and cook on 100% (full) setting for 3 min, stand for 5 min. Drain well.
2 Melt the butter for 1½–2 min in a 20–22.5cm (8–9in) round dish until bubbling. Stir in the mushrooms and peas, cover and cook for 4 min.
3 Add the prawns, shrimps or sliced seafood sticks and the noodles. Continue to cook for 2 min, stirring halfway through.
4 Heat the milk or water for 1–1½ min until boiling and beat into the eggs with salt and pepper.
5 Pour the eggs quickly over the hot noodle mixture and stir. Reduce to 50% (defrost) setting, cover and cook for 9–10 min. Sprinkle with the cheese and cook, uncovered, for a further 1½–2 min. Stand for 3 min before serving hot in wedges with green salad and french bread.

DO NOT FREEZE

Scallop kebabs (serves 2)
POWER LEVEL: 100% (FULL) (colour opposite)

The scallops are marinated for 1 hour before cooking.

5 scallops, cut into halves
3 × 15ml tbsp (3tbsp) oil
1 × 15ml tbsp (1tbsp) wine vinegar
1 × 15ml tbsp (1tbsp) lemon juice
salt and freshly ground black pepper
½ × 5ml tsp (½tsp) each paprika pepper and dried basil
4 rashers streaky bacon
25g (1oz) butter
50g (2oz) mushrooms, chopped
50g (2oz) frozen peas, thawed
75g (3oz) long-grain rice, cooked (page 216)
for garnish: chopped fresh parsley or dried basil

1 Place the scallops into the marinade, made by combining the oil, vinegar, lemon juice, seasonings and basil. Leave for 1 hr.
2 Derind the bacon and cut each rasher into half. Roll each one into a small bacon roll.
3 Drain the scallops and thread on to skewers, alternating each piece of fish with the bacon rolls. (If metal skewers are used, they must not touch each other or the interior of the microwave.)
4 Place the skewers into the microwave and cook, uncovered, for 4½–5½ min. Cover and allow to stand for 5 min.
5 Melt the butter for 1 min, add the mushrooms and peas and cook for 3 min. Stir in the rice and cook for a further 2 min, stirring halfway through.
6 Place the rice on a serving plate and arrange the kebabs on top. Sprinkle with the herbs and serve straightaway.

Special Omelette; Scallop Kebabs

Boston baked beans *(serves 4–6)*
POWER LEVEL: 100% (FULL) AND 50% (DEFROST)

2 large onions, sliced
2 × 15ml tbsp (2tbsp) oil
225g (8oz) belly pork, cut into strips or diced
225g (8oz) haricot beans, soaked (page 216)
4 × 15ml tbsp (4tbsp) dark brown sugar
850ml (1½pt) boiling stock (page 64)
2 bay leaves
½ × 5ml tsp (½tsp) ground ginger
1 × 15 tbsp (1tbsp) tomato purée
1 × 15ml tbsp (1tbsp) black treacle
2 × 5ml tsp (2tsp) mustard
salt and pepper

1 Place the onions and the oil into a large casserole dish, mix well, cover and cook for 5 min on 100% (full) setting. Stir in the belly of pork and continue to cook for another 3 min.
2 Add all the remaining ingredients and mix well together. Cover and cook for 3–4 min until boiling and then reduce to 50% (defrost) setting and cook for 50–60 min until tender, stirring 2–3 times throughout.
3 Allow to stand for 10–15 min before serving hot.

Vegetable moussaka *(serves 4–6)*
POWER LEVEL: 100% (FULL) AND 70% *(colour page 39)*

50g (2oz) butter
1 onion, finely chopped
1 clove garlic, crushed
225g (8oz) carrots, sliced
1 green or red pepper, deseeded and diced
350g (12oz) aubergines, thinly sliced
225g (8oz) can tomatoes
salt and freshly ground black pepper
2 × 15ml tbsp (2tbsp) chopped parsley
25g (1oz) butter, melted
25g (1oz) flour
225ml (8fl oz) milk
75g (3oz) cheddar cheese, grated
2 eggs, beaten

1 Melt the butter in a large soufflé dish for 1½ min on 100% (full) setting. Stir in the onion, garlic and carrots, cover and cook for 6 min.
2 Add the carrots, pepper and aubergines, mix well and continue to cook for a further 4 min. Stir well and add the tomatoes and seasoning to taste. Cover and cook for a further 5–6 min until the vegetables are tender. Stir in the parsley and press the vegetables down well in the dish to make a firm base for the sauce.
3 Blend the butter with the flour and stir in the milk gradually. Add salt and pepper to taste and cook for

4–5 min, stirring every minute until the sauce has thickened and cooked.
4 Add 50g (2oz) of the cheese and beat the eggs into the sauce. Pour the sauce over the top of the vegetables. Reduce to 70% setting and cook for 5–6 min until the sauce has lightly risen and set. Allow to stand for 5 min before sprinkling with the remaining cheese and browning the top under a hot grill.
5 Serve straightaway.

Note: *Double quantity of the sauce will be necessary if a large shallow dish is used.*

DO NOT FREEZE

Hot seafood dip *(serves 10–12)*
POWER LEVEL: 100% (FULL) SETTING

225g (8oz) crab meat, canned or frozen, thawed
175g (6oz) peeled prawns
2 × 400g (14oz) cans lobster or prawn bisque
1 × 15ml tbsp (1tbsp) chopped basil *or*
¼ × 5ml tsp (¼tsp) dried basil
salt and freshly ground black pepper
for serving: french bread

1 Flake the crab meat and chop the peeled prawns.
2 Mix together with the lobster or prawn bisque, herbs and seasoning.
3 Cover and cook for 6–8 min until heated through, stirring twice throughout.
4 Serve hot with bite-sized chunks of french bread for dipping.

Salad niçoise *(serves 4–6)*
POWER LEVEL: 100% (FULL)

175g (6oz) french beans
2 × 15ml tbsp (2tbsp) salted water
225g (8oz) tomatoes, thinly sliced
½ cucumber, thinly sliced
salt and freshly ground black pepper
1 × 15ml tbsp (1tbsp) freshly chopped herbs, eg basil, parsley
1 lemon, grated rind
100g (4oz) canned tuna fish, drained
50g (2oz) black olives, stoned and chopped
1 clove garlic, crushed
French Dressing (page 141)
8 anchovy fillets, halved lengthways
for serving: lemon wedges and brown bread and butter.

1 Trim the beans but leave whole, wash and place into a bowl or dish with the salted water. Cover and cook for 3–4 min, shaking or stirring once

throughout. The beans should be crisp. Drain and rinse under cold running water.

2 Arrange the tomato and cucumber slices in layers in a shallow serving dish. Sprinkle with seasoning, herbs and lemon rind.

3 Place small piles of the beans and tuna fish around the centre of the dish and scatter the olives over the top. Season again.

4 Beat the garlic into the dressing and spoon over the salad. Arrange the anchovy fillets in a lattice style over the top.

5 Leave to stand for 30–40 min before serving to allow the flavours to blend. Serve with lemon wedges and brown bread and butter.

DO NOT FREEZE

Sautéd kidneys and tomato *(serves 2)*
POWER LEVEL: 100% (FULL)

25g (1oz) butter
1 clove garlic, crushed
6 lambs' kidneys, skinned, halved and cored
4 tomatoes, skinned and sliced
3 × 15ml tbsp (3tbsp) sherry or stock (page 64)
1½ × 15ml tbsp (1½tbsp) tomato purée
salt and freshly ground black pepper
4 × 15ml tbsp (4tbsp) soured cream or natural yoghurt
for garnish: chopped parsley

1 Melt the butter in a bowl or casserole dish for 1 min. Stir in the garlic and the kidneys. Cover and cook for 4½–5 min, stirring halfway through.

2 Add the tomatoes, sherry or stock, tomato purée and seasoning to taste. Continue to cook for a further 2½–3 min until tender and the tomatoes are mushy.

3 Allow to stand for 5 min and then serve hot with the soured cream or yoghurt drizzled over the top and garnished with chopped parsley.

Creamy cheese pudding *(serves 4)*
POWER LEVEL: 100% (FULL)

Serve as a light lunch or supper dish.

225g (8oz) wholemeal bread *or*
6 medium slices brown bread
25g (1oz) butter
1 small onion, finely chopped
150ml (¼pt) single cream
2 eggs, beaten
150ml (¼pt) dry white wine
salt and freshly ground black pepper
pinch each mustard and paprika pepper
100g (4oz) gruyère cheese
paprika pepper for sprinkling

1 Lightly grease a 15–17.5cm (6–7in) soufflé dish.

2 Remove the crusts from the bread, cut into dice and place in the greased dish.

3 Melt the butter in a bowl for 1 min, stir in the onion, cover and cook for 4 min. Beat in the cream, eggs, wine and seasonings. Pour over the bread.

4 Sprinkle with the cheese and paprika pepper. Cook uncovered for 4–5 min, turning the dish if necessary every 2 min. Serve straightaway.

DO NOT FREEZE

Microwave/conventional cooking

One of the many advantages of the microwave cooker is that even when you want to cook or bake by conventional methods, the microwave can work as a tool for you in the kitchen, completing many of the stages of preparation for the final dish. Melting, warming and cooking operations can be carried out quickly and efficiently, very often in the same mixing bowl or dish to which other ingredients may be added, saving the use of messy saucepans and therefore cutting down on the washing up.

Joints or smaller cuts of meat and poultry can be partly cooked in the microwave before finishing in the conventional oven or under the grill to make the outside more crisp. Precooking by microwave is particularly ideal when planning a barbecue as it can help to cut down the cooking times and thus assist in preventing the outside of the food becoming charred before the inside is cooked through.

Dough for bread-making may be proved quickly in the microwave before cooking conventionally for those of you who prefer the traditional cooked and browned loaf, or it may be part baked by microwave and just finished off in the conventional oven. More information and a few recipes are given in the section on Bread and Yeast (page 202).

The grill, too, on your conventional cooker is invaluable for browning the top of food such as au gratin dishes after preparing and cooking in the microwave. Even the tops of foods such as bread and cakes may be lightly browned under the grill if you really prefer a browned finish but haven't the time to cook the whole thing conventionally.

Foods which have been frozen after cooking con-

ventionally of course can be defrosted and reheated by microwave, but pastry dishes and similar-baked items should be placed on or covered with kitchen paper towel to absorb the moisture from the food and therefore help to maintain a crisp result.

The selection of recipes in this section is intended as a guide to give you ideas how the microwave cooker can be of invaluable assistance to you in the kitchen when cooking some of your favourite recipes by conventional methods.

Dutch apple tart *(serves 4–6)*
POWER LEVEL: 100% (FULL)
OVEN TEMPERATURE: 200°C (400°F), MARK 6

450g (1lb) cooking apples, sliced
1 lemon, juice and grated rind
50g (2oz) almonds, roughly chopped
50g (2oz) sultanas
sugar to taste
225g (8oz) Rich Shortcrust Pastry (page 248)
raspberry jam
icing sugar, optional
for serving: cream

1 Place the cooking apples and lemon juice into a covered large dish or bowl or in a boiling or roasting bag.
2 Cook in the microwave for about 6 min, stirring the contents of the dish or shaking the bag 2–3 times throughout. The apples should be softened but not overcooked.
3 Pulp down the apples with a wooden spoon or fork

and stir in the lemon rind, almonds, sultanas and a little sugar to taste. Leave to cool.

4 Roll out the pastry and line a 17.5cm (7in) flan dish. Roll out the trimmings and cut into thin strips.

5 Spread a little raspberry jam over the base of the flan and add the cooled apple mixture. Make a lattice design over the flan with the strips of pastry.

6 Bake in a preheated oven for 30–40 min until golden brown. Sprinkle with a little sieved icing sugar if preferred before serving hot or cold with cream.

Coconut flapjacks *(makes about 24)*

POWER LEVEL: 100% (FULL)
OVEN TEMPERATURE: 190°C (375°F), MARK 5

100g (4oz) butter
25g (1oz) dark brown sugar
2 × 15ml tbsp (2tbsp) golden syrup
175g (6oz) rolled oats
50g (2oz) desiccated coconut

1 Cut the butter into pieces and place in a mixing bowl with the sugar and syrup.

2 Heat for 2 min in the microwave, stir well and then heat for a further 1–2 min until completely melted. Mix well together.

3 Stir in the rolled oats and coconut and place the mixture into a lightly greased tin measuring approximately 22.5cm (9in) square.

4 Bake in a preheated oven for 25–30 min until golden brown. While still warm, cut into fingers.

Yorkshire parkin *(makes 16)*

POWER LEVEL: 100% (FULL)
OVEN TEMPERATURE: 160°C (325°F), MARK 3

100g (4oz) plain flour
225g (8oz) medium oatmeal
25g (1oz) sugar
pinch ground ginger
pinch salt
150g (5oz) treacle
100g (4oz) golden syrup
100g (4oz) butter
2 × 15ml tbsp (2tbsp) milk
$\frac{1}{2}$ × 5ml tsp ($\frac{1}{2}$tsp) bicarbonate of soda

1 Grease and line a 20cm (8in) square tin.

2 Mix together the flour, oatmeal, sugar, ginger and salt in a large mixing bowl.

3 Place the treacle, syrup and butter into a seperate bowl and heat in the microwave for $2\frac{1}{2}$–$3\frac{1}{2}$ min until melted, stirring twice throughout.

4 Heat the milk in a cup in the microwave for 10 sec and stir in the bicarbonate of soda.

5 Add the treacle and milk mixtures to the dry ingredients and mix well together.

6 Pour the mixture into the prepared tin and cook for 55–65 min in the conventional oven until risen and firm.

7 Leave in the tin until cool. Serve cold cut into squares.

Pork fillet en croûte *(serves 2–3)*

POWER LEVEL: 100% (FULL)
OVEN TEMPERATURE 220°C (425°F), MARK 7 AND 180°C (350°F), MARK 4

1 fillet of pork, approximately 225g (8oz)
salt and freshly ground black pepper
$\frac{1}{2}$ × 5ml tsp ($\frac{1}{2}$tsp) dried sage
4–6 rashers streaky bacon, derinded
oil for brushing
175g (6oz) frozen puff pastry, thawed
beaten egg for brushing
for garnish: bunches of watercress
for serving: Rich Mushroom Sauce (page 134)

1 Trim the pork fillet, cut in half and place one piece on top of the other. Sprinkle with seasoning and the sage.

2 Wrap the streaky bacon rashers around the pork and secure with wooden cocktail sticks. Brush lightly with oil.

3 Cover and cook in the microwave for about 5 min, turning the pork over halfway through. Allow to stand and leave to cool.

4 Roll out the pastry thinly on a floured surface. Arrange the pork in the middle and wrap the pastry around to cover it completely. Dampen the edges and seal well.

5 Roll out the trimmings of the dough and make pastry leaves to decorate the top. Brush with beaten egg and place on a baking tray.

6 Cook in a preheated oven at the higher temperature for 15 min, then reduce the heat to the lower temperature and continue to cook for 20–25 min.

7 Serve hot, cut into slices and garnished with watercress. Hand the hot mushroom sauce separately.

Beef and walnut burger *(serves 4–6)*

POWER LEVEL: 100% (FULL) *(colour page 26)*
OVEN TEMPERATURE: 180°C (350°F), MARK 4

25g (1oz) butter
2 medium onions, finely chopped
2 tomatoes, skinned and finely chopped
675g ($1\frac{1}{2}$lb) lean braising steak, finely minced
75g (3oz) walnuts, chopped
1 × 5ml tsp (1tsp) paprika

salt and freshly ground black pepper
2 eggs, beaten
for garnish: tomato slices and parsley sprigs
for serving: jacket potatoes and coleslaw

1 Melt the butter in a large bowl in the microwave for 1 min. Stir in the onions, cover and cook for 5–6 min until softened.
2 Mix in the remaining ingredients and shape into a mound. Place on to a greased baking tray and flatten the top slightly.
3 Cook in a preheated oven for about $1-1\frac{1}{4}$ hr until firm and well browned. Serve hot, cut into wedges with jacket potatoes and coleslaw.

Spaghetti with aubergines *(serves 3–4)*
POWER LEVEL: 100% (FULL)

The sauce is made in the microwave and the aubergine is lightly fried until crisp.

1 large aubergine, thinly sliced
salt
3×15ml tbsp (3tbsp) oil
2 cloves garlic, crushed
1×425g (15oz) and 1×200g (7oz) cans tomatoes
2×15ml tbsp (2tbsp) tomato purée
1×5ml tsp (1tsp) oregano or basil
freshly ground black pepper
oil for frying
350g (12oz) spaghetti
grated parmesan cheese
for garnish: sprigs of oregano or basil

1 Sprinkle the aubergine slices with salt and leave for 1 hr to draw out the moisture.
2 Place the 3×15ml tbsp (3tbsp) oil in a bowl or casserole dish with the garlic, tomatoes, tomato purée and herbs. Season with salt and freshly ground black pepper.
3 Cover and cook in the microwave for 6 min, stirring once halfway through. Uncover and cook for a further 2 min.
4 Rinse the aubergine slices under cold running water and gently squeeze dry. Heat 1.25cm ($\frac{1}{2}$in) oil in a frying pan and fry the aubergine slices, a few at a time, until crisp on both sides. Drain on kitchen paper towel.
5 In the meantime, boil the spaghetti in salted water, either in the microwave (page 216) or in a pan on the hob in the conventional way.
6 Drain the spaghetti thoroughly and place in a warmed serving dish. Pour the hot tomato sauce over and add the aubergine slices.
7 Sprinkle with grated cheese and garnish with sprigs of oregano or basil before serving hot.

DO NOT FREEZE

Herby toad in the hole *(serves 4)*
POWER LEVEL: 100% (FULL)
OVEN TEMPERATURE: 220°C (425°F), MARK 7

The sausages are partly cooked in the microwave before being added to the batter and finally cooked in the conventional oven.

25g (1oz) lard
450g (1lb) pork sausages
100g (4oz) plain flour
pinch salt
1 egg
275ml ($\frac{1}{2}$pt) milk or milk and water mixed
2×15ml tbsp (2tbsp) chopped mixed fresh herbs *or*
2×5ml tsp (2tsp) dried mixed herbs

1 Place the lard into a 17.5×27.5cm (7×11in) shallow tin and heat in the preheated conventional oven.
2 Prick the sausages and arrange on a plate. Cook in the microwave for 5–6 min, turning the plate or rearranging the sausages halfway through.
3 Make the batter by mixing the flour and salt together; add the egg and, beating or whisking well, add the milk or milk and water. Stir in the herbs.
4 When the fat is hot pour the batter in the tin and arrange the sausages in the mixture. Cook for 35–45 min in the conventional oven until well risen and golden brown.

Crème caramel *(serves 3–4)*
POWER LEVEL: 100% (FULL)

The caramel is prepared in the microwave, and then the cream mixture is added before steaming conventionally.

100g (4oz) sugar
150ml ($\frac{1}{4}$pt) water
3 eggs, beaten
275ml ($\frac{1}{2}$pt) milk
25g (1oz) caster sugar
$\frac{1}{2} \times 5$ml tsp ($\frac{1}{2}$tsp) vanilla essence

1 Place the sugar in a $\frac{1}{2}-\frac{3}{4}$ litre ($1-1\frac{1}{4}$pt) basin with the water. Stir well and heat in the microwave for 30 sec. Stir again and heat for a further 15 sec. Stir until the sugar has dissolved.
2 Bring to the boil in the microwave and cook, without stirring, for 3–4 min until the mixture turns a pale brown. Remove at once from the microwave. Move the caramel around the bowl until the base and sides are coated. Leave until cold.
3 Lightly beat the eggs into the milk and add the sugar and vanilla essence. Pour into the basin with the caramel. Cover with aluminium foil or greaseproof paper.

4 Place in a steamer over a pan of boiling water or, alternatively, place in a pan of boiling water with a tight-fitting lid. The water should come halfway up the basin. When adding water to maintain the level it must be boiling.
5 Steam for 30–40 min until the cream is lightly set.
6 Run a knife around the sides of the basin and invert on to a serving dish. Serve warm or cold.

DO NOT FREEZE

Fish parcels (serves 6)
POWER LEVEL: 100% (FULL)
OVEN TEMPERATURE: 200°C (400°F), MARK 6

15g ($\frac{1}{2}$oz) butter
1 small onion, finely chopped
450g (1lb) white fish fillets, skinned
salt and freshly ground black pepper
1 × 15ml tbsp (1tbsp) chopped parsley
150ml ($\frac{1}{4}$pt) White Sauce (page 132 and method 2)
2 × 5ml tsp (2tsp) lemon juice
375g (13oz) frozen puff pastry, thawed
beaten egg for brushing
for garnish: 6 lettuce leaves

1 Melt the butter in a casserole dish for 30 sec in the microwave cooker. Stir in the onion, cover and cook for 3 min.
2 Dice the fish and add to the onion. Continue to cook, covered, for a further 4–5 min, stirring once halfway through. Drain off the liquid and use to make up the liquid quantity for the sauce.
3 Add seasoning to taste and stir the parsley, sauce, lemon juice and fish mixture together. Leave to cool.
4 Roll out the pastry on a lightly floured surface and cut out 6 × 12.5cm (5in) squares. Reserve the trimmings and roll out to make pastry leaves.
5 Divide the filling between the pastry squares. Damp the edges, fold each corner into the centre to cover the filling but leaving a small hole. Pinch the edges together. Decorate with the pastry leaves.
6 Place the fish parcels on a greased baking tray and brush well with beaten egg. Bake in a preheated oven for 25–30 min until well risen and golden brown.
7 Place each parcel on a lettuce leaf and serve hot or warm.

Onion tart (serves 4–6)
POWER LEVEL: 100% (FULL)
OVEN TEMPERATURE: 200°C (400°F), MARK 6

50g (2oz) butter or margarine
450g (1lb) onions, thinly sliced
100g (4oz) smoked streaky bacon, derinded
3 eggs
150ml ($\frac{1}{4}$pt) milk
150ml ($\frac{1}{4}$pt) single cream
salt and freshly ground black pepper
20–22.5cm (8–9in) flan case, baked blind (page 248)
for garnish: sprigs of parsley
for serving: mixed tossed salad

1 Melt the butter or margarine in a bowl or casserole dish in the microwave for 1$\frac{1}{2}$ min. Add in the onions, cover and cook for 5 min, stirring well halfway through.
2 Cut the bacon into strips, stir into the onions and continue to cook, covered, for a further 3–4 min. Leave to cool slightly.
3 Beat the eggs lightly, stir in the milk, cream and seasoning to taste.
4 Arrange the onion and bacon mixture in the base of the flan case and pour the egg mixture over the top.
5 Bake in a preheated oven for 25–30 min until set and golden brown. Garnish with sprigs of parsley before serving hot or warm with a mixed tossed salad.

Cheese gougère *(serves 4–6)*
POWER LEVEL: 100% (FULL) *(colour opposite)*
OVEN TEMPERATURE: 230°C (450°F), MARK 8

150ml ($\frac{1}{4}$pt) water
1 × 5ml tsp (1tsp) salt
100g (4oz) unsalted butter, cut into cubes
100g (4oz) plain flour
4 eggs, beaten
100g (4oz) gruyère cheese, grated
egg and milk to glaze

1 Place the water, salt and the butter into a large mixing bowl. Cook for 3–4 min in the microwave until the butter is melted and the water is boiling rapidly. Stir once halfway through.
2 Add the flour and stir well. Return to the microwave and cook for 20 sec then beat well until the mixture is smooth and leaves the sides of the bowl. Leave to cool slightly.
3 Add the eggs gradually, beating well into the mixture until smooth between additions. Add 75g (3oz) of the cheese and beat well into the paste.
4 Lightly grease a baking tray and place spoonfuls of the paste in a 20cm (8in) ring on the tray or pipe the mixture using a 2.5cm (1in) nozzle. Brush the egg and milk glaze over the ring and sprinkle with the remaining cheese.
5 Bake for 20–25 min in a preheated oven until golden brown and cooked through. Serve hot.

Chicken, ham and mushroom pie *(serves 4–5)*
POWER LEVEL: 100% (FULL) *(colour opposite)*
OVEN TEMPERATURE: 200°C (400°F), MARK 6

1 small onion, chopped
100g (4oz) ham, chopped
15g ($\frac{1}{2}$oz) butter
100g (4oz) mushrooms, sliced
$\frac{1}{2}$ green pepper, deseeded and chopped
225g (8oz) cooked chicken, chopped
1 × 15ml tbsp (1tbsp) chopped parsley
salt and freshly ground black pepper
275g (10oz) can condensed chicken or mushroom soup
225g (8oz) Shortcrust Pastry (page 248)
beaten egg for brushing

1 Place the onion, ham and butter into a bowl, cover and cook for 3 min, stirring halfway through. Add the mushrooms and pepper and continue to cook for a further 3 min.
2 Stir in the chicken, parsley, seasoning and soup. Mix well and place into a 17.5cm (7in) pie dish.
3 Make up the pastry, roll out and cut a narrow strip to place on the edge of the pie dish. Dampen the strip with water and cover the dish with the remaining pastry. Cut off the extra pastry. Reserve trimmings to make pastry leaves and arrange on the top, around the centre of the pie.
4 Make a small hole in the centre of the pie, brush with beaten egg and bake for 30–45 min in the conventional oven until golden brown.

Profiteroles *(makes 24)*
POWER LEVEL: 100% (FULL) *(colour opposite)*
OVEN TEMPERATURE: 180°C (350°F), MARK 4

40g (1$\frac{1}{2}$oz) butter
150ml ($\frac{1}{4}$pt) water
65g (2$\frac{1}{2}$oz) plain flour
2 eggs, beaten
whipped cream
for serving: Chocolate Sauce (page 137)

1 Place the butter and water into a bowl and heat in the microwave for 2–3 min until the butter is melted and the water is boiling rapidly. Stir halfway through.
2 Add the flour and beat well. Replace into the microwave and cook for 15 sec. Beat well until the mixture is smooth. Leave to cool slightly and then beat in the eggs.
3 Using a 12mm ($\frac{1}{2}$in) plain nozzle fitted into a piping bag, pipe small balls of the pastry, about the size of a walnut, on to a lightly greased baking tray.
4 Bake in a preheated oven for 15–20 min until well risen and crisp. Make a small hole in the side of each profiterole and leave until cold.
5 Pipe whipped cream through the hole into the centre of the profiterole. Pile them into a serving dish and drizzle the chocolate sauce over the top. Serve cold.

DO NOT FREEZE

Pancakes *(makes 6–8)*
POWER LEVEL: 100% (FULL)

The pancakes are made in the frying pan, filled and then reheated in the microwave.

for the pancakes:
100g (4oz) plain flour
pinch salt
1 egg
275ml ($\frac{1}{2}$pt) milk or milk and water mixed

Cheese Gougère; Profiteroles; Chicken, Ham and Mushroom Pie

1 Mix the flour and salt together and add the egg. Beating well, gradually add all the milk or milk and water until the mixture is smooth.

2 Prepare a thick-based frying pan by melting a little butter in it and coating the base and sides. Pour off the excess butter.

3 Pour a little of the batter into the pan and cover the base completely. Do not add too much or the pancakes will be too thick.

4 Cook until the pancake is golden brown underneath. Toss over with a palette-knife and cook the second side. Make all the pancakes, add fillings and reheat in the microwave as given below.

FOR THE FILLINGS:

Ginger and banana: mash some bananas with a little ground ginger and thick cream. Spread between the pancakes and roll up or fold each one and place on a serving plate. Cover and cook for 2–3 min until heated through. Allow to stand for 3 min before serving with cream.

Cream cheese: beat together 225g (8oz) cream cheese, 1 egg, 1 × 15ml tbsp (1tbsp) caster sugar and few drops vanilla essence. Spread the mixture over the pancakes, fold in half and half again. Cover and cook for 2–2½ min until heated through. Stand for a few minutes before serving with fresh fruit such as raspberries, pineapple or fruit salad.

Apricot and almond: chop 100g (4oz) dried apricots and place in a bowl with a little water to cover, sugar to taste and a good squeeze of lemon juice. Cook in the microwave on 100% (full) setting for 4–5 min until soft. Add 50g (2oz) chopped almonds. Fill and roll the pancakes. Cover and reheat for 2–3 min until heated through. Serve with cream.

Cottage cheese and prawn: mix 100g (4oz) cottage cheese with 50g (2oz) prawns, seasoning, 50g (2oz) chopped cucumber and a squeeze of lemon juice. Fill the pancakes and roll up. Place on to a serving dish or plate and cover and cook for about 3 min until heated through. Allow to stand for 2–3 min before serving with lemon wedges.

Chicken and ham: make a well-flavoured White Sauce (page 132) and add 100g (4oz) cooked chicken, chopped, and about 50–75g (2–3oz) chopped ham. Fill the pancakes and roll or fold into envelopes. Cover and cook for 2–3 min until heated through and stand for 3 min before serving garnished with parsley.

Mushroom and chives: make a Rich Mushroom Sauce (page 134) but do not purée. Stir in 2–3 × 15ml tbsp (2–3tbsp) chopped chives. Fill the pancakes and roll them to enclose the filling. Arrange on a serving plate or in a dish, cover and heat through for 2–3 min. Stand for 3 min before serving topped with spoonfuls of soured cream and sprinkled with extra chopped chives.

DO NOT FREEZE THE FILLED PANCAKES

Mushroom soufflé loaf *(serves 6–8)*

POWER LEVEL: 100% (FULL)
OVEN TEMPERATURE: 180°C (350°F), MARK 4

1 round loaf of bread
100g (4oz) butter
450g (1lb) mushrooms, finely chopped
salt and freshly ground black pepper
3 × 15ml tbsp (3tbsp) lemon juice
275ml (½pt) White Sauce (page 132)
2 eggs, separated
for serving: mixed salad

1 Cut a slice from the top of the loaf and remove most of the crumb leaving a 1.25cm (½in) thick shell.

2 Using 50g (2oz) of the butter, spread it over the inside of the bread, place on a baking tray and cook in a preheated oven for 10 min.

3 Melt the remaining butter in a large bowl in the microwave for 1½–2 min, stir in the mushrooms and cook, covered, for about 5 min, stirring halfway through.

4 Add seasoning, lemon juice and the white sauce. Beat the egg yolks and mix into the sauce. Whisk the egg whites until stiff and gently fold into the mushroom mixture.

5 Pour the mixture into the bread shell and sprinkle the top with a few of the scooped-out breadcrumbs, grated.

6 Bake for 25–30 min in a preheated oven until well risen and crisp. Serve hot with salad.

DO NOT FREEZE

Note: *The remaining breadcrumbs can be grated, browned in the oven and when cool, stored in an airtight box or in the freezer for future use.*

Piquant meat pasties *(serves 4)*

POWER LEVEL: 100% (FULL)
OVEN TEMPERATURE: 220° (425°F), MARK 7

25g (1oz) butter
1 onion, finely chopped
100g (4oz) belly pork, derinded and minced
225g (8oz) minced beef
40g (1½oz) seedless raisins
pinch ground cloves
salt and freshly ground black pepper
½ × 5ml tsp (½tsp) paprika
2 hard-boiled eggs, roughly chopped
8 stoned green olives, chopped
375g (13oz) frozen puff pastry, thawed
beaten egg

1 Melt the butter in a large bowl or casserole dish for 1 min in the microwave. Stir in the onion, cover and cook for 4 min.

2 Add the pork and beef, mix well with the onions and continue to cook, covered, for 8–10 min until well browned: stir 2–3 times throughout and break down any lumps with a fork. Leave to cool.

3 Stir in the raisins, cloves, seasoning, paprika, hard-boiled eggs and olives and mix well.

4 Roll out the pastry on a lightly floured board into a rectangle approximately 20 × 40cm (8 × 16in). Cut the pastry into 8 squares.

5 Place the meat mixture on one half of each of the pastry squares. Brush the edges with a little of the egg, fold over and crimp the edges to seal.

6 Arrange on a dampened baking tray, brush with the remaining egg and cook in a preheated oven for about 25 min until golden brown.

DO NOT FREEZE

Veal and ham pies *(serves 4)*
POWER LEVEL: 100% (FULL) *(colour page 23)*
OVEN TEMPERATURE: 220°C (425°F), MARK 7

25g (1oz) butter or margarine
225g (8oz) veal or pork, minced or finely chopped
25g (1oz) flour
150ml ($\frac{1}{4}$pt) milk
salt and freshly ground black pepper
1 × 5ml tsp (1tsp) dried tarragon
75g (3oz) cooked ham, chopped
4 hard-boiled eggs
for the pastry:
350g (12oz) plain flour
75g (3oz) butter or margarine
75g (3oz) lard or white fat
water to mix
beaten egg for brushing

1 Melt the butter or margarine for 1 min in the microwave, using a bowl or casserole dish. Stir in the veal, cover and cook for 3–3$\frac{1}{2}$ min, stirring with a fork and breaking down any lumps halfway through.

2 Stir in the flour and add the milk. Cook for a further 3 min until thickened. Mix well and add the seasoning, tarragon and ham. Leave to cool.

3 To make the pastry, sift the flour into a bowl and add a pinch of salt. Cut the fat into small pieces and rub into the flour until the mixture resembles fine breadcrumbs. Stir in sufficient water to make a pliable dough.

4 Roll out the dough and cut into 4 × 12.5cm (5in) rounds and 4 × 15cm (6in) rounds. Place the smaller rounds on to a baking sheet. (If preferred, the pastry rounds may be trimmed to a slightly smaller size to fit 4 large individual yorkshire pudding tins.)

5 Divide the filling between the rounds leaving a margin around the edge. Place a hard-boiled egg on

to each pile of filling and then push it down into the filling. Dampen the edges of the pastry with water and cover with the larger rounds of dough.

6 Press the edges well down and crimp. Roll out the remaining pastry and make leaves to decorate the tops of the pies. Dampen the pastry leaves and press on to the top of the pies. Make holes in the centres.

7 Brush the pies with the beaten egg and bake in a preheated oven at 220°C (425°F), mark 7 for 30–40 min, until golden brown. Serve hot or cold.

Haddock, prawn and mushroom jalousie
(serves 4)
POWER LEVEL: 100% (FULL)
OVEN TEMPERATURE: 220°C (425°F), MARK 7

Serve as a starter or a snack.

100g (4oz) smoked haddock fillet
50g (2oz) peeled prawns
50g (2oz) button mushrooms, sliced
15g ($\frac{1}{2}$oz) butter
15g ($\frac{1}{2}$oz) flour
150ml ($\frac{1}{4}$pt) milk
salt and freshly ground black pepper
175g (6oz) flaky or puff pastry
beaten egg for brushing

1 Place the smoked haddock fillet into a dish and add sufficient cold water to cover. Cover with clingfilm or a lid and cook for 3 min in the microwave.

2 Allow to stand for 2 min then drain the fish. Remove the skin and any bones and flake the flesh. Stir in the prawns and sliced mushrooms.

3 In a bowl or jug, melt the butter in the microwave for 15–30 sec and stir in the flour. Add the milk gradually, stirring well after each addition. Stir in the fish, prawns and mushrooms.

4 Cook for 3–4 min until thickened, stirring every minute. Cook for a further 1 min and then leave to cool. Add seasoning to taste.

5 Roll out the pastry into an oblong measuring about 25 × 17.5cm (10 × 7in). Cut in half length-ways so that there are two oblongs measuring 12.5 × 17.5cm (5 × 7in).

6 Place one half on to a baking sheet. Top with the filling and spread out to within 1.25cm ($\frac{1}{2}$in) of the edges. Fold the other half of the pastry into half lengthways and cut strips to within 1.25cm ($\frac{1}{2}$in) of the edges. Open out and brush the edges all the way round with water.

7 Place the cut pastry over the filling, matching the edges. Press the edges down well to seal them.

8 Brush the jalousie with beaten egg and bake in a preheated oven at 220°C (425°F), mark 7 for 30–40 min.

9 Serve hot or warm as a starter or snack.

Lemon meringue pie *(serves 6–8)*

POWER LEVEL: 100% (FULL) *(colour opposite)*
OVEN TEMPERATURE: 200°C (400°F), MARK 6
AND 180°C (350°F), MARK 4

for the pastry:
275g (10oz) plain flour
pinch salt
150g (5oz) fat—half butter or margarine and half lard
cold water to mix
for the filling:
65g (2½oz) caster sugar
40g (1½oz) butter
150ml (¼pt) water
2 lemons, grated rind and juice
25g (1oz) cornflour
150ml (¼pt) milk
3 egg yolks
meringue:
3 egg whites
100g (4oz) caster sugar

1 Sift the flour and salt into a mixing bowl. Rub in the butter or margarine and lard until the mixture resembles breadcrumbs. Add sufficient cold water to mix into a pliable dough.
2 Roll out the pastry and line a swiss roll tin measuring 17.5 × 28.5cm (7½ × 11½in). Prick the base and bake blind in the conventional oven at 200° (400°F), mark 6.
3 Place the sugar, butter, water, lemon juice and rind into a bowl. Heat in the microwave for 2 min and then stir until the sugar has dissolved. Heat for another 1–2 min if necessary. Leave to cool slightly.
4 Blend the cornflour with a little milk, add the remainder and then stir into the lemon mixture. Bring to the boil in the microwave, stirring every 30 sec until the mixture has thickened. Allow to cool slightly.
5 Beat the egg yolks and add to the thickened mixture. Beat well and then pour into the pastry case.
6 Whisk the egg whites until stiff. Add half the sugar and continue to whisk until stiff again and holding shape. Fold in the remaining sugar and cover the lemon filling with the meringue using a spatula or knife. Alternatively, pipe the meringue over the surface using a piping bag fitted with a fluted nozzle.
7 Bake in a preheated oven set at 180°C (350°F), mark 4 for 15–20 min until browned.

DO NOT FREEZE

Almond jam doughnuts *(makes 12)*

POWER LEVEL: 100% (FULL) *(colour opposite)*

The dough is proved in the microwave, shaped and then deep-fat fried in the conventional way.

75ml (⅛pt) milk
1 × 5ml tsp (1tsp) caster sugar
6g (¼oz) dried yeast
225g (8oz) plain flour
¼ × 5ml tsp (¼tsp) salt
50g (2oz) margarine or butter
50g (2oz) almonds, toasted and chopped
1 egg, beaten
water
2 × 15ml tbsp (2tbsp) raspberry jam, approximately
oil for deep-fat frying
caster sugar for coating

1 Warm the milk and sugar in the microwave for 15–30 sec. Stir in the yeast and leave to activate.
2 Sieve the flour and salt into a mixing bowl and warm for 30 sec in the microwave. Rub in the margarine or butter until the mixture resembles breadcrumbs.
3 Stir the chopped toasted almonds into the flour. Place the egg in a measuring jug and make up to 75ml (⅛pt) with water.
4 Add the egg and water to the flour and knead until smooth. Cover with clingfilm and prove in the microwave by heating for 15 sec and then allowing to stand for 5–10 min. Repeat until double in size.
5 Knead well and divide into 12. Shape into circles and place ½ × 5ml tsp (½tsp) jam in the centre and then draw the edges together to form a ball.
6 Arrange in a circle on baking parchment or a lightly floured plate and prove again in the microwave.
7 Heat the oil to 180°C (350°F) in a deep-fat fry-pan on the conventional hob. Deep fry the doughnuts until golden and cooked through.
8 Toss the cooked doughnuts in caster sugar and serve hot.

VARIATION

Cinnamon and apple doughnuts: Add 1 × 5ml tsp (1tsp) cinnamon and 100g (4oz) chopped eating apple to the rubbed-in flour and margarine before adding the liquid. Proceed as above, omitting the jam filling.

Almond Jam Doughnuts; Lemon Meringue Pie

Orange soufflé (serves 3–4)

POWER LEVEL: 100% (FULL)
OVEN TEMPERATURE: 200°C (400°F), MARK 6

25g (1oz) butter
15g (½oz) plain flour
150ml (¼pt) milk
25g (1oz) caster sugar
1½–2 oranges, grated rind and juice
3 eggs, separated

1 Melt the butter in a bowl in the microwave for 1 min. Stir in the flour and then add the milk gradually, stirring and beating well after each addition to produce a smooth sauce.
2 Cook in the microwave for 2–3 min until boiling and thickened, stirring every 30 sec. Add the sugar, orange rind and juice, beat well and then leave until cold.
3 Beat the egg yolks into the mixture. Whisk the egg whites until stiff and fold in carefully using a metal spoon.
4 Pour the mixture into a lightly greased 17.5cm (7in) soufflé dish. Place in a preheated oven at 200°C (400°F), mark 6 and cook for 30–40 min until well risen and brown.
5 Serve straightaway.

DO NOT FREEZE

Rich shortcrust pastry

175g (6oz) plain flour
pinch salt
75g (3oz) butter or margarine
2 × 5ml tsp (2tsp) caster sugar, optional
1 egg yolk
2 × 15ml tbsp (2tbsp) water

1 Sift the flour with the salt and rub in the butter or margarine finely. Stir in the sugar if using.
2 Beat the egg yolk with the water and add to the flour. Mix well, then knead together lightly.
3 Chill before rolling out.

Shortcrust pastry
Omit the egg yolk and add 1 extra 15ml tbsp (1tbsp) water.

Light wholemeal pastry
Half the plain flour is replaced by wholemeal flour.

Sweet rich shortcrust pastry
If preferred, 2 × 5ml tsp (2tsp) caster sugar may be added to the crumb mixture before adding the egg. This gives a sweeter pastry for dishes with sweet fillings.

Flan case
To line a flan dish
Using 175g (6oz) mixture of rich shortcrust pastry and a 17.5cm–20cm (7–8in) flan dish, roll out the pastry into a circle 5cm (2in) larger than the dish. Wrap the pastry loosely around the rolling pin and lift into the flan dish. Ease the pastry into shape removing any air under the base, pressing well into the sides and taking care not to stretch the pastry. Cut the pastry away but leave 6mm (¼in) above the rim of the flan dish. Carefully ease this down into the dish, or flute the edges and leave slightly higher than the rim of the dish (this allows a little extra height to the sides of the flan case to compensate for any shrinkage during cooking). Alternatively, run the rolling pin across the top of the flan to cut off surplus pastry. Prick the base well.

To bake blind—microwave
POWER LEVEL: 100% (FULL)
Using a long, smooth strip of aluminium foil measuring approximately 3.75cm (1½in) wide, line the inside, upright edge of the pastry flan case to protect this section from overcooking in the microwave. Place two pieces of absorbent kitchen paper over the base, easing around the edge and pressing gently into the corner between base and side to help keep the foil strip in position. Place in the microwave and cook on 100% (full) setting for 4–4½ min, giving the dish a quarter turn every minute. Remove the kitchen paper and foil and cook for a further 1–2 min.

To bake blind—conventional
OVEN TEMPERATURE: 200°C (400°F), MARK 6
Line the pastry flan case with a circle of lightly greased greaseproof paper (greased side down) or kitchen paper towel. Half fill the paper with uncooked beans, lentils, small pasta or rice which may be specially kept for this purpose. Alternatively, line the pastry flan case with foil only. Cook in a preheated oven at 200°C (400°F), mark 6 for 15–20 min, until the pastry is nearly cooked. Remove the lining and bake for 5–10 min until the base is firm and dry.

Acknowledgements

My grateful thanks to Rosemary Moon for her assistance with developing and testing some of the recipes, and for her help with the preparation of the food for photography.

Colour photography by John Plimmer, RPM Photographic, Havant, Hants. Line illustrations by Mona Thorogood.

Credits

The following companies have generously sponsored some of the photography and kindly supplied microwave cookers and equipment featured in the colour pages:

Thorn EMI Domestic Appliances Ltd, New Lane, Havant, Hants (pages 35, 107, 154, 171, 187, 231, 243 and 247).

Microwave Ovenware Ltd, Church Street, Teddington, Middlesex (pages 207 and 231).

Thorpac Group Plc, 1 Elliot Road, Lovelane Industrial Estate, Cirencester, Glos (pages 35 and 171).

Kitchen Devils Ltd, Sword House, Totteridge Road, High Wycombe, Bucks (pages 107—Kitchen Devil Professional Knives, and 175—Kitchen Devil Icing Set).

Other microwave books by Val Collins

Here is an ideal paperback that will give you all the background information you will need to become a microwave expert.

Val Collins explains in simple terms what microwave energy is and how it works. It is packed with ideas and appetising recipes too!

Probably more than any other food, fish benefits from being cooked by microwave as the moist texture and delicate flavour is preserved.

Val Collins provides a wealth of information and delicious recipes for a wide range of dishes: soups and starters; main courses such as haddock with orange and walnut stuffing and exotic dishes such as squid with mushrooms or scampi à la crème.

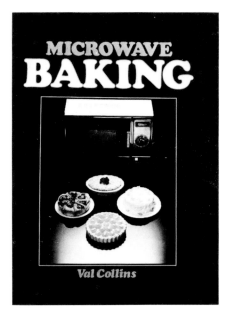

A wealth of information and mouth-watering recipes for the complete range of baking needs. Instructions are included for using conventional baking methods and combinations of microwave and conventional oven use.

Treat your family and friends to the real flavour of fruits and vegetables, cooked to perfection, looking and tasting better than those cooked by any other method. Details on freezing, blanching, drying herbs and suitable containers.

Recipe Index

251

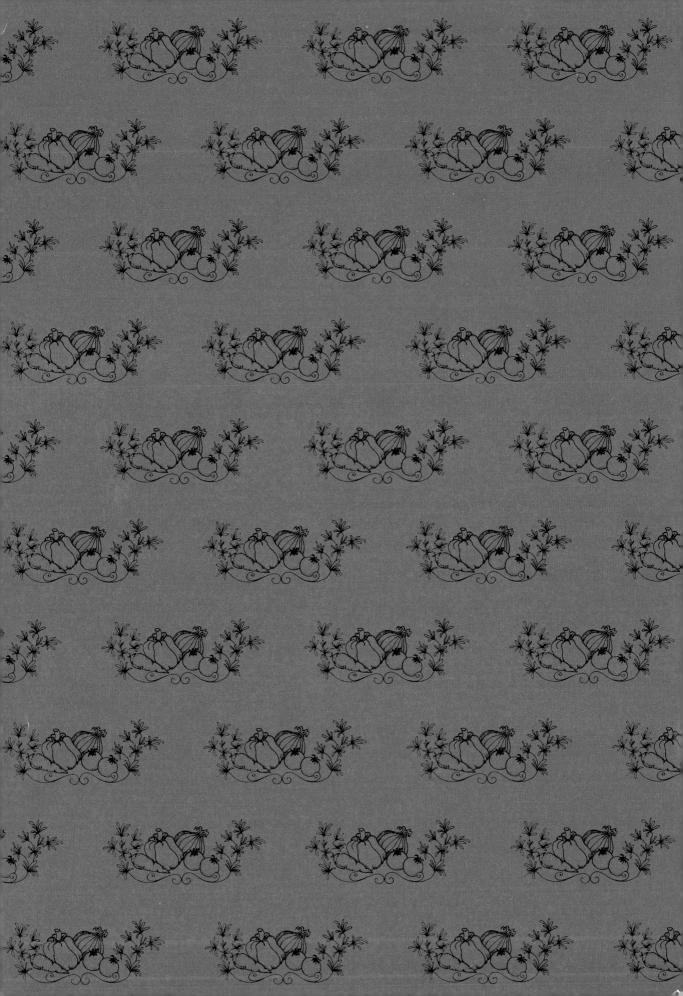